THE XBOX 360 UNCLOAKED

THE REAL STORY BEHIND MICROSOFT'S NEXT-GENERATION VIDEO GAME CONSOLE

DEAN TAKAHASHI

SpiderWorks

For more great books, visit us online at
http://www.spiderworks.com

Published by SpiderWorks, LLC.
http://www.spiderworks.com

ISBN-10:   0-977-78421-5
ISBN-13: 978-0-977-78421-5

Library of Congress Control Number is available from the publisher.

Edited by Dave Mark
Cover Design by Dave Wooldridge
Cover Background Illustration: mecaleha (istockphoto.com)
Interior Page Design by Robin Williams and Dave Wooldridge

Xbox 360 product images, screenshots of Xbox 360 games, and
photographs of Microsoft employees and events are provided
courtesy of Microsoft Corporation unless otherwise specified.
See the Photo Credits page for complete details.

For my 360 degree circle:

my wife, the girls, my parents, and my brother.

CONTENTS

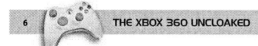

ACKNOWLEDGEMENTS

It's hard to count how many people have helped out with this book. I'd like to thank my wife; my mother the proofreader; my publishers at SpiderWorks, Dave Mark and Dave Wooldridge; and my agent, David Fugate. SpiderWorks has turned out to be a wonderful publishing partner. I highly recommend them for their speed and quality. I've come to believe that e-books are a disruptive force in publishing, and SpiderWorks really gets that. This book would never have happened without the hidden sources that I cannot name. You know who you are! The total number approaches 200 people.

I thank Donna Alvarado and Todd Woody, my bosses at the *San Jose Mercury News,* for their generous support. My blog and stories for the *San Jose Mercury News* have been better for the reporting that has come from the book. I was able to use most of the reporting for the book on my own blog, **Dean & Nooch on Gaming**, and I have borrowed liberally from both the blog and stories I have done for the newspaper.

Our gaming blog has benefited enormously from loyal blog readers such as SlipStreamBro, Fredo, Jason, Basheron, Bing, and Kidflash. They weighed in with their own insights as only gaming fans can do. Mike Antonucci has been a good sounding board, even if he is a Nintendo fan boy. I appreciate his wisdom. It keeps my own fan boy instincts in check. He has a sharp critical eye and isn't shy about what he likes and dislikes.

Dave Mark did most of the editing and did an outstanding job. In addition, volunteer editors who looked at parts of the book include my mother, Nicole Wong, John Boudreau, Therese Poletti, Geoff Keighley, Mike Antonucci, John Taylor, and Jon Peddie.

Melissa Wilson of Edelman tirelessly helped arrange interviews with Microsoft's team and its partners. Molly O'Donnell coordinated access to Microsoft's people and helped check facts. This book wouldn't have happened without them. John Porcaro and Yumi Huh sifted through hundreds of photos to find the ones in this book. The fact checking was an enormous task that had to be done quickly. The help from the PR team is a big reason I have been able to finish on time and I thank them for their efforts. David Hufford and Doug Free assisted as well but there are too many PR folks to name. Edelman's PR staff, including Denise Gocke, made my job much easier by arranging for interviews with Microsoft executives on *Mercury News* stories. I thank the Microsoft Xbox 360 team members who granted me official interviews, including Robbie Bach, J Allard, Peter Moore, Todd Holmdahl, Shane Kim, Mitch Koch, David Reid, Greg Gibson, Ken Lobb, Larry Hyrb, Scott Henson, Aaron Greenberg, Chris Satchell, Laura Fryer, Leslie Leland, Bill Adamec, Barry Spector, Chris Di Cesare, Don Hall, Jonathan Hayes, Larry Yang, Nick Baker, Joe Belfiore, Masoud Foudeh, Peter Birch, Jeff Andrews, Hugh McLoone, Rick Rashid, Jeff Henshaw, Don Coyner, and Greg Canessa. I appreciated the short on-the-record time and unofficial interview time I had with Bill Gates and Steve Ballmer, though most of their comments were pulled from the public record. I also used material from a number of public appearances by Microsoft and industry folks, such as James Miller, Russ Glaser, Paolo Malabuyo, Jen-Hsun Huang, Ken Kutaragi, Neil Young, Roger Perkins, Gareth Wilson and Nolan Bushnell.

A number of journalists, along with many folks at Microsoft's partners, suppliers, and industry insiders also helped out. Among these are Ed Fries, Brett Lovelady, Larry Probst, Jeff Brown, Trudy Muller, Brian Farrell, Bruno Bonnell, Pat O'Malley, Renee Brotherton, Jim McKusker, Bob Feldstein, Dave Orton, Dave Erskine, Steven Kent, Todd Mowatt, N'gai Croal, Jack Thompson, Leland Yee, David Thomas, Hal Halpin, Tiffany Spencer, Will Wright, Kevin Bachus, Seamus Blackley, Grant Collier, Bobby Kotick, Doug Lowenstein, Jordan Weisman, Jamil Moledina, Sibel Sunar, Tim Sweeney, Mark Rein, Cliff Blezinski, Lorne Lanning, Kevin Krewell, Anita Frazier, Steven Kent, Chris Morris, Jed Lengyel, Alex Seropian, Susan Lusty, Andrew "bunnie" Huang, Greg Zeschuk, Ray Muzyka, Greg Richardson, Darrell Rhea, Garth Chouteau, James Gwertzman, Chris Crotty, Matthew Day, Paul Steed, David Wu Alex St. John, Dennis McCauley, Stuart Moulder, Nam Hyung Kim, Greg Thomas, Scott Steinberg, Todd Hollenshead, Simon Jeffery, Chris Szarek, Dave Demartini, Colin Sebastian, Michael Pachter, Susan Lusty, Richard Doherty, Peter Glaskowsky, Van Baker, P.J. McNealy, Don MacDonald, Ian Bogost, Rob Enderle, Chris Evenden, and Rick Hagen.

Others who offered insights included David Kirk, Dan Vivoli, Marv Burkett, Mike Hara, Derek Perez, Calisa Cole, Reggie Fils-Aime, George Harrison, Perrin Kaplan, Julia Roether, Eileen Tanner, Beth, Llewlyn, Satoru Iwata, Molly Smith, Phil Harrison and Kaz Hirai. Special thanks to Hiko Ikeda for keeping me posted on news events. A load of gamers also helped. They include Mahdi Ashktorab, Shayan Khales, Chris Szarek, Mirik Smit, Josh Sattler, Richard Ouellette, Alfonso Chartier, Timothy Tripp, Bart Rader, Mohamed Ghandour, Sundeep Makhecha, and many others. My thanks to everyone.

Lastly, where I couldn't get interviews, I used sources from other media and I have acknowledged them in footnotes. I am indebted to all the journalists who share the joy of covering video games on a daily basis.

INTRODUCTION

*T*he people who make consoles are made of sturdy stuff. They take a lot of risks, but they don't always get much glory. In my first book on the Xbox, and in this one as well, I've tried to dwell on the humans behind the machine. This is their story.

I didn't land a publisher for this book until August, 2005. But I have been working on it in some fashion from the moment my first book on the chronicles of the Xbox ended in 2002. I wrote my stories on the evolution of the video game industry for *Red Herring* magazine and, later, *The San Jose Mercury News*, and I saved my notes like a pack rat. At first, I didn't think the subject would lend itself to a second book. Microsoft didn't conquer the world the first time around, so who would want to read a sequel? But I have run into a lot of people who felt the subject deserved another telling. Popular demand drove me to give it another try. I wanted to give this book an insider's take, a probe into a single project, with as much detail as possible, in the hopes of recreating a feeling that you're there with the team. This would be a story that you wouldn't get by simply following the public announcements about the project in chronological order. That's what Tracy Kidder pulled off with *The Soul of a New Machine*, and that has always been my beacon.

I proposed the book, as I had done with the first one, as an independent journalistic project. Microsoft isn't paying me for this book and they have no right of approval on its text. But I needed to talk to a lot of people at the company above and beyond my normal daily newspaper interviews. At first, Microsoft was so burdened with the duties of its worldwide Xbox 360 launch that it decided not to work with me on this book. This made sense to me, since laying a company's secrets bare for all to see isn't always the best policy. I kept collecting material. I made a pilgrimage to Amsterdam on my own dime, and there I made my pitch to Peter Moore, the corporate vice president who headed international marketing and publishing for the Xbox division at the time. Peter eventually accepted and directed the PR folks to work with me, when they could find the time. Molly O'Donnell agreed to work with me and assigned Melissa Wilson of Edelman Public Relations to coordinate all of the interviews. They have granted me access to most of the right people.

With that help as a springboard, I have filled in the blanks. I have spoken with a wide array of people to make this book happen. The list includes hardware engineers, chip designers, component makers, game developers, game publishers, analysts, CEOs, marketers, recruiters, and gamers. They helped me put together the puzzle, get a handle on the big picture. You draw from enough sources, and the 360 degree view emerges.

This book has consumed so much of my time for so many months that I haven't had time to play many games. That's the curse of being a writer who loves video games. But my kids didn't let me off the hook. Instead of watching Saturday morning cartoons, we are slowly making our way through one of Microsoft's first Xbox 360 games, *Kameo: Elements of Power*. It's an epic role-playing game where we take turns playing Kameo the fairy princess. Sort of like *The Seven Samurai* or its Western copycat, *The Magnificent Seven*, we are collecting a series of comrade creatures who will help us unseat the evil Thorn and his army of trolls that threaten the Enchanted Kingdom. As most gamers know, there are different ways of plowing through any game. You can take a straight shot through the levels, skipping all of the side missions and the dead ends. This is the quickest way to burn a path through Kameo. But you miss out on a lot of fun if you don't explore a few of the side quests along the way. Side quests are the equivalent of stopping and smelling the flowers.

I have come to look at the creation of the Xbox 360 the same way. There are 2,000 people working within Microsoft's Xbox division. Beyond that, the number of people who touched the Xbox in some way, from game developers to factory workers, amounts to more than 25,000. There is no way that I could have interviewed them all and still come out with a timely book. I have tried to capture as many of the side quests as I can, but by and large I have burned a path from inception to launch, interviewing the key players as I could. The stories I have collected range from the reaction to security breaches on the original Xbox to the genesis of some of the most interesting games for the Xbox 360. But I've also tried to stick to the fundamentals of the mission at hand. I follow the Xbox 360 crew on adventures through the Badlands, and am there as they catch glimpses of the Enchanted Kingdom. Some of the sources, such as Bill Gates and Steve Ballmer, could answer only a handful of questions when I had the chance to ask. Microsoft's PR team provided me with plenty of interviews with executives, but I had to supplement the picture they gave me with additional views. I hope that what emerges is a cross section of the humanity involved in the entire enterprise. No doubt some people will read this work and see stories that are missing. I invite everyone to tell me more, so that I can revise the book in future editions. As Peter Moore told me when it was all done, "All the complexities of doing a global launch are hidden. The incredible sweat, tears, anguish, euphoria." I hope that this edition brings those behind the 360 into the foreground, if only for a moment, before everyone returns to playing their games.

PRELUDE

*T*he Microsoft executives were gathered for a review of the Xbox video game business. The numbers reflected the grim losses of going to battle against Sony. The company was losing money, but its online game service was surprisingly strong.

Steve Ballmer, the CEO of Microsoft, was pounding his fist on the table. "Xbox Live is awesome! It's our differentiator." He believed Microsoft could beat out its rivals, Sony and Nintendo, with better online games and entertainment experiences. He hit the table again and again, shouting, "Xbox Live!" Peter Moore, the new game marketing guy from Sega, quietly watched Ballmer. Moore was astonished at the enthusiasm of his bald-headed boss, whose outbursts were both comical and legendary. Then Ballmer accidentally hit the Polycom voice conferencing phone on the table. It broke. Ballmer stopped pounding and looked sheepish. Ed Fries, the head of Microsoft Game Studios, turned to Moore and said with a smile, "Welcome to Microsoft."

CHAPTER ONE

LESSONS

Robbie Bach, the Chief Xbox Officer at Microsoft, was beaming as he stepped on stage during Bill Gates' keynote speech at the Consumer Electronics Show on January 7, 2002. Under the glare of the Las Vegas Hilton spotlights, where Elvis Presley once shook his gyrating hips in hundreds of performances, Bach didn't look at all like an entertainment mogul. The 6-foot-3-inch man stood rigidly straight in a blazer, as if he were a soldier getting ready to salute. There was no telling that the then-39-year-old Bach had worn a back brace for five years as a teenager to correct the curvature of his backbone. Bach was the kind of man who looked at adversity as a challenge. Whether it was playing collegiate tennis with a brace; engaging in bruising basketball games at 5 am at the Pro Sports Club in Bellevue, Washington, with Microsoft CEO Steve Ballmer; or leading the fierce charge against the rivals of Microsoft's Office software, he always played to win. And most of the time he did. [1]

Gates surrendered the stage. Bach was exultant. He spoke about the fact that Microsoft had sold 1.5 million Xbox video game consoles during the last six weeks of 2001. The 9/11 terrorist attacks had not dampened the holiday buying spirit in the United States. Bach smiled as he recounted a conversation in which film director Ron Howard told Jay Leno that he just couldn't get his son to stop playing the Xbox. The game console had buzz – that critical word-of-mouth marketing, vital to success in games. The Xbox had the brand, the positioning, and the image that it needed to distinguish itself from its rivals and stay in the game for the long term. Microsoft was preparing to launch it in Japan in February and in Europe in March.

Jonathan "Seamus" Blackley joined Bach on stage to show off Sega's *Jet Set Radio Future* game. Bach preferred his battles in the court or the boardroom. He never had the thumb coordination to be a gamer. If he played at all, it was the relatively cerebral *Age of Empires* strategy games that Microsoft published for the PC. Blackley, on the other hand, was a game fan in the extreme. He was the kind of guy who loved mashing buttons in the mano-a-mano tests of machismo fighting games. He was one of the four original instigators of the Xbox, and had a reputation among game developers as being cool and in the know. Normally graceful under pressure, Blackley choked on the game as he went sliding off the rails while attempting to ride a skateboard on a rollercoaster. That ended the demo early. "All right, that's enough from Seamus, the game expert," Blackley cracked in self-deprecation. "Unable to stay on the rail."

They showed a comic video that demonstrated how online gaming would work on Xbox Live, where gamers could play against each other on the couch or across the Internet. The punch line was that a little girl in a living room could project a menacing image and wipe out burly brutes in a game of online football. It was done in goofy Microsoft style, with a shrimpy kid masquerading as someone with a deep voice.

Robbie Bach, chief Xbox officer, and Seamus Blackley, co-creator of the Xbox.

It was funny, and Bach took the spotlight again to bring the talk full circle to the business view. Microsoft, once again embarrassingly late to a strategic market, was aiming its corporate firepower at video games because of the industry's central position in the emergence of digital entertainment. Bach made the point that video game revenues had exceeded the movie box office receipts in the U.S. The message was clear. Microsoft was in the video game business to stay. Since Microsoft and its publishers had sold more than three games for every box, the company had generated sales estimated at $750 million for the six weeks before the end of the year. That in itself was a remarkable achievement.

After the speech was over, several thousand people shuffled out of the auditorium. The guys from Redmond felt it was time for a victory lap. Bach's presence meant that the Xbox, which began with all the attitude of a start-up, had gone corporate. But Blackley was there to recall the project's renegade roots. Bach was the quintessential big company Microsoft insider, and Blackley, the ultimate game industry fanatic. Without both to balance each other out, the Xbox wouldn't have been conceived as an audacious plan to rule the universe or been funded as a major corporate initiative. They didn't know it at the time, but it was one of their last chances to be together as a single unified team. As one of Blackley's heroes, World War II general George S. Patton, said, "All glory is fleeting."

Success is a relative thing. Sony had launched its PlayStation 2 console in Japan in March, 2000, about twenty months ahead of Microsoft. By the end of 2001, it had sold more than 25 million consoles worldwide. Microsoft was late, even by its own standards. The company had entered into fruitless negotiations to buy Sega and Nintendo.

"What do you get if you buy Nintendo for $5 billion," Steve Ballmer, CEO of Microsoft, said in an interview later. "The assets walk out the door everyday."

It had taken so long to decide which vendors to pick that it didn't give them enough time to get their vital engineering work done, nor did it give game developers enough time to make games. Nvidia didn't sign its contract for the graphics chip until just before the Game Developers Conference in March, 2000. The schedule gave it barely a year to combine a couple of different chips into one. Nvidia usually took about eighteen months to two years to complete such a project. It might have finished on time, were it not for a bug in a power supply that kept its engineers puzzled for weeks. The company finished the chip late, and when it handed its designs over to Flextronics, the contract manufacturer wasn't ready to begin. The manufacturing database wasn't big enough to keep track of all of the components, and Flextronics had to retool its software. Manufacturing didn't begin until September, just weeks before the launch. Microsoft pushed the U.S. launch back by a week, and it had already delayed the rollout in Japan and Europe until 2002. So much for the original plan to launch worldwide simultaneously. So much for instantaneous world domination. No console maker had ever pulled off a worldwide launch before, and now Microsoft knew why.

A few months later, at the E3 Expo in Los Angeles, Kaz Hirai, president of Sony's U.S. game division, got up on stage and primped. "The console wars are over," he declared. Satoru Iwata, CEO of Nintendo, thought it was "an arrogant thing to say." But Hirai's blustering proved right. Neither Microsoft nor Nintendo ever caught up to Sony's head start. The PS2 had the biggest number of consoles in the market, and that meant that game developers had the widest possible market if they published on the PS2. Feeding on this "network effect," the game developers had gravitated to Sony's machine because it offered the chance for the biggest sales, and the fans would soon follow.

Clearly, the company that got into the market first with a next-generation machine had a huge leg up and the lead was theirs to lose. The PlayStation 2, however, had been considered late itself, when compared to Sega's Dreamcast. But Sony managed to blunt the acceptance of the decidedly under-powered Dreamcast. It announced its specifications early and convinced gamers that it was worth waiting for the better PS2. Electronic Arts decided not to support Sega, throwing all of its weight behind the PS2. The vaporware strategy – aimed at wowing customers with fancy demos so they would wait to purchase – dampened demand for the Dreamcast. Sega ultimately threw in the towel and became a game software company.

By the middle of 2005, the scorecard was clear. Microsoft had sold 22 million Xboxes. Nintendo had sold about 20 million GameCubes. But Sony had sold about 90 million PS2s. Game developers like RockStar Games had seen the wisdom of launching their best titles, such as *Grand Theft Auto: Vice City* and *Grand Theft Auto: San Andreas,* exclusively for the PS2. Also, the PS2 had extra circuitry in it that made it capable of running original PlayStation games. That kept Sony's momentum going and it kept the lead, except for a short period when it had to deal with manufacturing glitches. As publisher support for the GameCube dried up, Nintendo slipped further behind. By the end of 2005, Sony held 55 percent of the U.S. market, Microsoft held 24 percent and Nintendo held just 15 percent. And on a worldwide basis, Sony had sold three of every four consoles in Europe and four of every five in Japan.

Part of the reason for this lopsided market share was Microsoft's disastrous debut in Japan, where it sold less than 500,000 consoles in the first four years. It was the place where the gang from Redmond couldn't shoot straight. Its game plan was lost in translation. Literally. Some Japanese developers submitted their code to Microsoft and they got indecipherable reports back in English. [2]

Microsoft had started out with representatives in Japan who spoke Japanese but didn't truly understand the games business, its traditions, or its movers and shakers. Japan was the cradle of video games, and Japanese gamers had very distinct tastes. And here was this *gaijin,* or foreigner, coming in uninvited. Despite these obstacles, Microsoft was able to win over some key developers such as Tecmo, makers of the *Dead or Alive* martial-arts games. But overall in Japan, Microsoft went down in flames.

It wasn't for lack of effort. Microsoft hired Toshiyuki Miyata, a former Sony studio chief, to run the Microsoft internal game studio in Tokyo. The American company wanted a Japanese insider to lend respect to its efforts to create games for the Japanese fans. But Microsoft didn't pour a lot of money into the Japanese studio, and the majority of Japan's game publishers stayed loyal to Sony. Microsoft wasn't ready for its February, 2002, launch in Japan. *Halo,* its top-selling game in the U.S., wasn't completed yet for Japan, in part because it hadn't planned on adapting the game to Japanese audiences. Besides, Japanese gamers didn't like "first-person shooter" games. They liked story-based games, such as the *Final Fantasy* series of role-playing games, and other titles with cute characters. Because Microsoft failed in an attempt to buy *Final Fantasy* maker Square outright, and because it couldn't convince Square to invest in Xbox games, the *Final Fantasy* franchise was still exclusive to the PlayStation 2. A total of 12 Xbox games were ready, including samurai swordsman game *Genma Onimusha* and *Project Gotham Racing*. But there was no blockbuster.

Then there was the ill-conceived game controller for the original Xbox. The initial design was too big for the smaller hands of many Japanese gamers, so the company had to go through an embarrassing redesign of the controller for the actual Japanese launch. Microsoft had assumed that the design it had created for U.S. gamers was going to work worldwide. The box was also enormous. It was about the size of an old video cassette recorder. Peter Moore, a former Sega marketing executive who joined Microsoft, joked it was so big "it couldn't fit through the doorway in most Japanese homes." For laughs, he showed a picture to industry executives depicting a giant Xbox atop a construction mover to hammer home the point about how big it was.

"Xbox was the Humvee of consoles," he joked.

In spite of these missteps, the launch in Japan started well enough. The Xbox was priced at the equivalent of $263, or 34,800 yen, about 5,000 yen more than a PS2. A limited edition model, which came with a remote control for watching DVD movies and a serial-numbered key holder autographed by Bill Gates, was available for $300. At a 7 am launch at a Tsutaya video rental store in the trendy Shibuya district of Tokyo, Gates handed over an Xbox to Atsushi Ishizaka, one of 300 people who had lined up the buy the console on the previous night. "I am so honored," the 22-year-old student proclaimed. Microsoft had set aside 250,000 units for the launch. But then the curse of the gaijin hit. Within days, Japanese fans began to complain that the machine would scratch their DVD game disks, leaving them playable but visibly marred on the outer rim of the disk's bottom. At first, the company argued with its customers, saying that the disks still functioned perfectly. Retailers were aghast and some decided to stop selling the machine. In early March, more than two weeks after the complaints arose, the company had to offer free replacements and apologize. Game sites started calling the incident "scratch gate," and sales never recovered from the quality gaffe. Four years later, Bach admitted during a meeting with financial analysts, "We're not even on the track right now. I mean, no, really we sell literally hundreds a week maybe. I mean the Japanese business has not been successful. We've not done well there."

In Europe, Microsoft did better, but not better than Sony. Sales in the United Kingdom were strong, but they fell short elsewhere. Microsoft made the mistake of pricing the box in the new Euro currency so that it was the same in every country, even though the value of the Euro hadn't yet equalized across Europe. The price came out to an equivalent of $419. By April, just a month after the launch, Microsoft had to cut the price on the Xbox in Europe to the equivalent of $266.

Then there was the issue of costs. Microsoft had burdened every machine with an expensive hard drive, whereas a drive was an option on the PS2. Every machine that Microsoft sold at $300 ended up losing an estimated $125. This was a byproduct of rushing into the market with off-the-shelf PC parts. These parts were already cost reduced and they allowed Microsoft to enter the market with better quality graphics than Sony could offer. But Microsoft couldn't get the manufacturers to keep reducing component costs. The hard drive, for instance, started at a cost of about $50 but didn't decline in cost all that much. Storing eight gigabytes of data, the hard drive was already at a rock-bottom single platter and single spindle, the barest components of a hard drive. Typically, hard disk drive makers kept the prices of their drives the same. They just offered more and more storage on each disk. But for Microsoft, that didn't help. It had to keep the components in the machine the same so that game developers could have a consistent platform to target.

In short, the Xbox sucked money out of Microsoft's coffers as if it were a sink hole. Microsoft didn't disclose precise numbers, but it did break out losses for the Home and Entertainment Group (Xbox was the biggest part of this group, but it also included home consumer products, TV software, and PC games). Microsoft lost $2.6 billion in this group from June 2002 to June 2005. Insiders believed the total losses for the Xbox were $3.7 billion. That was a staggering $168 per box for a machine that started out at $299 when it debuted. Those numbers are not precise, but analysts believe they are in the right ballpark. This was worse than the nightmare scenarios when it started planning the Xbox in 1999. On Sept. 29, 1999, Rick Thompson, then the vice president in charge of the project, warned Bill Gates in a meeting about the risks he was taking.

"If you do this, you will lose $900 million over eight years," Thompson said, as he delivered a PowerPoint slide deck entitled "Hail Mary."

Thompson went on to say that if Microsoft were forced to match aggressive price cuts by Sony over time, the Xbox project was going to lose $3.3 billion over the same period.

Those numbers were the best guesses the company had at the time. They were revised later on. But they were the numbers that Gates used to decide whether to go forward with the project. Gates felt it was worth the risk to stop a big threat from Sony and to open a new avenue for Microsoft's products in the home. The Xbox was the key to creating a second "pillar" of Microsoft software. This one would rule the home, while Microsoft's Office software ruled the work place. This battle was going to play out over two decades, and Microsoft needed more than the PC to win it. Gates was willing to make a big bet in order enter the video game business.

The public knew what kind of gamble Microsoft was taking as well. In March, 2001, analyst Henry Blodgett of Merrill Lynch predicted that Microsoft would lose $2 billion on the Xbox before turning a profit in fiscal 2005. His assessment was overly optimistic. Video games operated on the razor and razor blade model. You lost money on the razors, and made money on the blades. Microsoft lost money on the Xbox in hopes of making money on the games. If the model didn't work, the consequences could be catastrophic. The tie ratio, or the number of games sold per box, was the key measure of success. That's where

Sony left Microsoft behind.

Worse, hackers had cracked the security in the Xbox. They figured out how to modify the machines and turn them into cheap computers or load hard disks full of pirated games. That was the same problem that helped doom Sega's Dreamcast. Microsoft stood to lose a considerable amount of money as the hackers bought the hardware with no intention of helping Microsoft making the razor and razor blades model work. [3]

On the matter of losing money, there was a split between Gates and Steve Ballmer, who became CEO in January, 2000, four months after the Hail Mary presentation. Ballmer was responsible for Microsoft's financial performance, so he looked at the Xbox from the perspective of the balance sheet. Over time, he wanted the Xbox to win, but not at any cost. He had a lot of battles to fight on a lot of different fronts, and he wasn't willing to flush all of Microsoft's resources on one project. He bore down on the Xbox team to improve its bottom line. While the Xbox advocates argued that a hard disk drive was a necessary feature to woo skeptical gamers to Microsoft's side, Ballmer looked at the cold financial numbers. Several years later, Ballmer had to admit, "Putting the hard drive in there was a bad business decision. It cost more but didn't allow us to charge a premium in the market." He meant that the hard drive's advantages weren't so overwhelming that gamers would pay more for Xbox hardware or games.

The more machines Microsoft sold, the deeper the losses got. That was OK for a company that had tens of billions of dollars in cash, thanks to its Windows franchise on the PC. But it was embarrassing to take that money from PC owners and donate it back to gamers. At its heart, Microsoft's leaders were business professionals. They knew they had to stop Sony from taking over the living room. Everyone was forecasting that someone would make a mint in the living room, providing consumers with digital entertainment devices. These devices would be a byproduct of the convergence of consumer electronics, computing, and communications and serve as portals into an unlimited world of entertainment choices on the Internet. Whoever controlled the gateway to the living room would dominate digital entertainment, and boxes such as game consoles were viewed as Trojan horses. They would enter the home as game consoles, but eventually be used as digital entertainment gateways. Microsoft *had* to stop Sony. The Japanese company had boasted that the console would supplant the PC as the gateway to the living room, making a direct connection to consumers and their wallets.

The Xbox was a publicly unspoken attempt to destroy Sony's biggest profit source. But Microsoft's executives knew that the Xbox business had to be sustainable in the long run in order to escape the fate of so many of Microsoft's other ill-advised expansion efforts, such as WebTV, the failed effort to make an interactive TV set-top box that could be used to browse the web and read e-mail. Sony, meanwhile, kept the pressure on, periodically redesigning its box to lower costs and then cutting prices. Over the years, the losses would build up into the billions of dollars. Costs became such a concern that Microsoft's contract manufacturer, Flextronics, had to dismantle its factory in Hungary and move it to China.

In contrast to Ballmer, Robbie Bach shrugged off the losses. In an e-mail to his staff on Nov. 14, 2001, Bach said it was "mind boggling" that Microsoft was able to accomplish all that it had in less than two years, all from a standing start. He wasn't going to rest until Xbox was a "central part of the interactive entertainment landscape."

"We knew going in that this was going to be one of those 10-year, 15-year type projects, not something in the market for two years and all of a sudden you'll have a big success," he said. [4]

In the end, the Xbox's failure to defeat the PlayStation 2 was all about the games. Microsoft could have overcome all of these handicaps if it had the games that gamers wanted. *Halo* was its first game to top one million units sold. It was a fine accomplishment, and the game development team at Bungie had done an excellent job converting the shooting game from the PC to the console. Taking aim with a controller was never easy compared to shooting with a mouse, but Bungie had done it. And it had created a balanced game with an intriguing storyline and a heart-pounding, haunting musical score.

But *Halo* wasn't enough to overcome the wave after wave of good games debuting on the PlayStation 2. There weren't enough new games coming out for the Xbox. Electronic Arts had supported the Xbox, but not as wholeheartedly as it did the PS2. Some of the cool titles that Microsoft had touted, like Peter Molyneux's *Fable*, were nowhere in sight. In many respects, Microsoft had out-maneuvered Nintendo on a variety of games, but the Japanese company could always pull out a well-known franchise such as *Mario* or *Zelda* to get gamers frothing. And Nintendo had locked up the kids market with its cute characters, and it held a virtual monopoly on the handheld market.

The *Grand Theft Auto* series, exclusive to the PlayStation 2 for a long time, along with the *Gran Turismo* racing game, sealed Sony's dominance of the top selling games list. This doomed Microsoft to a battle with Nintendo for second place. And, thanks to its near-monopoly on portable games, Nintendo was making a lot of money, while Microsoft was losing billions of dollars. For Sony, the business model of razors and razor blades – in which the company lost money on the console but made up for it through software and accessory sales – was golden. It was much closer to breaking even on its console at all times than Microsoft was, and it could afford to make big bets on games. Microsoft could only assume it would have 20 million or so customers at the most. But Sony could plan for about 100 million customers. That meant that Sony could afford to give a big advance to a game developer to make a game into a PS2 exclusive. It knew that royalties on selling games would pay off in the end, considering that many of the top games sold far more units because of the huge installed base of the PS2. Microsoft, with a smaller installed based, couldn't afford to outbid Sony on many exclusives, because the business case never justified big advances. Sony had a network effect going where one customer led to another, and the logical end of that process was monopoly power. Microsoft was the little guy in this fight.

Some things had gone right for Redmond, though. Microsoft, for once, had come into the market as the good guy. It was earning credibility as the company that could break the grip of the Japanese giants, winning over fans with its considerations for gamers and developers. It was the underdog, yet it had the power to upset the status quo. Those who hated Microsoft's monopolistic practices in software couldn't criticize it in the game arena. And that translated into a positive brand image. For the first time in years, Microsoft had introduced a product that made it seem like the coolest of companies. And Microsoft game managers such as Bungie's Pete Parsons could speak about "world domination" without spurring an antitrust suit. Seamus Blackley's passion was one of the key reasons that Microsoft was perceived in this way.

Bill Gates can play the "good guy" in the video game business.

Microsoft had taken the market share that Sega once held in consoles which, in the Dreamcast generation, was about 15 percent. Not only that, it had even surpassed Nintendo's market share in the low 20s. With its first console, Microsoft had edged out a company that had been in the games business for decades. *Halo 2* sold 2.4 million units in its first 24 hours when it went on sale in November, 2004. That generated cash register receipts in the U.S. and Canada of $125 million, which Microsoft claimed was a record-breaking day for any kind of entertainment. Microsoft had its first quarterly profit in its Xbox division in the quarter that ended Dec. 31, 2004, thanks to the launch of *Halo 2*. Analysts were projecting that *Halo 2* would top 10 million units sold, or more than $500 million in retail sales. *Halo 2* drove subscriptions to Xbox Live, which charged $50 a year, to a record 2 million. The hours played on Xbox Live exceeded 1.4 billion. Sales of Peter Molyneux's *Fable* also topped a million units. That helped Microsoft narrow the losses for the Home and Entertainment Group in fiscal 2005 to a mere $391 million.

"If you think about what we did with Xbox Live, *Halo 2*, *Fable*, and console sales, 2004 was a great year for us," Bach said.[5] "We grew share. We produced some great products; we had the No. 1 day in entertainment history with *Halo 2*. It is tough for me not to include ourselves on the list of people who had a good year."

Xbox Live, Microsoft's online gaming service that debuted in 2002, made possible the new careers of professional gamers such as Alfonso "Fonzi" Chartier, a 19-year-old Palo Alto student in his second year at Santa Clara University. He and three friends were part of Trademark Gamers, a sponsored team that specialized in *Halo 2* online multiplayer tournaments. They did a circuit of 13 tournaments during the year, winning the two tournaments in which they all played together as a team. The team traveled across the states, all expenses paid.

"It's the No. 1 cooperative game," Chartier said in an interview over Xbox Live's voice over the Internet communicator. "It's a thinking game. I played single player once and then forgot about it after I went online."

There were more than 400,000 clans that gathered on a daily or weekly basis to scrimmage with *Halo 2*. Full told, there were two million paying subscribers for Xbox Live, a number that had doubled since the previous year. This passion was why Bach had committed to spending $2 billion on Xbox Live over a number of years.

Sony had held on to two thirds of the market with the PlayStation 2, but it had no such following for its online games. While Microsoft managed the online game infrastructure, Sony left that chore to the game publishers, with haphazard results. It faced severe pressures from Microsoft's attack on its key profit maker. On two occasions during 2004, Sony made the mistake of not having enough PS2s on the shelves. In March, 2004, Microsoft cut the price of the Xbox by $30 to $149. It took until May for Sony to match the price cut, and by that time, a lot of damage was done. The price cut enabled Microsoft to double its Xbox sales in April, 2004. For one month, Microsoft even had the largest market share in North America. Then, again, in the fall of 2004, Sony ran short on PS2s as it transitioned from the older PS2s to a smaller, slimmed down design. The so-called "PS2 Slim" machines were nominally priced at $150, but by the end of November in 2004, they were selling on eBay for $230. Microsoft kept its stores fully stocked during the time, allowing it to gain market share and reduce its losses. In 2004, Sony sold 4.6 million units in the U.S., a number lower than the year before, while Microsoft sold 4 million Xboxes, according to the NPD Group. Microsoft made a million extra units beyond its plan, but it stopped short on the production because it was losing so much on every box. It didn't want to make the red ink spin out of control. The setback for Sony showed what happens when you are racing Bill Gates and you take your hands off the steering wheel.

J Allard, general manager for the Xbox platform, said in a message to his troops at the beginning of 2003, "If I needed to pick an introductory quote for the 'History of the Xbox,' I'd choose the following words spoken by Gandhi: 'First they ignore you, then they laugh at you, then they fight you, then you win.'"

Allard added, "It's a very relevant quote to Sony's attitude towards us in the console market. As we built the plan and started talking to partners in 1999, Sony wouldn't even comment or engage in the discussions. After we announced the plan publicly around the world and for the first couple of E3s (trade shows), Sony scoffed with the attitude that we would never be serious enough to do what it took and took a lot of cheap shots. Even at the launch, they acted as if they really didn't believe that we were serious and to the extent that they used any tactics with the press or retail, they were very cavalier."

"Today, it's pretty clear that they know we're here for real and are serious about the business. They are clearly reacting to the success and leadership we've demonstrated with Xbox Live. They are hard at work to hold us off at retail. As examples of this, witness (their move to) broadband-only in Europe; the late addition of voice support in *U.S. Navy Seals: SOCOM*; the money they are pouring towards third parties to hold up titles from simultaneous shipping; the advertising they are throwing at TV. It would be crazy to say that we have them on their heels or in a corner, but it's evident that they are feeling serious pressure from us and are trying to defend their installed-base lead. This holiday, we landed a couple of punches that have made them a little dizzy."

Sony's mistakes were relatively minor ones, but they were execution mistakes – enough to give Microsoft a chance to catch up. And they probably cost Ken Kutaragi, the tough-talking boss of Sony's game division, his chance to be the CEO of all of Sony. In March, 2005, Sony's two top executives resigned and the board appointed Howard Stringer, a *gaijin*, or foreigner, to head the Japanese consumer electronics giant. It was the first time an outsider had ever held the top post at Sony. It was an indication that Microsoft had rattled Sony. Stringer was an affable cost cutter who brought Sony's music and movie business back to life. He was viewed as an inspirational leader, while Kutaragi had developed a reputation as prickly. Nobuyuki Idei, the departing CEO of Sony, even criticized Kutaragi as not being a good listener when asked why Kutaragi didn't get the job. Stringer went on to announce a $1.8 billion restructuring and 10,000 job cuts. Microsoft, by contrast, had given tens of billions of dollars in excess cash to its shareholders – and still had $37 billion left in its coffers. It was more than enough money to buy every single independent game company.

"Sony and Microsoft look at each other as formidable competitors," said Larry Probst, CEO of Electronic Arts, the biggest independent game publisher. "It's a battle to the death."

Microsoft had hurt a big rival. Nintendo was still making money, but not as much as it once had. But in the big picture, it isn't clear that Microsoft took

aim at the right competitors when it moved into the game business. It had to pay out billions of dollars in antitrust settlements. And while Sony was hurting, Microsoft was clearly falling behind other rivals. The Internet companies – Amazon.com, Yahoo!, Google, and eBay – took off as a group as broadband penetration created new demand for online services. Microsoft's competing services were falling behind on most of these fronts. And Apple Computer cleaned up in digital music with the launch of the iPod. While Microsoft was successful, to a degree, in holding back its rivals in games, it had a lot of holes in its defenses elsewhere.

Still, Microsoft had the appetite and the war chest to go another round with Sony. That big cushion of cash was insurance for whatever losses the Xbox suffered as it experimented with business plans.

"Can we get to No. 1?" Ballmer said. "Yes, I think so. We have to have great products."

Microsoft was maneuvering to gain what it called "thought leadership," where it dominated the industry chatter if not the market itself, as it went through its gaming training mission. And the gains against Sony, though small and late in the season, kept the Xbox team going. That's why Bill Gates, in an interview with *Time* magazine, laughed and said, "The first generation, it's just like a video game. If you play perfectly, at the end, it says, 'You get to play again.' That's all it says!" Gates cracks up at his own joke. "You put your hand in the till. There's no quarter down there. There's no, like, even tickets to buy funny dolls or anything. It's just, Hey, play again."[6]

1. *Business Week*, "Robbie Bach is Ready To Rumble," by Jay Greene, Nov. 28, 2005

2. "Risk 360," *360 Magazine*, February, 2005, p. 48.

3. "Hacking the Xbox: An Introduction to Reverse Engineering," by Andrew "bunnie" Huang, No Starch Press 2003, p. 3

4. "Robbie Bach: New York Times Breakfast With Microsoft," Churchill Club interview by John Markoff, April 27, 2005

5. IDG Industry White Paper: "And They're Off," September, 2005

6. "Out of the Xbox," by Lev Grossman, Time, May 23, 2005

CHAPTER TWO

GAMES FAIL TO WIN THE CULTURE WAR

Not only did Microsoft fail to dislodge Sony, but the company also fell short of the larger ambitions that inspired so many of the talented artists of the game industry to join in its crusade. It is worth remembering the words of Ed Fries, who ran Microsoft Game Studios from 1995 through 2003. The Xbox division truly wanted to change the world. Fries had made a big prediction at Microsoft's *Gamestock* event in Seattle in 2001, where he first showed off games for the Xbox. He promised that the game industry was ready to "leave the cartoon world behind." Some of what he said was prescient. He had been right that the epic battle between the three gaming giants was driving innovation, much like the space race, at a very fast pace. He had challenged his colleagues to offer more than mindless entertainment.

"A great book, a great movie, a great play, they are about more than just killing time," he said, holding his audience of game journalists spellbound. "We need to reach out to our audience. We need to create things that are relevant to them. We need to change how they view the world. We ask the wrong questions. What kind of game is this? We should be starting to ask, 'What are you trying to say with this game?' What do you want it to mean to the people who play it? What I'm saying is, we need to create not just entertainment. We need to create art. I think that is the goal of all the other forms of media. It's really the only way to advance to where we want to get. If we take that seriously, if we focus on making art, not just entertainment, then I think for the first time we'll deserve to speak to the mass audience and inherit our rightful place as the future of all entertainment."

A few years later, Fries was no longer the chief at the game studios. He had quit because he didn't get to run the studio autonomously, not because gaming had failed to become an art form. Microsoft was disappointed that the original Xbox didn't become even more of a cultural force than it was. It had not succeeded in truly changing cultural attitudes about games. The prediction that Fries made in his speech did not really come true. Fries' words inspired artists to dedicate themselves to the large cause. The console makers were spending billions to grab a bigger share of entertainment dollars and a bigger share of the time that consumers dedicated to leisure. They said that the true competitors weren't the other video game companies. The competition was mass market TV – shows like *American Idol* that were vying for the same eyeballs. The "war for the eyeballs" that Intel CEO Andy Grove had predicted so many years before was finally coming to be. Microsoft and its competitors had promised that they would expand gaming as a mass media. Harkening back to the first advertisement that Electronics Arts created upon its founding in 1982, the game creators were going to produce games that could make you cry. They were going to enthrall the women and girls who had heretofore failed to get excited over testosterone-based games. Forget the similar broken promises of 3DO, Rocket Science, and convergence with Hollywood. Games were not just for geeks anymore. They had the potential to draw in everyone, like the mass appeal of Will Wright's family simulation game, *The Sims*, which was on its way to selling tens of millions of units, raking in revenues like a movie blockbuster. Worldwide, the various versions of *The Sims* franchise had sold more than 58 million copies by 2005. Gabe Newell, the CEO of Valve LLC in Kirkland, Wash., noted that his company's statistics showed that gamers spent several billion minutes a month playing *Counter-Strike* online – which was more than the time people had spent watching *Friends* on TV before the show ended.

At Microsoft's Gamestock event, Ed Fries pointed to an era where games dominated entertainment.

The market research companies were frothing at the idea of Gaming Uber Alles. Forrester Research predicted that the video game industry would triple from 2000 to 2005. International Data Corp. predicted that the percentage of households with video game consoles would double from 35 percent to 75 percent. Gaming was coalescing into a massive audience, as about 80 percent of kids played games. Over time, all the non-gamers were going to die off. And, based on the predictions in 2000, it seemed like all of those non-gamers would die off in the next five years, or convert to gaming.

It didn't happen. Doug Lowenstein, president of the Entertainment Software Association and the man who is paid to be the industry's biggest booster, had to bring everybody down to earth in his keynote speech at E3 in May 2005.

"How many of you of you have written at any time that the video game industry is bigger than Hollywood, or have heard someone in the industry make such a claim?" Lowenstein asked. "Let's set the record straight once and for all: it is simply not true – yet. It has never been true. Yes, when you add video game hardware sales and software sales together, you come up with a figure which exceeds the total box office take of the film industry. But including hardware sales in the figure skews the comparison. Why not include the sales of DVD players? And even if you think it is valid to include console, handheld, and related hardware sales in the calculation, it fails to account for the streams of additional revenue produced by Hollywood, from DVD and videotape rental and sales to syndication of films for broadcast and cable TV. In truth, the worldwide film industry stands at about $45 billion and the worldwide video game industry checks in at $28 billion." (Lowenstein had guessed low on the film industry, as others put the number well above $50 billion). Parts of the world were coming on strong. But Japan was in decline.

So this was the reality check. Four years had gone by, and the Xbox had not conquered all. Many mass market consumers still considered games the domain of geeks, or social misfits who had nothing better to do than to toil away in virtual dungeons. A good movie could garner an audience of a billion people. The real mass market was movies. In a good year, the movies could generate 1.6 billion individual ticket purchases at the theaters in the U.S., according to Exhibitor Relations. That was far above the number of gamers who played religiously every week. Not even Sony had vaulted the game industry to its desired goal of supplanting the movie industry. Microsoft had hoped that favorable demographics, the rise of gaming in youth culture, the pervasive spread to all corners of the globe, the creation of incredible games – all these factors were going to propel it to the top of the heap in video games. A rising tide of video games was supposed to lift all boats, even for the second and third place companies that couldn't overtake the leader. The game business was still cyclical.

Microsoft had lost money, and both Sony and Nintendo saw the percentage profit on sales shrink in the generation. Among those big players, there wasn't a clear winner. The biggest beneficiaries were those who got to ride on the coattails of the console makers. Electronic Arts was the biggest winner of all, growing its revenues from $1.4 billion in the year ended March, 2000, when the PS2 launched in Japan, to $3.1 billion in the year ended March, 2005. Net income had grown from $154 million to $504 million in the same time period. EA had supplied ammunition to all sides in the console war, making games for every machine. During the generation of the PS2, EA turned its Madden NFL football game from the top sports game to one of the top games period. Clearly, something was happening to fuel this growth.

There was no denying the fact that the subculture of gaming was gathering momentum. Todd Holmdahl, the Xbox hardware chief, noted that his own six and eight-year-old boys were playing *Toe Jam & Earl* instead of watching Saturday morning cartoons.

Halo had risen to the level of cultural phenomenon, with celebrities bragging that they played it. About six months after it launched, the *Halo* creators started getting solicitations from Hollywood about how to make *Halo* into a movie. On the web, kids were more likely to download the latest episode of *Red Vs. Blue* or *The Halo Chronicles* than to watch a show on TV. These shows were "machinima," or short videos that were captured on screen by manipulating the animated characters of *Halo*. For younger audiences, the films were much like the sitcoms of the gaming era. It was harder to find kids who didn't play games. Occasionally, the Hollywood studio chiefs would tip their hat to games. Michael Eisner, CEO of Disney, visited the Microsoft booth at the E3 show in 2004. After checking out titles like *Halo 2*, he said, "Movies are going to be harder to make now that games are so beautiful." Microsoft itself had captured hardcore gamers. In its first six months, Microsoft's Xbox.com web site drew 5.6 million visitors a month who viewed 97 million pages per month.

Girls were starting to play. By 2005, 43 percent of all gamers were female, according to the Entertainment Software Association. At casual game sites that featured puzzle games or card games, women were half the audience. Laura Fryer, a game producer at Microsoft who grew up as a bit of an oddball playing *Dungeons and Dragons* with her older brother, said that she was a rarity as a game player in high school. "I'm a game geek," she said, "But my younger cousin is a cheerleader and she plays games. The industry and the community of gamers are changing."

Heather Chaplin and Aaron Ruby, two video game journalists, tracked this subculture for five years and wrote about it in their book, *Smart Bomb: Inside the $25 billion Video Game Explosion.*

"Because of this new medium," they wrote, "There are millions of people around the world who consider themselves citizens of virtual planets; others spend countless hours trying to master tactical combat maneuvers, or even spend hundreds of dollars to hear an orchestra play the score from a cherished videogame. People around the world haunt video arcades, hopping to the electric rhythm of games like *Dance Dance Revolution*, or take their computers to gatherings in giant warehouses where they party and compete against their peers, playing videogames over local networks. Still others have banded together in clans, devoting themselves to the task of using game designers' own creations against them, disassembling popular titles and then rebuilding them as their imagination dictates. The military has gotten in on the game as well, tapping video game developers to build tools to train soldiers, and those very same tools are then repackaged and sold to consumers."

But the Xbox moved the ball forward without scoring the touchdown. Microsoft, and the video game as an art form, wasn't there yet.

"I don't have anything against *Halo*," said Ian Bogost, assistant professor of information design and technology at the Georgia Institute of Technology. "I like these games as much as anyone. But the Xbox certainly hasn't expanded the possibility space for video games. *Halo* is an entertaining game, but it's not what I have in mind. It's not Picasso's *Guernica*, for example."

What Bogost lamented was that the drive toward realism, or higher resolution graphics that approached verisimilitude, was viewed as a replacement for art.

"For video games to engage social change on a meaningful scale, we need a sea change in our understanding. We need to acknowledge that video games are a medium, a medium capable of a multitude of expressive possibilities, from catharsis to emotion to politics to social critique."

Stan Lee, the creator of Spider-Man, pondered the question as to whether video games would become an art form. Comic books had to struggle for decades for recognition as art. He thought video games were already art.

"Suppose William Shakespeare or Michelangelo were alive today," he said in his gravelly voice after a speech at a video game conference. "Let's say they work on a comic book or a video game. Would anybody say it wasn't an art form? Anything that has to do with creativity done for the public is an art form. It could be beautifully illustrated, well written, a piece of junk. Same goes for movies, novels and video games. They are either beautifully written or badly done. You have characters who could be as engaging as anything Mark Twain wrote. We have action that can compare favorably with the best motion pictures. To me, everything gets back to the story and characters. By that measure, video games can be one of the best art forms."

Some believed there was a vicious cycle that was keeping games from becoming more and more artistic. Lorne Lanning, the developer of the *Oddworld* series of games, lamented that the economics of game consoles didn't help. Imagine, he said, if the movie industry had to reinvent the camera every time it wanted to make a new movie. Game developers first had to master technology before they could go to work on their content. As consumers became spoiled by Hollywood special effects, they expected the same from their games. This forced game publishers to add more staff for each game.

Neil Young, a vice president at Electronic Arts, observed that it took 20 people to develop a PlayStation game, and about 80 to develop a PlayStation 2 game. He estimated it could easily take 150 people to develop a PlayStation 3 game. That amounted to $30 million in payroll costs for two years of development, he said. With those kinds of costs, publishers grew risk averse. They stuck with known franchises, sequels and licenses. Sex and violence, as with the movies, were an easy bet to draw an audience of hardcore gamers. Independent game studios were starting to go out of business, much like independent film makers. There was no equivalent of Disney's Miramax to promote the sleeper Oscar winners. Games with narrow niches, such as war games, were crowded off the shelves. The breakeven point for major games was rising toward 500,000 units sold. A very small percentage of the 2,000 or so titles produced each year ever sold that much. Trying to be creative with original content was risky. Like Hollywood, the game industry was starting to lose its creativity and narrow its entertainment choices.

Are games too violent?

Bogost said that video games were still forms of expression worthy of free speech protection. But as the game industry catered to hardcore gamers with sex and violence, others didn't think so. Instead, by the summer of 2005, the criticism of games as a corrupting influence had hit its peak. Like comic books before them, video games were much closer to being classified as corrupting influences as bad as alcohol, tobacco and pornography. David Walsh, director of the National Institute for Media and the Family, feared that game companies were in an arms race to outdo each other in producing more and more shocking, violent games to win over jaded audiences.

As their influence among youth in society grew, developers of violent games found themselves the target of what they viewed as a McCarthyesque investigation. Video game violence had been in the cross-hairs of conservative politicians and anti-violence advocates as the cause of mass school shootings from Paducah, Ky., to Littleton, Colo. The shootings began with 14-year-old Michael Carneal, who killed his classmates in 1997. Such shootings inspired copycat violence. Critics of games contended the shooters were alienated young male teenagers who sought refuge from schoolyard bullies in first-person shooter games such as *Doom*. Lt. Col. David Grossman, author of *Stop Teaching Our Kids To Kill*, argued that such games were "murder simulators."

State by state, city by city, the anti-games lobby proposed regulations against the sale of mature-rated video games to minors. The laws tried to define the type of violence that was inappropriate for young kids, but the courts struck down the laws as unconstitutionally vague and that they had chilling effects on the creation of content. As such, they were violations of the First Amendment.

No one crusaded harder than Miami attorney Jack Thompson. A medical malpractice attorney who defended doctors, he had cut his teeth early in the culture wars. In 1989, he led a campaign against the raunchy lyrics of 2 Live Crew's album, *As Nasty As They Want To Be*.

In 1999, he turned his attention to violent games. He filed a $130 million product liability lawsuit against various movie and game makers on behalf of the victims of Michael Carneal. The suit was tossed out in 2002. But Thompson vowed to continue his efforts, quoting the Bible and saying he had a holy mission to fulfill. Some media wrote him off as a right-wing lunatic. Thompson called Doug Lowenstein, the head of the game industry association, a morally bankrupt defender of the game industry, akin to Adolph Hitler, Joseph Goebbels, and even Saddam Hussein.

But while some disagreed with his methods, a number of parent advocates had taken up the anti-video game cause. The American Medical Association and American Psychological Association weighed in with their support for the regulation of violent media aimed at children. The Surgeon General didn't agree with them, but they decided that the weight of 1,000 studies showed that witnessing violence could make children more aggressive. A lot of parents were conflicted about the growing violence and realism of games. They thought it was appropriate to monitor what their kids played.

Even Nolan Bushnell, the father of video games and founder of Atari, said, "I felt that video games took a wrong turn in the 1980s when they became violent." There were very few kids around who were aware that video games started as a peaceful medium.

Henry Jenkins, director of comparative media studies at the Massachusetts Institute of Technology, was one of those who embraced the impact of video games on mass culture. He noted that youth violence was at a 30-year low in the United States. He cited the U.S. Surgeon General's report that stated the risk factors for school shootings included mental stability and the quality of home life, not media exposure. Jenkins noted that the laboratory context for studies on the effects of game violence were far different from real life, leading to suspect conclusions about "media effects." [1]

Moreover, he noted that the average age of gamers was 30, meaning that most video gamers were older than 18 and therefore not the targets of violent video games. Game audiences were becoming more diverse as young girls picked up games such as *The Sims*, a family simulation game which became the most popular game of all time because of its crossover appeal. As much as games were criticized for teaching violence, they were rarely praised for documented effects such as making gamers into better problem solvers and developing better hand-eye coordination. To those who said that games were socially isolating, Jenkins noted that most gamers played with other friends or family members, and that online play could be socially liberating. Fears that games would desensitize antisocial kids were overblown and based on a fundamental misunderstanding of what happens in games, he argued. [2]

Then "Hot Coffee" hit. In the summer of 2005, a hacker from the Netherlands discovered that there were hidden scenes on the disk for *Grand Theft Auto: San Andreas*. At first, RockStar denied that it created the hidden sex scenes, which depicted oral sex, nudity and simulated intercourse between the game's hero and various women who invited him inside for some "hot coffee." It wasn't clear at first if the animations were an "Easter egg" meant for gamers to find and unlock, or if they were simply scenes that had been deleted. Take-Two's press handlers later said that the scenes were inadvertently left on the disks during the editing process. In any case, advocates such as Thompson seized on the opportunity to heap criticism on RockStar. He called for a revocation of the mature rating on the game. The Entertainment Software Ratings Board, the industry group charged with rating the games, did just that, labeling the game AO for "adults only." Take-Two Interactive agreed to pull the game from shelves and replace it with a cleaned up version. As Thompson led the charge against games yet again, he received numerous death threats via e-mail. This was simply more evidence, he argued, that the minds of gamers had been warped by violent video games.

Parents were outraged at the thought that their kids had bought a video game that could expose them to pornographic images. Until "Hot Coffee" appeared, California state senator Leland Yee had little support for a bill banning the sale of ultra-violent video games to minors. But afterward, even California's Gov. Arnold Schwarzenegger came out in favor of the bill. It passed and the governor, who starred in various violent video games himself, signed it despite warnings that it wouldn't pass constitutional muster. Similar bills had been passed in Illinois and Michigan. Courts struck down these laws as unconstitutional, but each time the politicians who passed them got a little bit closer to the "magic language" that could succeed in balancing the rights of the creators with the need to protect kids. Some game developers privately fretted that RockStar's mistake was bringing a lot of unwarranted heat down on the industry. Even Walsh at the National Institute for Media and the Family, in his tenth annual report on video games, said that the system for rating games was broken. The report gave the industry poor grades for keeping harmful games out of the reach of kids.

"The industry's efforts to be good corporate citizens have not kept pace with its explosive growth," Walsh wrote in his MediaWise report for 2005.

New York's U.S. Senator, Hillary Clinton, jumped on the issue by introducing a bill in December, 2005, seeking to impose the California-style curbs on sales of violent video games to minors on a national level.

From politicians to cultural warriors, video games were an easy target. They were a relatively young industry that didn't have the kind of clout that established industries had. These forces sought to contain the spread of gaming as if it were a dangerous virus. And against them, it seemed that Microsoft was swimming upstream in its goal to make gaming a mainstream activity. The original Xbox fell short of that goal. The company had to try it again once again with the Xbox 360. As Bobby Kotick, CEO of Activision, said in an interview a few years back, "Microsoft is a version 2.0 company."

Over time, Microsoft's hope was that it would convert all of those non-gamers who feared the effects of games. They could be enticed with "casual" games that were much less intense than the hardcore violent games. From "Tetris" on a PC to "Jamdat Bowling" on a cell phone, these lightweight games could lure those who might have been intimidated by the games that took hours and hours to play. Microsoft had the hardcore gamers, but it had not made a dent in the mass market that Sony had won over. Expanding upon Sony's audience was the path to universal adoption. With the Xbox 360, Microsoft would pursue that goal aggressively.

1.   www.pbs.org/kcts/videogamerevolution/impact/myths.html

2.   www.pbs.org/kcts/videogamerevolution/impact/myths.html

CHAPTER THREE

THE XBOX GREEN BERET DIASPORA

*T*he original Xbox was built by dedicated souls who dealt with the stress of a fast-moving start-up and sacrificed long hours for the sake of getting the job done. They were elves in the workshops of Bill Gates, thriving on the thrill of fashioning something beautiful from chaos. The Xbox wouldn't have happened without them. But the Xbox team didn't survive the launch intact. It was like an army that had been exhausted by a long march. Not everyone was sticking around for the next fight.

The impact of these departures didn't change the course of what had become a multibillion-dollar business, but they weighed heavily on morale. Jonathan "Seamus" Blackley left Microsoft in April, 2002, just three years after he had joined. Most people credited Blackley for driving the Xbox to the market by sheer force of will. He was a game developer turned evangelist, and he supplied the passion behind the Xbox. He was the last of the four original co-creators of the Xbox to depart.

His primary co-conspirator, Kevin Bachus, had already left almost a year earlier. Blackley and Bachus had worked together like renegade brothers. The other co-founders, Otto Berkes and Ted Hase, had left the project even earlier, in mid-design, when the Xbox concept shifted from a Windows PC to a dedicated console. They split because they had philosophical differences with the direction of the program. Hase and Berkes both move back to the Windows group, working on technologies such as HomeStation, a dorm room computer which was never commercialized. Their work gave some inspiration to the team that put together Microsoft's living room computers, dubbed Media Center PCs. After that effort, Berkes enlisted Horace Luke, the industrial designer of the original Xbox, to join him in Microsoft Research to design handheld computers that ran the entire Windows operating system. Berkes was a Windows hawk, and probably more passionate about the PC than Bill Gates was. He felt the PC was the adaptable Darwinian beast. He wanted the PC to win, not the game boxes.

The Xbox team members followed a cycle. The gamers and other geeks inside Microsoft had the passion to come up with ideas like the Xbox and push them through. They ran into the buzz saw of cold reason. The dispassionate corporate veterans took those tech-heavy ideas and fashioned them into real business ideas. They then created the real product that fused the two opposite extremes personified by Seamus Blackley and Robbie Bach. The gaming evangelist gave the product its credibility with developers, who in turn convinced publishers to finance games. When the games grabbed the attention of the hardcore, the wannabes followed. Soon enough, the mass market embraced the product. But the corporate guys had to bankroll the gaming enthusiast's project, and figure out a way to make money. With more money behind a project, the more developers and publishers came on board. The corporate guys were really the ones who had the keys to the mass market. The two extremes needed each other.

The fusion created a product with momentum. By May, 2002, at the E3 show in Los Angeles, Microsoft announced that there would be 200 games available for the Xbox by the holiday season. Robbie Bach also announced that Microsoft would spend $2 billion on the Xbox Live online gaming service over the next five years. The business was a juggernaut. Many of the gamers on board felt it was foolish to stick around working on the console business when they could be making games for it.

Sometimes, the gamers and the business guys came together in a magical kind of union. Robbie Bach said the original team was a lot more like the United Nations. J Allard said that the group would never accidentally have met in the same bar. Blackley had a knack for inspiring the gamers and technologists to believe in the project.

"I was inspired by Seamus when he talked about his goal," said Jed Lengyel, a graphics expert who moved over from Microsoft Research to join the Xbox Advanced Technology Group. "This was a tool for the artists. An artist-centric platform. It turned out to be the best time I ever had working. Seamus was a kick."

But the work could be grueling. Allard later recalled in an e-mail, "We were far away from convincing developers, publishers or the press that we "got it," though. The standard reaction was 'This is Microsoft, right? The business software company talking about making a consumer electronics product to compete with Sony and Nintendo? Yeah, right.' We heard it all. 'You'll never get the developers!' 'All they'll have is crappy PC ports.''They can't make 2001.' 'Where's the CTRL-ALT-DEL buttons on it?' 'Will it green-screen instead of blue-screen when it crashes?' 'Will there be any memory left for the game when Windows is done loading?' 'It's a Trojan Horse to get MSN and Hotmail into the living room.' 'No kid will think that a system from Microsoft is cool.' 'They won't get it right until version 3.'"

Inside the company, the skepticism was just as tough. One crucial meeting illustrated just how excruciating the Xbox work could be. As the team sifted through the technical details, software chief Jon Thomason and technical leader

J Allard had concluded that the game console couldn't use Microsoft Windows as an operating system. It took up too much of the box's resources. Game developers wanted a stripped-down version so that the system's resources were reserved for running games. On Valentines Day, 2000, Bill Gates walked into the meeting and asked why the operating system had to be built in a way that threw out most of Windows. Robbie Bach and his men stood their ground against Gates. The gamers wanted Gates to go for it. They all convinced Gates, who was prepared to make a huge investment. At the end of the three-hour meeting, Gates, Steve Ballmer, and everyone else were on board. Microsoft had decided not only to do the Xbox, but its successor as well, which did not yet have a name. Allard said, "It was approving a 20-year vision." He added, "The thinking for the Xbox 360 was laid down before we approached the project initially." The meeting had been so brutal, it was known as the "St. Valentines Day Massacre." Bach later said, "None of us have ever forgotten that meeting." [1]

The brutal process seemed natural for starting any huge project. But on a human level, it took a toll. Whenever someone had a good idea, dozens of people had to jump on it and fashion it into the right idea. The passionate gamers had to compromise. They got chewed to pieces in the business discussions. This sometimes cost them the respect of the top bosses, who no longer listened to what was once considered wise counsel. Other people took over the ideas and made them their own. Nat Brown, one of the earliest Microsoft veterans to join the core group of Xbox founders, knew that this was a very natural thing at Microsoft. There was even a name for it: the handoff. When his time came, he stepped aside. The handoff went well as far as he was concerned. But Blackley and Bachus had to flail about for while as they tried to find new roles within a much larger project that they could no longer claim as their own. They didn't embrace a Zen-like acceptance of their fates.

As the Xbox idea became an Xbox business, Blackley and Bachus had to submit to the leadership of Rick Thompson, the chief of Microsoft's hardware division who, under threat of a swinging Steve Ballmer baseball bat, agreed to be the first general manager for Xbox. Thompson was a tough New Yorker business guy. He didn't like Blackley and, instead, he entrusted much of the technical leadership to J Allard and his buddy Cameron Ferroni. Thompson took off for a dotcom start-up just as Microsoft announced the project to the world. Bach stepped in and built an executive team around him to lead the various parts of Xbox. At that point, the project took on a momentum of its own and became a real business. Bachus found a role as head of third-party games.

"It went from a religious jihad to something that had to make money," said one Xbox insider. "The teen-agers started it, and the parents had to impose control."

Blackley established the Advanced Technology Group, or ATG, as it became known, to assist game developers in their quest to exploit the Xbox's technology. It was the perfect position for him because he became a kind of ambassador from Microsoft to the games community. It fed his desire to be the center of attention and to mix with the best creative talent of the industry. ATG collected the elite of the gaming industry within its offices. Laura Fryer, who was Blackley's No. 2, held the group together while he was traveling. She said, "ATG was really close knit. We all had the same vision. To make the Xbox as good as it could be from a game development view." ATG walked the line between developers and Microsoft, translating so that one could understand the other. This was the grease that proved critical as Microsoft eased its way into unknown territory. The message that Blackley and Bachus had spread was taking root. ATG was so effective that Rick Rashid, head of Microsoft Research, called it a competitive advantage.

"The idea of the Xbox was beautiful," said Lorne Lanning, co-leader of Oddworld Inhabitants, a seasoned game development company that was among the first to defect from the PlayStation 2 camp. "The machine was outstanding. It was friendly to content, so that we could focus on storytelling and not on the technology."

ATG was a few dozen people at the heart of what became a huge effort. The team worked tirelessly from early 1999 through the fall of 2001 to launch the Xbox. By launch time, the Xbox division had grown to 2,000 people, with more than half in game development and the rest in hardware, system software, marketing and support. Beyond Microsoft, tens of thousands of game developers were making games for the Xbox and publishing houses and independent development studios. There was now an ecosystem. When Microsoft successfully launched the box, they reached a natural reset point. It was time to ante up another 25 cents. They had to make some commitments to stay.

In May, 2001, even before Xbox launched, Kevin Bachus hit escape velocity. That prompted a host of rumors from those who wanted to believe that the Xbox itself was in jeopardy. But no single person could really make or break the project anymore. Everything was not turning out the way he wanted, so Bachus left. Things were a lot more corporate. Bachus wanted to get back into the business of making games.

"People have trouble believing that you just wouldn't stay," Bachus said, several years after leaving.

Blackley and Bachus wanted to make big bets on games, rather than invest heavily in the things that Microsoft's top brass wanted, such as a path to link Xbox and the Windows operating system over time. It just reached a point where it wasn't worth the battles. Even though the real job of defeating Sony wasn't done, it was easy to bite off a piece of the task and declare that it was all over. "Once you build a game console, there is nothing left to do," said Drew Angeloff, one of Blackley's cohorts in ATG. [2]

Blackley shared some of the same concerns as Bachus. He felt like the project was getting away from him as well. He moved off the ATG business to move into an evangelist's role as part of John O'Rourke's marketing group. But he felt a kinship with Bachus. He decided to join Bachus in a business that exploited the opportunities for making games that the Xbox created. Beyond evangelizing the platform to an increasingly accepting audience, there was no position inside for

him at Microsoft. He resigned on April 22, 2002, the same week a book about the Xbox appeared.

Blackley, the last member of the original Xbox group, said that after three years of proselytizing the Xbox – first within Microsoft, then with game developers, and finally to consumers – it was time to return to his first love: making games.

"It's not like I'm going home to rearrange my sock drawer and I was fired," said Blackley. "The Xbox is OK – I would never leave if I thought the Xbox was flagging. But from a personal happiness standpoint, I'm a game-development guy." [3]

In a parting e-mail, Blackley said, "Well, it's time for me to put my money where my mouth is. A few months ago me and a couple of other industry loonies had an idea for a new kind of games company that would enable games to get made that aren't being made today, and to build games in a way that maybe could get more of the creativity and fun out of the developer's heads and into the bits.

"Well, it turns out that the idea we had is pretty powerful, and a lot of people want to try it out. So instead of cheering from the sidelines as I have been, I made the very-very-outrageously-onerously-brain-bustingly-difficult decision to throw in with them to start this company... I love Xbox. Dearly, more than dearly. And you must realize – and sometimes it's hard because we're all so close to it – that being on this team is like being a Green Beret. I will sorely miss being a part of this organization....I want a huge installed base for my Xbox games, so you guys need to kick ass at E3, get the online service up and rocking, and a hundred other things. So what are you doing reading this crap? Get back to work!"

The company lost an intangible quality when some of those Green Berets departed. Bach and Allard were particularly weak on their knowledge of the Japanese video game market. They didn't have the inside connections or the historical appreciation of the different players. But the juggernaut continued.

Some people in Blackley's group also left. Rob Wyatt, a graphics expert who had lobbied heavily to get Nvidia's graphics chip into the original Xbox, left to work at Insomniac Games, which made the popular *Ratchet & Clank* games for the Sony PlayStation 2. Chanel Summers, who was married to Kevin Bachus, had been the audio evangelist in Blackley's ATG. She too decided to move on to something new. Jed Lengyel, the graphics researcher, also took off to live on an island with his family and work on a world simulation game. Even Blackley's trusted administrative assistant, Avril Daly, left Microsoft for another job.

Bachus and Blackley got together again to start their own company. They teamed up with a veteran game business attorney, Gene Mauro, and Mark Hood, a game producer, to form Capital Entertainment Group. They raised some money, saying they would create a new kind of middleman in games that would help bridge the frosty relations between creative developers and business-like publishers. Like Ron Howard's Imagine Entertainment in Hollywood, they would focus on production of video games, taking young development teams, helping them get their work done, and then matching them with game publishers who could get the games onto store shelves. The principal behind the business – that someone needed to help unleash new creativity in the games industry

– was not unlike the goal behind the original Xbox.

The start-up had a promising beginning, but it couldn't raise the amount of money it needed to finance big games. In November, 2003, CEG shut its doors. Blackley went on to become an agent at Creative Artists Agency, cutting deals that involved the union of game companies and Hollywood. Bachus became president of Infinium Labs, which unsuccessfully sought to create a free game console for the living room that played downloadable PC games.

Both Robbie Bach and J Allard would take sabbaticals after the launch of the Xbox and before the next-generation started moving swiftly. They both intended to stay, but they had to bat back rumors that they had had enough and were not planning to come back. Both of them came back. Like everyone else, they wanted to win.

At the highest level, Rick Belluzzo, who came in as president just as the decisions to launch Xbox were made, also left Microsoft. After some time off, he decided to take a job at Quantum, a much smaller storage company. He said that it was hard to make an impact at a company like Microsoft, even in a high position. He would go to meetings with customers and talk to them about a critical purchase, but he would have to move on to so many other things that he never found out what happened with those customers.

"I wanted to make an impact," Belluzzo said. "I wanted to be at a place where I could feel good or bad about making a difference. At Microsoft, I was making a difference but not in an immediate, tangible way."

Yet Bill Gates and Steve Ballmer were still running things at the top. Gates was still chairman, but by the time of the Xbox launch in November, 2001, he had fully transitioned into the job as "chief software architect." His job was to make sure that the company's 50,000 employees were all working toward the same goals and taking advantage of Microsoft's vast resources. As mentioned, he had been very upset that the original Xbox didn't use the Windows operating system. It was all the more galling when hackers installed Windows on the Xbox for the fun of it. But Gates wanted the successor to integrate more of Microsoft technology, taking advantage of advances in the PC, media, and other divisions of Microsoft. He also wanted to be in on the planning earlier this time to better understand it. Rick Rashid, the chief of Microsoft Research, wanted to see if the PC and the console could be brought closer together.

"I think people want to see their various computing experiences brought together," Rashid said. "They don't want a million different logins. One of the advantages we have today is, we can move stuff back and forth across those barriers much more easily."

On the original Xbox, Rashid made the resources of his labs available to game developers, including a team that was devoted to artificial intelligence. That team promised to make computer-controlled enemies far more realistic. He felt that his graphics teams and artificial intelligence experts had given the original Xbox team a competitive advantage over Sony. Many bright minds moved into the game division, including the Advanced Technology Group. Thanks to both

Microsoft Research and ATG, Rashid said, Microsoft stood out from the other console makers. He lent his teams again on topics from simulating cloth properly in games to making better artificial intelligence for racing games.

The phrase "better together" was the agenda that Gates pushed as the plan for the Xbox 360 came together. Gates wasn't just arguing that Microsoft should make use of Microsoft technologies to cut the costs of development or to give an artificial boost to any one division. He asked, "How can we do something that the competition can't do?" These were things that the original Xbox creators didn't care about. They wanted it to be all about the games. Gates' vision could be annoying because it distracted them from the mission of beating Sony in games.

Ballmer, as CEO responsible for the bottom line, wanted the machine to make money. For him, it was simple. The business had to be on the path to make money, or Microsoft would have to exit the business. Since Gates and Ballmer were signing the checks, the gamers inside the Xbox team had to deal with it. In this way, Microsoft handcuffed itself. In this David and Goliath battle, Microsoft had the money of an industry goliath, but it talked itself into thinking that it should behave like a David. One of the former insiders who was fundamental to the success of the original Xbox had to fret about the whole direction Microsoft was taking.

"It's the game enthusiasts versus the bean counters," he said. "What game people are left? The brand was all about the technology edge. I worry that they will lose the technology edge."

1. *Business Week*, "Robbie Bach Is Ready To Rumble," by Jay Greene, Nov. 28, 2005.

2. "Opening the Xbox: Inside Microsoft's Plan to Unleash an Entertainment Revolution," by Dean Takahashi, Prima Publishing, 2002, pg. 349.

3. Source: Jon Peddie, Jon Peddie Research

CHAPTER FOUR

REGROUPING

At 39, Robbie Bach had already led a remarkable life, having helped establish Microsoft's preeminence with Office, one of the most profitable products in software history. He was born in Peoria, Ill., and grew up in Milwaukee, Wis. He was a sharp student and learned both Dutch and French.

At 13, he moved to Winston-Salem, N.C. The year before, he grew eight inches. That gave him a condition known as kyphosis, a curvature of the spine. He got a brace with steel rods connecting from a girdle at his waist to a metal ring around his neck. He wore that brace for five years for as much as 23 hours a day at the beginning. [1]

"It was a huge hassle," he said in an interview, years later. "Everyone looks at you kind of funny. I grew up quicker than a lot of people."

He also grew up more competitively. Even with the back brace, he played tennis six days a week. In 1978, he reached the quarter-finals in doubles at the national boys tennis championship.

He was a gifted athlete and played competitive tennis at the University of North Carolina, Chapel Hill. In the dorms there, he lived one floor up from basketball players Michael Jordan and James Worthy. He earned an economics degree, and worked as a financial analyst at Morgan Stanley. He received an MBA from Stanford University. Pete Higgins, a Microsoft executive, met with Bach at Stanford for a job interview. He remembered Bach as intense but not abrasive. Bach joined Microsoft in 1987, just after Microsoft went public. He became a lifer at the company. Stock options made him enormously rich, and he was among the group of executives who had big homes on the shores of Lake Washington, just east of Seattle.

Bach wasn't about to give up. And he had a knack for keeping people on board and focused. His teams had never lost. He had worked on the Excel spreadsheet with Ed Fries when rival Lotus ruled. Under his watch, Microsoft's Office software suite moved to the front and center of productivity computing.

He wasn't much of a gamer. "My thumbs aren't coordinated enough," he said.[2] But Bach hired talented people and allowed them to run their own groups. He had developed a consensus style of management. On the original Xbox, he made decisions after hearing out opposing sides, and he rarely imposed edicts against the recommendations of the entire team. Among his protégés was Ed Fries, the game studio chief who looked to Bach as a mentor. If anything, said Steve Ballmer, Microsoft CEO, Bach had a track record of building teams that were winners.

Robbie Bach signed up for another war.

In his 13th year at Microsoft, Bach was ready to be the leader for Xenon, the code-name for the next-generation game console. He knew going into it that this battle would last more than one console generation. The team that put the Xbox 360 together was an amalgam of old and new. It had Xbox veterans and Microsoft newbies. It attracted some serious game veterans from the rest of the industry. It had drawn outsiders who had joined Microsoft in its new crusade.

Larry Probst, CEO of Electronic Arts, didn't always agree with Bach. But he thought Bach was good at listening, solving problems and making compromises.

Bach preferred to look at how much Microsoft had accomplished when he was talking about carrying on the fight. Not everyone had the unrealistic expectation that they were going to kill the Japanese giants, even though the original Xbox creators had code-named the project "Midway," after the decisive

World War II battle where the U.S. turned the tide on the Japanese Navy. The original Xbox managed to sell almost three times as many units as Sega sold of its failed Dreamcast console. It beat out Nintendo's GameCube for second place, especially in the American and European markets. Xbox scored a big hit with *Halo*. Altogether, Microsoft sold three games for every console. More than 40 titles were available at the end of the first holiday season. Most impressive, Bach said, was the "buzz" around the Xbox as the hot product that everyone wanted.

In January, 2002, Bach sent out an e-mail congratulating his division on the Xbox launch and detailing how the team would move forward. The memo explained that the executive team that had launched the Xbox would largely remain intact and that J Allard would take on an expanded role as the leader of the Xbox Platform Team. Allard referred to this group as the team that would create the infrastructure for Disneyland. Bach would remain the Chief Xbox Officer and would be in charge of the broader Home and Entertainment Division, while Allard would be the technical lead on most things Xbox.

(Left) Todd Holmdahl, Xbox hardware chief. (Right) Mitch Koch, head of Xbox marketing and sales.

Reporting to Allard, Todd Holmdahl would manage the manufacturing of the Xbox and peripherals. Holmdahl had to get the boxes through the supply chain and into stores. His hardware team had to work closely with suppliers such as Nvidia, Intel, and Flextronics to cut the costs of the box. Holmdahl was a giant of a man who had grown up in northern Washington in the town of Tonasket. The community had 1,000 residents and the nearest street signal was 25 miles away. Although Holmdahl grew up hunting with bows and arrows, his father wanted him to go into technology. He attended Stanford University, became an electrical engineer, and eventually commanded the hardware division's computer mouse business at Microsoft, where he made 20 million mice a year. [3]

When Rick Thompson, the head of Microsoft's hardware division, moved over to run the Xbox unit in 1999, Holmdahl followed Thompson to the Xbox division and took over Xbox hardware. After Thompson left, Holmdahl reported to Allard and was responsible for taking the marching orders from above and turning them into reality. He employed the 200 or so hardware engineers who had been working away on cutting the costs of the original Xbox. Rick Vingerelli was manufacturing chief. Larry Yang ran chip design. Glade Bacon headed product evaluation. Rob Walker supervised peripherals such as controllers. The crew had been through a trial by fire with the Xbox.

Asked why he stuck around again, Holmdahl said, "I love to compete. I worked at other places before. There's no place like this with respect to entrepreneurial mode and the resources Microsoft has. People here are amazing. The product lets you play at the highest level. It's a fun, very visible product. I find that incredibly satisfying."

In Xbox system software, Microsoft had its deepest deep bench of veterans. Jon Thomason, a Windows veteran, led a small group of elite programmers who built the operating system and helped with much of the programming for the Xbox Live online gaming service. Key technical thinkers included Tracy Sharp, Dinarte Morais, and Andrew Goossen. Sharp was a programming genius who figured out how to carve the right pieces out of Windows 2000 and then essentially create a bare-bones operating system that was ideal for games.

"Without Tracy Sharp, it would have been a disaster," said one former engineer on the Xbox project.

Goossen knew nitty-gritty details of graphics programming. Morais was both a programming wizard and a security expert. Without these technical brains, the original Xbox never would have shipped. There was almost no turnover in this group of 16 people. The team worked with the Xbox development kit (XDK) team to ship developers a new version of software tools and operating software almost every month.

Cameron Ferroni had worked for Allard for years in the Internet group. He had spearheaded the early stages of Xbox Live, and he worked closely with Jon Thomason to manage software for the Xbox. Ferroni would go on to lead the worldwide content services team, which included platform evangelism, support, publisher relations, game evaluation and events. Both Thomason and Ferroni frequently swapped duties and often backed each other up. Ed Fries would run the worldwide Microsoft Game Studios, while Stuart Moulder would manage PC games for Fries. Shane Kim would report to Fries to help run the studios with 1,200 game designers.

Within the ranks, Microsoft had people with deep experience. A. J. Redmer, a former Nintendo game production manager who defected to Microsoft in 2000, was one of the general managers in Fries' group. Redmer had been in the games business since 1986. He had worked on big games at places such as Maxis, LucasArts, Spectrum Holobyte and Orbital Studios. At Nintendo of America, he joined in 1998 to run the North American first-party studios. But when Howard Lincoln, the longtime chairman of Nintendo of America, retired,

Shigeru Miyamoto took the reins on first party games. Redmer was "retired" at the same time. Since Nintendo of America was just a short walk from the first location of the Microsoft Xbox team, Redmer took a job as a game studio general manager for Ed Fries. Many Nintendo staffers sneaked into Microsoft's cafeteria because it offered free drinks and better food. After Redmer made his move, dozens of Nintendo employees followed suit.

Mitch Koch ran the sales, marketing and operations efforts for all of Microsoft's retail products, including the Xbox. Originally a certified public accountant, Koch had spent a couple of decades moving up the ranks in entertainment. But despite his long tenure in Hollywood, he wanted to raise his kids in Seattle and move closer to his wife's family there. Before he joined Microsoft to head the Xbox sales and marketing effort in October, 2000, he was president of Disney's Buena Vista Entertainment. John O'Rourke ran marketing for the Xbox under Koch.

Bryan Lee, another Hollywood veteran who had joined midstream on the original Xbox, continued to lead the business strategy and planning efforts. Bach's group of executives was stable. They had years of experience. But with the exception of Fries, they didn't have much video game experience. They were die-hard corporate leaders.

But here and there, the team still had trusted lieutenants. Jeff Henshaw, a friend of J Allard's, continued to work on new ideas to make the Xbox more appealing to non-gamers. His group worked with Alex St. John's Wild Tangent game company to develop the Xbox Music Mixer, a karaoke sing-along system for the Xbox. Drew Angeloff, a sidekick of Blackley's who worked on the original Xbox prototypes, stayed aboard to help with software tools and "middleware." These tools made it easier for game developers to automate the process of making assets in games.

Lower in the ranks were people who were familiar with games, or at least had been through the Xbox on a trial by fire. When Seamus Blackley vacated the Advanced Technology Group job, his No. 2, Laura Fryer, was just the kind of person to pick up the baton. She wasn't a renegade like Blackley, but was the one who stayed in the office and held ATG together. She built it into a 50-person organization and managed it so Blackley could stay on the road. She was a 13-year Microsoft veteran. In one of her more forgettable projects at Microsoft, she worked with Melinda French (Bill Gates' future wife) and the twin sister of Ed Fries on "Microsoft Bob." Bob was Microsoft's attempt at creating a simple interface that was cute and non-threatening for computer neophytes. With a dog character to introduce navigation concepts to the user, it was supposed to be the next big thing in product innovation from Microsoft. It bombed.

Fryer's true love was gaming. A transplant from the town of Parker, Colo., she had a big brother who roped her into gaming. In the days when female gamers were rare, she loved all sorts of games, from *Magic Carpet* to first-person shooters. She had taught herself programming and started life at Microsoft as a lead game tester. She joined the game group when it had only 30 people and went on to produce a number of games, including the Internet dog fighting game

Fighter Ace and the combat flight simulator *Crimson Skies*.

Her game developer friends, Mike Abrash and Mike Sartain, had moved over to work for Blackley in ATG. They convinced Fryer to join them in March, 2000. For a while, she had to do double duty, working in ATG and trying to finish the production of *Crimson Skies*, which finally shipped in August. Blackley was the vision guy, but Fryer had the ability to juggle four or five things at the same time. She was an organized manager who had managed the dozens of creative people that Blackley had gathered. Her people were still the critical liaisons to the game developers, and ATG would prove crucial in the development of the specifications for the Xbox 360. Fryer thrived in a chaotic environment and she could think of nothing more exciting than working on the sequel. She was the perfect kind of person to come in and execute on the vision created by Blackley. Where Xbox people left and new ones took their place, transitions such as the one between Blackley and Fryer took place repeatedly, allowing the cultural assimilation that had to happen for the Xbox 360 to be born.

Chris Satchell was a game developer who had worked on titles such as "Project Gotham Racing" and "Rallisport Challenge." He had experience stretching all the way back to 3DO. But he no longer had the urge to make games himself. Rather, he wanted to help make other game designers succeed. So he signed up to work on advanced technology and software tools. Don Coyner, a former Nintendo marketer who had helped with the marketing on the original Xbox, took a job as director of platform planning alongside Cameron Ferroni.

"We mixed veterans and newcomers," Allard said. "The critical thing to preserve from the first time around was the focus on the customer and customer scenarios. We thought about the gamer. We thought about how they needed longer controller cords so they could sit on the couch instead of the floor. We created a delightful experience, and we wanted to preserve that. It came at the expense of others things. We weren't experienced. We didn't really have a business goal other than to get in the market."

Within Xbox, there were many changes of the guard. Many of the top executives stayed to fight Sony for the duration, even as those who carried a heavy workload underneath them departed. As the original team scattered, fresh blood moved in. George Peckham, a Microsoft veteran, replaced Bachus in third-party relations. Ed Fries brought aboard Blake Fischer, an editor at Next Generation magazine, as a game evangelist and to scout for games in the works that Microsoft wanted to own. He helped spread the Xbox gospel that both Bachus and Blackley preached on the original Xbox.

But it was Nintendo that provided experienced recruits for the Xbox. As the Nintendo people came on board, they boosted morale at Microsoft because they offered external validation of the belief that Microsoft could beat a Japanese company that had been preeminent in games for decades. Nintendo's aging CEO, Hiroshi Yamauchi, rankled the organization when he passed over Minoru Arakawa, his son-in-law and the longtime chief of Nintendo of America, for the CEO job. Yamauchi instead appointed Satoru Iwata, a 40-something game designer, as the successor. Arakawa retired after 22 years at Nintendo in 2002.

"When Mr. Arakawa left, that was a real blow for me," said Ken Lobb, a seasoned game producer at Nintendo of America. "He was one of the smartest guys I ever worked for. I was going to retire at Nintendo. I was loyal to him."

Lobb was devastated at Arakawa's departure. He had worked at Nintendo since 1993 and was born for video games. A Chicago native, he didn't take much notice of games until college, preferring the pool even though his girlfriend and future wife played *Space Invaders* in the game room. A friend who ran the game room dragged Lobb in one day to play *Battle Zone*. The friend rang up 20 credits on the machine. Since that day in 1979, Lobb had become addicted. He played video games every day of his life and had a collection of thousands of games.

Ed Fries decided to recruit Lobb. A. J. Redmer, who had worked with Lobb at Nintendo and now reported to Fries, invited Lobb to lunch one day at a Japanese smorgasbord called Todai. At first, Lobb thought it was a social meeting, but Redmer eventually gave him a hard sell. Lobb decided it was the right time to join. There were already dozens of Nintendo people at Microsoft. Hiring people like Lobb, who was such a game freak that he used music from *Halo* as the ring tone for his cell phone, gave Microsoft executives the confidence to keep up their battle and the knowledge that they were on target with the mission to understand games. It was victories like winning over Lobb that lifted everyone's hopes. He was tangible proof that Microsoft might really have a chance to overtake its rivals.

Those who stayed were itching to continue the fight. One person who started thinking about the future was Margaret Johnson, a programming manager who had a habit of coming to work at Microsoft in gym shoes. She had moved over from the Windows group. Microsoft had often been accused of reacting to Sony's leadership in the game industry. In typical fashion, Johnson was appointed director of Xbox Next as a knee-jerk reaction to a Sony announcement.

Sony had announced on March 12, 2001, that it was teaming up with IBM and Toshiba to create Cell microprocessors for the next-generation of game consoles. It was six months before the Xbox launch, and Sony still had years to go on the PlayStation 2. The plan was that the team would spend $400 million over five years to create the chips for the PlayStation 3. Not only would these chips be more powerful than IBM's "Deep Blue" supercomputer, they would be used in a wide array of consumer technologies. The new chips would have "broadband connectivity" built-in, allowing a network of systems to work together. It dropped like a bomb in Redmond.

"I was thinking, Oh my God!," said one mid-level employee in the Xbox group. "It scared the shit out of me. I could see that they would take the PlayStation 3 chip and then cost reduce it for a handheld, and then take four PlayStation 3s and make them into the PlayStation 4. It was a total unknown quantity."

The knowledge that Sony could be so far ahead on its thinking about the PlayStation 3 at a time when the PlayStation 2 was still beginning to generate sales showed just how far behind Microsoft was. Microsoft had to start moving. It was clear that Sony wanted to make a huge upfront capital investment in both manufacturing and engineering design so that it could race ahead of Moore's Law on performance and drive down costs on chips in subsequent years. As such, the Cell microprocessor represented the biggest bet anyone could make on video games.

Four days after Sony's announcement, J Allard sent a message announcing that Johnson would lead the thinking on Xbox beyond 2001. Everyone else was still preoccupied with the launch coming in November. But Johnson was assigned to chart "future scenarios for Xbox." She would report to Allard and explore compelling scenarios and new business models that could make Microsoft more competitive. The topics at hand included wireless and mobile gaming, the relationship with sister division WebTV and its Ultimate TV digital video recorder, portable music players and other Microsoft entertainment devices, the online platform, and the possibility of working with partners to take "Xbox everywhere." Much of her attention focused on new kinds of software that could remake the Xbox and its functions without radically redesigning the hardware.

Johnson matched one of the game studios that was working on a racing game with some Microsoft Research experts on artificial intelligence. They worked on a technology that would enable a computer opponent in a car race to drive the car as well as a human racer could. Jed Lengyel, a graphics researcher, recalled getting all sorts of queries from Johnson. She was looking at new kinds of input devices, such as the dance mats for the *Dance Dance Revolution* games. One of the ideas she explored was the Xboy. With a small group, she studied what it would take to move the Xbox into the handheld space to compete with Nintendo's GameBoy, which had about 97 percent of the market and was the cash cow that fueled Nintendo's growth. Johnson's group proposed a project.

R.J. Mical, the co-creator of the 3DO game console, caught wind of it. Mical and Brian Bruning had a new handheld game player dubbed Red Jade. Funded by Ericsson, they were making a handheld game player that would compete with the GameBoy. But in 2001, Ericsson pulled the plug on the handheld just as it was ready to launch. Mical and Bruning proposed a new company, dubbed Black Jade, to carry on. They pitched Johnson. Mical went to Redmond and had a series of meetings. It was never clear if he was going to sell Microsoft some technology or get hired. One interviewer even gave him a simple programming test. He laughed it off and took the test.

"Margaret Johnson was excellent," Mical said. "I loved her passion. She was very comfortable with herself, bee-bopping around in gym shoes. I talked to her a lot, but I had no idea what her plans were."

But Robbie Bach said he decided that Microsoft needed to focus all of its energy on the Xbox console business. Besides, some of Microsoft's mobile groups were considering their own ways of adding games to their cell phone and handheld computing products. And Microsoft couldn't really get the portable console going until it had a big library of games to shift from the console to the portable. Microsoft decided to pass on the Red Jade technology. It was a big disappointment for Mical, who would later say that what he proposed with Red

Jade was similar on a high level to what Sony would propose several years later in its handheld game player, the PlayStation Portable.

Another idea that came out of the planning process was "Freon," a code name for a cool project. It was a combination of Ultimate TV's digital video recorder and the Xbox game console. Bill Gates had said he was a big fan of a machine that could combine video services and games. Sony had been planning its own integrated DVR/PlayStation 2 machine, and Microsoft hoped to beat it to the market in 2004. [4]

But Microsoft shelved Freon. It would likely steer Microsoft off its focus on games, and the consumer demand wasn't there. Mid-cycle updates of hardware were never well received by consumers. That was one of the mistakes that doomed Sega. Schelley Olhava, an analyst at International Data Corp., worried that Freon would introduce too many features to the consumers, resulting in "feature creep" confusion. Sony, meanwhile, was worried that Microsoft would do something crazy. Shin'ichi Okamoto, then chief technology officer at Sony, fretted that Microsoft might launch an annual model, dubbed Xbox 2002, Xbox 2003 etc.

But there was no such plan in the works. During the plans for the original Xbox, the company had floated ideas for what it would do with the second machine. While the three-year effort to create the Xbox seemed like an intense, well-planned mission to beat the Japanese rivals in video games, it was really a strategic stop-gap measure. Most of the first year was spent deciding whether to go into the business at all. Then, from the St. Valentine's Day Massacre on Feb. 14, 2000, the team had 21 months to execute on its plan, barely enough to get good games in the pipeline and ready for launch. The Xbox launched with 19 games, compared to just a few for other game consoles. But many of them didn't stand out as spectacular games. Even *Halo* was a rush job.

J Allard liked to say that it was "ready, fire, aim." In an e-mail to the staff on the first anniversary of the Xbox launch, Allard described the chaotic process: "The hard disk was in, it was out. We'd decide that we would manufacture it and then, a week later, we'd decide to OEM it. We'd have it run PC games. Then it wouldn't. It would emulate PS 1. Then it would emulate Dreamcast, and then it would do both. Narrowband or broadband was the question of the week for about 20 weeks. All this was happening in real-time and no variable ever remained constant. On top of it all, people all over the company were adding their two cents. We eventually got enough of a plan together (and collected a lot of pennies) and stabilized this idea to convince the exec team that we had a shot and that this thing would be worth doing. It was clear to us all that this was vital to our 20-year corporate vision and that now was the time to get in."

Allard was a man who didn't like to lose. He was still immersed in the ground war with the other console makers. But his job was to worry about what was coming next. Xenon had to move to front and center. It would be his 28th product at the company.

One of the things he asked the new team to do was read a copy of *Snow Crash*, the 1992 science fiction novel by Neal Stephenson that described a virtual world known as "The Metaverse." In that world, a samurai-sword wielding character named "Hiro" wanders through the virtual city, encountering people with their own virtual selves known as avatars. During the dotcom frenzy of the late 1990s, Will Wright, designer of games such as *The Sims*, often ridiculed online game companies whose business plan was "a dog-eared copy of *Snow Crash*."

But Allard was serious. He wanted a billion people to play the next-generation consoles.

"*Snow Crash* was a fun way to get people to think differently on technology and the impact it can have," he said. "It rattled around in the back of my head."

J Allard, chief of the Xbox hardware and software platform.

Allard had been excited about virtual reality, the field popularized by VPL Research founder Jaron Lanier, who wanted to create worlds that people could interact with via data gloves and goggles. The technology of the late 1980s just wasn't up to the task, and Allard believed it was more about communities than goggles. But it was one of the things that inspired him to get a degree in computer science from Boston University.

Allard joined Microsoft in 1991, just before *Snow Crash* came out. A network programmer, his job was to build TCP/IP, the Internet communications protocol, into Microsoft's software. In 1993, he ran an unsanctioned project to link Microsoft to other web sites via the company's first Internet server. His goal was to make e-mail so easy that his mom could do it. He adopted a shortened form of his logon as his nickname: J without a period. [5]

It was his memo, penned on Jan. 25, 1994, that motivated Bill Gates to get excited about the Internet. At the age of 25, Allard had convinced Gates to bring all of Microsoft's resources to bear, squeezing tiny competitors such as Netscape

Communications on the way to the Internet gold rush.

The idea of virtual worlds again grabbed Allard's attention in 1999, when *The Matrix* debuted in theaters. The story of an artificial world created by machines to lull human beings into a slave-like state, *The Matrix* visually realized the vision of *Snow Crash*. Ken Kutaragi, the chief of Sony's game division, was so enamored with *The Matrix* that he played a DVD version of the movie in PlayStation 2 systems during a trade show before the console debuted. And in a famous story in Newsweek magazine, Kutaragi promised that fans could "jack into *The Matrix*." [6]

By the time Xbox had come to his attention in 1999, Allard had shipped dozens of products. He had been on an extended leave of absence, nursing a broken ankle, and contemplating whether to open an art gallery or a bar in Seattle's Capitol Hill area.

Contrary to popular belief later on, Allard did not start the Xbox. He arrived long after Kevin Bachus, Seamus Blackley, Ted Hase and Otto Berkes started it. He came along after Ed Fries, Rick Thompson, Robbie Bach and others signed on to support it. He had joined the Xbox project midway through and took over as technical leader on the Xbox project. At the time, the idea was more like a Windows machine that ran PC games and sold for around $500. Nat Brown, one of the original Xbox team members, had recruited him to take the technical lead on the Xbox. Allard's friend, Cam Ferroni, joined the Xbox team and also lobbied Allard to come on board. It was his zeal – and his credibility inside the company as a "shipper" of products – that convinced Gates and Ballmer to make a multi-billion dollar bet on video games. After some of the early team members left, Allard and the remaining group pushed the Xbox to be much more console-like than it was in its original conception. He was a cross of the crazy gaming fanatic and the respectable technologist who had enough credibility in both the technical and the business worlds to give Gates and the game publishers a reason to believe.

Allard had a medium build, a high forehead and a fondness for dyeing his buzz cut hair – until he shaved it all off. He looked like a Buddhist monk, wearing an earring. In an article, one reporter described Allard as pudgy and he went on an exercise binge. He loved to ski in places like Whistler, British Columbia, and ride mountain bikes down steep hills. He drove a red Ferrari and was part of what one public relations officer at Microsoft called the "Ferrari club." Wired magazine profiled Allard and described him as a "sturdier version of REM singer Michael Stipe." Steve Ballmer, Microsoft CEO, described Allard as "a little crazy" in the same article. [7]

Allard was a game fan who played games competitively with his friend Cameron Ferroni. At first, he didn't have many connections into the game industry. Yet, inside Microsoft, Allard knew how to get things done and how to get people on board a crazy new enterprise. He was good at recruiting other programmers to join in on his projects, and many became known as the FOJ, or "friends of J," including Jeff Henshaw, Scott Henson and Ferroni. At first, Xbox was just another renegade project. But its success was Allard's ticket to a vice president's title.

After the Xbox launched and started selling by the millions, Allard had the ear of upper management. He was in command of hundreds of people working on Xbox hardware, software and services such as Xbox Live. He had gotten so much attention he had been nicknamed by Business 2.0 magazine as one of the "baby Bills," or those who might one day replace Bill Gates as the chairman of Microsoft.

In the eyes of Jon Thomason, the Xbox software chief, Allard was "absolutely brilliant." But he saw how Allard could rub people the wrong way.

"His opinion could be random, and he could change his mind very quickly," Thomason said. "He's very bright and that can be disconcerting. He was passionate about arguments, and didn't always deal with people very well."

Allard wanted to ensure that Microsoft would move in a stealthy manner yet retain the same participatory approach that made the original Xbox successful. Game developers and publishers had long complained about the arrogance of the Japanese console makers. They felt they were shut out of decision-making and simply had to adapt their strategies to fit the needs of the console makers. Microsoft saw a wedge to exploit the perceived arrogance of the Japanese as it tried to find allies to support the Xbox. It would do the same as it created Xenon. The true gaming fans inside Microsoft were thrilled that they were making the right decisions for gamers.

The feeling didn't necessarily last that long. Xbox had become a big corporate enterprise, with many trade-offs to make for the sake of making money in the long run. But Allard wanted to preserve what the Xbox stood for, that feeling of being an underdog. Even though Microsoft was perceived as a giant elsewhere, in games it was the upstart. And for once, it could be viewed as the good guy against the established console makers. Game publishers complained about the power of the Japanese console makers, prompting David Sheff to write the 1993 book *Game Over: How Nintendo Zapped An American Industry, Captured Your Dollars, and Enslaved Your Children.* The book had painted Nintendo's leaders as domineering and cold. Such complaints enabled Sony to steal away Nintendo's game publishers in the PlayStation generation. But soon enough, similar complaints surfaced about Sony's growing domination of video games.

That was why Allard could picture himself as a warrior fighting against an impersonal machine. His people were the special, chosen ones who could upset the balance of power. On the Xbox, he had become a well-known figure among gamers. Using his *Snow Crash*-inspired gamertag "HiroProtagonist," he challenged gamers to embrace online games and fought them one-by-one in matches. Xbox had made him famous. But that wasn't good enough. He made his grudge against the leadership of Sony's game division personal.

"What gets me out of bed and into the office every day is the thought of Ken Kutaragi's resignation letter, framed, hanging next to my desk," he wrote much later in a memo at a retreat of Xbox senior executives. [8]

Allard reported directly to Chief Xbox Officer Robbie Bach. Since Bach's style was to delegate management, Allard had a lot of freedom to design Xenon as he saw fit. This time around, the team wanted to create an experience similar to those of magical products like Disney World, the Mini Cooper car, Apple's iPod, and Willy Wonka's chocolate bars.

"They feel as if they were created by one person," Allard said. "With Xbox 360, we knew that 20,000 people would be involved. How do you make it feel like it was created by one person?"

Allard had always wanted Microsoft to move quickly. Cutting off Sony's final profitable year would help Microsoft achieve its goal of keeping a threatening competitor from undermining their core business. By launching in 2005, he didn't think Xenon would beat Sony to market. Bach knew that Microsoft couldn't be second again. He and Allard assumed that it would be a tie. Allard looked at 2005 as a year for the "perfect storm," a perfect confluence of events. By that time, high-definition TV sets would start to become mainstream, and the new Xbox could exploit those TVs to deliver much better graphics. It was also the year when the old-generation consoles would be losing steam.

"It would be time to reinvigorate the market," Allard said. "It would be the knee in the curve for high-definition TVs. Let's catalyze that and ride it."

And by that time, broadband adoption would also be much more pervasive across the population. Microsoft could be at the forefront of the notion of connected gaming and connected consumer electronics devices. Moreover, retiring the old money-losing hardware sooner was a good idea to stanch losses. Microsoft could still sell the old software for a couple of more years. The timing felt right.

"We could wait later, but we were getting the most of our investment out of our first console that we were going to get," Allard said. "A soccer mom buying a $129 Xbox in 2005 just doesn't fuel our agenda. And it costs us money."

Allard acknowledged the importance of cost.

"It is a real object," he said. "We have real financial constraints. If we add more cost, it had to come out of some other cost."

Microsoft had settled many of the agonizing questions from their first go-round. They knew where they wanted to go this time. They had more time to plan their second machine. They knew they had to think of a different kind of name. Xbox 2 clearly wasn't appropriate because it would seem inferior to the PlayStation 3. Allard knew that the second box would really be the vehicle that could complete the strategy, take the lion's share of the market, and make money for the corporation.

In January, 2002, just after Bach made his executive announcement, Allard shuffled the leadership on the next-generation explorations which he had dubbed Xbox Next. Allard had appointed three seasoned technologists to start thinking about the future. Mike Abrash was a graphics wizard and was in charge of future Xbox architecture, Jeff Henshaw headed an effort known as alternative entertainment, or the world beyond games, while Margaret Johnson switched her focus to advanced software tools. Abrash had been part of Blackley's Advanced Technology Group and had helped game developers exploit Xbox technology. He knew its limitations and where it could be pushed in future generations. Henshaw had headed software development kits, but was now looking at ways to rope in more family members into Xbox entertainment through products such as a sing-along karaoke product.

The team didn't make a lot of progress at first. Johnson returned to the Windows team. When the team considered Xenon, most of the early thought went into establishing that all-important date: When should they launch the machine?

1. *Business Week*, "Robbie Bach Is Ready To Rumble," by Jay Greene, 11/28/05

2. "An Interview With Robbie Bach," By John Boudreau and Dean Takahashi, Nov. 26, *San Jose Mercury News*.

3. "Opening the Xbox," pg. 140-141.

4. Wall Street Journal "Secret Project At Microsoft Features An Xbox With Extras," by Khanh Tran, July 1, 2002.

5. "Opening the Xbox," pg. 135.

6. "The Amazing PlayStation 2," *Newsweek* magazine, cover story, March 6, 2000.

7. http://www.wired.com/wired/archive/13.06/xbox_pr.html

8. "The Xbox Reloaded," by Josh McHugh, June 2005, *Wired* magazine.

CHAPTER FIVE

GO FIRST,
GET HACKED

If you created a simulation of the video game console business, it might feel more like gambling than gaming. The scenarios could generate massive profits or nightmare losses. The spreadsheet for the business had so many variables that were moving targets. If you started making a console at a loss, the more units you sold, the deeper the hole got. If you scaled back on the technology to make the box cheaper, your competitor might come up with better technology that the fans wanted instead. Among the things you had to track were the royalty rates charged to third parties, the number of games you developed internally, the price of main memory chips, the amount of time it took to develop custom chips, the price that consumers were willing to pay, whether fans perceived the design of the box as cool, and how quickly your contract manufacturers could mass produce machines. Guessing wrong on any one of these decisions could easily cost you a billion dollars. This was a business that even Will Wright, inventor of the *SimCity* games, wouldn't have liked playing. He said, "It would be just like simulating any other business, but then the winner would be whoever gets *Grand Theft Auto* on their platform."

Microsoft understood the model for the personal computer. Operating systems took a few years to rewrite, and PC hardware raced ahead every six months or so. Graphics chip makers often took 18 months to design their chips, but they launched a new chip a couple of times a year. They did so by getting three teams of engineers to work simultaneously on staggered cycles.

Console makers, by contrast, launched new machines every five years or so. Sony launched the original PlayStation in the U.S. in the fall of 1994, and waited until the fall of 2000 to launch the PlayStation 2 in North America. Nintendo had launched its N64 in 1996, and waited until the fall of 2001 to launch its GameCube console.

It wasn't that it took more time to design and build a game oper-

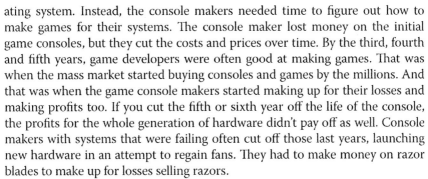

ating system. Instead, the console makers needed time to figure out how to make games for their systems. The console maker lost money on the initial game consoles, but they cut the costs and prices over time. By the third, fourth and fifth years, game developers were often good at making games. That was when the mass market started buying consoles and games by the millions. And that was when the game console makers started making up for their losses and making profits too. If you cut the fifth or sixth year off the life of the console, the profits for the whole generation of hardware didn't pay off as well. Console makers with systems that were failing often cut off those last years, launching new hardware in an attempt to regain fans. They had to make money on razor blades to make up for losses selling razors.

Going first had its risks. Japan's Sega was an example of what happened to a company that tried to interrupt the typical cycle. It introduced its blockbuster Sega Genesis console in 1989, capturing a big share of the video game market. But it dribbled out advances in technology. It launched the Sega 32X and SegaCD add-ons for the Genesis. Gamers wanted to play games, and they didn't want to constantly invest in new hardware. The big upgrade was the Sega Saturn, launched in 1995. But that console failed to win big fans and it was eclipsed by both the Sony PlayStation and the Nintendo 64 console. Sega quickly replaced it in 1998 in Japan and 1999 in North America with the Sega Dreamcast. But Sony's PlayStation 2, launched in Japan in 2000, was such a big advance over the Dreamcast that it killed Sega's last console. In the summer of 2000, German hackers figured out how to defeat the security on the Dreamcast proprietary disks, so that a standard CD-ROM disk could run on the console. Piracy ensued[1]. While the Dreamcast games dried up, Sony's kept on coming.

Sega had even tried giving away Dreamcasts for free if gamers signed up for an online subscription. Peter Moore, the U.S. chief of Sega, took a big gulp and made a conference call with journalists in January, 2001, where he announced that after selling eight million boxes, Sega would stop production on Dreamcasts. Sega wrote off $700 million and began transforming itself into a software-only company. To be "Dreamcasted" became a new verb. It meant that Sony's vaporware for the PS2 effectively killed off game developer support for the Dreamcast. Consequently, the pipeline for Dreamcast games dried up and so did consumer enthusiasm.

"If you look at our history, we've never gone first," said Kaz Hirai, president of Sony Computer Entertainment America.

Sony won because it played the game well. It launched powerful hardware and invited all sorts of developers to make games for its platform. It built up its own internal game studios and marketed the console worldwide.

After it launched the Xbox, Microsoft believed it had the clout to change the cycle, which was akin to changing the course of a river. The plan was to knock a year off the console cycle, so a new machine could debut in four years instead of five. Microsoft's team hoped to bring more of the PC industry's dynamics of big changes every couple of years to the video game industry. They wanted to cash in on the collective research and development invested in the PC. At first, the original Xbox advocates suggested that Microsoft try to upgrade its console every two years, taking advantage of the latest that PC hardware vendors had to offer. They thought they could get a jump on rivals by taking advantage of better graphics and microprocessors. But the more they thought the idea through, the more they backed off on the idea. Consumers didn't want to keep upgrading to new machines, and the software developers wanted enough time to learn how to master the art of creating games on the console before moving to a new one.

But the idea of capitalizing on the advantages of the PC model stayed with J Allard. From the outset, he saw that Microsoft's adoption curve was about the same as Sony's. But since Sony started 20 months before Microsoft did, Microsoft could never catch up. Not unless it launched ahead of Sony. By doing so, Microsoft could start taking market share and inflict some pain on Sony by cutting prices on its hardware well ahead of when Sony could be able to do so. It meant turning the tables on what happened to Microsoft in the Xbox-PS2 battle.

But Microsoft's executives found it hard to find time for long-term planning. Demanding tasks always interrupted the schedule. On Dec. 4, 2001, software chief Jon Thomason had to rally the troops to figure out how to deal with hackers who had started cracking the security on the Xbox.

"As you probably know, there's a pretty dedicated effort to hack the Xbox," he said in an e-mail. "Because information on these attempts tends to be distributed across a number of different places, you might run across information about hacking attempts that hasn't been seen yet. When you find information of this nature, I encourage you to send factual mail about the hack attempts, including links, to the Xbox Security Response Team alias."

Thomason cautioned his staff against correcting misconceptions in forums on the Internet or acting as if they were legal experts themselves. Since Microsoft had used an off-the-shelf Intel processor that was well understood, the hackers had pieced together enough clues to circumvent all of the security measures that the company had used to keep owners from illegally modifying their boxes or pirating software. While decoding the secrets of the Xbox security measures was a big job for any single hacker, the Internet and web sites such as XboxHacker.net made the effort into a collective enterprise of thousands of determined hackers. Under such pressure, Microsoft's security measures didn't protect the Xbox for long.

An MIT doctoral student named Andrew "bunnie" Huang received an Xbox as a present after Thanksgiving in November, 2001. A trained hacker, he began tearing it apart and found a way to decrypt the scrambled contents of the flash ROM, a storage chip that was used to start up the Xbox. He wasn't interested in monetary gain, and this was his idea of having fun. He posted some material about it on his web site in early December. Twelve hours later he got a voice mail from Microsoft's Jon Thomason, who asked him to take it down. Huang obliged.

"We were watching for the hackers," Thomason said. "I asked him to take down the copyrighted materials. He did. I wasn't very threatening. I had talked to our lawyers first, and he was posting things that were copyrighted."

Huang was only just becoming aware that he might be violating provisions of the Digital Millennium Copyright Act of 1998. The federal law made it illegal to publicize flaws in encryption technologies, likening the process to breaking and entering a home.

Initially, Huang hoped someone would take the flash ROM data and crack the system security so that he could write programs to run on the Xbox. He discovered that the code was a decoy, a red herring meant to distract hackers from code hidden elsewhere. Over the next couple of months, he used the tricks of his trade – home brewed logic analyzers, sulfuric acid baths for stripping chips of packages, and two-pronged soldiering irons – to tear yet another Xbox to shreds and uncover the real secret.

Without spending much money at all, he figured out how to monitor bits of data as it passed along the pathway connecting the Nvidia communications chip with the rest of the system. Consequently, he found the hidden security key inside the Nvidia communications chip that gave him the ability to take complete control of the Xbox. The big mistake Microsoft made was having a single key that unlocked not just Huang's Xbox, but every single console the company had made. With one "brute force" program that he ran at 5 am one day, Huang had cracked the security of every single machine. He created his own cheap version of the flash ROM and booted the Xbox so that it would run Linux and other software that Microsoft did not approve. Huang argued that he had hacked the box in the name of technical exploration, not financial gain, and he won representation from the Electronic Frontier Foundation.

The EFF attorney, Lee Tien, advised Huang to tell Microsoft that he held the key to the security on every Xbox they had made to date. He wrote a letter to J Allard. At that point, it was out of Thomason's hands. Allard himself called Huang back. After a number of conversations, Allard told Huang that Microsoft wasn't going to sue him. But Allard requested that Huang write his paper in an academic fashion, so that it didn't create a complete disaster for Microsoft. After a four-month legal tussle with Microsoft, he published his results. He did not say exactly how to engage in the more controversial acts such as replacing a hard disk drive (presumably with pirated games and other software).

"I didn't want to economically harm their enterprise," Huang said. "But I didn't want bad security to exist. Exploration was the reason I did this. My intentions were never to make a profit or to pirate. This is what I have done since childhood. It was like hopping on a wagon in the 1800s and going out west. This was the frontier."

Microsoft ultimately brought no legal case against him. But others were simultaneously working on the same problem. If he didn't publish his results, somebody else would have, Huang reasoned. Once the exploits of Huang and others were widely known, crackers, or criminal hackers, started modifying, or "modding," their Xbox consoles and selling them on the black market. Modders had to go to a lot of trouble. They had to create their own chip to boot the Xbox, pry the authentic chip out of their system, and then solder in the modified chip. But they didn't, as Microsoft had hoped, have to spend $25,000 on technology to discover the system's secrets.

"He used an innovative approach that didn't occur to us," Thomason said. "It wasn't that we thought it was impossible. We thought it would take a sophisticated approach to listen to the high-speed bus. There was a fear we could lose a chunk of sales. If you look at the PC gaming business, you could argue that piracy killed it."

Huang eventually wrote a book called *Hacking the Xbox.* The book had an academic twist. It wasn't a cookbook describing how to steal money from Microsoft. But the original book publisher, John Wiley & Co., dropped the title. Huang published the book himself, taking a big legal risk. Adding insult to injury, he had no kind words for Microsoft's hardware design skills. "The Xbox was pretty ugly," he said. "The internal architecture, the choices of parts. It was very rushed and hurried."

Microsoft tried to crack down on the crackers, but it was clearly losing money to people who were buying Xboxes with no intention of legally purchasing games. That was the nightmare scenario for the company. More than a few hackers realized Microsoft was really selling a fully capable computer in the Xbox for $300, a price that was lower than the cost of a cheap PC. It didn't cost much money to hack an Xbox, but the good thing for Microsoft was that it took a considerable amount of technical skill, even for someone who read Huang's book. Some modders would put a large hard disk drive on the machine, load it up with stolen software, and sell it for a profit. Those who bought such systems didn't spend much on games. Microsoft created a new security system with a new version of the Nvidia chip, but a British hacker named Andy Green cracked that system within a day. He had discovered that one of the security algorithms Microsoft used had a known vulnerability[2]. Chastened by the lessons that were coming up on a daily basis, Thomason assigned Dinarte Morais, one of Microsoft's most talented programmers, to absorb the security lessons from the first time around and try to come up with a more secure box the second time.

Other matters kept the staff occupied. As soon as Microsoft launched in North America in the fall of 2001, it had to regroup for the launch in Japan in February, 2002. The Japanese launch showed what happened when a company took its eye off the task at hand. Then came the European launch in March, 2002. Allard and Cameron Ferroni, his colleague from the Internet wars, were preoccupied with the launch of Xbox Live, which debuted in the fall of 2002.

In the top ranks, Bill Gates and Steve Ballmer had begun to weed out unsuccessful projects. They did a review of the Xbox business in June, 2002. By that time, Robbie Bach had proudly announced that Xbox had sold 3.5 million units in 20 different countries. Xbox had passed muster. Periodically, Microsoft CEO Steve Ballmer would drop hints about where Microsoft would go. In June, 2002, he told a Japanese newspaper that Microsoft might launch a new system in 2006. The device would have better Internet capability and fit right in with the rest of the living room as a digital home appliance. But at that point, no solid plan existed.

The leaders had to keep the troops inspired and ready to sign up for another five years. Robbie Bach needed to visit various places and tell his team members how valuable they were. One of his stops was Mountain View, Calif., where Microsoft now had a crew of hardware engineers who had nothing better to do than design a game console.

CHAPTER SIX

WEBTV'S REVENGE

he twisting path to the beginning of the Xbox 360 started not with the Xbox veterans, but with the engineers who traced their lineage back to both WebTV and 3DO, two of the greatest failures in Silicon Valley history. Indeed, the lineage of today's modern video game systems descended directly from those earlier machines, and those who created those early machines made lasting contributions – and sometimes even worked on – the machines that are appearing today.

When Bill Gates approved the original Xbox, the casualties piled up from the internal warfare for control of the project. On May 5, 1999, two sparring groups met with Gates in a meeting that became known as a beauty contest between two machines, the appliance-like WebTV machine and the PC-based Xbox machine. On the one hand were the Xbox advocates Seamus Blackley, Kevin Bachus, Ted Hase, Otto Berkes, Nat Brown and Ed Fries. They had their roots in PC games and wanted Microsoft to exploit the advantages of the personal computer in games. On the other side was a team that came from the appliance, or consumer electronics business, through Microsoft's acquisition of WebTV. That team included Dave Riola, Tim Bucher, Bruce Leak and their executive sponsors Craig Mundie, Ted Kummert, Nick Baker and Jon DeVaan. It wasn't an even match. The Xbox team had all the beauty and the right political support within the organization.

The WebTV crew had lost its credibility. Microsoft bought the Silicon Valley company in 1997 for $425 million. WebTV was making TV set-top boxes that connected to the Internet. The boxes were low-cost, dumbed down computers that allowed consumers to use the TV to check their e-mail, browse the Internet, and watch their TV shows. Microsoft bought it in order to jam its Windows CE software into it, but it wasn't really working and consumers quickly soured on the boxes. For one thing, the graphics and text on the TV screen looked terrible and were too be too big to be readable. But the team had video game

veterans. And they were pitching a version of the WebTV box that was much more like a traditional game console. They wanted to design and manufacture custom chips – with all the risks of delivery schedules and cost overruns.

Gates listened to proposals from both groups, but he liked what he heard from the Xbox crew best. WebTV went down in defeat. So began the journey to create the Xbox. In a bit of irony, when J Allard came aboard and remade many of the plans, he adopted more of the WebTV vision.

Over time, the WebTV gang found ways to come back and nibble away at pieces of the Xbox project. They pushed for a role in helping to design the common hardware that the Xbox and WebTV would share. The teams had bitterly opposed each other for several months, but eventually they started merging into one as everyone realized that Microsoft was woefully short of engineers to handle the difficult task of creating a console. The Xbox guys realized their machine had to be much more like a console than a PC, and the WebTV gang began to appreciate the value of screaming high-end performance. The Xbox general manager Rick Thompson brought the WebTV team back into the fold.

"We had always advocated more of the consumer electronics model," Baker said. "As the Xbox changed to be more like a console, we didn't have as much a problem with it. The consumer electronics model was the only way it was going to succeed."

Thompson figured the WebTV crew could save Microsoft a lot of money by designing more of the Xbox insides internally. The risks were so great that something might go wrong with a business deal that Thompson had to keep parallel tracks of teams working on different solutions, one of which might be used in the final Xbox.

In Palo Alto, California, dozens of WebTV engineers began architecting a graphics chip. They were working with GigaPixel, a start-up that had created a design for a new kind of graphics architecture. Most of the Xbox team wanted Thompson to go with Nvidia, which stood out as the top graphics chip company on the PC. But Thompson couldn't cut a good business deal with Nvidia. So he began to favor a proposal from WebTV's Tim Bucher, who suggested Microsoft license the GigaPixel architecture and design a chip based on it. He foresaw the day when WebTV's own next-generation set-top box could use a graphics chip based on GigaPixel's work. Microsoft agreed to invest money in GigaPixel and then moved GigaPixel's employees into the WebTV building. The team started designing the chip, but they were rudely interrupted. In March, 2000, at the last possible moment, just before announcing the Xbox to the world, Thompson and his lieutenant Bob McBreen finally negotiated a deal with the formidable CEO of Nvidia, Jen-Hsun Huang. GigaPixel and the WebTV hardware engineers were once again out of luck.

For George Haber, the CEO of GigaPixel, the news was devastating. His company never recovered from the setback and it had to sell out to another graphics chip company, 3Dfx Interactive. Eventually, Nvidia bought GigaPixel by purchasing the assets of 3Dfx. The WebTV engineers had a fallback plan. They were designing the next-generation set-top box, Ultimate TV, which was going to work with satellite TV provider DirecTV and record TV shows to a hard drive. Bill Gates showed off Ultimate TV at the Consumer Electronics Show in January, 2001. But Ultimate TV didn't really catch the interest of customers, since it was already lagging behind others such as Tivo and ReplayTV. Ultimate TV only sold about 150,000 units. Worse, EchoStar had made a bid to buy DirecTV, which was Microsoft's only big customer. Since EchoStar had its own hardware division, engineers such as Leslie Leland, who had been part of the WebTV team for years, started feeling nervous.

"I remember the pit in my stomach," she said. "It was like reading your fate on the front page of the Wall Street Journal. This was after September 11, and a lot of the jobs were drying up in Silicon Valley. It meant we didn't have a future."

By the end of 2001, the Xbox was taking off. Microsoft decided to pull the plug on Ultimate TV. On Jan. 22, 2002, Microsoft confirmed that it was discontinuing the product and laying off a third of the 500 engineers at the WebTV campus in Silicon Valley. Among those departing were Tim Bucher and, Dave Riola. Robbie Bach went down to Silicon Valley to welcome the Ultimate TV team to the Xbox group and to convince them to stay with the Xbox team. A recession had settled upon the valley, thanks to the bursting of the dotcom and telecom bubbles, as well as the September 11 attacks. The WebTV remnants needed jobs. J Allard also made a pitch via video conference, sharing his vision with them, while Bach visited in person.

"Robbie came down and pitched us," Leland said. "There was tension in the room. They were getting to know us. We had competed with them internally and lost our business. We started to connect on technical things with their people. I had learned what they went through. How fast they had to work. How many millions of units they were selling. I gained an incredible amount of respect for them. I wanted to be part of something that was selling those kinds of volumes."

For Leland and others, the death of Ultimate TV was a big heartbreak. Some of her colleagues were out of work. But working at a giant software company that had just plunged into the console hardware business, they knew Microsoft needed them. For Leland, it wasn't an easy choice. She wasn't much of a gamer. Some parents had come to her and asked her why games on the consoles had to be so violent. But she saw from the vision that Bach and Allard presented that they wanted the console to grow up.

"It was a clear there was a plan for blasting out of the hardcore gamer space," she said. "It was part of the connected home. You see that you have to bring a lot of different things together."

Most of the remaining team signed up with the Xbox group. By this time, Microsoft was preparing to launch the console in Europe and Japan. But the thing about consoles is that they're never really done. To gamers, the features stay the same. But engineers constantly redesign the insides of the box to make them cheaper to produce. As the sales volumes go up and semiconductor technology advances, the engineers can combine multiple chips into one, keeping the

features but making them smaller and easier to produce. Among the tasks the engineers had to deal with was why the DVD player was scratching disks in Japan. Troubleshooting was their specialty.

The Xbox hardware team, under Vice President Todd Holmdahl in Redmond, had the tough job of making the box more profitable. At the outset, on every machine bought for $299, Microsoft had incurred somewhere around $425 in hardware costs alone. The WebTV hardware engineers, such as Leland, who worked on product testing, had to join in on the cost reduction designs. Microsoft would redesign all of the components inside the box, while keeping the look of the box the same. Hackers who tore the boxes apart saw the differences with every new version. But most gamers never noticed.

"It was like, holy shit, we just launched this thing and now we have to cost reduce it," Leland said.

The problem was, the engineers couldn't squeeze out much cost. They had chosen Intel for the microprocessor and Nvidia for the graphics chip. While Sony eventually combined those two chips inside the PlayStation 2, Microsoft could never convince Intel and Nvidia to do the same. The suppliers were bitter enemies and had never cooperated in such ways before. Xbox also had a $50 hard disk drive that was getting somewhat cheaper, but not quickly enough. Every time Microsoft came up with a cheaper unit, it had to cut the price on the Xbox. So it never got ahead of the game on profits. That's why the losses mushroomed to about $3.7 billion, or $168 per box.

Holmdahl needed more engineers to keep driving down the costs. That was a good thing for Baker and the others who had lost their Ultimate TV jobs. Their group was a tight knit circle. They had all worked for Tim Bucher, who was a lead designer of the 3DO video game console that debuted in 1993. This team had led a tortured existence, and they were used to losing their jobs or moving to new owners.

3DO was the brainchild of Trip Hawkins, founder of Electronic Arts, the biggest video game software publisher. Hawkins wanted to control his own destiny, so he teamed up with R.J. Mical and Dave Needle, creators of the Atari Lynx game console. Hawkins bought the company that Mical and Needle had formed and plotted to bring their console, dubbed the 3DO Multiplayer, to market. In 1991, they were the first to design a game console that took advantage of the CD-ROM. At first, he operated it within EA. But after tensions developed between the hardware and game makers, 3DO spun off as a separate company. Hawkins became CEO of 3DO, while Larry Probst took over EA.

Hawkins had the novel idea of using contract manufacturers to license and build the 3DO hardware, the same kind of strategy that Microsoft would orchestrate with Flextronics years later on the original Xbox. Matsushita's Panasonic was the main manufacturer, but Goldstar, AT&T and Sanyo all licensed the 3DO technology and brought the machine to market at $699. Its high price doomed it. It was labeled a rich man's system, and, to make matters worse, the games made for it didn't really stand out from the pack. Sony's PlayStation buried 3DO with an avalanche of better games and a lower price.

"We had a great system with a stupid price tag," Mical said.

Hawkins tried to recover with a second machine, dubbed the M2. The M2 contained a few key technologies: DVD playback, MPEG-3 (a video compression standard), and a new chip set dubbed the MX that used two PowerPC 602 microprocessors. Announced in 1995, the 64-bit system was designed to leapfrog the 32-bit competitors from Sony, Sega and Nintendo.

"There was a lot of seminal research they did in digital video encoding and decoding," Hawkins said. "Compression technology. Critical aspects of architecture, CPU design. The team was familiar with the IBM Power PC architecture."

But Hawkins had to sell off the chip design division as a separate business as the financial picture worsened. Samsung bought the chip division and renamed it CagEnt, hiring more than 100 members of the team, which was led by Toby Ferand. Samsung gave the division a couple of years to make money. Meanwhile, Hawkins sold the M2 rights to Matsushita in early 1996. But Matsushita's Panasonic division never brought the M2 to the market as a game console. It did sell some pachinko and arcade machines that competed with Sega's arcade machines, but sales of those machines topped out at around a million. Meanwhile, Samsung failed to do anything with the chip engineering team. In late 1997, Nintendo visited CagEnt in search of a new 3-D chip set. 3DO transformed itself into a software company but it eventually went bankrupt in a war against EA.

Nintendo's N64 console wasn't selling as well as expected, and its relationship with Silicon Graphics was sliding downhill. In early 1998, Nintendo terminated the relationship with SGI and offered to buy CagEnt. Howard Lincoln, chairman of Nintendo of America, and Nintendo executive Genyo Takeda visited CagEnt in Silicon Valley. As the details of the negotiations were hammered out, CagEnt began planning to move the MX architecture to the MIPS microprocessor architecture that Nintendo used. The plan was to launch a new console to replace the ailing N64 in time for the holidays in 1999. But CagEnt's architecture, which was only an improvement on the M2 design, was starting to look less impressive with age. The talks between Nintendo and Samsung broke down. Nintendo chose to work with ArtX, a team of engineers who broke away from Silicon Graphics. ATI Technologies eventually bought ArtX.

"Life at CagEnt was getting a little old," said Nick Baker. "I started looking around." Jeff Andrews said, "To be honest, we deserved to fail. We weren't aggressive enough. If you looked around at others like Sony, they were more aggressive."

Then Microsoft stepped in. In April, 1998, it bought CagEnt and incorporated it within the WebTV group. The gang from 3DO was once again working for a company with ambitions in the video game market. Having come from Apple, Baker liked the idea of working for a systems company. And Microsoft's hardware engineers realized that they had a team of talented game console designers. For a time, the CagEnt crew was preoccupied with the UltimateTV project. But when

the company cut that project loose, about 70 of the WebTV team members, including CagEnt, joined the Xbox team. The group included electrical and mechanical engineers, materials management, silicon chip designers, and hardware quality and testing engineers. The CagEnt team would lend their graphics expertise so that Microsoft could launch a casual games business on UltimateTV. That plan for a casual games business would resemble the Xbox Live Arcade business that came years later.

"We need to use this time to prepare ourselves for the next battle, so we can continue to move the bar up on our development activities and business," Todd Holmdahl, the head of Xbox hardware, told his new teams.

It was through this series of setbacks that Nick Baker, Jeff Andrews, and the rest of the 3DO engineers fell into the Xbox 360 work. Both Baker and Andrews had ridden the 3DO rollercoaster together, as had about a dozen or so ex-3DO engineers who remained at Microsoft. They had been devoted to making hardware for game consoles since about 1993, but they all had yet to deliver a machine to the market. And, while they weren't the luckiest bunch of engineers, Microsoft was lucky to have them on board.

"By the time I got to the Xbox 360, I had worked on six game consoles," Andrews said.

All the other hardware engineers had begun to redesign the original Xbox to reduce its costs. That was an important mission, given the game industry's razor and razor blades model. To break even on those boxes, Microsoft had to sell a lot of games. Because game sales didn't meet targets, Microsoft was losing money in the nightmare scenario for the games business.

Roughly 50 hardware engineers undertook the redesign of the innards of the Xbox without changing any of the features that the consumers saw. Among those who joined this effort was Leslie Leland. She had assigned her mechanical engineers to become familiar with Xboxes by tearing them apart and examining each component. It wasn't the most thrilling work to Leland, who had been trained as a product design manager at places such as Apple, Sun Microsystems and WebTV. But she was enchanted with the potential of the video game console to grow up and become capable of more things. And it was also a good time to have a job as a hardware engineer in Silicon Valley.

The box would still be compatible with the games and its original controllers and sockets, but the insides would be made of cheaper components. In the first year and a half, Microsoft scheduled three major cost reductions. They were code-named QT, Xblade, and Tuscany. The target for those programs was to cut costs by 30 percent, bringing the box cost to just under $300.

The teams did so by taking advantage of improvements in manufacturing technology to combine two silicon chips into one or by switching from Thomson DVD drives to Samsung DVD drives, since Samsung had better factory yields, lower costs, and they had fewer playback problems. Later, they added Philips Electronics as a supplier.

The Mountain View team had to create two chips that would combine the functions of multiple pieces of silicon. They worked with Nvidia to shrink the graphics chip so that it could made with less material and thus could be made at a lower cost. Redesigning chips to be smaller meant that they could get rid of daughter cards, reduce the heat dissipation and get by with smaller fans. For the commodity parts, they held online auctions to get the lowest prices. The rise of Internet procurement helped Microsoft get the competitive bids they needed to help bring down costs.

Unfortunately, that wasn't enough. In May, 2002, Sony cut the price of the PlayStation 2 from $299 to $199. Microsoft had to match the price. At that point in time, it was still losing well over $100 on every Xbox sold. The bleeding wasn't stopping, even though *Halo* had turned into a smash hit from its first day of sales. Sony was still capturing most of the sales. Of the top ten games of 2002, Sony had seven titles, while Nintendo had one GameBoy Advance title and one GameCube title, while Microsoft had only *Halo*. *Grand Theft Auto: Vice City*, an urban crime game from RockStar Games, was a runaway hit on the PlayStation 2 and was a Sony exclusive.

With the Xbox, Microsoft regretted handing over so much control to Intel and Nvidia. Nobody had an incentive to reduce the costs of chips on Microsoft's terms. Nvidia had expended a lot of engineering capital on the project. It had devoted more than 200 engineers to finishing the chip at a time when its competitor, ATI, had more resources. Nvidia ran late on finishing the Xbox chip. Then it had to go back to fighting off ATI. It didn't have leftover engineers to keep redesigning the Xbox graphics chip for Microsoft to drive costs down. Microsoft, nevertheless, was obligated to ensure that Nvidia received a constant gross profit margin on every chip shipped.

Sony's own manufacturing of the chips for the original PlayStation was an object lesson in the magic of silicon miniaturization. In chip design, the size of a chip determines its cost. Chip makers process chips in the form of wafers, which are later sliced into individual chips. A big chip is hard to manufacture, because a given silicon wafer always has a few killer defects. If the chips are really big, chances are a killer defect will render a chip inoperable. But if you can fit 100 chips on a wafer, a few defects will only kill a few chips. The number of working chips out of the total number on the wafer is dubbed the production yield. If you had 97 working chips in a batch of 100, the yield was 97 percent. With high yields, the costs per chip are lowest. With big chips, yields were low. With small chips, they were much closer to 90 percent. Either way, the wafer cost was the same. So, if possible, it made much more sense to make smaller chips with high yields. Trouble was, the big chips had the best performance because they packed in so much circuitry.

Over time, the same type of chips could be made smaller. Chip designers could redesign the chip the next year so that it performed the same functions with fewer fundamental components, dubbed transistors, as if the designers stuffed the same chip into a garbage compacter. They could also run it through a new factory. Every couple of years, chip making equipment improved so that the system of lenses and light-bending machines could create finer and finer circuits on a chip. It was like getting a sharper pencil to draw thinner and thinner lines. As such, they could add more transistors on the same size chip. In doing so, they fulfilled Moore's Law, named after Intel co-founder Gordon Moore, who observed that the number of transistors which fit on a chip doubled every two years or so. That observation, made in 1965, had held up for decades. Every two years, chip makers worked their magic. They could double the number of transistors on the same size chip. Or, in a machine that had static functions such as a game console, they could put the same number of transistors on a chip that was half the size of the original. Sony had proven with the PlayStation chip that Moore's Law was alive and well.

In 1993, Sony created a big microprocessor for the original PlayStation, which was very powerful for its time. It ran at 33 megahertz, slower than Intel's 60-megahertz Pentium chips for the PC. But Sony made it for a lower cost than the Pentium and the chip didn't dissipate as much heat as the Pentium. The first PlayStation chip was 128 millimeters on a side. Five years later, after two rounds of miniaturization, the chip could perform the same functions, but now it was only 46 millimeters on a side. The new chip took up only 13 percent of the area that the original chip occupied. Hence, it could be made with fewer materials, reducing its costs. And since the chips were smaller, the yield on each wafer was much higher. This meant that, in 1998, Sony could afford to sell the PlayStation for a much lower price and still make a profit. It could even put the same machine into a much smaller box, which it dubbed the PSOne. All because of the magic of silicon miniaturization.

With the PlayStation 2, Sony started out with the same chip strategy. In 1998, it created a powerful "Emotion Engine" microprocessor that ran at 294 megahertz and had 10.5 million transistors. It also had a graphics chip with 10.5 million transistors which served as a companion to the CPU for rendering 3-D images. The microprocessor was 240 millimeters on a side, a huge chip with low yields. But Sony's chip designers worked furiously to reduce the size. The next year, they shrank it to 110 millimeters on a side. In 2001, they further shrank it to 75 millimeters on a side. The first graphics chip was 279 millimeters on a side, with yields so low that Sony had trouble shipping enough PlayStation 2 consoles in 2000. By 2002, the graphics chip was 77 millimeters on a side.

At the time, Microsoft didn't know it but Sony had an ace up its sleeve. By 2004, it would combine the Emotion Engine with the graphics chip in a single piece of silicon. That chip measured 87 millimeters on a side, taking up only five percent of the space that the original chips consumed. Since the graphics chip and microprocessor were the most expensive items in the PlayStation 2, Sony rode the cost curve down. It accordingly reduced the price of the PlayStation 2 from $299 in 2000 to $149 in 2004. And instead of losing money on the hardware, it was actually making a small profit on every box sold. Sony had seen the fruits of the major capital investments it had made in full custom chip design, chip factories, manufacturing process technology, and its own system assembly factories. By spending a huge amount of money up front, it could get cheap hardware by the end of the cycle that blew away the competitors who didn't invest.

While Microsoft didn't know how far it was outclassed on silicon, it knew it was behind. Microsoft couldn't motivate Intel and Nvidia to dedicate precious design engineers to cost reducing their chips in the Xbox. And under no circumstances would either company trust the other enough to combine the Intel CPU with the Nvidia graphics chip. Microsoft was stuck with high silicon costs on its machine, and consequently, in addition to having a high-cost hard drive, it had a machine that was a perennial money pit. Microsoft desperately needed silicon partners who understood these economics, but Microsoft didn't want to go to the trouble of creating its own silicon design teams, silicon factories, and all of the headaches that come with them. Companies such as Digital Equipment Corp. which were saddled with the costs of silicon ownership went down in defeat against the smaller but more nimble PC companies such as Dell.

The hardware team just couldn't bail out on the original Xbox. It had to cut its costs at the same time as it was trying to come up with the design for Xenon. This problem of balancing the needs of the current Xbox and the requirements for its replacement became the primary management problem at Microsoft. Besides cutting the costs of hardware, Microsoft had to continuously push the original Xbox forward by launching in new territories, releasing new versions of Xbox Live, unveiling new versions of the Xbox dashboard software, releasing new sets of tools to aid game developers, and rolling out new marketing programs. Some of those efforts were critical to pulling ahead of Sony in some markets in Europe and Asia. And they meant that Microsoft had to spend more money.

So the added reinforcements from WebTV were no longer viewed as outsiders. They were welcomed as relief pitchers, said Leland. The core group of designers from 3DO was just about a dozen people. They started their work. After sitting out most of the Xbox work, they were now the lead engineers for Xenon. It was time for their revenge.

While most of the Microsoft hardware engineers were preoccupied with cost reduction, J Allard assigned Mike Abrash, the game developer who had brought considerable graphics expertise to the Advanced Technology Group, to pull together a silicon team to for the next Xbox in January, 2002. Abrash asked for help from Todd Holmdahl, who in turn conveyed the message to Larry Yang, another WebTV veteran who was running the semiconductor engineering team in Mountain View.

Yang was a 37-year-old WebTV engineering manager who had taken over the chip engineering group after Tim Bucher left. Yang grew up in Los Angeles in a family that wanted him to be a doctor. He went to Stanford University, played around with computers and decided he wanted to be an electrical engineer. In particular, he liked semiconductor chip design because the smarts in an electronic system were always in the chips. It was the hardest thing to create. He joined Sun Microsystems in time to work on the Sparc microprocessors. He spent a decade there before leaving to join WebTV's custom chip development

team. With the 1997 acquisition of WebTV, he joined Microsoft. Now he led the few dozen or so chip designers at Microsoft's Mountain View campus.

The day after Ultimate TV bit the dust, Yang asked Nick Baker and Jeff Andrews, the senior system architects on hand, to work with Abrash. They also pulled in Greg Williams, a former 3DO engineer, to contemplate the memory system for the console.

They had been rebuffed at first. They had saved their jobs by offering their skills at cost reduction. But when Microsoft was looking around for more hardware engineers to start the next generation of video games, it had to go to the former WebTV team.

They rode a Trojan horse into the heart of the Xbox team, and then they took it over. Nick Baker himself didn't think of the Xbox as a defeat for the WebTV team. "After all," he said, "They came up with their proposal and we came up with ours. Then the two teams moved closer together. When they started, Xbox was more like a PC. When they finished, it was a console, like what we proposed."

Now the wheel of fortune had spun their way. For the Mountain View crew, their new role at the center of the project was a heady thing. It meant that all those years of struggle and failure had prepared them for something really important. The people who had gone down in defeat on WebTV were now calling the shots on the next Xbox. Trip Hawkins, who was now CEO of Digital Chocolate, a maker of cell phone games, felt some pride at the accomplishments of the 3DO offspring.

He remembered the group later as "the young Turks of the organization, the best and the brightest." He added, "There was a Kennedy Camelot feeling. Smart young idealists. But we got assassinated. Everyone looks at 3DO as a failure as a crop. But if you look at what those people have done, you know they were influenced by 3DO. What we contribute becomes part of human culture. Our society tends to over-rate success and under-rate failure."

By learning from failure and by clinging to survival with tenacity, the WebTV team finally had its revenge on the original Xbox team. And yet it didn't really matter anymore, since they had merged into one team. Leslie Leland said everyone understood the goals. Xbox 1.0 was to get into the market. Xbox 2.0 was to beat Sony.

"This time, they had a seat at the table," said J Allard. "They were full shareholders and citizens on this project. They were on the highest wire with the smallest net."

1. "Hacking the Xbox: An Introduction to Reverse Engineering," by Andrew "bunnie" Huang, No Starch Press, 2003, p. 3.

2. "Hacking the Xbox: An Introduction to Reverse Engineering," p. 143.

CHAPTER SEVEN

CODE NAME TRINITY

*I*t was already late to start planning the next generation. Little did the Mountain View team know, but they were again almost two years behind their counterparts at Sony, IBM and Toshiba. In early 2000, a group of five Sony engineers sat down with five IBM engineers in Austin, Texas. They started drawing up plans to create a new custom chip for the PlayStation 3. Michael Gschwind, an IBM engineer who attended the meeting, said they began the architecture of what they would eventually call the "Cell" microprocessor. It was going to be something monumental. In contrast to hot rods such as the fastest Intel microprocessors, it wouldn't have just a single engine for getting tasks done in a serial fashion. It was more akin to bees working in a hive together, said Jim Kahle, the IBM chief architect behind the idea for Cell.

Sony didn't announce until March, 2001, that it had created an alliance with IBM and Toshiba to develop Cell chips for use in a wide variety of systems, including the next-generation video game platform. As it had with the PlayStation 2, Sony was going full custom with the microprocessor and many of the innards for the PlayStation 3. Toshiba was exploring options to craft a graphics chip from the ground up to go with the Cell microprocessor. That meant that Sony was prepared to spend billions of dollars on its engineering teams and the factories for building its systems and its chips. If IBM was going to do this work for Sony, would it really have anybody left to work with Microsoft? And if Nintendo also chose some key partners before Microsoft did, who would be left to work with Microsoft?

Nick Baker gave the new Microsoft game console the code name "Trinity," named after Carrie-Ann Moss's character in the 1999 science fiction blockbuster film, *The Matrix*. It was a cool name that conveyed the idea that the next Xbox would unlock a virtual world where illusions were so real that they couldn't be separated from reality. They worked under that code name for a time, but eventually someone cross checked it with the active list of projects at Microsoft. Somebody else was already doing Trinity, so the team then changed the name to Xenon, an element on the periodic table that was a colorless, inert gas. Beyond having an X in the name, the code name didn't mean anything, and that was better than Trinity, which had too many interpretations from the Holy Trinity to the Trinity atomic bomb test site to the Trinity character in the movie. It was an inconspicuous birth. For Baker and Andrews, it was a job they had waited years to do.

Nick Baker, Xenon silicon architect

"I knew we were going to do it and I wanted to get going," said Baker. "Ultimate TV was going away. And the lead time on things like silicon was going to be so long. We looked at the workload and had to decide what we would be able to do. If it was going to get done, it was pretty much up to us."

"I was really excited about working on it," Andrews said.

Abrash was a big help at the start because he had programmed cutting-edge games such as id Software's first-person shooter, *Quake*. He had also been instrumental in the design of the original Xbox, working for Seamus Blackley in the Advanced Technology Group. He offered good ideas. One of them was to create a CPU and a graphics chip that worked together much more intimately than the typical counterparts would work in a PC. But Abrash resigned from Microsoft a month after Xenon began. He had enjoyed working with both Baker

and Andrews, but he had decided to leave to work with his friend Mark Sartain at Rad Game Tools. The start-up would create software development tools to more easily generate 3-D graphics. Abrash's vision for game development had always been to create simple hardware and build sophisticated tools that allowed developers to get the maximum benefit out of that hardware. That idea would live on at the Xbox division after he was gone. While at Rad, Abrash still consulted for Microsoft, helping to define how the graphics system would work.

The 34-year-old Baker had to step up as the technical ringleader. He was a smart man who had filled his head with the knowledge of computer graphics, but he wasn't much of a video game player. The son of a metal merchant, he had grown up in Canterbury, England, the setting of Chaucer's *The Canterbury Tales*. One day, when he was around 10, Baker's father bought him an electronics magazine.

"I was hooked," Baker said.

But he had a video game-deprived childhood. His parents would never buy him a game console. They did buy him a personal computer in 1985, and he started playing around with it. One of the early games that fascinated him was *Nethack*, a fantasy role-playing game that was created in the 1980s and ran on primitive, text-only screens. The game had no graphics except the ASCII text characters that were used to draw the outlines of its dungeon passages. Wagner James Au wrote, in an article on Salon.com, "*Nethack* is still one of the best games ever made." It was an open-source project, meaning anyone who wanted to could make changes to the game's source code, in order to improve it. It took a lot of imagination to visualize the game, since the hero's character was nothing more than an "@" sign. In the game, you could take a bunch of Orcs out with a "Wand of Lightning," but the blast would ricochet off the walls and take you out too. Baker played the game obsessively.

Thanks to that early computer, Baker grew up to be an electrical engineer. He graduated from Imperial College in London in 1990 with an electrical engineering degree. Baker went on to get his master's degree in electrical engineering. He would occasionally play games, but he became obsessed with only one game per generation. On the original Xbox, that game was *Project Gotham Racing*. Fortunately, he could talk to game developers about what they wanted in a game console. In college, one of Baker's friends worked at Apple. Baker got an interview with Apple and, at the age of 23, he immigrated to Silicon Valley to work in Apple's video capture card division. Beginning a long string of bad luck, the project got canceled. Looking around, Baker joined the exodus of Apple veterans who were taking a job at a new video game start-up, 3DO. There, in April, 1993, he joined as a video engineer. He learned more about graphics for game consoles from some of the best engineers of the day, such as Adrian Sfarti.

"Nick was quite good," recalled Robert (R. J.) Mical, the co-creator of the 3DO game console. "I didn't know he cut his teeth on graphics with us. He was that good."

Baker built up his expertise and eventually became one of the engineering

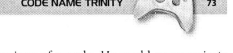

managers. He wasn't the most gregarious of people. He could communicate technically, but he often answered with just a few words.

Baker had been part of many failures. Apple had axed his video card division. At 3DO, the M2 technology he had helped create didn't succeed. At WebTV, he had lost his bid to build the first Xbox. And the Ultimate TV project had died an early death. But building hardware systems was his forte. His experience was invaluable.

His buddy and fellow 3DO traveler was Jeff Andrews, a computer engineer who grew up in Rockford, Ill. Andrews was the son of a community college teacher. His destiny was clear from the third grade, when he saw a ham radio for sale at a garage sale. His interest in technology continued to develop, and it was a momentous day when his father bought him a Commodore Pet, an early entertainment computer that debuted in 1979. He played games on the machine and wrote a crude, horse racing game for the machine.

Throughout high school, he took electronics classes and played games. He majored in computer engineering at the University of Illinois at Urbana-Champaign. In 1988, he made his way to Rolm, an early telecommunications hardware company, in San Jose. He designed some chips there but jumped to Steve Jobs' Next computer company as Rolm collapsed. That's where he met some friends, such as Tim Bucher, who made the migration to 3DO. Andrews joined 3DO in 1993, the year it launched its first console. He met Nick Baker as they worked on the chips for the M2 console. He took off for a brief stint at an "intolerable job" at Nvidia, where he worked on a console graphics chip for Sega, before joining Baker at CagEnt. Having been through the same rollercoaster as Baker, Andrews said, "You have to persevere. You have to absolutely stay competitive. You can't be doing something that is just OK."

After Mike Abrash left, the silicon team needed new direction. As the WebTV/3DO folks were working away at the chip architecture in Mountain View, Holmdahl assigned Greg Gibson to be the chief on the overall design of the Xenon hardware system in Redmond. He was going to be the customer of whatever the Mountain View team designed.

Gibson, then 31, grew up in Salem, Ore., and earned an electrical engineering degree from the University of Washington. Like a number of other Microsoft hardware engineers, he had worked at Fluke Corp. designing handheld test equipment for six years. He joined Microsoft in 1997 to work for the hardware group designing mice and keyboards. When the time came to put together the original Xbox, Gibson was one of the first that Holmdahl assigned to work on the engineering design. In September, 1999, he became a technical program manager in charge of working with Intel and Nvidia on the Xbox chips. Since the Xbox had been mostly outsourced, Gibson's role was to supervise and communicate with the teams at Intel and Nvidia that were doing all the work. Intel had agreed to provide the microprocessor and create the system board for the Xbox, while Nvidia had agreed to create a custom graphics chip and a communications chip. Gibson had to shepherd those projects through to completion, pulling out a few hairs as he was doing so. Holmdahl regarded Gibson as an essential contributor.

At the time of the Xbox launch in November, 2001, Gibson was running all the electrical-mechanical hardware development on the Xbox. While Nvidia and Intel had designed most of the innards of the original Xbox, Gibson's team was taking over those tasks on Xenon. Now it was overseeing the redesign of the motherboard, mechanical design, and software. The last thing that Microsoft had not yet taken over was silicon integration. That meant that Microsoft wanted to determine the schedule for redesigning chips, debugging the designs, and sending them to the factory. That was why the chip engineers in Mountain View were so important.

When he moved over to run hardware development for Xenon, he gave up command of 200 engineers and went to a team with just a few. In the spring of 2002, Gibson made the shift from Xbox to doing mostly Xenon. He had clear marching orders. Whatever happened, this time Microsoft couldn't be late.

Microsoft needed to know the competition's intentions. Baker hired Jon Peddie Research, a technology consulting company in Tiburon, California. Peddie had been around the graphics industry for decades and had a wide array of market intelligence at his disposal. Sony was applying for patents on the Cell microprocessor, so Baker, Peddie's staff and the rest of the crew analyzed them. Microsoft's people thought that Sony was making a mistake with the way it was designing the system. It would be too complicated and too costly to make games for. At one point, the team actually thought that Sony would put three Cells on one chip, for a total of 27 processors. The patents just didn't spell out Sony's intentions. But one part of Sony's strategy, which had the imprints of Ken Kutaragi, a semiconductor expert, was absolutely clear.

"It was a huge upfront capital investment and I didn't think that they would get their money back later when they were making masses of cheap chips," said Jon Thomason, head of software for the Xbox team. "We clearly didn't think that the capital investment was going to be necessary. So we looked for other strategies."

Microsoft wasn't going to copy Sony and create a full custom chip with its own factory. It didn't have the time or the inclination. Microsoft had to tailor the system to run video games, without going full custom in a risky project that might take years to finish. With the original Xbox, Microsoft had chosen mostly off-the-shelf parts developed for the PC. That saved a lot of time. But it meant that the Xbox life-span wasn't as long as a box that had custom-designed silicon. Other off-the-shelf parts would come along and quickly enable the PC to move ahead of the game console. Microsoft had more time to do custom parts this time, but still wanted to take advantage of PC hardware R&D. It also wanted to take advantage of the vast growth in contract manufacturing infrastructure around the world. It could use somebody else's factory instead of its own and use that to beat Sony, a cash-strapped company trying to fight off competitors on too many fronts.

Todd Holmdahl, the head of hardware for the Xbox, knew where he wanted to go. He had known how to make the mouse business work without owning

factories. Microsoft hired contract manufacturers such as Flextronics to make its mice and keyboards, and it did the same for the original Xbox. Running the business in a virtual way was natural.

Holmdahl had known about Nintendo's deal with graphics chip maker ATI Technologies on the GameCube console, and he also considered WebTV's experience in system design. ATI designed a graphics chip for Nintendo, but it allowed Nintendo to take the design to a contract chip manufacturer and have it fabricated on its own timetable. ATI generated profits on engineering fees and royalty payments for every box sold, but Nintendo owned the designs and didn't have to pay ATI a margin for making the chips. Nintendo owned the intellectual property that ATI had created, and that mattered a lot in terms of profits. Holmdahl wanted the same for the next Xbox.

"The first time, we had a short period of time and it didn't afford us the opportunity to make these relationships," Holmdahl said. "The whole intellectual property business, sharing IP, was just in its infancy. The lesson we learned is you want to control your destiny." [1]

Holmdahl knew that the rush to get to market had forced Microsoft to sign some contracts that it eventually came to regret. The company tried to lean on suppliers to cut costs as much as possible, but Nvidia's CEO, Jen-Hsun Huang, had fought back. The battle spilled into public. Both companies sought a resolution in an arbitration process, which was the only thing that prevented them from going to court.

Huang wanted to redo the contract because the yields on his chips weren't as high as expected. Nvidia had to scale back the speed of its graphics chips to get better yields, but the problem persisted. Huang threatened to stop shipping chips. Microsoft objected, and the arbitrator sided with Microsoft.

The lesson inside Microsoft was clear. Holmdahl wanted more control over the design and manufacturing of its chips. That would give him more leverage over suppliers. This was the key for Microsoft to control the costs of the box. From Microsoft's point of view, Nvidia and Intel had kept too much of the control in terms of cost-reducing their chips and determining the price changes on their own schedule. Because they didn't cut the costs quickly, Microsoft could not cut the prices on the original Xbox. Yet, for the sake of compatibility, it seemed Microsoft was stuck with those vendors. It was almost a given that old Xbox games had to play on Xenon.

The last thing Holmdahl needed was a repeat of the PC story. In 1981, IBM was in charge of the design of the system for the personal computer, but in its rush to market it unwittingly gave away most of the technical decision-making – and profits – to Intel and Microsoft. IBM eventually exited the PC business, while Intel and Microsoft became dominant firms in PC technology.

"We didn't know what we were doing the first time," said Gibson. "If we did, we would have been more terrified about what we were getting into. It was such a barn burner just trying to complete development on time. There wasn't a lot of time to step back. We had this vision to change video games and the industry. We put our heads down on how to get that product on the shelf. When we were still putting our team together, the PlayStation 2 was already on the shelf in Japan."

Gibson began to assemble a team of electrical and mechanical engineers who would craft the system design. He asked the Mountain View group to cast a wide net in their search for relevant technologies for the key chips. The Mountain View crew looked at everything in the technical universe, including architectures for supercomputers, corporate servers, Macintosh desktops, standard PCs, set-top boxes and even cell phones.

"We wanted to look at everything with a computer in it," Gibson said. "We had an open mind."

To flesh out the chip manufacturing strategy, Holmdahl discussed his ideas with Larry Yang, who was running the silicon team in Mountain View.

"One thing I learned," Yang said, "was the strategy toward partnerships had to be different. In a standard PC, they increase performance but keep the selling price the same. It's different with a console. You want to fix features and drive costs down. It's hard to engage with a merchant semiconductor company and hit cost objectives. They typically double up on a chip's performance for the same cost. They don't ship the same chip for seven years. It's not in their DNA."

Yang's team started figuring out how Microsoft could control the schedule for reducing chip costs and integrating components together. Fortunately, globalization was on Microsoft's side. Foundries such as TSMC and contract manufacturers such as Flextronics were now much bigger and able to handle the demands associated with large console volume sales. In every aspect of hardware, from the design on through the finished product, specialists could handle a single task extremely efficiently. While each middleman player took its own profit, its specialization advantages could give the company that used it in an outsourced manufacturing model an advantage over the vertical companies that owned everything. Even the big Japanese electronics giants, Sony included, were now adopting outsourced manufacturing, said Jim McCusker, a senior vice president at Flextronics and the project lead on Xbox. Microsoft didn't need to enter the hardware or chip manufacturing businesses, but it did need to control the key parts of the supply chain to make some magic happen.

"The point of globalization is that it broadens the number of partners you can work with to get a product out without making it yourself," Yang said. "If you control the key points in the supply chain, that's what matters. Then you tap the key players who can do the work for you and all they do for a living is that one thing. You can control your own destiny."

Inside the Mountain View campus, Yang's team would grow to include chip architects, design verification engineers, physical designers, operations people, supply chain managers, and planners. The team saw an opportunity to create one of the necessary chips for Xenon, a TV encoder that would enable the machine to record and play back video, from the ground up. It would take no more than 10 engineers, partly because Microsoft owned encoder technology thanks to its Ultimate TV project. This was one case where the WebTV experience paid off.

But Microsoft stopped short of becoming a hardware company. It didn't need to turn itself into Sony in order to take on the Japanese electronics giant. Rather, Yang, Gibson and Holmdahl all saw a chance to outdo Sony with a hybrid model. They could use their internal expertise to get chip vendors to come up with a semi-custom design. That design would be tailored for the console market, but it could tap into the vast amount of engineering work that was already being done for the PC.

"We built an overall business model for the entire Xbox 360 generation," Yang said.

All of the decisions were contingent on just one decision: when was the console going to launch? By looking at the Cell project, Microsoft deduced that Sony would be able to launch a console as early as 2005. That determined the schedule for Microsoft's own console. From Steve Ballmer to Robbie Bach to J Allard, launching at the same time or earlier than Sony was an absolute requirement. If that didn't happen, all hope of gaining market share would be lost.

"Before we had the conceptualization, the 2005 number was there. We said it was important for us to start the next generation of gaming in 2005," said Holmdahl.

"Given that, how much time do we have?" Yang said. "We worked our way backward."

It would take about two years to get everything critical done, from creating marquee games to designing semi-custom chips. That meant that everything critical had to get started by the fall of 2003. More time might even be necessary.

---

1. *Electronic Engineering Times,* "Microsoft Bets On Xbox 360 To Beat Sony At Its Game," Nov. 14, 2005.

CHAPTER EIGHT

THE ADVANCE SCOUTS FROM 3DO

Nick Baker, Jeff Andrews and Greg Williams worked alone for a time in Mountain View. They needed to define what a game console was and what it needed to deliver in terms of performance. The critical parts were the microprocessor, the brains of the system, and the graphics chip, which produced the animations that the console displayed on the TV. They had to know the ins and outs of these kinds of chips.

Both parts had to make calculations at blinding speeds, and they had to be customized to handle exactly the tasks they needed to run. That meant that they had to be specially designed. Those chips cost the most and would get the most attention, but there would be hundreds and hundreds more components in the system.

The team had to decide what it needed, and then see what kind of chips were already in development. If there was something close to what Microsoft needed already in development, it could shorten the timetable by taking such a chip and tailoring it. It would be a mostly custom effort, but with a lot less risk and time than Sony's effort.

For sure, the graphics would get better. But one of the problems of game consoles was that they always lagged behind the PC. The resolution of the TV set, with only 480 lines of dots for creating images, wasn't as sharp as PC monitors. But high-definition TV had been coming for a long time and it promised a big leap in image resolution.

Clearly, one of the requirements would be that a next-generation game console would have to be able to handle wide-screen high-definition TV resolutions. The original Xbox could display graphics in regular analog TV or the lowest-resolution format for digital TV, dubbed 480P because it could show 480 vertical lines in a progressive format. This time, the engineers thought that they should take a step up to true HDTV, with resolutions at 720P, or 720 vertical lines. They also had to consider versions of HDTV that were still in the pipeline and could offer even more resolution. The difference was similar to what gamers noticed when they switched from 800 x 600 resolution on a computer display, and when they played the same game running at a resolution of 1024 x 768. The images were sharper, clearer, more defined, and better focused. For gamers, they would now be able to notice blades of grass, the skin on a basketball player, or the way a character's muscles moved. [1]

That meant they would have to push billions of polygons through the graphics processor. The graphics chip companies were already quite capable of rendering animations at such resolutions on personal computer monitors, which actually could display more detail than TVs. But the consoles couldn't cost as much or consume anywhere near as much power. The task boiled down to defining the kind of games that the console would play, the performance that those games needed, and comparing that to the practical technology that was available from the best vendors.

"For us, 2002 was about understanding what the technology could do," said Greg Gibson, who joined Baker and Andrews in the spring.

For the first half of 2002, the Mountain View team was busy looking into the realm of technological possibilities. The scouts quizzed everyone and anyone who had ever designed a microprocessor or graphics chip. The choice of these two components was critical because they would determine how good the games running on it would look, and together they were likely to account for more than half the cost of the console.

Jeff Andrews visited Stanford University, where a team headed by computer science professor Bill Dally was working on "Imagine," a chip architecture that had a novel "stream processor" for doing graphics and imaging tasks. Andrews was intrigued at the design, the first version of which had been built in April, 2002. But it was complicated to program and in some ways resembled Sony's Cell architecture. Consulting with software experts at Microsoft such as Andrew Goossen and Tracy Sharp, Andrews knew that Microsoft wouldn't go for a complicated programming model.

"We were a software company that has hardware engineers," Andrews said. "There is no way we would have taken an architecture like Cell and jammed it down the throats of people in Redmond."

Andrews also met with chip suppliers such as PMC-Sierra, Transmeta, and Broadcom. The latter, a feisty communications chip maker in Irvine, Calif., had bought SiByte, a microprocessor start-up, for $2 billion in stock during the Internet communications frenzy. Andrews liked the Broadcom solution, but he had reservations about working closely with the unproven microprocessor architecture.

The Microsoft team figured they had to match Sony's launch in 2005, so they asked what the vendors would have ready by that time. They also had to talk to the chip foundries, or the contract manufacturers that would take the designs and actually fabricate the chips for them. That was because they had to balance a chip design with the right manufacturing technology to hit the right mix of performance and cost.

Chip-making processes were measured in terms of the width of the circuits they could fabricate. Measured in nanometers, or a billionth of a meter, the circuit widths in most chips in 2002 were about 180 nanometers. By 2005, miniaturization technology would proceed so that chips could be built with 90-nanometer circuit widths. The significance of shrinking the circuit widths was huge in terms of cost. The same chip design that was fabricated with 180-nanometer equipment was many times larger – and therefore many times more expensive – than the same chip fabricated with 90-nanometer technology. So Microsoft not only had to pick the right chip design, it had to pick the right manufacturing technology.

The problem was that manufacturing technology could be hit or miss. It was always risky to bet too early on a new manufacturing technology. It sometimes took months, or even years, to work out the bugs in a new chip-making process. Chip designers would design for a new manufacturing process, only to discover that it couldn't be used to make reliable chips until sometime after the production deadline. This was why a microprocessor designer said that designing such chips was like playing Russian roulette. You wagered years ahead of time, but then you would find out much later whether you had shot yourself in the head. By going to the chip foundries, Microsoft had to determine whether those companies were going to have enough factory capacity at the right circuit widths to produce chips by the millions in 2005.

The team expanded to handle the chores of checking out each option. Bill Adamec, a WebTV veteran in the hardware group, joined as the 12th engineer on the project in the middle of 2002. While Nick Baker was the technical lead on the graphics chip architecture, Adamec served as program manager, taking charge of the business and schedule aspects of the key chips. Under him worked Masoud Foudeh, the program manager of the graphics chip, and later he added Dan Cooper, the program manager for the microprocessor.

Andrews had made an initial visit to IBM but didn't see anything impressive on the road map. Adamec set about finding what IBM could offer in terms of microprocessor technology. For a time, it seemed that IBM really wasn't serious about making a bid. It was already locked in with Sony and was likely to supply chips to Nintendo again. It didn't seem like it wanted the Microsoft business too. And IBM's engineers were especially worried that there just wasn't enough time.

Andrews huddled for hours at a time with Dave Shippy, one of IBM's microprocessor experts. Adamec, who had once worked for IBM for two years, guessed that IBM would be an ideal partner. Six months before Microsoft started looking, IBM had started a new business for its chip engineers. It was going to offer design and engineering services. That meant it was going to take some of its best chip talent and hire them out to other companies. They would design chips for the outsiders and then fabricate the chips in IBM's own big factories. In particular, IBM needed to fill a factory in East Fishkill, N.Y., where IBM was investing billions of dollars.

"The formation of that group was perfect for us," Adamec said.

After two or three discussions, IBM brought the right people together. Charlie Johnson, a distinguished IBM engineer who specialized in the pre-sales process, finally opened the kimono, revealing the technologies IBM had to offer. Included were some microprocessor cores, or prefabricated designs that could serve as the heart of a custom chip, especially suitable for what Microsoft had in mind. Adamec got on a plane to go to Rochester, N.Y. As he entered the sprawling IBM campus, he realized that he was an ambassador for Microsoft. He could help thaw the Cold War between the companies. On his way to his first meeting, he passed by an open door with dozens of people inside. That couldn't be his meeting, he thought. But they invited him inside. There were 26 people in the room, and each one of them had a presentation to make to Adamec. The IBM team had just finished work on a low-cost server. Adamec toured the labs and liked it all.

The Mountain View team also had to learn the product road maps for the graphics chip makers. Masoud Foudeh, then a 38-year-old engineer, joined the small group with this purpose in mind. A computer scientist with a couple of degrees from UC Davis in computer science, he too had been through the long ordeal at 3DO and at UltimateTV. He joined the Xbox hardware team to help cut the costs on the original Xbox. He wasn't much of a gamer, but Foudeh would become the engineering program manager for the Xenon graphics chips. He started talking to the graphics chip makers about what they would be able to do in the next round of consoles. That job wasn't as tough this time, since Nvidia and ATI were now billion-dollar companies and pretty much the only graphics chip companies that had the wherewithal to design a custom graphics chip. Microsoft still tried to consider ideas from other sources, such as S3, a smaller graphics chip company, which pitched an intriguing low-cost design. They also checked out the technology at 3Dlabs, a workstation graphics company in Milpitas, Calif.

"Our view was to use something that was already going to be out there in the markets," Baker said.

ATI had reported weak results for a couple of years. It was targeting sales of $1.0 billion in sales for the year ended August, 2002, but that was below sales of $1.3 billion in 2000. It had lost money for two years in a row, and royalty revenue from its deal with Nintendo wasn't coming in as highly as they'd anticipated. But in July, 2002, ATI introduced a PC graphics chip that finally blew Nvidia out of the water on the high-end of the gaming business. Two years in the making, the Radeon 9700 Pro took the performance lead from Nvidia for the first time in years. This leadership was a good bargaining chip that could convince Microsoft to favor ATI's technology, even if it wasn't cheap.

Dave Orton, then president of ATI, and Bob Feldstein felt they had an opportunity to win over Microsoft. They had a team in Santa Clara, California, in Silicon Valley. That team, where Orton himself came from, had been the spearhead behind the graphics chip for the Nintendo GameCube, which debuted in September, 2001, in Japan. The Santa Clara team was already contemplating its next move for the successor to the Nintendo GameCube. But ATI also had

sizable teams in Toronto, Florida and Massachusetts. If they could just make sure to keep those groups completely separate, it was possible for ATI to do graphics work for both Nintendo and Microsoft.

Feldstein sent a group of engineers to do some early architectural work, even though ATI had not yet signed a deal. They had been thinking seriously about next-generation console designs and had some ideas that could address the need for high-performance *and* keep costs down, all at the same time. They called their project "C1." Rick Bergman, another ATI vice president, said that the key was that the solution they came up with couldn't be just another PC derivative. It would deliver what Microsoft wanted in terms of a high-definition experience for gamers.

"We were doing a console graphics chip from the ground up," Feldstein said.

Nvidia also got the same visit from the Xenon crew. The Santa Clara chip design firm was not getting along well with Redmond. Nvidia's engineers had run late on the design of the original Xbox graphics chip. They had faced a perplexing bug. The chip prototypes had passed muster, but when they were plugged into test boards, the systems didn't work right. One test of a dolphin swimming worked well for weeks at a time, but when another application was loaded, the dolphin program crashed. Nvidia's engineers took weeks to figure that a power supply had been poorly designed. It sent surges of electrical feedback into the system periodically, causing the failures. The delay cost months of production time, causing Microsoft to scale back its launch.

"A lot of us still have bad dreams of that dolphin," Holmdahl said. [2]

Because of ATI's progress, Nvidia was feeling pain. It was on its way to $1.9 billion in sales for 2002, and it had had the upper hand on ATI for many quarters. But Nvidia's engineers had gone down the wrong path in their designs for the power-hungry GeForce FX line of chips. The engineers had created special hardware to suit *Doom 3*, a hot new game being designed by John Carmack and his team at id Software. But the game had slipped its schedule. Nvidia's engineers also had to anticipate what Microsoft would put into the graphics hardware standard, known as Direct X, and they guessed wrong. Thanks to the Xbox, Nvidia was able to enter the chip set business, a big market for support chips for the PC. At times, Xbox was accounting for 20 percent of Nvidia revenues. But relations weren't good anymore. Microsoft and Nvidia were still in the midst of arbitration over pricing for the original Xbox graphics chips.

They had settled one arbitration case when another arose. In the second case, the companies quarreled about one of the smallest details. Bryan Lee, the head of business development for Microsoft's Xbox business, didn't want to let Huang get away with anything. Lee tried to make his mark as a new numbers guy by riding Nvidia hard. Microsoft alleged that Nvidia had promised a 100 percent yield on its chips, but Huang had agreed to no such thing. It backfired. Huang fought back. That second case wasn't settled until February, 2003, well into the planning stages for Xenon. By the time the matter was settled, there was less than $100,000 at stake. Microsoft felt it had a bad partner, and Nvidia felt the same way.

"There was never any question we wouldn't work with Nvidia," said one Xbox executive. "There was just too much conflict."

"It was unbelievable," said an Nvidia veteran. "We really didn't want to work with them again."

The investigation into new ideas for hardware took months, but it covered a lot of ground. As the task ballooned, more and more engineers joined the project. The team had to figure out what kind of architecture they wanted. They had to know more about what kind of games the hardware would run. They had to keep an eye on the competition. The team had to keep tabs on what the chip vendors could practically do in the next couple of years. And they needed to know what the foundries, or the contract chip manufacturers, were capable of making for Microsoft. They had to build simulations of the processing inside the box to determine what they needed to include in the system. The technical discussions covered everything imaginable.

As an example, this time Microsoft wanted to make sure that gamers would be able to send instant messages to each other. On the original Xbox, because of the configuration of the hardware and the software, there was no way to make that happen. This time, communication had to be baked into the chips. Another matter was security. Dinarte Morais had decided that the security algorithms had to be built into the hardware and the CPU had to be compatible with any scheme to protect the integrity of the box from embarrassing hacks. He had dreamed up approaches that would prevent consoles from being "modded" with fake ROM chips, that would secure a networked box with a unique encrypted key, and that would verify if a console was using legitimate software and other components, according to patents Microsoft filed on his behalf.

IBM, meanwhile, had figured out how to bake an encryption engine, which would accelerate the decoding and encoding of data traffic, inside the microprocessor itself. Andrew "bunnie" Huang and others had taught Microsoft that anyone could "listen" to traffic on a data pathway leading from one chip to another with inexpensive equipment. But this time, IBM would allow encrypted data to flow straight from memory into the CPU. Someone eavesdropping on the data pathway between two chips would only be able to intercept scrambled bits. The encryption accelerator would sit right next to the processors within the CPU chip. Hence, it could encrypt or decrypt data just before it was used. Charles Palmer, senior manager of security and privacy at IBM, declined to talk specifically about Microsoft. But after the launch, IBM described a technology called "Secure Blue" which it used to build encryption into hardware systems. In describing Secure Blue broadly, Palmer said in 2006 that it was already in use. He added, "Up until now, trusted security from end to end, at the hardware level, was hard to do. The system is only as secure as the weakest link."

Huang himself said he believed that Microsoft had learned its lesson and probably included a scheme so that if one chip's security algorithm was cracked, the key that the hacker discovered would only be useful in breaching security on that one machine. This kind of system would be much harder to crack.

"They probably have a different key for every machine," Huang said.

By the second half of 2002, the picture was becoming clearer. Microsoft's silicon team knew what they wanted to do on Xenon. And Baker and Andrews wanted to test one of their own ideas for how to get a lot more performance for a given amount of money spent on silicon. They understood that they had to pack a lot of processing power into an inexpensive box. The trend with PC microprocessors turning the machines into hot rods, with a lot of processing power but also a lot of heat. They were nothing but speed demons and brainiacs. The heat they were generating was going to melt the box someday if the trends continued. Going bigger and hotter wasn't appealing.

By sticking a few smaller processors on one chip, Baker and Andrews thought they could strike a balance between speed and power consumption. The idea was that they could throttle back on the actual speed and thereby reduce the amount of heat. But since they had several processors working at the same time, they could get more work done in a given amount of time. Each processor, or core, could work on a different thread, or subprogram, at the same time. This multicore approach had been tried before, but it wasn't really fashionable. The chief objection was that it was complicated to spread a software task out among so many cores or threads. There was a natural trade-off.

But Baker and Andrews had looked at supercomputers and servers where multicore, multithreaded solutions were already in use. They were not just chip designers. They had spent their time creating systems. They were not allergic to hardware with difficult programming challenges. And they knew that it did no good to have a screaming-fast microprocessor if the rest of the system wasn't balanced. The PC, for instance, had blazing fast Intel microprocessors. But the data pathways and the memory chips hadn't kept up with the same advances. The system was often out of balance, and the design of PC microprocessors had been distorted because of that. Greg Gibson reiterated the need to balance schedule, power consumption, performance, and cost.

As for the difficulty of programming with multiple cores, Baker and Andrews figured that if the team came up with the right programming tools, the game developers could learn how to develop the new software. If they went with a modified version of a well-known architecture, such as the PowerPC, software programmers could exploit the well-known tools for the architecture. That would help mask the complexity of the multicore system from the game developers. This was an idea that Abrash championed. The idea gathered momentum, and they returned to the vendors to ask what kind of multicore solutions they had in the works. But they were getting ready for the notion that they would have to switch away from Intel, Microsoft's longtime partner, and Nvidia as well.

"Within the first couple of months, we realized we'd go with multicore and multithreading," Baker said. "You get more computing for a given amount of power. But we were early in this thinking. We knew it would be a hard sell."

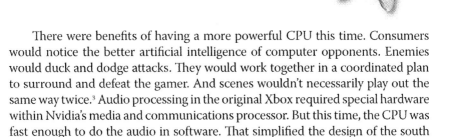

There were benefits of having a more powerful CPU this time. Consumers would notice the better artificial intelligence of computer opponents. Enemies would duck and dodge attacks. They would work together in a coordinated plan to surround and defeat the gamer. And scenes wouldn't necessarily play out the same way twice.[3] Audio processing in the original Xbox required special hardware within Nvidia's media and communications processor. But this time, the CPU was fast enough to do the audio in software. That simplified the design of the south bridge (Nvidia's media and communications processor in the first generation), which could minimize the amount of hardware-based audio functions in it.

Baker and Andrews estimated they could fit eight or 16 cores on one chip. They knew these decisions in favor of a multicore, multithreaded machine would cause some monumental changes in the intricate alliances that Microsoft had built over time. They kept it to themselves until they could gather all of the ammunition to win the argument.

Andrews primed the pump by writing a white paper on Microsoft's options for silicon architecture. He described three ideas. The company could go with a pure Intel solution. It would be hot and fast. Microsoft could also use a couple of chips, one with one big Intel core and several smaller cores. A third option, which Andrews said was the best option, was to use the multicore processor from IBM. In early September, Bill Gates took the paper with him on his "Think Week." Once a year, he went off by himself to contemplate matters and study importance issues. Back in 1995, after soaking in a paper from J Allard during Think Week, Gates wrote his famous memo about the Internet tidal wave and how Microsoft needed to marshal its resources to deal with it. Gates read the paper during Think Week and seemed to agree with everything that Andrews suggested.

"I was expecting somebody to yell at me," Andrews said.

Because they had hit upon a controversial idea so early, they were the first of the Xenon planners to schedule a meeting with Bill Gates and Steve Ballmer. Gates was wearing his hat as the Chief Software Architect. He wanted to hear about big projects when they were in their nascent stages. He didn't like it when a team presented a plan to him that was almost complete. He wanted the ability to make suggestions and monitor progress early on so he could nudge the project along the right road. Larry Yang went into the meeting with some trepidation.

It looked as if IBM's PowerPC chips were the best solution. Baker and Andrews had helped design 3DO's M2 solution around a PowerPC chip, so they were familiar with what the architecture could do. Baker was so nervous in the first meeting with Gates that he just read his slides, keeping his head down. Afterward, Todd Holmdahl said he did fine but he should look up once in a while. They all asked Gates and Ballmer whether Microsoft really had the stomach for an alliance with IBM, the company that lost its monopoly on computing because of Gates' wily maneuvers to control the PC operating system. They boned up for the meeting, and they found that both Gates and Ballmer were willing to listen and consider it.

"It was a surprise and relief that they had an open mind," said Yang.

Gates and Ballmer liked what they heard well enough to start cutting checks to the chip vendors, who would in turn begin formal development. There was no signed deal yet, but Microsoft was prepared to sign up the companies that came up with the best designs.

"We were glad, because politics is the death of good decision-making," said Jeff Andrews.

Adamec informed IBM that its proposal for a microprocessor looked good. That was enough for the companies to draw up a statement of work, meaning that IBM would start assigning engineers to the project while a contract was worked out.

"At that point it becomes a trust," said Todd Holmdahl. "No piece of paper will ensure something will get delivered on time. You have to establish a relationship and go through a few fires with them. That's where you get the magic."

The code name for the project would be "Waternoose," the spider-like monster with multiple legs and multiple eyes in the animated film *Monsters Inc.* Foudeh also told ATI that its proposal for a graphics chip would also be on the short list. There would be many more months of parallel negotiations with vendors on all sides. But Microsoft was inching toward its first decision on what the heart of its next video game console would be.

1. http://www.xbox.com/en-US/hardware/xbox360/nextgengraphics.htm.

2. *Opening the Xbox*, pg. 313.

3. http://www.xbox.com/en-US/hardware/xbox360/artificialintelligence.htm.

CHAPTER NINE

XENON: WE COULD TELL YOU ABOUT IT BUT THEN...

*T*he Mountain View group toiled earlier than most of the planners on the new Xbox. The chips were the first thing that had to be put into motion. But J Allard knew that the rest of the team had to get started as well. He decided that the rest of the Xbox team had to start a parallel track to work on other details of the system, its games, the marketing strategy, and other work that had to be done simultaneously.

Allard knew that Microsoft didn't have a winning schedule the first time around. They were out of the playoffs even before they started playing the console game. Now, in the classic Microsoft tradition of learning from mistakes and improving each new version, Allard wanted another stab at greatness.

For the time being, planning for the perfect storm had to wait. Even after the Xbox launch, Allard and Cam Ferroni had to see through the launch of Xbox Live, the online gaming service that Microsoft had pinned its hopes on as its competitive advantage over Sony and Nintendo. That service wouldn't launch until November, 2002. Allard had to delegate work on Xenon to lieutenants.

Xbox Live itself was going to be a key part of Xenon, so Microsoft had to get it right. The company had made a series of decisions about how to implement the online service, and not everyone was happy with them. Larry Probst, CEO of Electronic Arts, didn't like the way Microsoft had crafted Xbox Live at all. Thomason and Ferroni had decided that Microsoft would maintain its own servers and authenticate users as they signed on to the service. That way, Microsoft could guarantee a consistent quality of service for consumers. It could handle billing so that the game publishers didn't have to bother with it. And it would create and maintain records so that gamers could have a single sign-on known as a gamer tag that they could use in any Xbox Live-enabled game. Gamers could build up their reputations and take the same identity from one game to another. Some of these problems plagued the Dreamcast when

Sega launched their online service. The team decided that this approach was the only way they could launch the next-generation of online gaming.

But EA had invested heavily in its own servers, and Probst didn't like the idea that Microsoft would know exactly who was signing on to play an EA sports game, particularly when Microsoft sold competing sports games. Microsoft was charging $5 a month to connect to the service, and it wasn't sharing any of that revenue with the companies that made the games that enabled people to go online. Probst believed that Microsoft was demanding too much control over EA's online games and was coming between EA and its customers. When Xbox Live launched, EA was mysteriously mum about it. It did, however, voice its support for Sony's PlayStation 2 online gaming service, which launched in August, 2002, along with a network adaptor accessory. Kaz Hirai, president of Sony's U.S. games unit, enjoyed pointing out that Sony gave its online game publishers more choice about how they could offer their online games, using Sony's servers or their own. Sony allowed their publishing partners to charge any kind of fees they wanted.

(Left) Larry Probst, CEO of Electronic Arts, thought Microsoft sought too much control over online games. (Right) Cameron Ferroni launched Xbox Live and was a key Xenon planner.

EA's absence hurt because this was the service that Microsoft had hoped would differentiate its console from the others. At E3 earlier that year, Allard had gone on stage and promised that online was going to be as big a shift for gaming as the shift from two-dimensional games to 3-D. It was eerily similar to the time, years earlier, when EA snubbed Sega and decided not to support the Dreamcast.

On launch day, Nov. 15, 2002, everything went well. More than 9,000 retailers had Xbox Live starter kits. Six Xbox Live games were on the shelves. Starting at about 8 am, about 2,000 new users created accounts every hour. The Xbox team threw a celebration in the cafeteria with a live DJ and toasts from the executives who commemorated the first birthday of the Xbox launch at the same time. Fountains across the Microsoft campus were tinted green. Before the day was over, Xbox Live had 10,000 simultaneous users.

Microsoft was able to support the large number of users because it relied upon Level 3, a company that had built a 20,000-mile intercity network to provide the backbone of a broadband network. As Microsoft added subscribers, Level 3 would allocate more of the network bandwidth in its 74 data centers around the globe to Microsoft. Since Level 3 had its own Internet backbone, it could guarantee good network connections, a key quality factor whose absence had killed off earlier online gaming networks. Less than 1 percent of the data packets being sent across the network were lost, and the average time it took to send a message from one part of the network to another was 40 milliseconds. That made voice communications over the network possible, adding a feature that could dramatically enhance the fun and sense of community in a game. On just about every measure, Microsoft could outdo Sony's network for online gaming.

The team got a little nervous Friday evening when users had trouble getting into games. The problem was diagnosed around midnight and a fix was put in place to enable improved matchmaking service for gamers. By Sunday night, Ferroni declared Xbox Live a huge success. About 80,000 gamers signed up since Friday morning, and 12,000 were playing by Sunday evening. On Monday, hackers with modded Xboxes, some of whom took apart the system and installed a bigger hard drive with illegally copied games, were booted off the system. That amounted to 2 percent of the machines. The number came as a kind of relief. It meant that, despite the flaws in the Xbox, the pirates weren't selling lots of modded consoles.

Hassles popped up. America Online users couldn't connect to Xbox Live. But in Microsoft's opinion, the launch went far better than the debut of Sony's network adaptor. Sony had chosen to enable both broadband and narrowband for the accessory that consumers had to buy in order to play online games. Though their service was free, Sony didn't lay much groundwork with broadband providers to prepare them for a surge in technical support calls. The broadband providers simply told gamers to call Sony if they had problems connecting.

Xbox Live became an advantage for Microsoft. More than 200 broadcast media stories covered the launch. But the reality was still pretty stark at the end of December, 2002. Sony had sold more than 36 million PS2s worldwide, while Nintendo had sold 9.1 million and Microsoft 5.8 million, according to Forrester Research.

As soon as the Xbox Live launch was over, Xenon rose higher on the list of things to do. Ferroni, who would become a key player on the Xenon team, was happy with the Xbox Live launch because it proved that Microsoft was on the right path. Xenon would be a natural evolution of the first Xbox as online took on much greater importance in the next generation.

"We could look at Xbox as a great learning experience," Ferroni said. "We knew we weren't going to beat Sony in the first round. In 1999, we wanted to be a good partner to retailers, developers and publishers. We wanted to build a good box and set ourselves up for the second round. Xenon was a natural evolution."

After the Xbox Live launch, Allard wanted to get serious about Xenon. Robbie Bach reassigned responsibility for third-party games from Allard to Ed Fries, ostensibly to allow Allard to focus on Xenon but in part because third-party games needed a boost. The silicon team under Todd Holmdahl, Greg Gibson and Larry Yang was making stead progress throughout 2002. Around December, 2002, Allard assembled a small band of general managers who worked for the chiefs.

The first trio of planners were high-ranking managers from the different functional units, and their charter was to make their decisions jointly, so that each part of the business worked together. They were the delegates who took the place of the executives who were too busy with their day jobs. The team included Chip Wood, a business development manager; A.J. Redmer, the former Nintendo game studio executive who represented the games group; and Jon Thomason, who headed the system software team for the Xbox. Greg Gibson, the head of system design, was supposed to represent hardware on the team but he wasn't able to attend all of the meetings.

"J's conceptualization was for a broad, far-reaching group of people," said Todd Holmdahl, the corporate vice president in charge of Xbox hardware. "This time around we wanted an integrated perspective. We would develop a platform from the group up to deliver great gaming experiences. We had to have hardware, software, marketing, sales. It was an integrated group."

Wood had been with the Xbox group since December, 2001, and had been at Microsoft for more than six years. A former Hollywood finance guy, he had worked at MSN and in the mobility group trying to get carriers to sign up with Microsoft's cell phone software. Redmer couldn't disengage from his day job. Ed Fries had sent Redmer to Japan to relieve Toshiyuki Miyata, the former Sony game studio chief whose big fighting game, *Kakuto Chojin*, wasn't in good shape. The staff was staging a mutiny and Miyata was leaving. Redmer had to undertake the controversial job of laying off many of the game developers in the office in a country where it was illegal to conduct a mass layoff. The job took him months to accomplish, and it was remembered as a big shock among the game developers in Japan. Redmer didn't really join Thomason and Wood until late in the spring. When Redmer returned, he was supposed to swap jobs with Stuart Moulder, the PC games chief who would go to Japan to run the game studio there.

"The pressure was on Ed to get me working on Xenon, and the pressure was on me to start," he said. "When Ed gave my name to Jon, he hunted me down and forced me to engage."

In the meantime, Wood, Gibson and Thomason absorbed a lot of data. Allard had conducted an informal post-mortem on the Xbox and so the team knew the problems that Microsoft wanted to avoid the second time around. Wood created the PowerPoint slides for the group and kept all of its records. He was a PowerPoint wizard, and his assignment was to make sure the project stood on solid financial ground from the start. Redmer's job was to keep Xenon focused on great games. He had to define the next-generation experience based on what the hardware could do for games. And then he had to take that vision and give it to the game developers so they could get started on games that fulfilled the vision. And he had to offer his thoughts to the engineering team so that they could make the right trade-offs on technology. Thomason represented some of the technical know-how that was needed to make the console come together. They knew what the primary mission was. They would come to call themselves Xe3o.

"We had to be fiscally responsible," Thomason said. "That was the drumbeat from Steve Ballmer. The genius was doing the technology for an acceptable cost."

While the members of the small group wanted the authority to design the product themselves, the executives wanted more people on the team. When the team finally all met together for the first time in the late spring of 2003, they threw out so many ideas that one member felt it was like "drinking from a fire hose." Thomason spoke in such a rapid fire cadence that it was hard to keep up with him. J Allard wanted the team to launch the console simultaneously, worldwide, in markets such as Japan, Europe and the United States. But Jon Thomason wasn't sure about Japan. He thought it was a lost cause. But he believed that Europe was a failure mainly because it had been treated as second-class citizen.

The team also thought about entering the handheld business. But they decided not to do anything at the time. Thomason thought they could have mustered the people to make it happen, but the financial outlay was a big risk. It would have cost a lot of money to get the program started. They would have had to buy a lot of chips, hardware, inventory, and make sure they had a machine that was both low power and powerful enough to run original Xbox games so that the porting process would be easy. But the overriding reason for postponing the handheld was the need to focus on one task, making the next console, and doing it well.

The team didn't know that Sony and Nintendo were hard at work on new handhelds. And they knew almost nothing about the PlayStation 3 beyond Sony's patents and the Mountain View group's assessment of it.

They established a rule to make decisions jointly. They did a good job at that. They were senior enough to authorize people to do the necessary work underneath them. They could enlist human resources people to recruit staff for projects. But they lacked the highest authority. Convincing their bosses to go along with the decisions they made was hard. One meeting between the small Xenon planning group and the executive staff took place at the Pro Sports Club in Bellevue, Wash., where Robbie Bach regularly played early morning basketball with other Microsoft executives. Bach wasn't there. But the discussion was contentious, with each of the executives going through the gauntlet one at a time as they discussed the different contributions they would make to Xenon. Each executive wanted to back off on firm commitments. It was the same old internecine warfare that had delayed the original Xbox.

"We were a united team," said one team member. "The executives were not. We were mad at them. We had a couple of meetings where all they did was shout at each other. It was massive arguments."

Thomason didn't want the team to become a committee. That would make the console feel as if it was designed by a committee. On the flip side, he understood that the group approach, while more bureaucratic, would achieve an earlier buy-in from more parts of the company.

At that time, Sony was about to launch one of its worst experiments ever. It had decided to pack a 250-gigabyte hard disk drive into a PlayStation 2. It called the machine the "PSX." The idea was to combine the games of the PS2 with the digital video recording capability that came with a big hard disk. Sony launched the $800 machine in January, 2003. It sold poorly and the company shelved it.

The lesson for the planning group was clear. Just packing a lot of technology into a box wouldn't do. In need of broader thinking, the group invited input from hardware gurus, software, marketing, game makers, and technical wizards from the Advanced Technology Group. The approach this time would be guided by integration. Allard wanted to make sure that hardware, software and services would all be brought together to deliver the right experience to consumers. The point was to ensure that box and everything connected with it would feel as if it were designed by the same person, not a committee or a huge corporation.

"The biggest change was the forced collaboration," said one team member, who was confined with his fellow planners in a windowless conference room. "We had these silos that didn't talk to each other."

This time, Allard wanted to make sure that they were prepared to take on the rivals, with plenty of time to plan.

"We are playing our game this time," he said.

That meant that the Xbox division would also work with the other parts of the company. Bill Gates wanted tight integration between Windows and Xbox. While the teams appeared to compete with each other on some level, they had strong ties among the leadership. Jon Thomason had spent most of his time in Windows, managing the development of key parts of the operating system with Joe Belfiore, who had since become one of the chiefs in eHome, the part of the Windows team that focused on making the PC into a digital entertainment center for the home. Belfiore had taken J Allard to lunch on the day that Allard came in for a job interview at Microsoft. Jeff Henshaw, who was heading alternative entertainment on the Xbox, had worked with Belfiore on Internet Explorer. And Belfiore's boss, Rick Thompson, had been the hardware chief who became the first general manager of the original Xbox business.

The eHome division had been formed in 2001 based on the vision of Mike Toutonghi, who had taken some time off from Microsoft. He tried to get his PC to run on a big screen TV and had an awful time. He figured that Microsoft could do a lot more to make the PC into a consumer electronics-like device, operated by a remote control and displaying its output in the living room. Microsoft ran with the idea and by the fall of 2002, the eHome division launched its flagship product: the Media Center PC. This included a version of Windows that had an interface that could be viewed from 10 feet and operated by a remote control. This way, it was easy for a consumer to integrate entertainment such as music, recorded TV, DVDs, and digital photos. The eHome division and the Xbox folks could become natural allies over time.

Allard also spent some time working with Jim Stewart, the head of Xbox industrial design at Microsoft. Stewart's job was to make a box that was much better looking than the original Xbox. Together, they explored a wide variety of concepts. Stewart had worked with Leslie Leland, the former WebTV product designer who had joined the Xbox team in Mountain View, Calif. They drew dozens of pictures, and even enlisted the help of the industrial design team at Flextronics. The problem was, they just couldn't get any of the designs to click.

The Millennium office park, home to the Xbox division.

Mitch Koch, head of sales and marketing, assigned Andrew McCombie to join Thomason's group. McCombie could only help part-time because he had to help out with the European launch of Xbox Live. Jon Thomason and Cam Ferroni swapped jobs on an almost regular basis, with one leading Xbox Live and the other system software at any given time. At the beginning of Xenon, Thomason handled the operating system and the Advanced Technology Group. Ferroni represented Xbox Live. The team gathered for its meetings in the central conference room of Millennium D. It was a room with a long wooden table and silver metal sheets covering white boards. At one end was a huge digital TV set and walls with acid green paint that always reminded everyone they were in the middle of the Xbox universe. The building itself had horrible parking and a view of a gravel pit. It wasn't ramshackle, but compared to the Microsoft campus a few miles away, it was inglorious.

"It was a yucky place to work compared to the rest of Microsoft," Thomason said.

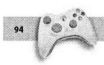

Laura Fryer, the head of ATG, also joined the meetings periodically. She began working with a broader group of managers who worked underneath the main planners to start executing some of the Xenon plans. She saw this phase of the console as the fun stage. That was why, she thought, only a handful of her people left ATG after the launch of the original Xbox and the departure of Seamus Blackley. Starting with a blank piece of paper and designing a console was exactly the kind of thing that her group lived for. The group included tools experts, demo makers, artists, game designers, and hardware geeks. She directed her group to collect all of the data related to the original Xbox games. One of the things that everyone noticed was that the microprocessor, not the graphics chip, was always the bottleneck for performance in the system. The next Xbox needed more oomph for the CPU.

One of her key explorers on the next-generation technology had been Mike Abrash, who had left Microsoft but was still consulting for her. Together, they wrote a white paper on game development for the original Xbox. Fryer looked through all the post-mortems on game projects that ran in Game Developer magazine, the Bible of technical game development. She discovered that everyone was still having problems with the game development tools. Xbox used PC software development tools that were well known. But as the game programming became more complex and the art work ballooned, programmers and artists were falling behind schedule.

Fryer wanted to keep the problems of game developers front and center in the minds of the next-generation box and software designers. Once or twice a week, her group and game developers would meet with the hardware gurus. They all wanted to know about the technical failings on the original Xbox. Everyone weighed in on the idea that Nick Baker and Jeff Andrews liked: multiple CPU cores on a single chip. It would be harder for developers, Fryer knew. But something had to break the logjam for artistic creation. She didn't criticize the idea outright because she knew that developers, much like consumers who couldn't visualize a product that they couldn't hold in their hands, could also be wrong about future products. Last time around, many of them counseled Microsoft to abandon its broadband-only networking strategy. The original Xbox didn't use a more primitive phone modem because it would have dragged down the performance of the online service. Broadband-only games, which included voice chat, were far superior as an experience. In the end, Fryer believed it was the right choice and that most of the game developers had been wrong. Fryer started pushing her team and the software experts at Microsoft to overhaul the company's programming tools in an effort that came to be known as XNA. J Allard would later start an effort, code-named Neo, which took those ideas and turned them into a real project.

The Xbox group was big and keeping secrets was a concern. The division shared its news in periodic newsletters, dubbed *X and the City*, that circulated by e-mail. On Oct. 29, 2002, the latest issue carried the headline, "Xenon: We Could Tell You But Then…" It noted that many people had been asking questions about the next generation of Xbox. The newsletter said that even the name "Xenon" was confidential and should not be used outside the group.

It said that product-specific information about Xenon was not being shared widely. "We have already experienced a significant information leak to one of our key partners, which is unacceptable. As you may know from Xbox 1.0, leaks of this sort can have a major impact on our business profitability." It noted that anyone who leaked information on Xenon could expect to be fired and prosecuted. Microsoft wanted to instill a culture of secrecy that had never really existed at the company. Most of the time, Microsoft's teams collaborated in transparent ways. The cost of that openness inside the company was that it wasn't very good at keeping secrets. By comparison, few details of Sony's plans ever leaked out before it was ready to share them.

The memo directed anyone with questions about Xenon to see Greg Gibson, and that over time more information would be shared. Gibson was the common link between the silicon architecture team and Thomason's planning group. The newsletter promised that the Xenon team was not working in a vacuum. The product specification and initial architecture were being reviewed over the next couple of months.

Xenon was still going to be about "games, games, games," Ferroni said.

Everybody agreed on this, said Mitch Koch, head of sales and marketing.

"It was clear for a long time that the primary thing we are selling, the primary proposition, the primary consumer value is about a gaming console," Koch said. "You've got to always think about why are you there. If you look at the soul of the project, the Xbox exists as a gaming console. If you can do other things, that's fine. At the core we are a making gaming system. You don't want to sacrifice a great gaming system."

But the memo said that Xenon would benefit from cross-fertilization with other parts of Microsoft. Maybe it wouldn't be a full fledged entertainment center unto itself. But it could be an excellent "digital amplifier" of devices that consumers already had in their household. Microsoft was consulting with game developers and with a Microsoft-wide technical review board that included leaders from Windows, the eHome living room PC group, and Microsoft Research to ensure that Xenon fits well with other corporate entertainment initiatives. The key person in charge of making sure that the divisions talked to each other and coordinated strategy was Bill Gates, who was still chairman but had settled into his role as the chief software architect at Microsoft. Gates checked on the progress of Xenon every six weeks or so. The Xenon group held meetings to evaluate technical decisions and get feedback directly from consumers as well.

There were as many dangers as there were benefits in working with the rest of Microsoft. The Xbox team could tap into the vast resources of the rest of the company. But Microsoft also ran the risk of making Thomason's fears about "design by committee" come true. If they asked too many people for feedback, they would create a kitchen sink project. And that would cause them to move in slow motion.

CHAPTER TEN

DREAMCASTED

*P*eter Moore, the marketer who launched Sega's Dreamcast console in North America in 1999, didn't start out as a game industry guru. He started his career as an athlete. He was the son of pub owners in Liverpool, England. He had once been a professional soccer player, and then a physical education teacher. He had broad shoulders and a solid build, capped with a balding head and a signature goatee. He loved the athletic life.

"I thoroughly enjoyed it," Moore said. "But then one snowy day on a North Wales mountain, freezing my you-know-what off, I thought, 'There's got to be a better life than this.'" [1]

In 1981, he and his wife moved to a trailer park in Long Beach, California. Moore had gotten a $10,000-a-year job selling soccer shoes to retailers for a French company, and he was working for a former professor on a sports training program. He managed to triple shoe sales in four years. He went on to pursue a master's degree in physical education at California State University at Long Beach.

In 1992, he switched stripes to Reebok, where he started the company's soccer shoe business. He built a factory for soccer ball production and signed tennis players Venus and Serena Williams to an endorsement deal. Moore had an infectious enthusiasm for all things sports related. He rose to senior vice president of footwear. In 1995, he became the head of global sports marketing. He had a big battle on his hands, as the underdog to the dominant shoe company, Nike.

"I've always liked to be the feisty underdog," he said.

Then Sega came calling. Bernie Stolar, president of Sega of America, needed a marketing guy to help launch the Dreamcast. Stolar wanted someone who understood branding. He had a plan for the Dreamcast brand, and it involved a lot of attitude. Stolar found Moore and hired him.

"We make video games," Sega executive Hayao Nakayama said to

Stolar. "Why do you bring me a shoe guy?" [2]

Stolar replied, "I said Peter did not understand games but he understood branding. Sega's brand was hurt by all the previous hardware systems it tried to launch. We had to convey that this was the best system Sega ever came up with."

Moore joined just a few months before the launch, which was scheduled for 9-9-99 in the U.S. Stolar had done much of the work already, and Moore's job was to execute the plan. Moore helped fill out the details in the marketing campaign that touted the intelligence of the machine and its beast-like power. The campaign commercials touted the Dreamcast's ability to learn from players and adapt to their style of play. "It's thinking," and "It knows it's alive" were the slogans. Stolar thought Moore executed well on the plans and he had a graciousness and cordiality that allowed him to make friendships quickly.

Peter Moore joined Microsoft in January, 2003

Following on Stolar's plan, Moore forged a partnership with MTV Networks and became a sponsor of the Ozzfest Tour. He made employees watch an attitude video so they could get in touch with the youth market. Just before the U.S. launch, Sega's Japanese executives fired Stolar. The Japanese brass put Toshiro Kezuka in charge of Sega of America. The Dreamcast was a dud when it debuted in Japan in November, 1998, in Japan, selling barely 200,000 units in its first holiday season. But thanks in part to Moore's aggressive marketing plans, it sold 1.8 million units in four months in the U.S.

As Sega was faltering, observers admired Sega's spunk. They saw in Moore's combative rhetoric the epitome of a fighting spirit. Sega had launched clever viral marketing campaigns that would come in handy in later console wars. But Sega was bleeding red ink. Electronic Arts had refused to support the console, and consumers had grown skeptical of Sega's frequent hardware revisions. Worse, the Dreamcast suffered from a dearth of games after its launch. Sony and Nintendo took the market back.

Sony launched the PlayStation 2 in March, 2000, in Japan, selling nearly a million units in its Japanese launch. Its console had more power, and it also sported a DVD drive that the Sega box didn't have. Newsweek did a cover story on "The Amazing PlayStation 2" on March 6, 2000 that talked about how the box would transform living rooms. It was stories like that which helped dry up demand for the Dreamcast. Remembering that story later, Microsoft executives said, "We didn't want to get 'Dreamcasted.'"

Japanese movie fans saw that the PlayStation 2 was actually cheaper than a DVD player, so they bought the console as a cheap DVD player. Sony didn't sell many games at first, but it had the better selling console in Japan as a result. In October, 2000, Sony also had a stellar launch in the U.S. The games for the PS2 looked better, and companies such as EA invested heavily in it. With games like *Metal Gear Solid 2*, *Gran Turismo*, and *Grand Theft Auto III*, the PS2 won over fans. Ken Kutaragi, the maverick executive in charge of Sony Computer Entertainment, had outmaneuvered the Dreamcast with better technology and a richer pipeline of games.

Sega bailed out of console hardware in January, 2001. The Japanese company turned its crosshairs on becoming a worldwide software powerhouse that could publish games on any platform. But that meant that Sega was going to go into a bruising battle against Electronics Arts in sports games.

Moore repeatedly went to Japan to appeal to the Sega executives to expand their software development efforts in the U.S. and Europe. He was tired of pitching Japanese games, designed for Japanese audiences, to western gamers. Sega's studios churned out spectacular games such as *Shinobi*, *Panzer Dragoon Orta*, and *Shenmue*. The latter started with an initial $23 million budget, which ballooned even higher, but the game didn't catch hold beyond a small enthusiastic crowd. These Japanese games had characters that western audiences couldn't identify with. Consequently, they weren't big sellers in the U.S. or Europe.

Moore had gotten along well with Microsoft's Robbie Bach. He joined Bach on stage at the E3 show in May, 2001, to voice Sega's support for the Xbox, which had yet to debut. It was a lonely feeling, given the relatively weak support that Microsoft had generated. But Moore liked Microsoft. "I felt that a spiritual baton had been passed from Sega to Microsoft, which was promoting online gaming and community." Moore hoped that Sega's line of 2K sports games would go over well on the Xbox. Sega went on to announce that it would do eleven games for the Xbox. Microsoft and Sega had a relationship that went back years. Microsoft convinced Sega to include Microsoft's Windows CE software on the Dreamcast, but the deal never went anywhere because game developers bypassed Microsoft's software and instead wrote games in the assembly language of the machine so that they could eke out better performance. Microsoft also tried to buy Sega before it launched the Xbox, but the talks had stalled. Sega still wanted to hold out for a glorious comeback as a software publisher for all platforms, and it saw online games on the Xbox as key to defeating Electronic Arts.

But Larry Probst, CEO of Electronic Arts, had anticipated the threat from Sega. After E3, he returned to the company's headquarters in Redwood City, Calif., and held a post mortem on the show. Sega was clearly a threat, and EA had to step up to make its sports line-up better. Probst unleashed a big budget of more than $30 million for TV advertising. The companies got into a war of words throughout 2001. Moore painted a target on EA and signed a licensing deal with ESPN sports. He earmarked $35 million to advertise two of the company's sports titles.

Jeff Brown, vice president of communications at EA, said, "They're the Burger King of video game sports – they can brag about extra pickles, but they'll always be the second choice." EA had all the firepower in the battle. It had celebrity athletes jumping at the chance to be in its games and commercials. It had John Madden, the veteran game announcer whose voice was synonymous with video game football. And EA had the brand that resonated.

"Bring it on!" Probst said in an interview. "It will keep us on our toes, it will make us build better products. At the end of the day, the consumer benefits and the industry benefits." [3]

Moore gave it his best shot, but EA crushed Sega.

"We went from euphoria to abject sorrow at Sega," Moore said. "It was time to move on."

Probst considered hiring Moore at EA, since he was a skillful marketer. But Probst said EA didn't have an appropriate marketing job for Moore.

Moore made a few more trips to Japan to appeal to the Japanese bosses. They listened, but didn't take enough action. During the holiday break, Robbie Bach called to wish Moore a Merry Christmas. He invited Moore to join Microsoft if things weren't working out at Sega. Moore felt that Microsoft was picking up Sega's slogan of "taking gaming where gamers are going."

"It was clear that Peter was going to leave Sega," Bach said. "We had an opening. He and I had a pretty good relationship. I wanted to strengthen the team, deepen our talent. He was an addition that was just needed. We had a good team. But there were not enough of us. Not enough competencies in all the areas."

Microsoft needed a pitch man that knew the European and Japanese markets well. Bach knew that the efforts in those territories had fallen short, and Moore brought both expertise in games – albeit quickly learned – from Sega, as well as years of experience with overseas markets. Moore had lunch with Steve Ballmer and was caught up in the pitch man's enthusiasm for digital entertainment in the living room. Microsoft had big plans, and Ballmer wanted Moore to come on board. The enthusiasm was infectious, and Moore said, "It swayed me."

Landing in a vice president's job at Microsoft wasn't an easy task. Microsoft's culture favored home-grown executives and it had a way of chewing up and spitting out foreign objects. But Bach knew the team needed more heft in its marketing ranks and he felt that Moore could do the job. Moore was assigned to handle international Xbox marketing in Europe and Japan. The executive team on Xbox was growing up. Staffing for Xenon projects was under way, from game development to hardware engineering.

And Moore had arrived just in time to assist with the plans for Xenon. He had joined at just the right time to launch another big war.

1. "Peter Moore," by Fast Company, www.fastcompany.com/ftalk/sanfran/moore.html

2. "Moore's War," by Geoff Keighley, *Business 2.0* magazine, Oct. 26, 2005.

3. Wired magazine, "Sports Rule!" by Evan Ratliff, January, 2003.

CHAPTER ELEVEN

EXECUTIVE ORDERS

At an executive retreat in the fall of 2002, Bryan Lee, the top finance chief of the Home and Entertainment Group, floated an idea for Xenon. He was a numbers guy who had spent 13 years at Sony Pictures. While he had an easy-going personality, he lived up to the stereotype of the businessman who cared only about the bottom line.

"He was agnostic to technology," said one observer who worked with him. "Others were passionate. Bryan could care less. It was like, 'insert technology here' in his plans."

Lee knew that Microsoft was losing a lot of money on the Xbox and he wanted J Allard to focus on something radical that would change the economics of the business. Lee brought up the CD-ROM lesson. The CD-ROM was an optical disk which Sony popularized with the original PlayStation. The CD-ROM helped Sony turn the tables on Nintendo, whose N64 console used the older cartridges which used memory chips known as mask ROMs (for read-only memory, or memory that could be recorded only once). [1] Mask ROM chips were quicker than CD-ROMs in terms of the speed of memory access. But with mask ROM chips, Nintendo had to wait until the chips went through the factory, with the games burned into them along the way. It took around 10 weeks to move the silicon wafers through the dozens of processes until they came out the other side as finished products, ready to be sliced into chips. With such a long lead time on the chips, both game publishers and retailers had to bet far in advance on exactly how many copies they needed for a game. If they guessed too low, it would be another few months before they could replenish store shelves with more games. And even then, within two months, a popular game could go out of fashion. Such a system broke the backs of a number of game companies that guessed wrong about demand.

With Sony's CD-ROMs, the story was much different. The CDs went through the factory as blank media. They could store 650

megabytes of data, or much more than the mask ROMs, so that they could lead to richer games. After they went through the manufacturing process, they could be burned with game data. So it was only a matter of days between the time it took to order and the time the CDs could be shipped to store shelves. The inventory replenishment and ordering system took a lot of the risks out of judging demand for games. The CD-ROMs were also cheaper to produce than the ROM chips. Sony could price its games at $40, while Nintendo had to keep its games at $50 or $60. The better economics allowed Sony to draw far more game publishers to its platform, and Nintendo never recovered from those defections.

Lee believed Microsoft could use a different royalty model to beat its rivals. Along the lines of the CD-ROM lesson, the goal was a simple one: win more friends. The idea was to offer the industry's game publishers much lower royalties than either Sony or Nintendo were willing to offer. It was, in short, a bribe. Microsoft could give publishers a big break if they would publish games on its platform. This would solve a lot of problems. More games would be published on the Xbox platform. Sony could no longer count on big third-party exclusives like "Grand Theft Auto." Consumers would flock to the new Xbox because of the exclusive content. Above all, Lee wanted to see if Microsoft could entice Electronic Arts to make exclusive games for Microsoft. That was a tall order, since Microsoft would have to fork over a lot of money in order to convince EA that the profits it could generate from one platform would be enough to make up for the profits it would lose if it no longer released games on several platforms at once. No one had ever truly succeeded in making such a convincing argument to big publishers.

Ed Fries liked the idea because it meant that the publishers who had been on the fence about supporting the Xbox would have come over in waves. That would have taken the pressure off Microsoft's own internal games group to supply all the hits on its own.

The downside was clear. Trip Hawkins had the same idea on the original 3DO game console. But the business model didn't work. The executives had earlier shot down the same idea on the original Xbox because a royalty-free platform would be just like the PC. Poor quality titles would swamp the platform, and consumers would get fed up with the junk. On top of that, Microsoft couldn't make money on the console business without the royalties, unless it assumed that it would sell an astronomical number of games and consoles. Microsoft stood a chance of losing even more money. It was already looking at losses of $1 billion a year. The Xbox 360, still known only by its code-name Xenon, was struggling to be born. But it wasn't ready yet. Within a short time, the team pitched their idea to Bill Gates and Steve Ballmer. And shortly after that, they came up with a ruling. They had shot down the idea, and wanted something better.

"We pushed back hard," Ballmer later said in an interview.

Lee's argument was one of many that the executives bandied back and forth. They looked at the cell phone model, where they could give away hardware in exchange for monthly subscriptions. That business model was untested in video

games, and it posed even bigger risks than then no-royalty proposal. It, too, went down in flames. "It's goofy to reduce royalties," said one planner.

Two natural opponents were the leaders of hardware and software, represented by J Allard and Ed Fries. It was always tempting for one to fault the other when something didn't seem to be going right. Allard, who ran third-party games during 2002, was in charge of the hardware platform. Fries ran first party, the division that made games internally. Allard kept urging Fries to come up with some winners for the Xbox platform in the fall of 2002. Allard wanted Fries to put Bungie to work on another version of *Halo*, either an expansion pack or a version of the first *Halo* that worked with Xbox Live. But Bungie had an independent streak and it always tried to make a big leap forward when it undertook a sequel. For *Halo 2*, the studio wanted to do something spectacular. Fries agreed with them. He didn't want to churn out bad titles that would erode the value of the franchise. He made one concession and had an outside developer, Gearbox, make a PC version of *Halo*. But he considered the talent on the Bungie team to be a finite resource. If they were assigned to do an expansion pack, that would force back the dates for the true sequel. Fries had a long-term view and he appreciated the creative element in developing games. The game group viewed Allard as having a software engineering mentality. He had always shipped products that hit their budgets and schedules, from server software to networking software. He thought that brute force could work on getting games out the door. At some companies, such as Electronic Arts, that's what happened. EA never showed up late with a football game when the real football season started. He wanted the games to ship on schedule down to the quarter.

"It was unthinkable to J that *Halo 3* wouldn't ship at the launch," said one observer. "He had a strong core belief that engineering could be managed. J's position was, this is Bungie's job. Go do your job. This is the single most important thing. When we tried to explain it to him, he couldn't rationalize it."

Fries wanted the game developers to produce their games without unreasonable pressures. Allard wanted the company to behave much more like Electronic Arts. When pressed to make commitments for first party on Xenon, Fries didn't want to and couldn't produce a schedule for launching games every quarter after the launch. He understood that making games was more of an art form than a technical undertaking. Game developers were on his side in this respect. Greg Zeschuk, co-CEO of BioWare, a successful developer in Canada, said that great games couldn't be pumped out on an assembly line. Instead, they were "lovingly crafted." Noah Falstein, another veteran game designer, said, "Games aren't spreadsheets. It's still an art form." Even though it was an art form, game developers also acknowledged they had to compromise on vision and balance it with practical attention to both technology and business principles. The consequence of the unpredictable nature of making art was galling for others. Thomason was frustrated with first-party, a reference to internally produced games at the console maker.

"First party was always behind on the planning," Jon Thomason said.

Fries won one internal battle. Bach decided that Allard should focus on technology and the next Xbox, so he relieved Allard of control of third-party publishing and gave that to Fries at the close of 2002. That wasn't such a bad move. Under Allard, the third-party division had failed to spot *Grand Theft Auto III* as the killer application. Allard had organized a group of game managers to evaluate proposals for games. They asked questions of developers, such as, "What would a gamer do in 60 seconds of game play?" The process was secretive, and it had been nicknamed "The Star Chamber," after a 1980s Michael Douglas movie where a group of judges meted out street justice in secrecy. (The movie itself was named after a secret medieval society of judges who vindictively abused the powers of the courts). Unfortunately for Microsoft, the Star Chamber turned down the proposal from RockStar games for *Grand Theft Auto III*. The Star Chamber members sent the proposal back to RockStar Games with the suggestion to beef up the game. When RockStar later cut a deal with Take-Two Interactive to create an exclusive for the PlayStation 2, Microsoft didn't even get a last-minute chance to bid for the deal itself. It wasn't Microsoft's kind of game, since it was a gritty crime game with foul language, abusive treatment of women, and cop killing. Microsoft had a corporate image to maintain and, like Electronic Arts, it avoided that category. Gamers, however, increasingly loved the anti-establishment themes in the games and the ability to roam free without any rules. The game became the runaway hit of the PS2, and it proved the ineffectiveness of the Star Chamber. To its credit, the Star Chamber did greenlight the RockStar proposal before its exclusive deal became public, but the Star Chamber team didn't know about the Sony exclusive until too late.

While Allard criticized Fries for failing to come up with a credible launch plan for games, Fries pushed back and wanted more out of hardware, either better cost-cutting or more technological improvements that would generate more console sales. Despite these turf battles, the executives knew they couldn't succeed with a silo, or fiefdom mentality.

"You try and look at the business holistically," said Mitch Koch, the head of retail sales and marketing who tried looking at the business from both his own view as a marketer and on a high level. "You look at it from your subject matter expertise and also look at it as a member of the overall project and management team. It was like being a Senator, where you want to represent the country and the state at the same time."

Most of the executives who were in on the planning for Xenon didn't want the hard disk drive in the system. It had been the boat anchor of the original Xbox. The hard disks had started out costing Microsoft about $50 each for every Xbox, a cost that neither Sony nor Nintendo had to carry. It was an albatross.

And the only reason that Microsoft was able to get those 8-gigabyte disk drives for $50 or so was because suppliers like Seagate Technology were willing to make a big bet on the brand new business. A disk drive had bare bones components such as a spindle, a platter, and control chips. The chips could be redesigned to be cheaper over time, but the platter and spindle couldn't really be cost reduced.

Seagate executive Steve Luczo directed finance executive Pat O'Malley to come up with a winning bid for the Xbox drives so that Seagate could pioneer the use of the hard disk drive in consumer electronics. It was a loss leader. The first drive that Seagate proposed was clearly going to lose money, but O'Malley's team planned it so that they could substitute new drives that met the same specifications over time. These new versions of the drive would be cheaper to produce. By doing this, Seagate drove the costs own to $30 dollars or so. Seagate made money on them, and it gave unexpected price breaks to Microsoft.

Overall, it still wasn't enough to make the Xbox profitable. Ed Fries had been an advocate for the hard disk on the original Xbox because it was a way to differentiate games. But the critics such as Bryan Lee said it didn't allow Microsoft to differentiate its games or charge a higher price for its console. Multiplied by more than 20 million consoles, the hard drive itself was responsible for big losses.

Fries decided to go for it again and find other ways to cut costs out of the hardware. Why was Sony able to make money on *its* hardware? Fries had talked to Ballmer and noted that Sony was managing to produce its hardware far more cheaply than Microsoft.

One of the problems was that Allard's group had not yet come up with anything that yielded the kind of economic advantage that the CD-ROM had given to Sony. The hardware wasn't exciting. Chip Wood was trying to keep everyone important in the loop with meetings every week. The problem was that all of the executives doing the planning were also in the middle of their day jobs running the current generation Xbox business. They had a number of meetings, but often times the executives couldn't attend. They had to send lieutenants in their stead, and that meant that nobody was sticking their necks out or making decisions that moved Xenon forward. Wood, A.J. Redmer of the games group, and Jon Thomason in software convened regular Xenon meetings.

The planners were getting frustrated because they would wrangle through the decisions for weeks, only to find that the executives didn't understand the rationale for them or didn't agree with what their delegates had signed them up for. Ed Fries kept asking, "Why is this machine exciting?" The group had to backpedal often and spend hours bringing the executives up to speed. The executives were too busy to do the work themselves, but didn't like the decisions of the delegates.

"In a normal world, somebody does more detailed work, then goes to another level of review and approval," Mitch Koch said in defense of the executive team. "Very rarely does it help the organization if you have a complete rubber stamp. If it is a rubber stamp, you should just delegate. The fact you have a review means you are not completely authorized to make calls. Different people see things different ways. The great thing about marketing is that everyone has an opinion on it. Engineers talk about their views on marketing."

Thomason felt that the executives would water down plans. If he signed his

bosses up to deliver something specific, they would balk at the commitment. J Allard wanted Ed Fries to come up with a date for the launch of *Halo 3*, but Fries thought it was much too early to make such a commitment. The game was more a work of art than it was a spreadsheet. Thomason sometimes regretted the fact that Microsoft had no tyrannical dictator, like Steve Jobs of Apple, who could make decisions quickly and put an end to the debate. Robbie Bach might have been the most powerful executive on Xbox, but he refused to play the role of the dictator.

"It was definitely a committee project," Thomason said.

To deal with the inevitable bureaucratic slowdowns and cross-divisional rivalries within the Xbox empire, the executives had created what they called the "Decision Council." This team of top executives came together to resolve issues that crossed the lines of multiple groups, such as game development, marketing, publishing and manufacturing. For instance, if Microsoft chose to start selling the Xbox in a market such as China, it had to be ready on a variety of fronts. The manufacturing had to be in place. The game studios had to consider making localized games for the market. The marketing team had to line up partners well in advance of the launch. It had to be coordinated. This council was a byproduct of Robbie Bach's consensus-oriented management style. It was a committee that was supposed to break deadlocks. But because Xenon crossed all the lines, it was hard to say that anyone, even Allard, owned the project.

"Decisions weren't getting made," recalled one executive. "The Decision Council forced decisions."

One of the things that the council, and the Microsoft board of directors Directors itself, made a decision about was Rare. Since 1985, Rare had been making video games from its headquarters in Twycross, England. It was a partnership between brothers Chris and Tim Stamper and arcade pioneer Joel Hochberg. For years, Rare had gained a reputation as an outstanding second-party game developer for Nintendo, meaning it was an independent company that made its games exclusively for the Japanese company's video game platforms. Nintendo owned half the company.

Nintendo noticed Rare in 1994, when the Stamper brothers showed a level of *Donkey Kong Country* to Ken Lobb, a Nintendo of America game producer, and to Tony Harman. Lobb looked at the demo and immediately told his bosses that Nintendo had to have the game. The title sold more than 8 million copies. The company went on to become one of the most productive studios in the industry, selling on average 1.4 million units per title. It came up with best sellers on the N64 such as *GoldenEye 007*, *Donkey Kong 64*, and *Banjo-Kazooie*, and *Conker's Bad Fur Day*. Over time, Chris Stamper took the lead on technology, while Tim led creative efforts.

Nintendo had the right to buy all of Rare, but it had to do so before an approaching deadline. The relationship with Nintendo wasn't a good one. Speculation about a split was rife when Rare sent out a Christmas card in December, 2000. On the card was a green Christmas tree with a black box

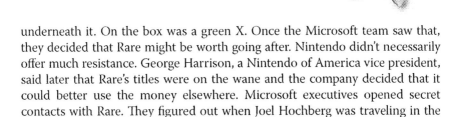

underneath it. On the box was a green X. Once the Microsoft team saw that, they decided that Rare might be worth going after. Nintendo didn't necessarily offer much resistance. George Harrison, a Nintendo of America vice president, said later that Rare's titles were on the wane and the company decided that it could better use the money elsewhere. Microsoft executives opened secret contacts with Rare. They figured out when Joel Hochberg was traveling in the same city as Ed Fries and passed along the information.

Fries wanted the studio, and he had been courting the Stampers for a long time. Both men showed up at the E3 press conference that Microsoft threw in May, 2002. Their presence stirred a lot of rumors.

It was no coincidence that Ken Lobb, the former Nintendo game producer who had managed the relationship with Rare, was now working for Ed Fries. Fries asked Lobb a bunch of questions about the valuable properties within Rare. Lobb enthusiastically lobbied to get Fries to make the purchase. Rare could be key to winning over a broader group of gamers, like the Japanese gamers who loved cartoon-style games.

"They were super talented and always pushed the edge of the envelope," Lobb said. "I was biased. But when I left Nintendo, I couldn't work with Rare anymore and that left a hole in my stomach."

The Rare teams kept making proposals for big-budget games, but Nintendo kept asking them to go back and see what they could do for a smaller amount of money. It was clear Nintendo and Rare were going in different directions.

"I think the real reason Nintendo didn't buy them was they didn't believe the future of the game industry is $20 million games," Lobb said. "They think it is $3 million games with small teams. Nintendo kept going back to Rare and asking them, 'Can you do that game with $2 million?' It was driving Rare nuts."

Lobb kept telling executives to visit Rare to see for themselves. When they came back, they were sold on the idea that it was a special company. Fries himself made the pitch to buy Rare to Microsoft's board of directors. Rare had a lot of properties that it owned altogether, something that most other developers didn't have. If Microsoft bought them, those franchises could move to the Xbox platform.

On Sept. 24, Microsoft announced it was acquiring Rare for $375 million in cash. Ed Fries got up on stage with Chris Stamper and Tim Stamper to announce the deal at the company's annual European games event, X02, in Seville, Spain. Harrison at Nintendo of America said that the Japanese company would take the money and more wisely invest it in a large number of game titles.

"These guys are an amazing development company," Bach said when the deal was unveiled. "Their track record goes back 25 years. They generate 1.4 million units per title. Really creative work. Nintendo had to figure out something to say because they lost their premiere developer. These guys will add a lot of value to the business. They will help us broaden our demographic."

Bach expected that Rare would release five major Xbox games in the next 12 months to 24 months. That prediction wouldn't come true. With the deal behind him, a big part of Ed Fries' game plan was in place. But since Rare was so expensive, he came under pressure to cut costs. It didn't help that Rare's first title, *Grabbed by the Ghoulies*, sold poorly. Bach had been clear. "If we spend a lot of money on Rare, I don't want to spend a lot of money on other things."

1.   "Revolutionaries at Sony," by Reiji Asakura, McGraw-Hill, 2000, pgs. 93-97.

CHAPTER TWELVE

3-30-300

noqualmie Falls is a memorable sight. About 30 miles outside of Seattle, it is a place that is famous as the opening scene for the *Twin Peaks* TV series of the early 1990s. Water from the Snoqualmie River hurtles 268 feet from the top of the rocky cliffs to the gorge below. Visitors can walk down the winding path to bottom of the falls, where they can feel the mist from the falls spray their faces. It's a dreamy place, the site of the creation myth of the Snoqualmie Indian tribe.

The Salish Lodge & Spa sits nearly atop the falls. The place was built in 1916 with only five guest rooms. It was a stopping place on a logging route, and it is still surrounded by Douglas firs, western hemlock, and Sitka spruce trees. The new lodge was built atop the old one in 1988. The spa was added in 1996, making it into a retreat destination. The dining room has an aerie-style view of the falls and the nearby Cascade Mountains. Its wine cellar has nearly 1,300 different selections. The new rooms have fireplaces and whirlpool baths. If you leave the window open, you can hear the thunder of the falls. Not a bad place for making visions.

In February, 2003, the Xbox leaders descended upon the lodge. They were a grizzled bunch of veterans now. In the face of withering skepticism, they had launched the Xbox video game console worldwide and were celebrating the successful launch of the Xbox Live online gaming service, which was now rolling out around the world. Hundreds of titles were available. Some of those titles, such as *Tom Clancy's Splinter Cell*, had a chance to prove the Xbox was more than the "*Halo* console."

But it was already late to start planning the next generation. Sony's Cell alliance was moving quickly. Bach thought that Sony made the mistake of signaling its intentions too early. But the announcement was useful. The Cell microprocessor sounded like a formidable technology, the kind that would probably race far ahead of the PC components that

Microsoft might rely upon for Xenon. It was time to get to work.

They had gathered to talk about how to run the team. But at the Salish Lodge, the executives also tried for another stab at a plan for Xenon. They stuck big sheets of paper on the wall with all of the factors they had to consider. They knew they couldn't be late. They figured that Xbox Live would be a competitive advantage over the rivals. Bach had announced that Microsoft would spend $2 billion over five years on Xbox Live, though many in the industry didn't understand how Microsoft could possibly spend so much money on something with a relatively small development team and outsourced bandwidth partners. Another Microsoft executive said, "It's marketing math, if you throw in everything Microsoft was spending on online." Still, it was the big gamble of Microsoft's foray into games. It would lead the opportunities for new business models, such as spectator events, downloadable demos and game expansions, and an alternative means of distribution for content from small independent developers.

And they knew that the integration of hardware, software and services would be key. They debated whether a hard drive should be in every box, or if they should have more than one version of the box. But they really decided upon how they would operate the Xenon team and codify the process for moving forward.

At the offsite meeting, they created strategy for proceeding. Based on a suggestion from J Allard, they called the process "3-30-300." They drew a pyramid on a white sheet and separated it into sections. Robbie Bach would set the high-level strategy in a three-page memo with the basic principles of the plan. J Allard would create a 30-page memo that detailed the guts of what Xenon would be. He was supposed to describe what it was, why it was cool, and what it would achieve. His small group of a dozen leaders would define the project and write the memo. The pressure was on Allard to come up with something exciting that everyone could get behind. The 300 part referred to the detailed description of the strategy that the much larger team would implement. They left the meeting satisfied that they had a way of moving forward.

Bach soaked in a lot of ideas from Allard and the rest of the team. Bryan Lee had created a model for the business. If the system architects made a decision to add a $2 component to the box, they could see the impact multiplied millions of times through a number of fiscal years, Allard said. It made executives see how their budgets fit in with everyone else's, and it made them see that their success was linked to someone else's.

"We threw out every idea to improve the business model," recalled Peter Moore, who had moved over from his job as chief of Sega of America to head part of international marketing in January, 2003. "We pushed the chips across the table."

Bach decided he wanted the Xbox division to be profitable in 2007. At the retreat, Bach zeroed in on the ideas that he liked and decided that he had enough to set the direction for the future of Xenon. In March, 2003, Steve Ballmer sat down with the Xbox executives for a review of the Xbox business. He wasn't happy with the losses in the division and wanted something to be done to contain the costs. Ed Fries, head of the games division, had to agree in principle that Microsoft should now shave back its B-titles and focus only on the best possible games. How to do that was up to Fries. But Ballmer liked the idea that the pervasive deployment of Xbox Live among all gamers would turn out to be the competitive advantage that Microsoft had against its rivals. Cameron Ferroni, one of the leaders on Xbox Live, had persuasively argued that online was fundamental. At some point, he said, connecting Xenon to the Internet would be as important as connecting the console to the TV set and the power cord to the wall. You wouldn't think of not doing it.

"The business model is one that assumes that you get a lot of things attached to each console and you make a little bit of money on everything attached – every peripheral, every accessory, every game, online subscriptions," Ballmer said later. [1]

Bach took the ideas from Allard, Lee and others and synthesized them into a three-page memo while flying back from a trip to Mexico for a golf vacation. Bach ran the draft by everyone. It really was just three pages, "I didn't cheat by changing the font." The memo was for Bill Gates and Steve Ballmer. While the console would exploit all opportunities in digital entertainment, gaming would trump any other functions that the box would serve. The gamers would be at the center, and they would have the opportunity to personalize their console to suit their preferences.

Bach assumed that Sony would stick to a typical five-year cycle. That was the expected plan, based on Sony's press release about the Cell. Bach wanted Microsoft to be there with its own console on time in 2005. It was his manifesto for success, not just for launch, but in the first several years. Microsoft would also try to contain its costs by owning more of the hardware and the intellectual property for the silicon embedded in it. This console would gain market share, doubling Microsoft's share to at least 40 percent of the business. And it would make Microsoft money.

By this time, Larry Yang's team had narrowed down their search for chips to about three vendors for each kind. For the graphics chip, they favored ATI. And for the microprocessor, they wanted IBM. Again, while Bach made sure that Microsoft would take advantage of the silicon IP ownership, he didn't spell out who Microsoft would use.

Bach had listened to arguments about launching globally, but he didn't specifically say so in the memo. Microsoft had the strongest brand equity in the U.S., but it had weak market shares in Europe, and the weakest of all in Japan. If Microsoft could launch worldwide, the advantage was that it could treat all regions on an equal par, with none feeling like a second-class citizen. A global launch was hard to pull off. Microsoft had tried and failed in its first attempt in 2001. But the benefits could be enormous.

"The first to market is a benefit," said Mitch Koch, head of sales and marketing. "The sooner you are in, the more benefit. The Europeans felt like second-class citizens. It would be positive if you get the product there sooner."

Just like Ballmer, Bach wanted build out Xbox Live into a ubiquitous service for most gamers, not just the 10 percent that it had reached with the first version. This would be the competitive advantage over the rivals. With Xbox Live used more universally, Microsoft could introduce new business models such as downloadable games. In doing so, it could allow more game developers to reach gamers even if shelf space at retail stores was tight. Moore said, "We could become the Miramax of game distribution."

Being early, or at least on time, had its pluses. Bach was a student of strategy. The games that he did play included *Age of Empires*, Microsoft's big hit for the PC. In those games, the player had to make quick decisions about how to deploy soldiers, which kind to create, how to allocate resources so that the army and fortresses were ready for war. In multiplayer Age of Empires games, it was always important to be on guard for the "early rush." In this kind of battle, one of the players created everything needed to launch a surprise attack. The aggressor built up military units and struck with speed at an enemy who wasn't yet entrenched in an impregnable fortress. If the enemy was caught off guard, they might never recover. The strategy that Bach had articulated was the equivalent of the early rush. Microsoft wanted to deliver a knock-out blow before its opponents knew what had hit them. It was classic *Age of Empires* thinking.

Bach revised the draft once and then sent it to Ballmer and Gates on April 2, 2003. They signed off on the memo without any questions. Both had been in the discussions and understood the plans. They had been meeting with the Xbox executives every six weeks or so, and were plugged in. Gates did say that he wanted to read the 30-pager, but it wasn't done yet. In fact, it wouldn't really be done for six months.

Next, Bach arranged to present the memo in a PowerPoint presentation to about 50 Xbox managers in a two-hour meeting. Some people asked questions about why it was the right decision to launch in 2005 and why it made sense to do so on a worldwide basis.

Bach thought that 2005 made sense in terms of technology. A "perfect storm" waited in the offing, one that would compel consumers to buy high-definition television. They would get tired of the old game machines, and Microsoft could truly distinguish itself with a new generation of games.

"That started to bake that into the team," Bach said.

The meetings "socialized" the memo so that everyone would understand what they had to deliver. On the original Xbox, Bach felt as if the team wasn't aligned. Previously, factions dominated. Now, the team would have a playbook. Everyone from first party game developers to hardware would know it. And no one would misunderstand the schedule.

"The conversations largely ceased," Allard said, referring to questions about delaying the launch.

After that, it was time for Bach to step back. He had made his decision about the schedule. Now he was going to step out of the engine room. The executives, as a team, wanted to push the decisions lower into the organization. Bach would help with the partner communications but leave a lot of decisions to the team.

Bach didn't describe product decisions in the memo. He thought that the team should make those decisions, much of the time without the need for his approval. The team had more experience now and could run with the plan. But time was running short. Microsoft had to start committing to deadlines. Bach wasn't going to impose a decision. That wasn't his style. But he wanted the company to start moving.

On the original Xbox, too many decisions piled up.

"You discover that 90 percent of the decisions you make aren't right or wrong," Bach said. "The most important thing is to make them. On about 10 percent of the decisions, those matter a lot and affect the outcome. The important principle was to get the decisions made. The difference with Xbox and Xbox 360 is, we didn't let the decisions percolate."

1. "Microsoft Previews A New Breed of Xbox," by Dean Takahashi *San Jose Mercury News,* May 13, 2005.

CHAPTER THIRTEEN

LIFTING A VEIL

After the first decisions, there was no backing down. Robbie Bach, Ed Fries, and other executives hit the road to tell the biggest U.S. video game publishers that Microsoft was going to launch Xenon in the fall of 2005.

Bach visited New York and Los Angeles, while Ed Fries hit San Francisco. Both of them visited Electronic Arts in Redwood City, Calif. A.J. Redmer went to Europe to fill in developers such as Rare, Lionhead Studios, and Bizarre Creations. His agenda included telling them about the vision for next-generation games.

The executives limited their comments to 45 minutes or so. They talked about the current Xbox business and Xenon. By that time, some of the hardware thinkers had been tinkering with Xenon plans for more than a year. Only a few decisions had been made, but it was time to start bringing the allies on board to make games.

The Microsoft leaders didn't say much. It was early, and they had made few decisions so far. They told the publishers they were determined to launch the console in the fall of 2005 and explained why. They also said that they wanted to continue with the strategy of making the games easier to program. Microsoft wanted to make life easier for publishers who were beset with the problems of rising production costs, the squeeze on shelf space, and the drift toward expensive license-based games. Microsoft offered its assets such as its superior software testing groups, user research, and its Advanced Technology Group, which helped developers finish games and exploit the best features of the hardware.

With Xbox Live, Microsoft would have a competitive advantage over Sony, which had tepid results for its online strategy, and Nintendo, which never moved beyond one online game with the GameCube. Microsoft had accomplished the near-impossible task of getting gamers to pay for online play. It wasn't much, at $4 or $5 a month, and it didn't

do much to defray the Xbox Live start-up costs. But it was an investment that would pay off as more households adopted broadband Internet service. The next generation of games would come out of the gate with much bigger online components.

As Microsoft had argued in the first round, it wanted to be the publisher's friend. In contrast to the arrogance of the Japanese console makers, Microsoft wanted to continue to be the good console maker that offered a variety of choices for publishers. They wouldn't play favorites by giving royalty breaks. And they would invest more heavily in the marketing and software tools to make sure that the console got off the ground.

Bruno Bonnell, the CEO of Atari, met with Bach in the lobby of a New York hotel. The Nintendo Revolution and Sony's PlayStation 3 were still just rumors. Bonnell listened intently as Bach described the plan. "The brilliant part was that he was not putting this out as a hardware wonder," Bonnell said. "It was on the software side of the console where they would make big improvements. It was a no-brainer that we would do games."

Bonnell had never heard a console maker emphasize software and services as much as Microsoft had, and he believed that Xenon would broaden the market for games. Bach had said that Microsoft was a software company. It would match the hardware coming from Sony, but it would pull ahead because of software. Brian Farrell, CEO of THQ in the Los Angeles area, also felt like the plan was solid and worth getting behind. He believed that Microsoft would truly hit its schedule for 2005 because he knew it was losing tons of money on the original Xbox.

"I felt this was the right strategy, and that they would hit it," said Farrell. "They gave us lead time so that we could plan. They understand how long it takes to do software."

He knew that Microsoft was losing money on its console and that it had good reasons to launch a replacement console early.

"I believed them," Farrell said. "It made sense they wanted to get there first."

Bach had said that game development kits would be coming on a timely basis and that all publishers would have access to them as needed.

The development kits were often critical to a successful game launch. Microsoft had scored many game developers the first time around because its tools were complete. Developers understood them because they were essentially PC software development tools that had been around for years. By pumping out lots of the kits early, it seeded the game developers with the tools they needed to support the Xbox. Sony's console, by contrast, was harder to program and required a steep learning curve. Were it not for its head start in the market, the PlayStation 2 might have suffered based on difficulty of programming.

When Microsoft, a software company, guaranteed that its SDKs would be ready and on time, CEOs such as Farrell could bet on it. Farrell, who had run THQ for many years through several cycles, felt the timing of Microsoft's console matched THQ's own ambitious plans. Farrell had watched Take-Two

Interactive rise to prominence with new franchises on the PS2. At the time of that launch, THQ had 50 internal developers in two studios. It had now built its internal studios up and had expanded staff dramatically. The plan was to have around 11 studios and 1,000 employees by the time of the Xenon launch.

"Everyone remembers the lesson of *Grand Theft Auto III*," Farrell said, referring to the game that made the PlayStation 2 take off.

Both Bach and Fries met with Electronic Arts CEO Larry Probst, who had a positive reaction to Xenon. He believed they were serious about making the 2005 launch.

"Launching a year or so ahead of Sony made sense to me," Probst said in an interview. "I remember them saying they wanted to get to an installed base of 8 million to 10 million units ahead of Sony and the PlayStation 3. Their idea was enter the market first. Try to go quickly and aggressively. Get a meaningful installed base prior to Sony's launch and do better in Japan. As a launch strategy, it made a lot of sense to me. We encouraged them along those lines. We said we hope you price it aggressively and bring a lot of machines to market quickly."

EA didn't support every platform equally. It ditched the Sega Dreamcast altogether in favor of the PlayStation 2. But it had supported the Xbox, and Probst believed that the console did much better than expected given Microsoft's newcomer status. Six months after a console launch, EA reevaluated how much support it should give that console. Over time, EA's support for Nintendo's GameCube dwindled. Nintendo has to step up with its own guarantees and money to keep EA on board. Probst and his executives supported any system that they felt could get to 10 million units within 18 months and stand the test of time. They looked at whether the console maker could support a launch around the world and put a business model in place that made sense of EA. Xenon would clearly be one of those.

"A lot of those things go into the assessment, and lot of those things were well known with respect to Microsoft in the second generation," Probst said. "Our technical guys said later, this is a viable technology."

It would take months of technical disclosures before EA formally committed resources. The technical folks concluded that Microsoft's box would likely be ten times faster than the old machines. The groundwork was laid for EA, the king maker of the game industry, to throw its support behind Microsoft again. Probst started thinking about how EA could have the leading market share on Xenon with the most titles at launch.

Oddly enough, though Sony had started earlier on its chips for the PlayStation 3, it hadn't said a word to game publishers about when it was going to launch the new video game console. Bach was assuming they would show up in 2005.

Probst had faith in Microsoft's ability to launch hardware, but he didn't go along with everything it wanted. EA was still in a big fight with Microsoft in an ongoing dialogue about Xbox Live. Probst didn't like the fact that subscribers to Xbox Live paid Microsoft money, even if they were playing EA games. He wanted a share of the online revenues that came from EA customers. Also, he didn't like the fact that Microsoft collected data on EA gamers, who Probst considered to be his own customers. That was troubling, since Microsoft was battling EA in sports. Probst told Bach that EA was going to go exclusive with Sony's online service.

"Robbie, you don't need us, and we don't need you," Probst reportedly said in a meeting just before going public with his concerns. [2]

At E3 2003, the problem boiled over. The *Wall Street Journal* ran a front-page story on May 13, 2003, saying that EA would announce that it would make online versions of its sports games exclusively for Sony's console. Probst said in the story, "There's a 100-foot wall between us. We are not going to capitulate on this." He slammed Microsoft for collecting all the fees and keeping all of them. The defiance was a rare event for Microsoft, which was used to steamrolling both rivals and allies. It left a dark stain on the company's ability to partner with game companies.

Microsoft's booth at E3 2003

At the time, Probst felt the disagreement touched on issues of trust. In most other markets, Microsoft came off as a monopolistic predator. Its behavior on Xbox Live seemed to fit this pattern. And Microsoft was very powerful. Kaz Hirai, president of Sony's U.S. game unit, declared at the same show that Sony's free online service was friendly to publishers, promoting openness and choice for both gamers and publishers.

With the *Wall Street Journal* story, EA had embarrassed Microsoft and shown everyone where the real power was in the video game industry. The EA story overshadowed other news at the show. Microsoft cut the price on the Xbox

from $199 to $179 at the E3 show. It was unusual for Microsoft to lead the price war, considering it was losing so much money. But it also wanted to head off an even bigger cut from Sony.

At the Microsoft press conference in an all-green theater in Los Angeles, Robbie Bach, Ed Fries and J Allard talked about their line-up. Bach spoke about how the Xbox had inaugurated a "digital entertainment lifestyle" that brought connected gamers together. Fries showed off some exclusives, such as *Doom 3*, *Ninja Gaiden* and *Forza Motorsport*. *Doom 3* looked far superior to other titles, but it would show up first on the PC and look much better on that platform. Fries touted Rare's first Xbox title, *Grabbed by the Ghoulies*, which received a lukewarm reception from the crowd and the press. Microsoft was still trying to get the Japanese market stoked on Xbox Live, this time with *True Fantasy Live Online*, which would be an ill-fated and expensive enterprise.

Ed Fries, Robbie Bach and J Allard at E3 2003

Allard unveiled the *Xbox Music Mixer*, which was Jeff Henshaw's project, an attempt to bring karaoke sing-along and, hopefully, non-gaming family members, to the Xbox. He discussed plans to allow Xbox Live to send live alerts to gamers, and how *XSN Sports* could link a player into a world of online stats. A demo of *Halo 2* stole the show, particularly when Bungie showed that you could hijack an alien's "ghost" craft and take it over in mid-flight. But *Halo 2* wasn't anywhere near being done. Steven Kent, a veteran freelance journalist, felt that Sony and Nintendo had again out-classed Microsoft on games.

Nintendo had cool titles such as *Resident Evil 4* and an exclusive *Star Wars Rogue Squadron III* title coming. PlayStation 2 titles such as Sony's *Gran*

Turismo 4 would leave their rivals in the dust. Sony had some clever technology in its *Eye Toy* video camera that could be used to monitor movements that could, in turn, control the play in PS2 games. John Riccitiello, president of Electronic Arts, demonstrated a bunch of EA sports games that relied, exclusively, upon Sony's online gaming solution. All in all, Microsoft cemented the impression that it was a spirited underdog but was hopelessly behind the market leader. Kaz Hirai said that Sony had sold more than 51 million PlayStation 2s, and 96 million original PlayStations.

Behind the Microsoft confidence, there was struggle. A team of consultants from AT Kearney had spent eight weeks in a conference room analyzing everything they could about the Xbox operation and its supply chain. The team, dubbed ex10, came up with recommendations on ways Microsoft could shave $300 million in costs through various moves. They assessed how much control Microsoft should have over its design process and its 45 different contract manufacturers. They were going to consolidate the way Microsoft purchased components from different suppliers so that it could exercise more buying power. It wanted to leverage relations with contract manufacturers, such as Flextronics, which made both mice and Xbox hardware for Microsoft. The grand total saved was more than Bach had called for when he asked managers to come up with $250 million in cuts. Yet Microsoft was still losing around $1 billion a year.

For all the scrimping and saving, software sales were picking up. *Tom Clancy's Splinter Cell, Panzer Dragoon Orta, Ninja Gaiden,* and *Star Wars Knights of the Old Republic* were fueling sales. And in most of the cross-platform games, Blake Fischer said evidence was mounting that gamers thought the games looked better on the Xbox. The Xbox group enjoyed some perks. They had a lousy view of the gravel pit from their windows, compared to the serene and wooded main Microsoft campus a few miles away. About the time of the publisher visits, Microsoft installed four big lounges in the Millennium D headquarters of the Xbox team. The lounges were set up as living rooms, with Xbox consoles and big-screen TVs where employees could take breaks or show off new titles to visitors. The morale folks staged game tournaments with prizes once a quarter. Microsoft needed morale boosters in the grueling console war.

1. "The Xbox Reloaded," by Josh McHugh, *Wired* Magazine, June, 2005.

2. "Video Game Giant Electronic Arts Links With Sony, Snubs Microsoft," by Rob Guth, *Wall Street Journal*, May 13, 2003.

CHAPTER FOURTEEN

EMISSARIES

he planning team picked October, 2003, as the time that they needed to get a green light on their plan from Bill Gates and Steve Ballmer. That meant that they couldn't spend a lot of time in trial and error. They had to start talking to the partners who would make it all happen. Before it was over, Microsoft would have to sign contracts with dozens of parts suppliers and purchase more than 1,700 distinct parts, from the tiniest passive components to the metal enclosures for the box.

"The magnitude of the project was just enormous," said Masoud Foudeh, the program manager for the Xenon graphics chip.

The chip and hardware designers started drawing up formal specifications detailing their needs. They'd create a request for proposals, which is jargon for a bidding sheet. Larry Yang, the Microsoft semiconductor chief in Mountain View, California, said that the matrix of requirements was mostly technical. But chip vendors also had to meet some business requirements. They had to be able to deliver on time and staff up so that they had enough people on the project.

The early evaluations were complete. In the fall of 2002, the team made it out the door to get some serious bids from each potential supplier. By the spring of 2003, they had a short list of contenders for the main components.

Going out to get bids was always a bit of a comical experience. Microsoft didn't want to tell the vendors all of its plans out of a concern about leaks. For the same reason, the chip makers didn't always want to share every last detail about their upcoming chips. But both sides knew that Microsoft was prepared to spend a ton of money buying chips, and that it had to get them from somewhere. And so the dance started.

Barry Spector, a business development director who worked for Xbox finance chief Bryan Lee, had the job of visiting the chip vendors with the proposed contract requirements in hand. Spector had the spreadsheets and business model that Lee had developed to make the overall business work over eight years or so. If Spector cut the right deals, he could make that business model work. If he failed, it could be a financial catastrophe.

"You had to get it right because there were billions of dollars involved," Spector said.

Spector visited ATI Technologies, the top graphics chip maker, in Thornhill, Canada, during the fall of 2002. Spector, who had been at Microsoft for a dozen years in various sales and finance positions, was a tough negotiator. He sat across the table from Bob Feldstein, vice president of engineering at ATI. Both men had attorneys at their sides. At the outset, Spector said, "I reserve the right to wake up smarter tomorrow. I reserve that right for our team and for you too. We will solve problems in real time. Maybe you get an idea. You can pull it off the table. And so can we."

Spector came with a list of terms. Microsoft had to meet its 2005 launch schedule. It required a certain level of performance. The company wanted intellectual property rights and flexibility. It wanted to tie ATI's interests with Microsoft's. And it wanted control of the total costs of the program.

But as prepared as Spector was, the negotiations didn't start out on the right foot. ATI had been used to the PC business, where it made 25 cents on every dollar of sales. Microsoft said at the outset that such profit margins wouldn't work in the console business, where low-cost hardware mattered the utmost. In return, Spector said that ATI would be able to earn returns on the sales of tens of millions of chips. Feldstein said this was new and unfamiliar territory, where ATI gave up its intellectual property rights.

The talks hit a brick wall. The discussions became heated. That was why Feldstein said that, while he respected Spector's skills, he remembered Spector as an "emotional guy." Feldstein acknowledged it took a while for ATI to understand the sense of Microsoft's desire to own a lot of what ATI would typically own in a chip design deal. Microsoft didn't want to be held hostage to a single supply source. It wanted to play competitors off against each other, as a check on price gouging. If either side met or missed schedules, they would face bonuses or penalties.

Spector offered advice to his own team.

"We have a hard problem," he said. "It doesn't do good to rehash our position over and over again. That doesn't get us anywhere. The car is still in park."

Spector would drive the ATI executives crazy because he would say, "I want to drive a BMW, but I can only afford a Yugo. I really can't afford to pay for a BMW."

The fact that he was coming from Microsoft, one of the richest companies on earth, didn't escape the notice of the ATI listeners. But Spector said that his division was a separate part of Microsoft without access to all those billions. It had to stand on its own merits or it wouldn't be a long-term business.

Spector would also start out by saying, "I don't understand the technical details, but...." Then the ATI executives would push back, trying to explain the technical details that prevented them from doing what Spector wanted.

Spector said it was emotional on both sides, with different personalities and

different backgrounds. To try to break the ice, Spector invited Feldstein to his house for dinner. It was the first time that Spector had done that in a dozen years at Microsoft. "Microsoft was really making sure that they would bound the problem in many aspects," Feldstein said. "They were feeling their way around it. They were learning our business model. Why is it hard for ATI to do this?"

As the deal with ATI began to sour, Spector got frustrated and began to talk to others. Even Nvidia came back into the talks. To Nvidia, Microsoft was falling into a familiar pattern. It wanted the high end graphics for Xenon, but didn't want to pay for it. It was helpful that Microsoft knew exactly when it was going to launch. But Nvidia's executives knew that there wasn't much time to finish a chip for 2005. If the chip were more like the standard parts Nvidia was creating for the PC, then Nvidia didn't mind doing the deal. But it couldn't pull hundreds of engineers off other critical projects to do something special for Microsoft without enough money.

"They wanted a custom design, but they didn't want to pay the price," said Marv Burkett, chief financial officer at Nvidia.

The Microsoft emissaries also sought bids from the microprocessor vendors. Intel had made a PC chip for the original Xbox. The 733-megahertz Pentium III was fast in 2001, but it was downright primitive compared to newest processors coming out. Intel was never that thrilled to be making $20 chips for Microsoft in chip factories that were better employed making $200 PC microprocessors. But Craig Barrett, then-CEO of Intel, realized that it was important to be in the living room and that game consoles were growing in popularity. Microsoft felt that it had gotten a reasonable price from Intel on the chips. Intel had a chip in the works, a new version of the Pentium 4 code-named Tejas, that promised to run at speeds faster than 4 gigahertz. It was due to debut in 2005. Intel never offered Tejas, but Microsoft asked for it, and at a far lower price than Intel wanted to sell it for in 2005.

Microsoft and Intel had been partners for a couple of decades on the PC. The companies had their differences, and former CEO Andy Grove described the companies as fellow travelers on the same road. One of the goals of the rest of the corporation was to get Windows running on the Xbox 360. Intel pushed this idea and noted how easy it would be to do so with Intel chips. Rick Rashid, head of Microsoft Research, liked this idea so much that he had his team hack together a version of the original Xbox that ran Windows. They proved it would work, but Windows running on a machine with 64 megabytes of main memory just wasn't very impressive. It slowed down the machine and detracted from its ability to run games at the greatest possible performance. A game console just didn't have enough memory to run a program that was a memory hog.

Intel held sway over Microsoft in many ways, and its executives tried hard to get Microsoft to stay with its chips. Intel didn't want to license its design so that it could one day be combined with the graphics chip. That integration move was the end game in the cost reduction that Holmdahl envisioned. By not surrendering that right, Intel shot down its chances. Microsoft's planners sensed what Intel wouldn't say: the chances of Intel licensing its core x86 microprocessor architecture were about as likely as Microsoft licensing Windows to another company.

Some of the game developers such as Tim Sweeney and John Carmack favored the Intel architecture for the simplicity of programming a single core. They hammered that point home whenever they were consulted. Multiple cores came with huge debugging hassles. David Wu of Pseudo Interactive thought multiple cores would work just fine, thanks to advances in programming languages.

The early intelligence helped the game developers get started on their own forward-looking work. Toward the end of 2002, Sweeney and his team had begun work on a new software engine, which was called a renderer, that would exploit new features in graphics chips. Sweeney invested a lot of effort into shader technology, which was a new way to add detailed nuances to an image such as fur on an animal character. He bet that the Microsoft's future game console would make use of it.

"We made a bet of our own," he said. "We hoped all the next-generation consoles would move in that direction, and that we would license this technology broadly."

Microsoft also sought bids from Advanced Micro Devices, which had just missed getting into the original Xbox thanks to a last minute bid by Intel. Dirk Meyer, one of the key architects at AMD, said that the company decided to pass on the deal at the outset. AMD didn't have the resources that Intel had and it couldn't spare the engineers. AMD had launched the Opteron, an original chip aimed at Intel's server business, in April, 2003. It was starting to fill its factory and didn't need the extra business from Microsoft.

"You have to make choices," Meyer said. "It not just deciding what to do, but deciding what not to do."

Microsoft's hardware engineers also went to see IBM, which was already working with Sony. Over the years, the love didn't bloom between Microsoft and IBM. But business was business, old feuds or not.

Some partners weren't ready to go along with Microsoft's ideas. Neither Nvidia nor Intel liked the idea of giving ownership of the chip intellectual property to Microsoft. They wanted to build chips. This time, the partners had to be willing to let Microsoft run the system design. Microsoft also wanted to take the chips and have them fabricated in a factory of its choosing. The resistance from Nvidia and Intel wasn't total. But it hurt their ability to stay in the running for the contracts.

The process took months, even from the point where Microsoft knew who it wanted to work with. In the spring and summer of 2003, Microsoft engineer Jeff Andrews was getting nervous, concerned that they would run out of time.

"It was extremely stressful," he said.

Since Greg Gibson, the system designer on Xenon, didn't know what deal would be worked out, he assigned his engineers to come up with all sorts of scenarios, guesses at what the system would look like, given the presence of

a variety of vendors in the box. He didn't know how much main memory, or dynamic random access memory chips, would be in the final box. Main memory chips were a critical component that determined how large a program or piece of art a game could process at a given moment. It had to be balanced with the processor in the machine, and its presence could determine whether or not the games loaded quickly enough or the animations looked realistic. But DRAM chips were commodities subject to wild price swings. If the prices rose, Microsoft could get stuck with an enormous bill just to pay for memory chips. So Gibson needed to give the executives some options. He had the designers create a system that could take anywhere from the bare minimum 256 megabytes all the way up to 1 gigabyte. Any smaller than that, and the machine would be weaker than a low-end PC. Above 1 gigabyte, the machine would have too many chips, given the memory capacity of each one. The original Xbox had 64 megabytes of DRAM. Gibson's team started looking closest at the speediest of DRAMs, the graphics chips known as GDDR chips. A new one was scheduled to debut just before the Xenon launch.

As decisions approached, the competitive picture on the different bids kept changing.

"We made different cuts, and would get to the final two or final three," Yang said. "Then someone would scream at us and then they would get back in. It was fairly straightforward. We negotiated with the finalists in parallel."

IBM and ATI wanted the business more. J Allard wasn't directly involved in the negotiations, but he was paying attention. He said that IBM showed more vision than Intel about the future of multiple cores on a chip. IBM also had to make sure its $2 billion factory in East Fishkill, N.Y., had enough business to keep it busy.

Figuring out how many cores to put on a chip, and how fast each of those cores should be, wasn't an easy decision. Big Blue proposed to do a three-core PowerPC processor, with each core capable of running two threads at a time. The cores weren't the most powerful that IBM could design, but Big Blue was confident that it could manufacture them at the right cost and stay within the power consumption targets. The good news was that work was already under way on parts of the chips because those parts were already part of the future roadmap for other chips.

Such a design, Gibson's team saw, would likely have staying power, even compared to the ever-changing PC, because multiple cores weren't anywhere on the horizon for many other chip architectures.

"They wanted partnership and flexibility," said Jim Comfort, an IBM vice president in charge of the Microsoft relationship. "We were willing to do that."

But even so, it would be many months before Microsoft signed a contract on microprocessors, and the clock was always ticking. And one of the big technical problems loomed before Microsoft if it was really considering making the switch from Intel and Nvidia to IBM and ATI. How would the old games for the original Xbox ever work on Xenon?

CHAPTER FIFTEEN

CONSULTING DEVELOPERS

At the same time as the hardware team was figuring out its chips, the rest of the Xenon design team had to figure out what the gamers and the game developers wanted. The gamers would know what they wanted when they saw it, but the developers were the ones that had to understand the meaning of next-generation much earlier in the process.

The first time around, Seamus Blackley rounded up a team of game developers such as id Software's John Carmack, Epic Games' Tim Sweeney, and Pseudo Interactive's David Wu. They were the cream of the crop of PC game developers and they lobbied heavily for technologies such as Nvidia's graphics chip.

Gibson and the hardware team did the same thing this time, but they were aware that too much consulting could give away their secrets. They brought in Laura Fryer, the director of the Advanced Technology Group that Blackley had started. She was in charge of making the Xbox game developers' lives easier by offering technical support.

ATG's job was to know the Xbox inside out. It provided reactive support to help developers make better Xbox games. Fryer wanted her team to provide answers to questions within 24 hours. The team was getting and answering more than 6,000 questions a year from developers, about five times the number that Microsoft's usual software developer support teams handled. ATG also documented all bugs they had found, logging 1,152 of them in 2002 alone. And ATG provided hundreds of evaluations a year for developers, reviewing the code, content and game play.

Fryer kept Blackley's Xbox advisory group together. The small group was consulted on big decisions. But the broader group of game developers was periodically briefed on decisions. ATG collected information such as what kind of tools really worked well in the last generation and had to be moved to Xenon. The group helped educate developers on multithreading programming techniques, and got feedback about what was wrong with the earlier software development kits.

Now that Microsoft had a much bigger internal game development team, the experts were inside the company. Gibson approached the graphics experts at Bungie, Microsoft's hot game studio that produced *Halo*. They were in the midst of creating *Halo 2*. But graphics experts like Chris Butcher took time to offer their advice.

Butcher, one of the lead programmers at Bungie, wanted more memory in the system. And he didn't like some of the choices that the hardware team had made. For instance, the system had only a single memory controller which could control a data pathway from one part of the system to another. The CPU would have to go through the bus and the graphics chip to seek data from main memory. This so-called "unified memory architecture" would save on the costs of having a separate graphics memory, but it would cause a long delay in fetching critical data for a CPU that, with a few cores, could process data a lot faster than it could actually get the data. Butcher feared this design would bog everything down. Adding a new memory controller into the system, however, could complicate things and make the whole system more expensive. The original Xbox used unified memory as well, but in the Xenon architecture, the traffic would be much greater. The CPU could run six simultaneous hardware threads, any one of which could stall the traffic. And the graphics chip itself could also stall things. That was why ATI had proposed using embedded memory, a small amount of memory that the graphics chip could address directly and thus lighten the overall bus traffic. Game developers were also concerned about the small amount of embedded memory.

Gibson could be much more frank with the developers inside Microsoft because they were all part of the same team and understood the value of secrecy. Gibson could ask those inside developers what tradeoffs they would make if they were designing the console. For example, if they wanted more main memory, what would they give up to keep the costs in line?

The responses came in. The developers were mostly concerned about the choices Gibson's engineers were making as far as specifying the graphics chip vendor, the microprocessor, the amount of main memory in the system, whether every box would have a standard hard drive, and which kind of storage drive, whether DVD or a successor technology, the box would use.

"The biggest thing that came up was parallel processors for the CPU," said one game developer who was present at the first meeting. "Could you really handle more than one processor? Some said no and they just wanted something fast."

Sweeney wondered if they should just stick a 6-gigahertz, single-core CPU in the box. But it was clear to the engineers that Intel would hit the brick wall on power consumption before it could create a 6-gigahertz chip. Then some of the developers came up with their own calculations. "It didn't make a lot of sense to go with one processor," the developer said. "We could get three processors running at 3.2 gigahertz, or one processor running at 4 gigahertz. It was better to have the three."

The more threads, or programs, that a processor could handle simultaneously,

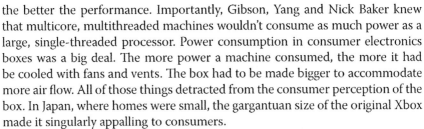

the better the performance. Importantly, Gibson, Yang and Nick Baker knew that multicore, multithreaded machines wouldn't consume as much power as a large, single-threaded processor. Power consumption in consumer electronics boxes was a big deal. The more power a machine consumed, the more it had be cooled with fans and vents. The box had to be made bigger to accommodate more air flow. All of those things detracted from the consumer perception of the box. In Japan, where homes were small, the gargantuan size of the original Xbox made it singularly appalling to consumers.

On top of that, microprocessors were running into a brick wall. Intel had been increasing the frequency of its chips so that they performed one task faster and faster and faster. That came at the cost of other performance measures. And it drove power consumption higher and higher. Typical PC microprocessors were dissipating over 100 watts, far too much to be used in a sleek and small consumer electronics device. Intel took advantage of advances in manufacturing technology to make its chips faster. It would use the latest lenses and chip-making equipment to create finer and finer circuits on chip. By making circuits smaller, everything got better. The distance between electrical paths was shorter, so the speed of the circuit went up. By making the chip smaller, it used less material, cutting costs.

So chip makers could shrink a chip and make it for half the cost at the same performance. Or they could keep the chip size the same and pack more transistors on every chip. That usually equated to performance, but now the performance gains were slowing down. And with every miniaturization, a new problem arose. The leakage current, or the amount of power that a chip consumed even when it was idle, was going up with each generation of chips. Transistors were less like switches for electrical currents and more like dimmer switches. Pat Gelsinger, chief technology officer at Intel, predicted, in 2001, that if the leakage trend continued, the density of heat in a chip would approach that of a nuclear power plant, or even the sun. Something had to be done.

Unfortunately for Intel, others were thinking ahead. As Intel was preoccupied with cranking up the megahertz on a PC, IBM had already launched its first dual-core microprocessor in the business server market in 2001. It was working on multithreading and addressing the power problem head on even as Intel was creating the world's fastest single-core microprocessors. And Bernie Myerson, head of technology in IBM's division, convinced a talented Intel chip designer named Ilan Spillinger to leave the world's biggest chip maker and move to IBM to work on low-power processor designs.

Everyone knew who was winning the graphics battles in the PC market. ATI was beating Nvidia for a change. As to the microprocessor, the outside game developers might have cared much more about which vendor Microsoft chose. They used to code their games in hard-learned assembly language. Assembly was low-level code that was tied specifically to a particular chip architecture. But now game programmers were writing their code in high-level software languages. Software coded in those languages could run on any type of microprocessor.

The developers would have preferred four cores instead of three, but understood the limits of silicon technology. The offerings from both IBM and ATI seemed like they were the best deals. So much so, that one of the developers who was consulted felt like Microsoft had made up its mind before it sought outside advice.

One issue in particular was a flashpoint. Tim Sweeney wanted the hard disk drive in the box again. Some developers had used the hard disk drive to cache data, such as a piece of art for an animation, so that the art could be more quickly flashed onto the screen when needed. Fryer's group consulted a wide group on opinions about the hard disk drive, and all sorts of opinions came back.

"For a game to have a useful online component, it has to have a hard drive," Sweeney said. "You have to download maps. You can get new teams for sports games. New levels. Significant updates to improve functionality."

If a gamer tried to download a new level into a box, it might take a lot of minutes. Gamers couldn't do that every time you logged in to play an online game. And if the hard drive wasn't there in Xenon, how could the machine run games for the old Xbox, particularly when those games looked for a hard disk to save a game?

Advocates such as Ed Fries had argued that the hard drive would unleash more creativity and become a competitive advantage. The assessment that came back from everyone else on the first round was that the hard drive was nice, but that not enough of the game developers used it to make games that put the PlayStation 2, which had no hard disk built-in, to shame.

Even Steve Ballmer, CEO of the company, was painfully aware of the hard disk drive's cost, which accounted for perhaps $1 billion of the $4 billion in losses on the original Xbox. Each eight-gigabyte drive cost about $50 or so, but since those drives consisted of the bare-bones parts – one disk platter and one spindle – the drive makers couldn't reduce the costs in the drives. Seagate drove the cost toward $30 or so. But that was still too much. It was clear that Microsoft, which had a fifth of the market, couldn't charge more for the Xbox than the PS2 just because of the hard disk drive.

Ballmer said, "Putting the hard drive in there was a bad business decision. It cost more but didn't allow us to charge a premium in the market."

Sweeney felt that the hard disk drive didn't get a good test. Because Sony dominated the market with the PlayStation 2, he said that game developers targeted their efforts at the PS2, a machine with no hard disk. Then they adapted their work to run on the Xbox. As they did so, they didn't add capabilities to take advantage of the hard disk. But if Microsoft had more market share, it would work the other way around. The developers would target the Xenon system with a hard disk, and fully exploit it.

Sweeney could never tell exactly what Microsoft would do with his advice. But Gibson could be much more open with Bungie and other developers inside Microsoft. For now, they had come up with a decision that would allow developers some latitude. They might split the product line into two parts, a premium product with a hard disk drive and an entry-level machine without one.

Nick Baker's crew had decided that they needed to leave the hard drive decision to the executive team. That meant that game developers might have to start working on games without knowing whether it was there or not. The solution was "virtualization." The system architects would create the box so that a game could always assume that mass storage of some kind was present. But that storage could either be an internal hard disk drive or a much cheaper flash memory unit with a smaller storage capacity. Hence, when a player reached a point in the game where it would save progress, the game would be saved to the virtualized storage device. In that sense, the games didn't really care if a hard drive or a memory unit was present as long as there was storage.

Fryer passed along the bad news on the hard drive. She told them that they couldn't assume that every box would have a hard drive. She left some room for changes down the road, but that, she said, was the current plan.

Sweeney didn't like the virtualization decision because it still meant that the developers wouldn't be able to assume the presence of a hard disk drive in every box. Optional hardware never really sold that well, reaching maybe 20 percent of total audience. That meant that developers couldn't design a game that required a hard drive and hit the highest possible audience of gamers. They would have to develop games for the lowest common denominator, meaning they would have to make games assuming there was no hard disk drive. But that was the decision he was stuck with.

Microsoft had a lot of trade-offs to make. Gibson kept his options open. He kept the parallel design efforts going for as long as possible until Microsoft had enough information to make a bet and stick with it. It would all be decided based on contracts, partners, technologies, and business decisions that were still to come.

Regardless of what was going to be in the box, Laura Fryer knew that she would have to inspire game developers to dream big with their next generation games. One of the brilliant maneuvers that Seamus Blackley had pulled off with the original Xbox was to wow both gamers and developers with outstanding demos. Every step of the way, from showing a chaotic room of full of snapping mouse traps and flying ping-pong balls to Monarch butterflies flying over a Japanese *koi* pond, to a gigantic robot performing martial arts moves in tandem with a fetching woman named Raven, Blackley made everybody's jaw drop with canned animations. Visuals were the key to everyone's hearts.

Fryer was well aware that she had to follow suit and get ATG to make demos that could show off the power of the system that Microsoft had in mind. Dan Duncalf, a developer at Pipeworks in Oregon, had made one of the original Xbox demos that depicted ping-pong balls bouncing around on springing mousetraps. He signed up to do another demo. Fryer and her demo tech Drew Angeloff started kicking around ideas. They thought that next-generation physics would be a cool thing to show off with the new console. Together, they dialed David Wu on the speaker phone.

Wu was always happy to provide advice to Microsoft. But he should have known better than to answer a business call from Microsoft. A muscular guy with a boyish face in charge of a young game development studio in Toronto, he was always willing to hear Microsoft out, even though he had had terrible luck working with the folks from Redmond. Wu was a good friend of Blackley's and had believed in the same religion – that physics would one day make games more realistic and fun. Wu had conceived of a car combat game, *Full Auto*, for the PC, back in the late 1990s. In the game, cars tricked out with heavy weaponry would race each other and fire everything from machines guns to rockets. The game had moved along well, but another Microsoft developer, Digital Anvil, had also conceived of a similar game. Microsoft decided to ax Wu's game in mid-1999.

As the Xbox gathered steam, Ed Fries made up for that move by green lighting another physics-based game that Wu had proposed. Combining the loony style of cel-based cartoons with cars that could stretch the laws of physics, Wu thought he had a winning Xbox launch title. But on Christmas day, 2000, Microsoft called again to deliver more bad news to Wu. The company had to cancel *Cel Damage*. Wu sucked it in and found another publisher, Electronic Arts, that was willing to publish the game for the Xbox. The game debuted as one of the launch titles, but it didn't sell that well.

When Fryer called in the spring of 2003, Wu needed another project. He said he would happily create a demo for Xenon. It would combine state-of-the-art graphics for animating cars with a truly accurate physics engine that would use finite element simulation to determine the paths of objects as they collided with each other. Wu wanted to make cars that would deform in the same way that real cars would when they hit each other. It would take a huge amount of computational power to implement the "finite element analysis" needed to accurately depict the destruction of the car and plot where the debris would fly as the car slammed into a wall. It required a lot of math, particularly the kind known as "floating point," all of which had to be done simultaneously.

But once Wu programmed the proper physics into the game, the animations in the game would flow much more easily. In the old days, if two cars collided, a programmer would have tell the computer exactly how they deformed and impacted and crumpled. But with physical laws accurately programmed into the behavior of the environment of the game, the cars would crash into each and then they would accurately collide on their own and crumple on their own. If a car crashed into a tree or a car or a building, the damage it took would be precise and automatically generated based on the physics program. The programmer wouldn't have to specifically program the result for each kind of crash. This actually saved the programmer a great deal of time. He described his plan to Fryer and she gave him the go-ahead to create "Crash."

"We knew we could make a really cool crash, and that we would want to rewind it so that we could watch it over and over again," he said.

Wu started thinking that he could revive *Full Auto* as a realistic physics-based game for Xenon. He knew it was a huge risk to work with Microsoft again. But he bet his company that the demo would turn into a huge amount of attention, and

that would help him secure a publisher and funding for the game.

"It was a game I wanted to do for a long time," he said. "No one has ever done vehicular combat the way that it should be done."

They got help on the textures for the cars from Paul Steed, an artist within ATG who was a computer animator extraordinaire. Steed helped out a lot with the textures for his cars, but he was working on his own demo.

Steed had cut his teeth at id Software, the makers of the *Doom* games, and at Origin Systems, on the *Wing Commander* series. Steed was a fiery character. He had left id after joining in on public feuds with some of the former id founders who had left to start a rival Dallas game development house. John Carmack, the programming genius at id, wrote on his *.plan* file (a kind of early blog on the Web) that Steed had been fired in the midst of a battle over which game id was going to pursue. In that debate, Carmack himself had been overruled and voted down by the two artists who had majority ownership of the company, Kevin Cloud and Adrian Carmack.

Steed went on to work at Wild Tangent, the Redmond, Washington-based web games company founded by former Microsoft DirectX evangelist Alex St. John. He built a game dubbed *Betty Bad* that combined the old arcade game Tempest with a sexy character modeled on the body of a public relations maven. There, Steed also started working on dancing girl visualizers. The sexy girls would bump and grind and gyrate to the beat of the music. His aim was to create the perfect female body, with all the right animated movement and physics, so that the model's breasts would bounce as realistically as they would in real life. He created model after model for the visualizers, which fans downloaded by the millions as the craze for pirated MP3 music took off thanks to companies such as Napster. The dancing girl visualizers were a way for Wild Tangent to distribute its software, as well as a way to pitch users to pay to upgrade for more.

Steed quit Wild Tangent to work on the dancing girl models full time. Then he was recruited to join Microsoft's ATG. His job was to create art that would help show off the power of the hardware platform. Steed was a self-taught artist who took time during 60-hour work weeks to write books on computer animation. The topics in these books included how to build a mesh, Garaud shading, and manual vertex assignment.

Steed had something special in mind that would show off the power of Xenon. He started his "research" on a woman he called Eva. This involved studying the pictures of hundreds of beautiful models and interviewing them in person. He held casting calls. In them, he attached a bunch of sensor electrodes to their bodies and captured their movements, a process known as motion capture. He pushed the limits of accurate motion capture measurement down to the millimeter. Then he scanned the data into a computer and ultimately tried to use the images to build an animated character that looked and moved like a real woman.

Over eight months, the vision of Eva came into focus. She was a busty siren in black-and-white noir shades, with a hat that covered her eyes. The only flash of color on her was her red lipstick. She sat in a chair holding a cigarette, tapping it on a table. She was an amalgam of a lot of real women, with shadows falling across the face as accurately as if she really were sitting underneath a lamp. Eva consisted of about 80,000 polygons, the basic shapes that computers used to create animations, while most current generation Xbox characters only had a few thousand polygons. That translated into an image that someone could easily mistake for a character in a film noir movie of the 1940s. She had a drink that showed what real water would look like. The only thing missing that Steed really wanted to show off was 3-D animated smoke, but he couldn't get it to work in time. It was exactly the kind of testosterone-pumping image that could get game developers excited about the coming technology. It was one of the demos that would rivet the whole crowd.

"I was going to put a hot chick in everything, but they said no," Steed said.

CHAPTER SIXTEEN

MASTER FRIES AND MASTER CHIEF

*E*d Fries was a Microsoft lifer, a company man if there ever was one. He worked at the company because he wanted to, not because he had to. Stock options had made him rich. As the head of the game studios at Microsoft, he had a responsibility to fulfill to keep a division of 1,200 people headed in the right direction. He was a gamer who had deep ties into the community of game developers. Like Seamus Blackley and Kevin Bachus on the original Xbox team, he was Microsoft's ambassador to the gaming community and one of the reasons why the industry supported the Xbox.

For all that stature, he wasn't a big man. He was thin and had wavy brown hair with a casual attitude that masked a sharp mind. He had grown up in Bellevue, Wash., and he had raced motorcycles around the fields that eventually became Microsoft's corporate headquarters. He started in 1985 as an intern at the company. He created the software used to create and display online tutorials. He was hired permanently and programmed code for Microsoft's Excel spreadsheet software. He rose through the ranks at Excel. He became the technical lead on Excel, working on the first version of Excel for Windows at a time when Lotus was far bigger. The team did seven versions of Excel in five years and, at the end, Microsoft beat Lotus.

Ed then moved on to the Microsoft Word group, where he managed a team of 60. With the transition to Windows, Word beat out its chief competitor, WordPerfect. When Microsoft went public in 1986 and saw its stock rise like a meteor, Fries became a rich man, as did his siblings at Microsoft. He and his wife bought a one-acre plot on the shore of Lake Washington, where many of the Microsoft nouveau riche built big homes, including Bill Gates. [1]

With no worries about money, Fries could indulge his passion for games. When he was in high school, he designed a knock-off of the hit *Frogger*. A game publisher named Romox tracked him down from a post he made on an electronic bulletin board and paid him several thousand dollars to revise his *Frogger* knockoff into a real game, re-titled *Princess and Frog*. Ed moved over to run the games division in 1995, when the games group had only 150 employees and four game development teams. The division was known for its lucrative but decidedly uncool *Flight Simulator* games.

Many of his friends thought he was committing career suicide. Microsoft was far behind the big kahuna of video games, Electronic Arts. Friends in the industry described EA as "the evil empire," a title that was often reserved for Microsoft and its domination of the PC software business. Yet he slowly built the business.

Robbie Bach was Fries' boss, and he mentored him in the ways of business, while Fries had free rein to pursue the right products. Fries found and nurtured Dallas-based Ensemble Studios, which made the blockbuster PC game *Age of Empires*. Once that game debuted in October, 1997, it sold millions. Microsoft became a contender in games.

"I wanted to build a new business," Fries said. "It was my show to run. I didn't have to pass decisions by a committee."

Fries was one of the group of talented young executives who, like J Allard, had been dubbed "Baby Bills." With the money he got from *Age of Empires*, Fries acquired a number of small studios in the late 1990s, including Fasa Interactive and Access Software. The deals never cost more than $30 million. But he made some expensive mistakes. Fries had fronted a lot of money to Austin-based Digital Anvil, founded by Chris and Erin Roberts, the creators of the *Wing Commander* series. They promised to create *Freelancer*, a science fiction game with a pirate-bounty hunter theme, and a series of other games. But Chris Roberts got caught up in directing a poorly received movie version of *Wing Commander*, and Freelancer fell embarrassingly behind schedule. Digital Anvil ran out of Microsoft's advance money before it completed its work. Microsoft took over Digital Anvil. After five years, it eventually shipped *Freelancer*, which fell short on sales goals. Fries didn't mind taking chances like that, but he knew that too many bombs would cost him his job.

At the beginning of the plans for the Xbox in 1999, Fries had 400 internal game developers spread across 10 studios. He had funded another 20 game development companies that worked on games one-by-one. By 2000, he had planned to launch 20 games, and the division was generating about $200 million a year. But by 2001, because of Xbox, he needed to expand to twice that number. During the Xbox generation, he funded a lot more external developers, bought Bungie, and eventually acquired Rare. He built a huge sports studio and funded a racing game team called *Forza Motorsport*.

He had successfully navigated Microsoft Game Studios through the Xbox launch. He had less authority over the games business as it expanded to include the Xbox console business. Mitch Koch, who ran sales and marketing, took over game marketing and pulled the embedded marketing people out of Fries' game studios. That gave Fries' teams less say about how their games would be marketed.

But the expansion was exhilarating, since for the most part his division had had to live off the *Age of Empires* profits. As Fries expanded, he moved the division away from its roots as a Microsoft company. It was becoming a game company, full of industry veterans who were not Microsoft lifers. They were part of the company because they did games, not because they had worked on Office. Fries was a unique hybrid of these two cultures, having worked on games and Office, too.

Just about every executive had advice for Fries. One common suggestion was that Fries buy up the best players in the industry. But while he paid good money on occasion, Fries didn't like to just buy publishers left and right. In addition, it was hard to go into a place like Japan and buy a publisher because of all of the interlocking ownership relationships the game companies had with other companies. Fries focused on building relationships over a long period of time.

Cranking out a big game wasn't just a manufacturing process. It was a labor of love, and those backing it really had to make a leap of faith. They had to believe in the team, the game play, the story, and everything else that could make it come together like a symphony. All of that took time to bring together. Sometimes it worked, as with *Halo*.

Fries had been the big believer in the original *Halo* when there wasn't a lot to believe. As first conceived, *Halo* was an Apple Macintosh game that was going to be a real-time strategy game with big outdoor environments and online play. It was like a science fiction version of the predecessor *Myth* games that Bungie made. The game didn't have much of a story to it, and it wasn't a first-person shooter.

Bungie Software, a Chicago-based developer, never had a mega hit. Alex Seropian created the company in 1991 while studying computer science at the University of Chicago. Seropian self-published a game, *Operation: Desert Storm*, for the Macintosh. Upon graduation, he had offers for programming jobs at Microsoft and Morgan Stanley. His father, a doctor, counseled him to work for a while before trying to start his own company. But Seropian didn't take the advice. He got serious about the game company, shipping the disks from his apartment. The folklore at Bungie was that he had stolen disks from Microsoft (where he had interned) to create the floppy disks for *Operation: Desert Storm*.

"There was never any proof of that," Seropian said.

He convinced another Macintosh-loving classmate, Jason Jones, to join him at Bungie after Jones showed him a build of a game called *Minotaur: The Labyrinths*. Seropian thought it was a very cool game. They sat together hand-assembling copies of *Minotaur* in Seropian's apartment. More than 25,000 copies of Desert Storm sold, but only about 2,500 copies of *Minotaur* sold, partly because it required the use of a computer modem for networking. Then, Jones and Seropian created a game called *Pathways to Darkness*, which would become the first 3-D texture-mapped game on the Apple Macintosh.

For two years, Seropian didn't make any money. Maybe he should have taken that job at Morgan Stanley. His girlfriend financed him, and he later made the smart move of marrying her. In the middle of *Pathways to Darkness*, Seropian thought that they could really have a future doing this for a living. Both Jones and Seropian were still writing code, but Seropian handled the business side. As *Pathways* took off, he finally hired a company to package and send out disks to customers. They moved to an old concrete school building in Pilsen, near the South Side of Chicago. By the summer of 1994, Bungie had a half-dozen people.

After *Pathways*, Bungie broke out with a title called *Marathon*, a first-person shooter, set aboard an interstellar colony space ship. Bungie became a star in the small community of Mac game developers. Seropian thought that pulling together Bungie by the bootstraps had a good effect. The company relied on a do-it-yourself mentality, and it grew organically, learning things on its own over time. It also listened to its fans. Macintosh fans were a captive audience, since most game companies ignored them. Seropian's team would go to trade shows and play games with fans and listen to what they thought was cool in the game space.

Bungie followed with games such as *Myth*, but those titles never sold more than about 350,000 units, small by modern sales comparisons. They expanded in size, tapping the talents of musician Marty O'Donnell in 1996, and began porting their games to Microsoft's platforms. The Apple market share was dwindling and it was becoming clear that Bungie needed a new platform. Jones was still able to work on just one project at a time, but Bungie now had three teams and had a publishing division run by Peter Tamte. Seropian felt the days of being an independent developer were numbered, and he started looking around for buyers. Bungie needed a fundamental change in the way that it operated. Self-publishing was going away. When word of the Xbox surfaced, Bungie gave Ed Fries at Microsoft a call.

Bungie's crew wanted to break out with their new game. The team stole the show at the Macworld Expo in early 1998. Then it created a stunning demo of *Halo* at the E3 expo in May, 1999, complete with pulse-pounding music and spectacular 3-D effects such as a realistic outdoor environment. Fries saw potential in the deal. One of his business development managers, John Jordan, negotiated a complicated deal to buy Bungie. It wasn't an easy to deal to pull off because Bungie had committed to making titles for Take-Two Interactive Software.

The allure for Bungie was clear. It needed time to iterate over and over again on *Halo*. It needed to modify the game and test it, and repeat that cycle until the game was good enough to ship. Slowly, Bungie's team pulled the camera in closer and closer until the game became a first-person shooter.

"The chance to work on Xbox -- the chance to work with a company that took games seriously," Jones said in an interview posted on Bungie's web site. "Before that, we worried that we'd get bought by someone who just wanted Mac ports or didn't have a clue." Jon Kimmich, a planner for Ed Fries, visited Bungie with Stuart Moulder. As they were negotiating, Seropian realized that he had been an intern in Kimmich's group at Microsoft, where Seropian had worked on a programming tool. "It was funny how things come around," Seropian said.

The deal was announced June 19, 2000. Microsoft spent an estimated $30 million. Under the terms, Take-Two got the rights to Bungie's old properties like

Myth, and Bungie's California team had to complete a Japanese "anime" style game called Oni for Take-Two. The Chicago Bungie team voluntarily moved to Redmond in the fall of 2000 so that they could be close to the Xbox hardware team. Almost every member of the staff moved out. Seropian was the studio manager, while Jones spearheaded the development of *Halo.* They had barely 14 months before they had to finish *Halo* for the launch of the Xbox. As the deadline neared, even Steve Ballmer and Bill Gates wanted to know when it would be done. The game was released on Nov. 15, 2001, along with the Xbox.

It was a wonderful gamble. No one had really pulled off a fantastic first-person shooter for a video game console. In that sense, *Halo* was critical in pulling over fans from the PC to the Xbox. It was far easier to point and shoot at something with a computer mouse, where you could just quickly point directly at your target using a single hand, than it was to use two thumbs to position a target with a game controller. Jones' *Halo* team was experimenting with the hardware prototypes and game controllers.

After an initial assessment, they ditched the Internet multiplayer game, saving that project for *Halo* 2. They decided that they need to focus on getting single player right and the project would be too complicated if they focused on multiplayer as well.

Instead, they built a single-player game with a strong story between a Clint Eastwood-style Spartan male warrior and a wise-cracking female computer avatar. The Master Chief and Cortana actually had some funny lines. Bungie had found the right balance of game play and story. The story revolved around the conflict between humans and an alien race called

Master Chief at Xbox headquarters

The Covenant. The aliens find a powerful artifact on a ring-shaped planet named *Halo.* The artifact promises to shift the balance of power in the war, and only the Master Chief, the Spartan warrior, can stop them. The story had borrowed from science fiction literature. But it was reasonably original, and Bungie eventually tapped a writer, Brannon Boren, to be the keeper of "The *Halo* Story Bible," a closely guarded document that described the *Halo* universe in all of its detail, from the history of the Spartan bioengineering warrior program to Master

Chief's childhood. Another writer, Eric Nylund, wrote a novel, *Halo: The Fall of Reach*, that filled in the back story.

Within that narrative there was a lot of action. In 30 seconds, the game player would engage in something fun that they would repeat over and over again. The enemies had the smarts to dodge out of the way when attacked, and the objects in the world had real physics behind them, such as a *Ghost* motorcycle-like hovercraft that could coast into a group of enemies and knock them over. The player would maneuver his warrior, fire his machine gun, toss a grenade or two, switch weapons to dispatch a different type of enemy, pick up some ammo and move on to the next group of enemies. Variations on this theme could keep the gamer occupied for 20 hours.

The team that came up with this basic mechanic was small. Jones and his crew had relocated to Redmond so quickly that Jones didn't have time to change his Illinois license plates. When the *Oni* team in Los Angeles finished its work, Fries transferred the people to Redmond to help finish *Halo*. A team of about 50 artists, programmers, designers and others assembled to crank the game out. They worked like crazy to get the game done, ferreting out more than 10,000 bugs before they shipped.

Among their brilliant accomplishments was figuring out an intuitive way for players to target and shoot with the thumbsticks and buttons on a game controller. They built in a little bit of an assist – making the cross hairs stay on top of a target for a split second longer than normal – without making it too easy to shoot down enemies. Players who practiced with the controller could get a hang of the game within a matter of minutes. The game experience was thus a mixture of both fast-paced action and skill – a thinker's shooter. Not since *Golden Eye 007* on the Nintendo 64 had a shooter succeeded so well on a video game console.

"We were proud that we nailed the controller," said Pete Parsons, who headed the marketing of *Halo*.

The game also made use of the hard disk drive. The game transferred images from the slow DVD drive to the faster hard disk, constantly caching enough images to keep the game from slowing down. While players on other consoles had to constantly wait for new scenes to load, the *Halo* gamers didn't have to wait as long. The game also used the hard disk to constantly store saved games so that players wouldn't have to restart a level from scratch after their character died.

Fries had made a lot of gambles in his career. With the exception of the *Age of Empires* series, none had worked out as well as *Halo* for the original Xbox. The game kept on selling more than a year after its launch, and it was the reason that people bought the console. The game had sold well over 10 million copies, often with brand new Xbox consoles.

"The cult status, the amount of fan fiction that was being written, the tournaments and *Halo* parties all showed that people cared a lot about the game," said Pete Parsons, who helped market the first *Halo*. "It was striking a chord for people, a pop culture phenomenon."

While *Halo* was taking off, most of the other Xbox games were not. *Project*

Gotham Racing, a new franchise based on city car racing, sold well. But Microsoft launched bombs such as the role-playing game *Azurik: Rise of Perathia*, that featured a blue-skinned hero.

With Bungie inside Microsoft, Fries staffed up the division and poured more resources into *Halo 2*. Getting this game out the door was the top priority for the current generation Xbox, which sorely needed more hits. Sony had a variety of exclusives, such as *Gran Turismo, Grand Theft Auto: Vice City*, and the *Final Fantasy* series. Consequently, the PS2 was outselling the Xbox five to one. The pressure was on to keep pace. Now the fans of *Halo* wanted to make sure that Microsoft took proper care of their beloved franchise.

Coming up with the hits was as tough a job as creating hit movies in Hollywood. Like any game business chief, Fries had a variety of options to pursue in order to produce hits. He could fund sequels such as *Halo 2*, but he couldn't rely upon such games to garner brand new audiences that Microsoft had never had before. Thus, he had to constantly find and develop new talent to make brand new games. He could buy the rights to big movie or book franchises such as *Harry Potter*, but he was easily outbid by companies such as Electronic Arts, which could guarantee the biggest audience for a franchise property by making versions of the game for all of the game platforms, reaching the largest possible audience. While Microsoft was rich, its budget wasn't unlimited and it couldn't flush much money away on expensive licenses.

Fries' answer had always been to work closely with the talent. He had continued playing games passionately. He was a real insider in gaming circles. He believed that gamers were artists and he loved keeping up with the latest. He personally returned the phone calls of game developers who were pitching new games. His team of game producers included business development scouts whose job was to find and secure new game teams for the best price. Fries always showed up at the Game Developers Conference, a trade show for developers that drew 10,000 of them to the San Jose Convention Center every year. That was where he poached developers, such as Oddworld Inhabitants, from Sony's PlayStation 2 camp.

"A lot of deals got done at the GDC," he said.

Fries didn't believe in buying big publishers for a ton of money. He felt that was a waste. The original Xbox chief, Rick Thompson, made the rounds with big publishers asking them if they wanted to sell out. He went into negotiations with Nintendo, but the aging CEO, Hiroshi Yamauchi, quashed the deal. Thompson made the rounds to Sega, Capcom, Electronic Arts and most other publishers, with no luck.

Fries was relieved, since he wanted to build Microsoft's success in games organically. The acquisition of Bungie fit perfectly with Fries' philosophy because it wasn't an expensive deal, and the talent had been overlooked. For the original Xbox, Fries had such a short timetable that he signed up dozens of game developers in a brief time, cashing in on all of his personal relationships. Some of the games for the Xbox bombed outright, but a hit like *Halo* could pay for a dozen failures. Still, the pace of adding new studios had been too torrid, and once Fries had enough to cover all the basic genres, from sports to adventure, he pulled back.

Since Fries had run the games division for so long, he had built credibility with Bill Gates and Steve Ballmer. But mistakes accompanied every hit. Because of that, Fries faced some additional oversight. He had always been teamed with a numbers guy, Shane Kim, since the beginning of his tenure in the game division. Kim wasn't much of a gamer. Like many people, he got nauseated playing first-person shooter games. But Fries liked to think that he taught Kim about games, while Kim taught Fries more about business.

Bryan Lee, the chief financial officer of Microsoft's Home and Entertainment division, wanted tighter financial controls. Lee had joined the company from Sony's entertainment business. He came in as a purely financial guy. He was following Ballmer's marching orders to cut costs in every division of the company. So Lee proposed a process where he approved every game from a financial perspective. Lee was staging a showdown. He called these approvals "Ultimates Meetings." Fries sat in on one of them and it was "incredibly confrontational."

Fries resisted what he considered to be interference. He suggested that the spending controls and marketing should be put under Peter Moore, the ex-Sega marketer. Fries respected Moore because he understood the video game business, while Mitch Koch and Bryan Lee came from Hollywood. But Moore and Koch shared duties, splitting up marketing and sales throughout the world. Fries thought that marketing under Moore would give him back control of his business and his game marketing strategy. The new approvals process slowed down the speed at which Microsoft could get talent on board. It was bureaucratic, but it would steer Microsoft toward profit-making deals. Fries also had to meet his financial goals for every fiscal year. If something slipped, as most complicated game development projects did, then Fries had to come up with either more hits or cuts in the budget in order to compensate.

Financing games always involved some difficult accounting judgments. When publishers such as Fries approved a game, they almost always gave an advance to the developer to start working on it. That advance was supposed to cover the cost of making the game. Usually, to keep control of a project, the publisher doled the money out in pieces. With each milestone reached, such as working code, the developer got more money.

At first, Microsoft booked the advances as loans. The debt got paid back as the game started generating revenue. At any given time, Microsoft had $100 million or $200 million loaned out for games. As it canceled games, it wrote off the loans as bad debt. But the bulk of the loans didn't show up as expenses in any given quarter. The problem with this kind of accounting was that it made canceling bad games harder than it should be, since it resulted in a big shock for expenses in any given quarter upon cancellation.

Then the company switched to more conservative accounting, booking the advances as expenses. As Microsoft built up its portfolio for Xenon, it recorded a lot of upfront advances as expenses, making its financial picture seem even worse. Either way, Fries always saw the expenses as a form of political capital. He had to justify the spending to both Robbie Bach, his boss, and Bryan Lee, the numbers guy.

The acquisition of Rare was a far bigger gamble than buying Bungie. Rare was, for the most part, a developer, not a publisher, and so it appealed more to Fries' style of finding and nurturing talent. But after that $375 million deal, Fries was once again under the gun. Bach wanted cutbacks in other parts of the game business in order to keep a lid on costs.

Fries wanted to keep expanding the empire and making big bets on a variety of games. Accounting could vary for game development expenses. He saw the Catch 22 on the Xbox 360.

"Spend less, sell more games," he said. "I don't know how to do that."

Fries felt that there was no way to beat Sony by spending less than Sony did on games and developers. Microsoft had to spend more, precisely because it was the underdog. Sony's brand name and huge console sales were natural draws to the most talented game developers and their publishers. To win them over to its side, Microsoft only had the argument that its technology was better and would allow the game developers to fully express themselves as artists. This worked for some talented visionaries such as Peter Molyneux, an English developer whose titles almost always sold more than a million copies. But most of the Japanese game developers and publishers made tepid commitments to the Xbox. With the current Xbox hemorrhaging money, he couldn't win that argument. Fries needed more hits to get more money.

That wasn't the best way to run a "first party" publisher, a publisher that was part of a console maker's company. After all, part of the duty of first party was to show all the other game publishers what could be accomplished on the platform. Fries saw the duty of first party as more than just making money. It had to give people a reason to buy the platform in the first place. It ought to make the biggest investments to pave the way for others to follow. Moreover, first-party publishers operated at a disadvantage to other independent publishers. Electronic Arts could develop a game and then publish it across six platforms. But Microsoft had to make exclusive games to show off the Xbox, publishing a game on only one platform. That wasn't conducive to maximizing profits.

"How should you view first party?" Fries asked. "Is it a business or is it a marketing platform to sell the console?"

Bach forced an answer upon Fries. Now that Rare was on board, plenty of other franchises could be jettisoned. The executive group decided that it was time to scale back on investments in experimental games.

It made business sense. With the first Xbox, Fries needed to throw a lot of money around to find new franchises for Microsoft's first console. It didn't have the credibility to steal away some of the best developers and publishers from Sony and Nintendo, so it fed a lot of money into small developers.

Now that Xbox was off to a good start in both the U.S. and Europe, developers were starting to come on board on their own. No longer did they need to be bribed. They saw the Xbox as a stable platform that had grabbed the high-end gamer.

Third party support was growing tremendously for the Xbox. Electronic Arts had played coy for a long time. But now the biggest independent game publisher was in talks to support Xbox Live and move all of its sports titles to the Xbox. Since Microsoft received a $6 or $7 royalty on every third-party game, some executives questioned whether Microsoft needed the first party group to work on "filler" games that weren't going to be blockbusters.

From the perspective of the money guys, Microsoft had to impose some limits on its grand adventure in games. It couldn't spend like crazy to put the rivals out of business. That could lead to a huge loss, and it could also draw the attention of antitrust regulators, who looked down on any attempt to use monopoly profits from one market to squeeze into another market. Such predatory practices were considered illegal for monopolists to use.

At about the same time that Nick Baker and Jeff Andrews started dreaming up the Xenon chips, Bungie got started on its next games. It had devoted one team to a game where players laid siege to a medieval castle. That project wasn't working out, and Jason Jones canceled it. Bungie had access to nearly 70 people now. But some of the early magic was dissipating. Against his initial wishes, Jones had to pour almost all of Bungie's available resources into *Halo* 2.

1. "Opening the Xbox: Inside Microsoft's Plan to Unleash an Entertainment Revolution," by Dean Takahashi, Prima Publishing, 2002, page 58.

CHAPTER SEVENTEEN

BACK AND FORTH

nce Bach gave his green light in the memo dubbed "3," J Allard's team went to work on "Xe 30," using 3 as a guide. The Xe 30 document had to articulate the strategic plan laid out in 3 in much more detail. But to create his memo, Allard really needed to get his team working on Xenon. He launched them and reviewed their feedback. Each functional team within the group started transferring and hiring more people to get the work done. The dedicated Xenon team assembled itself to figure out what the soul of the console was going to be. Everyone knew it was going to be a game box, but what else would it be able to do? What could Microsoft do differently than the competition? What would be its unique contribution?

Starting in April, 2003, the teams took Bach's original memo and raced to layout their pieces of the puzzle. The decision making started at the highest level of the hardware architecture. The emissaries from each group weighed in with their proposals. Larry Yang's crew had scoped out the chip makers during 2002 and they had a good idea of the prospects for Xenon's core architecture. The microprocessor and the graphics chip had to work in tandem. It was as if the microprocessor built the skeleton of an image in a game, and the graphics chip put the skin on it.

On the original Xbox, Greg Gibson felt the box contained wasted performance and wasted silicon. Some pieces of the system were imported directly from the PC and had no relevance in a game console. They were wasted resources. This time, Gibson wanted to spend all his money on real performance.

To Peter Glaskowsky, then-editor of the Microprocessor Report, Microsoft could have coasted on the platform that it created. The easiest thing would have been to go with the next generation of Intel microprocessors and Nvidia graphics chips. The box would have been backward compatible with all the original Xbox games, and it would have been simple to program. Microsoft could draft in behind the R&D

of the PC industry, and it could ask the chip makers to customize a version of the PC chips for the console again. "That would have been the path of least resistance," Glaskowsky said.

Intel's engineers said that they would be able to ship a chip that would break the 4-gigahertz performance barrier. Code-named Tejas, the chip was a single processor with screaming performance. It would be built with 90-nanometer production process (something that only the newest chips could take advantage of in 2005) and debut for the PC in the second quarter of 2005. That was just in time to suit the schedule for the launch of Xenon. It would have new instructions for improved audio multistreaming, speech recognition, and Dolby Digital. It would be more than enough for game developers looking for a leap forward, and it would likely be much simpler to program than the complicated Cell microprocessors that Sony was making.

But the chip came with a high price. Microsoft couldn't afford to eat a lot of cost, but it needed Tejas' performance. Moreover, buying an Intel chip brought other headaches. The chip's predecessor burned well over 100 watts of power, and this chip promised to be just as hot. Fitting such a chip and the cooling mechanisms inside a game console was a challenge. That was part of the reason that the Xbox was so big in the first place. Already, word was coming back from marketing loud and clear that the box had to be smaller to take off in Japan. Intel had only just started to pay attention to power.

To Gibson, the key measurement for the choice of chip was performance per watt per dollar. That is, the chips had to balance speed, power efficiency, and costs in order to fit in a low-cost video game console. The chips also had to balance both customization and familiarity. A custom chip could ultimately be the fastest and the lowest cost to make, but designing one from scratch could take a long time and it required high upfront development costs. If it fell behind schedule, a more general-purpose chip might wind up being faster. And it had to have a familiar architecture so that game developers could learn its nuances quickly.

"It was going to be a series of trade-offs," Gibson said. "The schedule, performance, cost of goods for each part, and development costs. Our No. 1 priority was schedule for strategic reasons. We wanted to beat Sony to market, and didn't want them to beat us."

On top of the power problem, neither Intel nor Nvidia were inclined to share their intellectual property with Microsoft. This time, Holmdahl continued to insist that Microsoft had to own the rights to the design. It was critical to bringing down the costs of the hardware and making money on the whole Xbox endeavor. He wanted to be able to take the design and cost-reduce the chips on his own schedule. That meant redesigning the chip, shrinking it so that it used less material and was easier to fabricate. He wanted to have the right to have the chip made in any factory so that he could play manufacturers off against each other on pricing. And he eventually wanted to be able to combine the CPU and the graphics chip into a single chip in order to drive costs out of the box. Those elements were essential to making money on Xenon.

"That's not our traditional way of doing business," said Don MacDonald, an Intel executive.

Intel typically owned its own designs, redesigned its chips on its own schedule, and made them in its own captive factories. Nvidia did the same, with the exception of making its chips at either IBM's factories or those belonging to Taiwan Semiconductor Manufacturing Co. Neither Intel and Nvidia would ever trust each other enough to share their chip designs with each so they could be merged into a single chip. Negotiations with those vendors hit a brick wall.

To Nick Baker and Jeff Andrews, that was OK. They saw that ATI was starting to take the lead in PC graphics chips. ATI was a $2 billion company with 3,000 employees. Its Radeon 9700 chip that came out in August, 2002, was retaking the high-end of the graphics chip market for the first time ever for ATI.

Bob Feldstein, vice president of engineering at ATI, gathered a dozen ATI veterans, including Clay Taylor and Steve Narayan, to contemplate graphics for a game box. They knew that Microsoft wanted to highlight high-definition gaming and launch in the fall of 2005 at the price of a traditional video game console, about $300. They also knew that Microsoft wanted to own the design that ATI would create and fabricate it in a factory of its choosing. While that was a tough hurdle for Nvidia, ATI's Santa Clara team had done such a deal with Nintendo already. It received a fee for the engineering work and a royalty on each console sold. It wasn't as much money as if ATI had made the chip for Nintendo, but it was money that floated to the bottom line.

With that information, they contemplated what they could do, using different teams than the Santa Clara engineers who were again going to work for Nintendo. Feldstein tapped engineers in Marlboro, Mass.; Orlando, Fla., and Toronto, Canada.

"We were doing a chip from the ground up," Feldstein said. "It was kind of liberating. We had long pursued the ideal of photorealism. We could see it up there just on top of the hill. We thought we could deliver fluid reality, and that would truly be a next-generation experience."

They didn't have to worry about making a chip work with all sorts of display resolutions. All they had to worry about was making it run on standard TVs as well as high-definition TVs. (In this case, running at 720P). The engineers tapped pieces of the PC chips that were already in the works to shorten the development schedule, but they also proposed several unique pieces that made the chip different from a PC graphics chip. In essence, they needed to create a machine gun that fired a bunch of dots at a display screen, and they had to make sure that the machine gun never ran out of ammo and never overheated.

Their alternative to the expensive PC graphics chip was to simplify it. They took two different processors that handle separate jobs on the PC graphics chip, and then combined them into a single processor that could handle both jobs. They called this combination processor a "unified shader." A shader is a program that the graphics chip runs to make a 3-D illusion look real. Two types of shaders were necessary. One type noted where an object was in 3-D space. The other gave it the proper lighting, color, and surface texture.

In the ATI design, the unified shader was smart enough to juggle between the two types of shaders. The graphics chip would have 48 unified shader pipelines running at the same time. It wasn't as many as the 64 that Nick Baker originally wanted, but it was better than the 32 the team had expected. But because it was more efficient at balancing the load of work at any given moment, it might actually be able to keep up with a graphics chip that had many more of the separated shaders. The design for this graphics chip was similar to a cook in a fast food restaurant with 48 arms, making both pizzas and tacos at the same time. The result in the restaurant would be more food served, and the result for gamers would be more detailed visuals. Now, games would have objects with realistic fur, hair, grass or cloth.

Jon Peddie, a graphics expert and analyst at Jon Peddie Research, believed that the unified shaders would be an experiment for the entire industry. Microsoft would be taking a chance by being the first to undertake it. The question was whether the unified shaders could balance the workload or not. The system had to efficiently allocate the shaders to either type of processing at any given moment. The unified shaders were less likely to be wasted. But they were complicated.

"Are they more efficient? The answer is yes, no, maybe," Peddie said. "Some observers think unified shaders are not the obvious right answer right now, that we as an industry just have to learn more about how to exploit them, the Xbox360 is a great laboratory. However, in the long term, we expect that the industry will migrate toward a unified architecture, because we'll solve all of the problems with a unified design, and maybe the efficiency will matter less than the flexibility."

The Microsoft engineers also thought about the bottlenecks in the PC and how to deal with the limited amount of memory in the machine. The Xbox had only 64 megabytes of main memory, and Greg Gibson, the system architect, figured that Microsoft would be able to afford about 256 megabytes in Xenon. This was such a scarce resource in PCs that most graphics cards came with their own dedicated memory. This PC approach wasn't an option in a game console because it drove up the costs dramatically. Without that dedicated memory, the graphics chip had to wait a long time to get data from memory. That slowed the machine down, and it was often the reason why console graphics lagged behind the more expensive personal computers that hardcore gamers bought.

So Feldstein's team came up with a solution. They would include a separate chip that held nothing but memory for the graphics chip. The amount of memory was small, about 10 megabytes, but it would allow the graphics chip to keep itself busy with processing tasks rather than go out over the long pathway to main memory. Dubbed "intelligent memory," this added some costs to the box, but it reduced the bottlenecks without requiring a lot more memory. At first, the memory would be a separate chip that was connected to the graphics chip in a common package, or multichip module. Over time, this memory created by

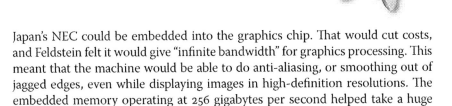
Japan's NEC could be embedded into the graphics chip. That would cut costs, and Feldstein felt it would give "infinite bandwidth" for graphics processing. This meant that the machine would be able to do anti-aliasing, or smoothing out of jagged edges, even while displaying images in high-definition resolutions. The embedded memory operating at 256 gigabytes per second helped take a huge amount of traffic off the data pathway to memory.

Lastly, ATI would combine the system memory controller, typically a separate chip in a PC, into the graphics chip itself. With the memory so close, the graphics chip itself didn't have to be as powerful as a PC graphics chip. That made it smaller and easier to produce. Again, that would cut costs. Microsoft's own engineers had to build some specialized translation software to make this new kind of shader work.

Nick Baker and Jeff Andrews sent their engineers back to evaluate the proposal. They wanted to make sure that this would work well with the solution being proposed by the microprocessor vendors. Feldstein favored Intel because of its track record, while IBM was a bigger risk. But he complied with Microsoft's request to come up with a joint solution with IBM. By the spring of 2003, ATI still didn't have a contract. But it had enough confidence to move forward, putting an engineering team to work.

IBM started working on the bus, or data pathway, that would have common elements inside the microprocessor and the graphics chip. This meant that IBM was proposing to design part of the graphics chip. IBM proposed a bus that could transfer data at 22 gigabytes per second, much faster than a PC. This was the kind of collaboration that Microsoft needed to make sure that the solution for Xenon was properly customized. They didn't want a solution for a personal computer.

The technical solutions on the graphics chip were moving along swiftly, but the contract negotiations were starting to drag out. It was always very hard for chip designers to figure out what prices they could charge for chips that weren't even designed yet. So much depended on the yield, or how many good chips came out of every batch. Typically, costs were fixed for a silicon wafer. If that wafer had low yields where only a few chips worked, the chips had to be priced high. But if the yield was high, and the wafer produced 90 working chips, then each chip could be priced lower. These were unknowns a few years from shipping. Who was responsible for cost reduction, which often meant lots of engineers working on a redesign? Who was going to take the profits when yields improved in the factory?

"There was both a terror of losing the contract and the terror of winning the contract," Feldstein said.

The contract teams started their negotiations, leaving both companies room to opt out. Nvidia, despite its aversion to working with Microsoft again, was still in the bidding. It was proposing its own solution, and the Microsoft team knew life would be so much easier with the backward compatibility to the original Xbox that Nvidia offered. Nvidia could also offer the option of lowering prices on Xbox 1 graphics chips, where it was making healthy profit margins, much to

Microsoft's irritation. Still, ATI met most of the requirements that would enable Microsoft to proceed with more profitable hardware from the beginning of the Xenon launch. Hence, ATI didn't know it, but it had the inside track.

Nobody inside Microsoft was demanding backward compatibility at the time. IBM was also far ahead of Intel in designing multicore microprocessors that operated at low power. IBM had launched its first multicore Power 4 microprocessors for supercomputers and business machines in 2001. It had the right technology that could put a supercomputer in a game box. Jim Comfort, a vice president at IBM, had said that IBM was willing to deliver Waternoose, a custom microprocessor, to Microsoft. It was also willing to accommodate Microsoft's wishes on owning the design that its engineers came up with, for the most part.

IBM had 450 engineers working with Sony and Toshiba teams on the Cell chips in Austin, Texas, but IBM could tap plenty of other design teams in places such as Rochester and East Fishkill, New York, and Burlington, Vermont. Microsoft wanted to separate the microprocessor into separate pieces. Microsoft would own the intellectual property, or the specific design that they came up with. IBM would create the design, using both custom engineering work and its existing library of PowerPC designs. And Microsoft wanted to be able to use either IBM's factories or anyone else's who could make the chips for the right price.

Doing custom design work was right up IBM's alley. In contrast to Intel, IBM didn't mind loading its factories with designs from all sorts of customers. It even operated a design services business. That is, it hired out its chip designers to create chips based on what its customers wanted. Lou Gerstner, then-CEO of IBM, was emphasizing services businesses over hardware, so he liked the idea of chip designers hiring themselves out for engineering fees.

IBM's designers had just finished working on a PowerPC chip for a blade server, a low-power commercial machine for serving up web sites to Internet surfers. Another team at IBM had finished designing a dual-core microprocessor, the PowerPC 970MP, for Apple, which was going to use it in its G5 machines due to launch in 2003. IBM assigned Ilan Spillinger, a former Intel chip guru, to manage the program for Microsoft, while Dave Shippy would work as the projects chief engineer. They brainstormed with Jeff Andrews from Microsoft about the kind of system they wanted to put together. Since Microsoft had chosen to launch in 2005, they calculated the schedule by moving backward in time, taking into account all of the things they had to do. It would likely take two years to get the chip into production. That meant that the design had to start in the fall of 2003. IBM started doing some work, but it had to hold back until the contracts were signed. It figured that it would use a 90-nanometer manufacturing process to build the chip, the same one that it would use to create the Cell chips for Sony.

IBM knew that it could make a derivative of the efficient PowerPC core that it had created for Sony without a huge redesign effort. It anticipated that it would be able to include a feature known as out-of-order execution. With this feature, a processor could run faster because it could take instructions and reorder them for the most efficient processing. The drawback was that it took up more space on a chip than the simpler, in-order execution of earlier processors.

Using a low-power Power PC core, IBM expected that it would create a chip that ran at a clock rate of 3.5 gigahertz and put three processing cores on a single chip. Each of the cores would also be capable of running two programs, or threads, at the same time. In terms of performance, the machine would be capable of running six times the number of threads on the original Xbox. And it would run four times faster in terms of megahertz. The cores would also be small, meaning that they wouldn't be extremely costly.

In the same amount of time it took a single-core processor to get one task done, this CPU would do six tasks. A multicore chip wouldn't have the highest megahertz. That meant that a single core chip would likely get one task done the fastest. But a multicore chip would be much faster at getting six tasks done at once. PC users often made the mistake of buying a new machine purely on megahertz, which measured single-task performance. But they often didn't consider multitasking results which were harder to understand.

Andrews wanted to include some new instructions for the PowerPC architecture that would make it more suitable to games.

"We were willing to fully customize to whatever they wanted," Spillinger said. "Even if that meant changing the instruction set."

One of the problems they decided to attack was the replication of objects in 3-D scenery. Typically, artists would create one kind of tree and use it over and over again. That's why forests looked so bad in games. Every tree looked the same. If the developer hired more artists, it could create different types of trees. [1] Even then, storing the data for all those unique trees in limited main memory was a problem.

With the Xenon CPU, Spillinger's team decided to store high-level descriptions of the trees in main memory. The CPU would take those descriptions and generate the trees on the fly, a technique dubbed "procedural synthesis." One part of the processor, which was running on a separate thread, would determine the location of the trees. Then the graphics chip would fetch that data from the CPU directly, render the details, and then output the image to the screen. Using this method, the team thought they could create the forest with a lot less data in memory. In a sense, the CPU would take a compressed image and determine its location, and then the graphics chip would decompress the image. It was like making a quilt. The CPU would determine the size and location of the patches, and the graphics chip would create the patches and color them appropriately.

Mike Abrash, Nick Baker, Jeff Andrews and a programmer, Andrew Goossen, also came up with an idea to keep the graphics chip even busier by allowing it to fetch data from the memory, dubbed the L2 cache, within the IBM microprocessor. They would lock down a portion of that memory so that it could make its data available to the graphics chip, which could bypass the much longer route to main memory again. This pathway would operate at a speed of 10 gigabytes per second. The idea was so novel that they filed for a patent on the idea.

Some game developers didn't like the multicore solution, but it grew on them as they started to understand that power consumption, cost, and performance all had to be balanced. Adding the multiple cores was better than creating a hot rod that burned hot and heavy. And Microsoft figured that most of the tools that developers used for making games for the Xbox could be converted to create games for the PowerPC architecture. That would give developers a familiar environment in which to work.

Nick Baker and Jeff Andrews commissioned teams to run simulations to evaluate the performance of this kind of chip. They liked what they saw. Choosing IBM would cost them backward compatibility. But they could either choose not to make the new console compatible with the old games, or run the old games in emulation, a layer of software translation that simulated the old Xbox within the new environment. The new machine would be so fast it would be able to run the translation software without slowing the game down to unacceptable speeds.

Though IBM was designing Sony's chips as well, the Xenon microprocessor, dubbed Waternoose, would be far different. Bill Adamec, the Microsoft program manager for the chips, believed that the system the team was designing would be more powerful than any PC on the market, and possibly even more powerful than any PC that arrived on the market at the same time as the Xenon machine. He believed that Microsoft did a good job tossing out the technology from the PC that it didn't need in a game console and designing the parts that they needed for the console so that everything would work better together. And, as a result, that was why he thought games running on the Xenon console would look better than games running on a PC whose parts were designed much later.

The IBM teams weren't even allowed to talk to each other. Spillinger noted that his company badge wouldn't work in buildings where work was being done on Sony's chips. A Toshiba engineer in Austin, Texas, once made the mistake of sending an e-mail asking Sony game developers what they wanted in their game machines. The Sony developers worked in a separate division that wasn't even cleared to know anything about Cell. The Toshiba engineer was gone the next day.

Microsoft's engineers decided they could trust IBM. But that decision wasn't an easy one. Part of the problem was that picking IBM to create the CPU was a huge political problem. IBM and Microsoft had never been friends, ever since Microsoft's control of the operating system in IBM's original PC proved to be the undoing of IBM's technology monopoly and led to the great shift in power to Microsoft. IBM was still fighting Microsoft on a lot of fronts, the biggest of which was its promotion of the Linux operating system in large businesses. While IBM had a lot of business to gain by working with Microsoft, it could also gain by hanging Microsoft out to dry.

"There were a lot of meetings inside IBM over whether we should do any business at all with Microsoft," said one source knowledgeable about the matter. "Should we ally ourselves with Sony and let Microsoft twist in the wind? Why should we help them when we competed with them? Who had forgotten what they did to us on the original PC?"

Robbie Bach said that Bill Gates had to weigh in on the choice of the chip at least three times. Part of the reason was that it meant kicking out Intel, which had been Microsoft's partner on the PC for more than 20 years. Nick Baker and Jeff Andrews readied their slides and made their case to Gates and the other executives in late 2002. Dave Cutler, a brilliant operating system guru; Jim Allchin, the head of Windows; and Rick Rashid, the head of Microsoft Research, all weighed in with their opinions.

"Silicon was the thing that Bill was most involved in," Bach said. "It was the big level in cost structure. It's something that you are stuck with for seven years or so. Once you make a choice, it has ten downstream things that it affects. Bill has insight because he has been focused on the semiconductor industry for 30 years."

Gates came back for a couple of more meetings to discuss the IBM choice. One of the options still being considered was whether Xenon would be a full-fledged PC running Windows. If Windows ran on the computer, it made sense to keep Intel in the box. But no appropriate version of Windows existed. Windows XP, which launched in the fall of 2001, required a lot of memory just for its own purposes and it wasn't appropriate in the living room. Windows XP Media Center Edition was aimed squarely at the living room, but it was going to require hardware that cost about $2,000.

Everyone agreed that the technical solution from both IBM and ATI fit with Microsoft's plans, particularly on reducing the costs of the new machine. As 2002 turned into 2003, each team began the hardcore engineering work. All they had to do was sign contracts.

"On both sides, we thought the schedule was aggressive," said Adamec.

Once the IBM and ATI choice became the front runner, Allard's group reconvened. They had a schedule, their favorite chips, and the overall plan to beat Sony. Now they needed to fill in the rest of the picture. Larry Yang's silicon design team went to work on a video encoder, code-named "Ana," which they would design themselves. This chip would allow the machine to handle complex video or picture processing tasks. Under the direction of Microsoft engineer Greg Williams, Silicon Integrated Systems started working on an input-output chip, or "south bridge." And the buyers started sorting through all of the other commodity parts that they could use to fill out the rest of the system board. Companies such as Marvell Technology began working on wireless Internet networking chips, dubbed WiFi. Microsoft hadn't decided if it wanted to build wireless networking into the box, but now was the time to get the work done. Another team had to look at whether they could make the controllers wireless. Gibson's group of hardware engineers gradually grew as they undertook more tasks.

Once again, storage was going to be a huge decision. Microsoft wanted to judge whether the hard drive should be on every box or an option. It also had to decide whether the drive should be easily removable, so that consumers could swap out the drives or carry them wherever they wanted to go. The buyers engaged with the hard disk drive makers again. Seagate had become the sole supplier of the hard disk drives by the end of the Xbox cycle. The Scotts Valley, Calif., company had pleasantly surprised Microsoft by taking the cost per drive down from more than $50 at the start to something over $30. Seagate wanted the business again.

This time, Seagate had more time to prepare and it figured that it would customize a drive for Microsoft, but still take advantages of the high-volume economics of its PC drives. Since the box had to be smaller, Seagate started with a 2.5-inch drive for notebook computers. But since the Xbox 360 wasn't going to be moved around a lot, Seagate could remove some of the features that added costs. For instance, notebook drives had sensors that could detect whether the consumer had dropped the laptop. It would initiate an emergency mechanism that would lock the drive head so it didn't damage the disk during the fall. Laptop drives also had power management features that preserved the ability to run on batteries. In a wired Xbox 360, that wasn't necessary.

But even with the changes, Seagate would be able to adapt drives headed for laptops, meaning it could take advantage of the lower costs for the high-volume laptop drives. Most of Seagate's drives had relatively short product life cycles in terms of how long demand for each drive lasted. But now it had to plan to make a factory that would be in operation for several years. Seagate also made plans to reduce the costs of the chips that it used to control the drives. Instead of coming up with a $50-plus drive, Seagate said it could build a 20-gigabyte drive for $30 to $40. Last time around, the capacity of the drive was only eight gigabytes. It was a lot closer to the "Yugo cost structure" that the Microsoft finance guys wanted, said Pat O'Malley, senior vice president for finance for storage markets at Seagate. With this pitch, O'Malley figured that the drive business was Seagate's to lose.

Then the team debated what kind of storage disks to use for the games. The Xbox used the same DVD disks that movie studios used for home videos. Thanks to the PlayStation 2, it had become the standard in the industry. But now Sony and Toshiba were in a fight over the successor technology, which would hold at least five times more data and could store a film in the high-definition format. Sony wanted to use Blu-ray, a technology derived from its research into blue lasers. Toshiba wanted to evolve the traditional red laser with a technology it called HD DVD. Microsoft didn't want to get stuck with Betamax if the industry moved to VHS. But it looked like the drives for the new disks would be expensive and they would only begin to debut in 2005. For now, Microsoft sidestepped the question by assuming that it would continue to use DVDs. Most game developers didn't mind, since the data could be compressed on the DVDs and the DVDs would likely be faster at moving data into the machine than an HD drive.

"No one really thought that Blu-ray would be the paradigm shift," said Cameron Ferroni.

As these decisions came together, the mechanical engineers got a good idea of how large the box would be and how many components it would have to accommodate. They tried to figure out how to make the machine smaller so that it fit into audio-visual cabinets more easily, especially in places like Japan. Jeff Reents, the lead mechanical engineer, saw that the machine would still need one or two fans.[2] So the hardware engineers decided that it would be best to remove the power supply from the box and put it into the power cord. This was often done in laptop computers and other portable devices, but it made the cord look like a big snake that has swallowed something huge. In the case of Xenon, the power supply was so huge it would be like a boa constrictor choking on a tire. But it made the console itself much smaller.

1. "Inside the Xbox 360," Ars Technica, http://arstechnica.com/articles/ppaedia/cpu/xbox360-1.ars/2

2. "360: The Guts," Xbox.com, http://www.xbox.com/en-US/hardware/xbox360/xbox360theguts.htm

CHAPTER EIGHTEEN

WHO LET THE MARKETERS IN?

*O*nce the technical teams figured out some of their options, the marketing team could lend its voice. Throw a marketing guy in with a group of engineers, and you get trouble. In the spring of 2003, the tug of war over what would be inside the Xenon console was in full swing. Even as the executives gave their blessing to the 2005 launch date, the planners beneath them were going around in circles on the design.

After Robbie Bach put together his three-page memo on the Xenon strategy and J Allard began work on his thirty-page memo, known as "30," more planners got involved. That memo was essentially the go-ahead for those reporting to J Allard to launch full scale technology investigations. The Xenon team was staffing up. Now more people focused on it full time. Chip Wood, Andrew McCombie, and Jon Thomason had started early. They were joined by A.J. Redmer from the games group; George Peckham, who headed third-party game developer relations; system designer Greg Gibson; his boss, Todd Holmdahl, the hardware chief; Mike Groesch from finance; Par Singh from the Japanese subsidiary, Cameron Ferroni, representing Xbox Live, and J Allard himself. Groesch took the minutes and kept the team on schedule. This team started as the Xe 30 team, and it later morphed into the Xenon Integration Group, or XIG, pronounced "zig."

As time went on, the top executives joined in. Bill Gates received an update on the progress every six weeks or so.

David Reid was the first marketer to be assigned full-time on Xenon. He took over from Andrew McCombie, who had been handling the Xenon marketing strategy on a part-time basis. Though Reid was a late arrival in the summer of 2003, he helped guide the so-called "North Star" process, which meant synchronizing Xenon with the rest of Microsoft. It was a union of marketing and product development. Working with Jeff Henshaw, who was focusing on alternative entertainment for Xenon beyond games, Reid could help gather the list of features that

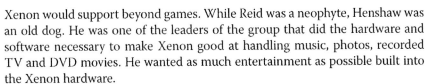

Xenon would support beyond games. While Reid was a neophyte, Henshaw was an old dog. He was one of the leaders of the group that did the hardware and software necessary to make Xenon good at handling music, photos, recorded TV and DVD movies. He wanted as much entertainment as possible built into the Xenon hardware.

At 33, Reid had been at Microsoft for a few years. He had gotten an MBA at Wharton's business school and did a brief stint at Hasbro Interactive. Then he took a job at consulting firm McKinsey & Co., handling marketing for online businesses. He decided he wanted to work in games and was hired into Mitch Koch's marketing group to work on PC games marketing. He moved over to Xbox, and his background was sufficient to horrify any self-respecting engineer. In July, 2003, he joined the Xenon team. His job was to lend a marketing voice to the design process so that Microsoft would hit the right market. Adding the right functions from the rest of Microsoft's resources, from digital music to Internet video playback, could play a key role in making the box more appealing.

"The process was to get agreement up front," he said. "It started with a list of 150 things people were working on, but here are the 10 that are the most important."

Jon Thomason, a former Windows executive who ran Xbox software, had close ties to the rest of the company so he consulted them early on matters such as where the Windows Media Player was going with video playback and how to make Xenon connect with handheld music players such as the iPod. While those who advocated Windows in the Xbox had lost out the last time around, they were happy to some degree that Xenon would benefit from a piece of Windows.

Joe Belfiore and Dave Alles from the eHome group in the Windows division decided to go to lunch with their friends in the Xbox division, Jeff Henshaw, the head of alternative Xbox entertainment, and Chris Pirich, one of the software chiefs. At the Redmond Brewery, they ordered pizza and beers and chatted as friends at an outdoor table. Version 2 of the Windows Media Center PC would ship in the fall of 2003. The eHome was also planning to build extenders for the Media Center PC so that the content on the PC could be played in another TV in the house. The extenders were simple pieces of hardware. They would plug into the home network on one end and into a TV on the other. They would include video playback hardware, and cost perhaps $50.

As the group talked, they realized that the Xenon console would be a perfect candidate to have a built-in Media Center Extender. It already had all the technology it needed to include an extender at no extra cost.

"Listen," Belfiore said. "We think the Xbox is a killer platform. As you guys work on Xbox 2, you will want more multimedia to go with it. We think this is going to be a great match." Around the table, everyone started thinking about how to make the built-in extender for Xenon happen.

To Henshaw, the idea fit with his vision for alternative entertainment. The Xbox had the hardcore gamers. But how could it become more appealing to the rest of the people in the household? Sure, it could play movies and music. But if it could fit snugly with a Media Center PC, the Xenon machine stood a chance to be more broadly appealing to wider audiences. This fit with J Allard's vision of reaching a billion people, including a lot of people who weren't gamers. The team took the ideas back to their respective staffs, and Belfiore authorized the eHome team to work with the Xbox team to build the extender for the Xbox.

Part of Reid's job was to analyze why Microsoft scored so well with the hardcore gamers last time but lost the battle to Sony with the mass market. Allard was serious about reaching a billion people. But Reid didn't think that hardcore route was the way to get there.

"It was clear to us that we built a product that didn't appeal to everybody," he said. "We built credibility with the core. But we needed to appeal to the broader range of people without alienating the core."

Reid's purpose was to hammer home the trends that mattered so the rest of the planners could see what was important. "I had to be the voice of the consumer," Reid said. "From outside, people think we do a good job of designing for Redmond."

He thought that online, high-definition penetration, personalization and connectivity of gadgets were important themes for Microsoft. Social networking was catching on with the spread of things like text messaging on cell phones and instant messenging services. People were putting on faceplates and downloading ring tones to personalize their gadgets.

A sizable marketing team supported Reid on Xenon. Bill Nielsen managed overall strategy for Xbox marketing, including media strategy, partnerships, licensing, promotions and sponsorships. His team included Albert Penello and Don Hall, who moved into the role of director of Xbox Brand Marketing. Hall's team included Brenda Ng, who supervised all large-scale marketing research projects. Aaron Greenberg headed the Xbox Business Intelligence Group. Justin Kirby worked with Don Coyner on the positioning, naming and visual identity of the brand for Xenon.

Reid's people looked at market intelligence. Apple's success with the iPod was beginning to show that people were ready for digital entertainment. People wanted to take things that were stored on their computers, such as digital photos and home videos, and view them in places like the living room.

"The game console had to play well in this connected environment," Reid said. "You plug it in and it works."

Microsoft's twin targets, the gamer and the digital entertainment enthusiast, often had identical interests. Since it was becoming clear that the cost-effective game box wouldn't run Windows and the hard disk drive wasn't going to be huge, using Xenon to store movies, music, and digital photos wasn't much of an option. This box wasn't going to be the kitchen sink for the living room. It would be more like a digital amplifier. As such, it ought to be able to display a digital picture on a TV, but it didn't have to store it. In this lesser role, it became easier to define what it should do and what it shouldn't. The PC would be the hub of the digital home, most often viewed from just a couple of feet away, while Xenon as

an entertainment box, or amplifier, would be viewed from 10-feet away.

"There was no mandate to use Windows," Reid said. "But Microsoft had a lot of assets and we should exploit them."

For instance, if someone wanted to rip a CD and then transfer it into Xenon, they should be able to do so without hassles. They could then take that music and use it as the themed music for the particular game they were playing. In a snowboarding game, the experience would be like taking an iPod with your own custom play list out on the slopes. Customizable sound tracks scored high among those who wanted to personalize the box.

Marketing had input on everything, such as what kind of games should be available at launch. Would *Halo 3* be needed? Reid didn't think so, because consoles would be in short supply during the launch no matter what. And the marketing team also believed that launching Xenon on a worldwide basis was also going to be important.

Microsoft considered the global launch for the original product but quickly backed off once it realized the logistics involved. It wound up launching the Xbox in the U.S. first and then a few months later it rolled out the machine in Japan and Europe. Sony and Nintendo had always done this too. This kind of launch always left Europe feeling like a stepchild. But it turned out that Europe was key to defeating Nintendo on a global market share basis. Robbie Bach, Mitch Koch, David Reid and the rest of the executive team thought it was time to stop treating Europe like a third-class citizen behind the U.S. and Japan. And if the manufacturing plans came off smoothly, Microsoft would do well to gain share against its rivals before they launched in those areas. The details would be decided much later. But the idea was put out there. It would become known as "sim ship," or simultaneous shipment.

Of all the different debates going on within the XIG group, Reid zeroed in on the issue of backward compatibility as extremely important for marketing purposes. His boss, Mitch Koch, didn't need any convincing on that subject.

"The consumer market research listed the things that were important, and the backward compatibility was there," Koch said.

Many of the engineers thought that backward compatibility was overvalued. The data from owners of PlayStation 2 consoles showed that they didn't really play their PlayStation games. Drew Angeloff, one of the game experts in the Advanced Technology Group, went round and round with Reid on the necessity of backward compatibility.

"It is completely secondary to having great titles on the box," Angeloff said. "The money for backward compatibility is better spent on one more exclusive title because the hardcore gamers just want the new titles."

The early adopters were the ones who would buy the console in the early days, when people would actually care about compatibility. Over time, they would stop caring. The mass market might be more interested in backward compatibility, but it would be a long time before those gamers began buying the new console. Reid brought in the marketing research that showed how much people cared about it. Some thought the studies were bogus, but they were able to sway the XIG leaders.

The problem grabbed the attention span of the executives. J Allard had been frustrated that marketing didn't seem to place as much importance on backward compatibility before the company chose its chip vendors. Then, as the issue became more of a flash point, the issue gained in importance. Allard was upset about the flip-flop on backward compatibility. And he was convinced that it was an "incredibly expensive" technical task, and Robbie Bach was inclined to believe Allard. Ed Fries, however, had a technical background. He threw a huge fit. He said it was possible and that Microsoft had to make the machine backward compatible.

"You guys are lazy," Fries argued. "Technically, it can be done."

For sure, it wasn't an easy task. Sony's PlayStation 2 included circuitry that enabled PlayStation games to run on the PS2. Most of the old games did indeed work, but even with the hardware included, some of the games just didn't run.

The issue of backward compatibility kept raising more questions. Even if Microsoft's software writers could write emulation software to mimic the functions of the Intel and Nvidia chips on the PowerPC and ATI machine, they weren't sure if they could legally do it without the permission of Nvidia in particular. Redmer thought that if Microsoft dangled enough money in front of Nvidia, they would eventually cave because of their obligation to shareholders to make money. On top of that, Microsoft didn't abstract the storage in the first console. Games looked for hard disk drives for caching or storage. That meant that the second Xbox would have to have a hard disk drive to be backward compatible.

Eventually, the team assigned Drew Solomon, a hardcore graphics expert and low-level operating system guru, to head a group of top-notch programmers and engineers. Their mission was to research backward compatibility and assess whether it would be technically possible. Allard referred to this group as the "ninjas," after elite Japanese assassins. No one would hear a definitive answer from them for a long time. The team had to pursue several different paths to get to their goal of making backward compatibility work through a software emulator. They dubbed this effort Fusion. Solomon got help from a variety of quarters, including Microsoft's research division in Beijing.

Redmer noted that the Xbox Live community wasn't automatically going to shift if games such as *Halo* 2 weren't moved over to Xenon. Reid took that idea and ran with it. He insisted that backward compatibility was going to be more important on the new Xbox in part because of the success of Xbox Live. Online games were so appealing to certain types of gamers because they loved playing against live opponents who could out-think any computer opponent. That's why those gamers played the same games over and over again on Xbox Live. If those gamers bought a new Xbox, and if the new games weren't as appealing on Xbox Live as the old ones, they would still want to play the old games on the new machine.

"Those online communities don't dissolve overnight," Reid argued. "They will want to keep playing, regardless of what the PlayStation 2 data is telling you."

The issue was so contentious that J Allard stormed out of one meeting, delivering a speech that was the equivalent of "you are all a bunch of idiots." He fretted that he was going to have to assign some of his most talented people to deal with the backward compatibility issue. In the face of such resistance, Redmer credited Reid for sticking to his guns. Peter Moore, who was amused at all the fighting, said in an off-the-cuff way, "Is this what it's really like at Microsoft?"

The Xenon project was going down a lot of different tracks. People were working on technology, branding, industrial design, games, third-party support, connectivity with other gadgets. For most of those, neither Allard nor Bach were consulted on many of the big decisions. That was the payoff that resulted when the executives moved out of the engine room. But the backward compatibility topic was generating a lot of debate throughout all the teams. The issue naturally flowed up to Bach.

The ninjas had not yet reported on the prospects of doing backward compatibility with the IBM-ATI solution. There were a few ways to do it. Nick Baker started thinking about how Microsoft could design the new chips so that it wouldn't be as hard to emulate the older Xbox hardware on the new system. Other ideas were floated.

One plan was to remaster all the old disks and then to give a new version of an old game that would run on the new console. That plan was dismissed as ridiculously expensive. A more measured plan was to create a software layer on the new machine that would recognize the old games and convert them on the fly. This solution would require some intense programming and might even require a big development team that would convert games one-by-one so that they could run on the new machine.

Baker was confident that this plan would work. The new system would be so powerful that it would be able to run the old games just fine, even if the machine had to go through the compute-intensive process of translating the old games into a form that would run on the new system. But creating an emulator represented a huge commitment in engineering talent. The upside of creating an emulator was that it was the key to making Windows run on the Xenon console. For that reason, the small investment in the backward-compatibility team promised a payback in the eyes of Bill Gates.

The ninjas were up to doing it. They would remain a small team because their work required an intimate knowledge of the operating system. It would take some of the smartest people at Microsoft to make it happen. They estimated that they might have 50 old games compatible with Xenon by 2005. The answer still wasn't clear. If it was possible, Bach wanted to make it happen.

"Is it worth devoting time and money and resources?" Bach asked. "We ultimately said yes."

CHAPTER NINETEEN

XE 30

Allard followed Bach's memo with a plan dubbed Xe 30. It was a document that dozens of people would work on throughout the summer of 2003. The man in charge of making it happen was now Cameron Ferroni, who was the stand-in for J Allard, who still had to manage other parts of the business in addition to minding Xenon. Ferroni ate, drank, and slept Xe 30, night and day. He had joined Jon Thomason, A.J. Redmer, and Chip Wood.

"It was my life that year," he said.

The first draft of Xe 30 came out on paper, so that the executives had to put their comments in the margins. One executive who saw Xe 30 described it as a mess, not a vision for an exciting product. It wasn't very descriptive.

The document included a rant on everything that was wrong with the video game industry. One of the problems was that it was becoming too expensive to develop games. As with movies, the budgets were starting to move into the tens of millions of dollars, particularly when advertising costs such as TV commercials were added in. The industry consisted of nearly 100 active console software publishers, but the top 20 publishers accounted for 90 percent of retail game sales.

Doing the art for just a single character in a game was getting more complex. The number of polygons, the shapes that were assembled to create the skeleton for a 3-D object in a game, were climbing from a few hundred per character to thousands. If the tools for creating more art didn't keep up with this pace of change, then game developers would have to hire more artists. Consumers had begun to expect outstanding graphics in games akin to the special effects in movies like *Jurassic Park*.

Developers would also have to hire more programmers to handle difficult tasks. Already, overtaxed workers were starting to complain that life inside a game company wasn't paradise after all. They were more interested in quality of life issues, like seeing their families, than working in crunch mode all the time.

Funding was also getting tight. As companies poured more money into each title, they couldn't afford to undertake as many projects. That created an effect similar to the problems in Hollywood, where producers could only afford to take risks on the blockbuster movies. Independent games were getting squeezed off the store shelves the same way that independent films were vanishing from theaters. Executives such as Activision's Bobby Kotick were predicting fewer game companies would survive the transition to the next generation.

Echoing Laura Fryer's attitude, Allard wanted to find a way to make game developers more productive. That spoke to Microsoft's core strength as a software company. Microsoft had always triumphed by creating better tools for programmers, winning them over to its camp so that they would create applications that run on Microsoft's operating systems. Microsoft was a software company, while Sony and Nintendo clearly were not. By making game developers more productive, Microsoft could recruit more of them to its platform. Winning those game developers over was the first step in getting enough good content that would get consumers on board with the console.

It was a familiar argument. Microsoft had made the same pitch on the original Xbox. Developers liked making games for the Xbox because it used the same familiar tools associated with the PC. That helped Microsoft surpass Nintendo, with more than 500 games developed for the Xbox. But it wasn't able to overtake Sony's advantage in sales volume. If a developer considered making a game exclusive for a console, it made the most business sense to make the game exclusively for the PlayStation 2, which was outselling the Xbox five to one. Though software productivity was an arrow in Microsoft's quiver, it wasn't a decisive one.

What was frustrating was that Xenon, as it existed in early 2003, wasn't a big leap forward that deserved the title of "next generation." It was still a product of a schizophrenic business strategy, where emphasis on gaining market share was diametrically opposed to the emphasis on shaving costs and making money.

Microsoft's costs were so high that they limited its design choices, and some thought that would come back to haunt Microsoft. It was easy to shoot down innovative ideas. Ideas such as building wireless Internet, or WiFi, support into every box just turned out to be too expensive.

The Xbox executives offered their written feedback on the paper memo, and they sent Allard back to rework the proposal. Conservative business plans just weren't going to win the war against Sony.

"We got our ass handed to us," said one member of the group.

Allard sent the group back to create a better plan. The planners had a tough time because they would hash out issues and then have to go back to convince their bosses that they had made the right calls. A.J. Redmer and George Peckham, who represented the games group on the plan, tapped Blake Fischer to help them with the writing of their section. A former Next Generation game magazine editor and a talented writer, Fischer was a big help crafting the right

words. The content team had identified the key characteristics that would define a next-generation game.

These so-called pillars included high-definition, wide screen games with a resolution of 720P and 5.1 channel Dolby sound. They knew that Sony would tout HD as its next-generation pillar, but they wanted to target the sweet spot of the market of HDTV sets that were better than standard TVs but were affordable as well.

Another pillar for the next-generation games would be the procedural geometry that Nick Baker and Jeff Andrews were specifying for the IBM microprocessor. That technique would enable game creators to build much richer worlds, including forests thick with trees or stadiums filled with spectators, all of whom looked different.

Redmer's team also wanted to create games that were accessible. That meant games that could be started and completed by anyone. They wanted shared interfaces to make the game learning curve easier to master. Pressing the "A" button on a controller in one game would yield a similar result in a different game. The games would have spectator modes so people watching a game could learn from the best gamers.

Each game would be enabled for Xbox Live. And if advances in artificial intelligence stayed on track, players would have a hard time seeing any difference between single-player and multiplayer modes. The games could include cooperative modes that could be played in either the single player or multiplayer modes. The games would not require a hard disk drive, and they would be targeted for the base platform.

The earliest plan for launch titles included a game in progress at Epic Games, the North Carolina developer run by graphics wizard Tim Sweeney. At the time, it was given the placeholder name "Epic Warfare." The plan also included new racing and sports titles. Microsoft figured that if it had eight games scheduled for launch, maybe four might fall out of the schedule and four might make it on time.

But much of Redmer's initial plans for first-party's portfolio goals were watered down. Ed Fries didn't want to tie the game development studios down into an arbitrary schedule. Redmer reminded everyone that two years before the Xbox shipped, Microsoft had no clue what the blockbuster titles would be for the launch. He suggested that some of the big titles could be snared from another console and converted to run on the Xbox 360 a year or two before the launch. The acquisition of Bungie and *Halo* had proven that strategy. The marketing plan was also in development, but very little of it was codified in Xe 30. The group kept pushing for some kind of loyalty program to reward hardcore gamers, but Mitch Koch, the head of marketing, was against it. Jon Thomason worried that so much of the document was being watered down.

"There were some people maybe who had unrealistic expectations of when is the right time to have all the answers," Mitch Koch said later. "I remember on being on other side. It's a waste of resources to plan things two years or a year ahead that we will have to throw out and change 32 times."

The group took another six months revising the memo and building out the detailed plan. On the top of the list was the recognition that people would buy the machine to play games. Sony succeeded with the PlayStation 2 during an early dry spell in spite of the weakness of their games, primarily because the machine had a DVD player that was cheaper than a stand-alone DVD player. Microsoft had to succeed on games, driven by a strong first-party line-up that showed off the power of the box.

Ferroni liked the idea of making the Xbox Live service free to gamers. It would be integrated into the dashboard of the console, and you might even click just a single button on a controller to go online. Enhancing communication would only broaden the box's appeal. Plugging in the network cable had to be as important as plugging the box into the TV set. Making it free would differentiate the box. But the team could still consider charging for some piece of the service. By the end of the Xe 30 process, the plan was to have both a free service and a premium service for Xbox Live.

One of the benefits of this would be downloading games or even pushing advertisements to all gamers, who could then click to download a demo version of a game or even buy it outright. If the gamers wanted to engage in multiplayer combat, an activity that uses the most bandwidth, they could upgrade for a fee.

James Miller wanted the Xbox Live Marketplace to be a destination of its own. It would be the place where people would go to buy games, download HD game trailers or pictures from new games, grab some art that they could use to personalize their console's dashboard and, eventually, a place to subscribe to new kinds of services. Gamers could go to the video download section and listen to an interview with a great game creator. They could sign up to watch a live tournament. And since the marketplace would use its own currency, based on some points that they could win, it could create new possibilities for commerce. Consumers wouldn't have to sign up with a credit card. They could go to a store and buy a pre-paid card with points. They could also win points in promotions and use them to buy things on marketplace.

Throughout the summer, the team of a dozen people wrote different sections of the report. The document grew and grew as more decisions were formalized within it. Allard would take small groups to meet with Bill Gates to discuss different parts of the program, such as the chips or the strategy for Xbox Live.

Allard went off to Ferroni's house at a skiing haven in Whistler, British Columbia. He spent a week in isolation, soaking in all of the ideas from his staff. When he came back, Pete Kelly in product documentation helped round the document out. The plan was supposed to be 30 pages, but by September, Xe 30 was about 80 pages, a thick wad of paper.

A set of principles were solidified and detailed in Xe 30, reflecting contributions from Gibson's team, the chip architects, the game developers, as well as the finance and marketing teams. Allard wanted the console to tap into everything around it in the digital living room, giving a 360 view on everything. That ultimately provided the seeds for the name of the console.

In all of their discussions, the group wanted to put the gamer at the center. Sony's motto was "Live in your world, play in ours." To Ferroni, that meant that the world belonged to Sony. It wasn't the gamer's world. It was Sony's world. But Microsoft wanted to distinguish itself by putting the gamer at the center. Everyone knew that they couldn't call the box the Xbox 2, because Sony's PlayStation 3 would seem more advanced. It didn't matter if it could be explained away. In a world of brief media descriptions, Microsoft might never get past that comparison.

"We didn't want to deal with that long explanation as to why the Xbox 2 was as good as the PlayStation 3," Ferroni said.

The idea of putting the gamer at the center evoked the image of 360 degrees. Don Hall, director of Xbox global brand marketing, ran with the idea and developed an entire campaign around it. They passed the concept to the industrial designers who were trying to come up with their own theme, who in turn had their own suggestions. In a short time, "Xbox 360" became the favorite choice for the name of the new console. But the branding group had to put together not only the brand name, but the look and feel, positioning, and the back-story behind the brand.

The original Xbox launched without a true brand message beyond its dark, hardcore, muscle-bound image that signaled energy and power. But after the launch, the brand marketers zeroed in on the caption, "the ultimate social magnet." They felt the brand should reflect the idea of gaming as a social experience. It could be richly personalized, with "you at the center of the experience," Hall said. "We saw socially connected gaming as our difference."

Robbie Bach, Peter Moore and J Allard liked what they heard on brand strategy. The branding group started working on new logos that were lighter in color and more inviting to a broader group of consumers. It would be more optimistic and hopeful. It would be well into 2004 before all the work was done. For now, Xenon persisted as the code name that everyone used.

The 2005 timing was good because Allard saw a perfect storm gathering. By 2005, the consoles would be showing their age. High-definition TVs were just beginning to gather momentum, and by 2005 they would be available to the mass market. With HD visuals, the games would take a step up above current-generation graphics and catch up with the quality of PC monitors. Customization and personalization were gathering momentum.

At the end of the Xe 30 memo, Allard did something special. He had commissioned a fake news article that explained the kind of story that Microsoft hoped would be written about the new console on the first day of its launch by a magazine dubbed "News Time," a play on *Newsweek* and *Time* magazines. It was a glitzy production with pull quotes and pictures. Allard had been obsessed with a similar article that ran in *Newsweek* on March 6, 2000. The cover story carried the headline "The Amazing PlayStation 2" and it had one of the highest bullshit levels of hype of all time, according to J Allard and others at Microsoft. In the article, PlayStation visionary Ken Kutaragi said, "You can communicate to

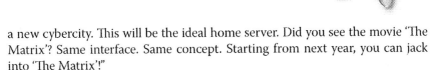

a new cybercity. This will be the ideal home server. Did you see the movie 'The Matrix'? Same interface. Same concept. Starting from next year, you can jack into 'The Matrix'!"

Allard wanted the same kind of article on Xenon. Pete Kelly did the layout so that it looked like the real thing.

"We circulated the 18-page article," Allard said. "That was how we socialized the dream of the Xe 30 memo."

By October, 2003, they were ready to present Xe 30, which was really 80 pages, to Bill Gates and Steve Ballmer.

CHAPTER TWENTY

THE HALO OF XBOX 2

*M*aking games for Xenon was the responsibility of Ed Fries. In December, 2002, Robbie Bach shifted responsibility for third-party games (games from outside Microsoft) from J Allard to Fries. That was a small victory for Fries in his smoldering rivalry with Allard. Allard had become busy with the Xenon product definition process, and he had many responsibilities associated with the Xbox Live service. He couldn't concentrate on relations with third-party publishers, which consumed a lot of time.

Fries had to be careful that he didn't mix third-party pitches with first-party (Microsoft internal games). Microsoft had to have a "Chinese wall" between potential competitors. First-party couldn't steal ideas for games from third-party and visa versa. The shift in responsibility meant one thing. The success or failure of games for the Xbox 360 fell at the feet of Fries once again.

With 50 projects under way at any given time inside Microsoft Game Studios, the management job was complex. Fries had four lieutenants working for him by the end of 2002. They included Stuart Moulder, who managed the studio managers in charge of Bungie, the simulation games, and Ensemble Studios. Shane Kim managed the MSN Gaming zone, the sports team, and overall business strategy. Phil Spencer headed the teams that included the racing games, Rare, and Zoo Tycoon. A.J Redmer ran the studio in Japan and managed Digital Anvil, the Salt Lake games group and FASA.

All told, 1,200 people worked for Fries, not counting independent contractors. But that firepower was split between the Xbox and the PC. Most of the studios had roots in the PC, and a number still focused on PC games. For instance, Blue Fang Games made *Zoo Tycoon*, Big Huge Games created *Rise of Nations*, Gas Powered Games made *Dungeon Siege*, the flight sim team focused on *Microsoft Flight Simulator*, and Ensemble Studios worked on *Age of Empires* games. Ensemble had

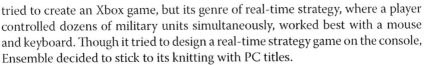

tried to create an Xbox game, but its genre of real-time strategy, where a player controlled dozens of military units simultaneously, worked best with a mouse and keyboard. Though it tried to design a real-time strategy game on the console, Ensemble decided to stick to its knitting with PC titles.

It was one of the largest game development teams in the industry. But by no means was it the biggest. By comparison, Nintendo had an estimated 1,500 game developers among its 3,000 employees. Sony had a dozen studios with 2,000 game developers at the time, and it was on the growth path. And Electronic Arts was approaching 4,000 at the time, and growing its ranks as well.

"The view I have is as a first party organization, we have a responsibility to innovate and grow the market," said Phil Harrison, Sony's top studio executive. "We have a philosophy of participating in genres where we can be best."

On Xbox, Fries had expanded rapidly to create first-party content. He had acquired Bungie and was spending perhaps $240 million a year internally. But about half his budget went to external developers who worked on one project at a time. Among those were Oddworld Inhabitants, maker of the *Oddworld* series of games, and BioWare, which was working on console role-playing games such as *Star Wars Knights of the Old Republic* and *Jade Empire*. Fries had funded entrepreneurs like Tim Schafer, an innovative Lucas Arts developer, who had gone off to start Double Fine Productions. Schafer was creating a new Xbox franchise called *Psychonauts*. These companies didn't mind getting funding from Microsoft, but worked better as independents.

Halo had bought Fries time, political clout, and recognition that made up for some of the losers in his portfolio. But with the Rare acquisition, the pressure was on again. Fries had to start looking for the next *Halo*.

In early 2003, he didn't yet have a firm idea of what would be in the next Xbox. Fries had delegated the job of representing the first-party game development staff at the Xenon meetings to A.J. Redmer and George Peckham. Like the other executives, Fries had the difficult balancing act of juggling the needs of the current Xbox business with the need to start planning for Xenon. Fries was concerned about the slow progress on the hardware vision because the job of making awesome games that exploited the hardware fell to him. It took about two years to create an outstanding game, and sometimes the big titles slipped to three, four or five years. With maybe 2.5 years before the scheduled launch, Fries felt he was already running behind.

He had some cool titles in the works. Among the candidates for Xenon launch titles were games from Rare such as *Kameo: Elements of Power*, and *Perfect Dark Zero*." These games were slated for the Xbox, but they might be held back. Bizarre Creations was planning on creating another racing game in its *Project Gotham Racing* series, and it was going to get help from artificial intelligence experts in Microsoft Research.

But Fries needed to go out hunting for big game. His team of planners once again scoured the game development community for the best talent and the best games. In February, 2003, Fries himself went to Las Vegas for the an industry summit dubbed DICE. It was where just a few hundred elite from the ranks of the game development industry gathered each year to hand out the equivalent of the Oscars of gaming and to hear talks about the state of game development. It preceded the Game Developers Conference, which typically drew 10,000 people to San Jose, California.

DICE had been conceived a couple of years earlier as an intimate affair. It was always oversubscribed, and the recreational location helped. This year it was at the Hard Rock Casino and Hotel off the Las Vegas strip. At the reception, Fries ran into Cliff "CliffyB" Blezinski, a game designer at Epic Games who wanted to live the rock star life. CliffyB was a geek who got hazed in school when he was young. He started making games when he was 17, sending them out to customers in Ziplock bags just as the Bungie guys had done. Now in his late 20s, he was lead designer at Epic Games.

Cliff "CliffyB" Blezinski, game designer at Epic Games

He hooked up early on with Tim Sweeney, a tall and thin programmer. Sweeney started Epic on his own in 1991 as Epic MegaGames in Rockville, Md. For his first game, *ZZT*, (a text-based adventure that came with its own kit for modifying the game), Sweeney packaged the disks and shipped them out, just as the Bungie founders had done. He brought aboard CliffyB, who was then still in high school, as a designer. Mark Rein, who had worked briefly at id Software, joined to head marketing. And James Schmalz joined as a second programmer. They worked on titles such as *Epic Pinball, Jill of the Jungle,* and *Jazz Jack Rabbit.* That helped fund a tour de force in graphics, dubbed "Unreal," starting in 1994. By that time, Schmalz had left to start his own game company. Sweeney gathered a crew to make *Unreal*, but the handled most of the 3-D programming work himself. *Unreal* was one of the first to challenge id Software's *Quake* for first-person shooter supremacy. When *Unreal* debuted for the PC in 1998, it quickly demonstrated the value of the new 3-D graphics cards on computers and sold a million units. In 1999, the company changed its name to Epic Games. The realistic look of the game quickly established Sweeney as one of the leading minds on 3-D graphics alongside id's graphics genius, John Carmack. As Epic expanded, it moved to Raleigh, N.C., and churned out one *Unreal* title after another. And it licensed its graphics engine to all comers who wanted to exploit the latest 3-D in their games.

To go with his new stardom, CliffyB dressed in white suits accented with bling bling gold jewelry. CliffyB had a quick wit and a foul mouth that could talk a mile a minute. At one conference, he bantered with Mark Rein, the vice president of marketing at Epic, who said, "Look at you in that white suit. You look like a pimp!" CliffyB replied, "You're my ho." That was what CliffyB later acknowledged as his "mack daddy phase." At DICE, CliffyB had a grunge rocker look, with dyed red hair, orange-tinted sunglasses, and a fur-trimmed coat that hung to his knees. But CliffyB had grown tired of *Unreal*. At the bar at the Dice Summit, CliffyB tapped Ed Fries on the shoulder and said, "Going to make me the *Halo* of the Xbox 2." [1]

Fries responded, "I might give you that chance." And to an eavesdropping reporter: "You didn't hear this." CliffyB let out a celebratory whoop. [2] It wasn't yet a deal. But it was the beginning of something. It's the kind of encounter that Fries loved. It meant that all that time spent in Las Vegas, chatting at the poker tables or playing golf, actually qualified as real work.

1. "Smartbomb: The Quest For Art, Entertainment and Big Bucks in the Video Game Revolution," by Heather Chaplin and Aaron Ruby, Algonquin Books, 2005, pg. 25.

2. "Smartbomb," pg. 27.

CHAPTER TWENTY-ONE

ROLLING THE DICE

eyond the deal making, drinking and gambling, Fries and the other attendees at the DICE Summit got to hear from the spiritual chief of the Xbox, Seamus Blackley. Blackley was toiling away at his new start-up, Capital Entertainment Group, trying to produce games from promising developers who couldn't get sequel-obsessed publishers to take risks on their ideas for original games.

In a speech entitled, "No, You're Wrong!" Blackley held the crowd spellbound. "The industry has evolved into a broken state that's holding us all down," he said. "There's stuff that's just plain broken. There's stuff that has evolved into brokenness. And there's stuff that's just our fault."

One problem, he said, is that developers were designing games for publishers, but not the audience. Developers were too focused on hitting milestones for publishers so that they could get their next project payment. The royalty structure of the industry, he said, was set up to encourage lying and discourage communication and creativity. Publishers, he said, live in a world of revenue targets, portfolio management, risk management, and investor expectations. They look for predictable results, meaning sequels. That, in turn, takes away the ability for developers to refine their ideas.

Focus testing, he observed, was often improperly used by publishers. He said that developers ought to be using it to scope out ideas. He said that both were good at misunderstanding customers.

"The average person walking into Wal-Mart to buy your game does not own a complete set of *Resident Evil* action figures and does not know what DICE is," he said.

He thought that more focus should be put on mass-market consumers and suggested that "gamer culture is new and, frankly, has a strongly negative social connotation." Games that last 10 to 30 hours are aimed at hardcore gamers, not the masses. For the business to be on par with movies, music and TV, Blackley said that designers need a safe place to iterate on ideas and refine them until they become powerful.

The sobering but honest talk left some developers, like Mark Cerny, deeply moved. Then the gang began a night of heavy partying and schmoozing. They kicked it off with their version of the Academy Awards. Inside the cool "The Joint" inside the Hard Rock, the elite audience gathered for food and drinks before the televised ceremonies.

The event was hosted by actor Dave Foley and the awards were presented by a combination of industry luminaries like Ed Fries and some young, attractive Hollywood actors. Microphones hanging on booms, spotlights, and TV cameras gave the audience a surreal sense. This can't be the geeky game industry that is holding an event worth watching on TV. G4, the 24-hour game cable channel, televised the presentation to millions of households.

CliffyB, playing his rock star role, presented an award with Nina Kaczorowski, a hot actress who had a small role in the *Austin Powers* movie. He was so excited that he giggled on stage and the crowd applauded in apparent understanding. The evening went on, with a long string of similar fame-by-association moments. After the show, drinking, dancing and gambling continued.

The conference went on for another day. The late-night partiers staggered into the room late, but some in the audience listened intently to the presentations. But a couple of developers stayed out at the computers outside, surfing the web. They were looking over a series of patents that have been posted on an Internet web site. They appeared to describe the chips for the PlayStation 3 from Sony.

Just before the Game Developers Conference in San Jose in 2003, the *San Jose Mercury News* popped the lid on the Sony patents on its front page. Developers at the show started poring over the patents to see what clues they offered about making games.

The patents were truly scary for the crowd at Microsoft. The assessments of game developers were overblown at the time. The PlayStation 3 wouldn't really be as staggering as described at that early stage. But the significance of the patents was clear. If Sony, IBM and Toshiba fulfilled their promise for "Cell microprocessors" that could compute in small clusters like bees in a hive, they would be able to build the chips into a wide range of devices, from supercomputers to handhelds. Each Cell would consist of a PowerPC chip with eight auxiliary processors. The chips would tap into broadband networks to accumulate more processing power. The patents didn't say exactly how many Cells would be used in a video game console, but it was clear this kind of power could challenge the dominance of Intel in computing. If Sony truly penetrated a wide range of markets, it could achieve volume economics that surpassed even the PC microprocessor, and that would ultimately make Sony's chips cheaper than anything that Microsoft could use for Xenon. It was the craziest of gambles, yet it had the kind of shrewd plan for world domination that just might work.

"This is a new class of beast," said Richard Doherty, an analyst at the Envisioneering Group. "There is nothing like this project when it comes to how far-reaching it is." [1]

Shin'ichi Okamoto, the chief technology officer of Sony's game division, had set as his target in a speech the year before the goal of a trillion floating point operations per second. That represented performance equivalent to 100 Intel-based personal computers. Kunitake Ando, president and chief operating officer of Sony, had said at the recent Consumer Electronics Show that the much-vaunted "home server," a repository of all entertainment in the home, and the PS3 could be the same thing. Sony's plan was to leapfrog the normal progress of chip performance. Moore's Law dictated that chips doubled their performance every two years. But that wasn't enough for Sony to deliver the kind of boost in game performance that it wanted. Game developers who studied Sony's plans figured that its chips would be finished in 2004 and that the system would launch in 2005, or about the same timing that Microsoft had scheduled for Xenon.

But no one knew that inside Sony, something was going terribly wrong. Sony had created a new game system, dubbed GS Cube, with 16 Emotion Engine chips. It proved to be a technological dead end. In parallel, IBM fellow Jim Kahle had proposed Cell, a radically different computing architecture. Instead of a microprocessor and a graphics chip, the system for the PlayStation 3 was originally supposed to have two Cell microprocessors. One would handle the system while the second one would handle graphics. The game developers couldn't make heads or tails of this non-traditional architecture. Sony scrapped that plan. Then it commissioned both Sony's and Toshiba's chip designers to create their own graphics chip. The graphics chip was going to be a screaming monster that relied totally on one kind of processing, dubbed fill rate, to handle the graphics. That was what Sony and Toshiba's engineers knew how to create, based on their work on the PlayStation 2. But in the meantime, both ATI and Nvidia had pioneered the use of shaders, which were subprograms that added the nuance and texture to the surface of an object. This technique simplified the process of creating art for games. To create a new effect, the developer had to simply create a new shader. The Sony and Toshiba team were far behind on shader technology. Game developers once again objected to the solution that they were proposing. Sony had to cancel the graphics chip altogether. The console just wasn't going to launch in 2005.

"They had a lot of problems getting off the ground," said Kevin Krewell, then-editor-in-chief of the Microprocessor Report. "I think the game developers had the most say in where they eventually moved."

Meanwhile, it had been clear that Microsoft and Nvidia were not going to be working together. Jen-Hsun Huang, CEO of Nvidia, said that the Xbox had been tough on his company. Xbox chips had accounted for 20 percent of Nvidia's sales, but the two companies were in a dispute over pricing. And Nvidia had been distracted from its core market of graphics chips for desktop personal computers. Rival ATI Technologies was putting Nvidia to shame in that market.

"We would be delighted to work with Microsoft on the next Xbox," Huang said in an interview. "But we are a company with many opportunities." Nvidia was exploring the idea of working with Sony on the PlayStation 3. The odds were unlikely of such a marriage, since Sony was working on its own graphics chip. But Nvidia saw its opening as the Sony graphics chip unraveled.

To most people in the Xbox division, and even some working on the Xenon team, this news was disturbing. But for Nick Baker, the Mountain View engineer charged with evaluating the Sony architecture, it wasn't terrifying. Baker had done some calculations and figured out some problems with the Sony approach. It clearly wasn't going to be friendly to game developers. The system had a lot of processors working parallel, but it didn't appear to have the kind of memory system it needed. Keeping all of those processors busy all the time was a task that game developers wouldn't enjoy. A simpler architecture could deliver a lot of the advantages of multiprocessing. And paired with a traditional graphics chip, Baker thought that Microsoft's solution was going to be much easier to program and deliver much more bang for the buck.

"We had good competitive intelligence, not because we did anything special but because we made good educated guesses," Bach said.

1. "Sony Chip To Transform Video Game Industry," by Dean Takahashi, *San Jose Mercury News*, 3/3/03.

CHAPTER TWENTY-TWO

GEARS OF WAR

t the 2003 Game Developers Conference, Epic was showing off a new graphics engine. The demo showed incredible details of monstrous characters that were properly lit by all the right sources of illumination, as if there really were a sun or a lantern shining light in exactly the right places, producing all the right shadows. A Microsoft business development manager, Jim Veevaert, saw the demo. He pressed Mark Rein, vice president of marketing at Epic, for details.

"I was interested in pursuing a war franchise, and the technology was very impressive," Veevaert said. "I knew there was a great game in the works."

Rein said that it was a new version of *Unreal* which had the working title of *Unreal Warfare*. Veevaert wanted to sign it up for the Xbox 360. In the subsequent weeks, Rein and Epic business chief Jay Wilbur negotiated to free the *Unreal Warfare* property from the publisher that Epic had found for it.

Everyone at Epic wanted to expand beyond the *Unreal* franchise. CliffyB in particular needed to stretch his wings. He had almost quit Epic Games after the first *Unreal Tournament* debuted. He wanted to work on a new property, something, ironically, more epic. He loved horror games such as the *Silent Hill* and *Resident Evil* series, where fear was the prevailing emotion.

"Remember that phrase about how 'the only thing we have to fear is fear itself'?," he said. "I say, 'Fear, it sells.'"

Since high school, he had wanted to make a game he called *Over Fiend*, a horror game where a character lost his wife to demons in a post-modern city. It was a single-player story-based game, in contrast to Epic's multiplayer online melees. John Carmack, the graphics wizard at Epic's rival, id Software, had once said that a story in a first-person shooter game was as gratuitous as a story in a porn flick. CliffyB thought that notion was ludicrous.

"This is a medium that can be used to tell stories," he said.

But he didn't get a chance to prove Carmack wrong. More *Unreal* sequels came along. CliffyB adjusted himself to market conditions. One of the sequels coming was a title called *Unreal Warfare*, a game that would allow players to engage in huge battles with ultra-modern marines in realistic terrain. But the team at Epic was getting overloaded, so they stopped work on *Unreal Warfare* in order to ship *Unreal Tournament 2004*.

One of CliffyB's programmers suggested they switch the *Unreal Warfare* game to a second-person view, with a perspective where the gamer could see the character that he or she was playing, as if they were just behind and looking over the shoulder of the character. CliffyB liked the idea and wanted to use it with *Unreal Warfare*. When he saw videos for Capcom's upcoming horror game, *Resident Evil 4*, he saw how the second-person view looked in practice. "That's totally the way to go," he said. "We had to go to this view because the character would look so fucking great."

The game, now code-named *Project Warfare*, would be very different from Epic's previous fast-action shooter games. Its pace would be slower than the typical first person shooter. The character would partially obscure the view of the player. By this time, the graphics team had a graphics engine, and CliffyB had pieces of a story. In some ways, CliffyB said, "It was the tail wagging the dog." He started thinking about all of the things he wanted to say. He had been stunned by the fall of the World Trade Center towers in 2001. He was struck with the notion that a surprise attack could bring down something so grand. The ruins of a cathedral reminded him of the last scene of the film *Planet of the Apes*, where Charleston Heston comes upon a fallen Statue of Liberty. He recalled the hysteria about Anthrax and people going to buy duct tape to protect themselves against terrorist chemical warfare attacks. The idea of "destroyed beauty" stayed with him, and it mixed with the demons from *Over Fiend*. CliffyB wanted to call it *Apex War*, after a sleepy suburban town near where he lived in Raleigh, N.C. He thought of ruined cities during World War II, where soldiers had to take shots and hide under cover, rather than run with guns blazing through the streets.

"What if you had enemies that take cover?" he wondered. "They're smart and they think about what they're going to do."

He had made sci-fi games for so long that this time he wanted the enemies to come from underground. That matched the kind of graphics technology that Sweeney's group was working on. The enemies would be vaguely humanoid, and pale. He would call them "locusts."

CliffyB had admired "*Halo*," which did have some smart enemies. The game had taken the first-person shooter genre from the PC and moved it to the console with grace. CliffyB had been frustrated with the hassles of the PC, and he wanted a console experience. He had to talk the rest of the team into it. One thing that helped him in his quest to do a new kind of game was that the *Unreal* brand had been associated with the PC. It hadn't worked really well on the consoles yet.

One phrase that stuck with him was "The gears of war lubricated with the blood of soldiers." It brought to bear the image he had in mind. He did a search on the name, *Gears of War*, and found an anime comic fan owned the web site. Epic made an offer to buy it and obtained the rights. Now that CliffyB had a game in mind, he became impatient to do it. He knew that *Halo 2* was running late. He could extrapolate that Microsoft would need something else to launch with its next console. He knew that gamers with a new console would want something "bad ass."

"I got impatient," he said. "I wanted to go, go, go."

Tim Sweeney's demo at the GDC was the groundwork that he needed for his new graphics engine, *Unreal Engine 3*, which would power the intricately detailed characters and scenes in the games. The engine would feature the kind of spectacular graphics that Sweeney and his programmers and artists loved to create. Among the highlights was something called "high dynamic range." That meant that the graphics would illuminate a wide range of bright images and dark images in the same picture. The resulting effect on realism would be stunning. They didn't know for sure, but they had made a bet that the kind of graphics they were creating would be perfect for Microsoft's next game console.

In March, 2003, Epic merged with Scion Studios, a start-up which had been working with Epic on derivative titles. The company needed a new building and Sweeney had decided that now was the time to dramatically expand. In contrast to boutique studios such as id Software in Mesquite, Texas, Epic recognized that game development was becoming so complex that it needed bigger teams and budgets.

The company finally had enough people to feed the *Unreal* franchise and start new titles as well. They then pitched the game as a story-based shooter that had the horror elements that CliffyB wanted to have.

"It was clear that the game Cliff and the gang were making was going to be different and that we should break it out as a new intellectual property," Sweeney said.

As CliffyB and his team refined the concept, the story took shape. It was an original science fiction title where mankind was engaged in insane wars, only to fall victim to a surprise attack on "emergence day," as a subterranean monster race surfaces. It was the game that CliffyB always wanted to do. CliffyB created a universe behind the game with foul creatures, destroyed cities, and massive humans who looked like bodybuilders decked out in body armor. The main characters were two buddy marines who would fight together. The story would unfold with "forced looks," which were canned cinematic sequences that forced the characters to look in a certain direction where they could see a piece of the plot unfold. These sequences would fit seamlessly within the actual game play. CliffyB now had enough material for a whole trilogy of games. The company filed dozens of trademark names for the game, some of them red herrings to throw off spies. One of the names was *Gears of War.*

CliffyB went to Redmond to make his pitch. On the morning of the presentation, he was nervous. He did 60 push-ups. In the meeting with

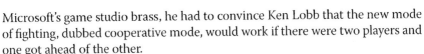

Microsoft's game studio brass, he had to convince Ken Lobb that the new mode of fighting, dubbed cooperative mode, would work if there were two players and one got ahead of the other.

The Microsoft planners negotiated for an exclusive. Epic wanted a big check to get the development going. Epic's Mark Rein was also dangling something else interesting in front of Microsoft. Sweeney was busy at work on his next graphics engine, the underlying code that would be able to render outstanding graphics that exploited the best technology in just about any platform, PC or game console. If Epic came on board, it could also encourage its licensees for its engine to come on board with the Xbox 360. And that meant that dozens of developers might make games for the Xbox 360. Epic never considered taking the *Gears of War* title to Sony, which hadn't even begun to court developers for the PlayStation 3.

"Microsoft showed a lot of enthusiasm for it," Rein said. "What makes or breaks a game is marketing. If a publisher wants a game bad enough and it's strategic to them, they will spend the money on marketing to get the game the attention."

Scene from Gears of War

Epic had its fans inside Microsoft. Studio manager Bonnie Ross and ATG chief Laura Fryer loved the idea. In fact, she liked it so much she used the game as an excuse to leave the Advanced Technology Group and shift back into game production as a producer working with Epic. Scott Henson, one of J Allard's buddies and a former boss on Xbox Live, filled the gap at ATG and replaced her. Fries liked the pitch, but he was also entertaining another pitch from a hometown company. Valve LLC, run by former Microsoft programmer Gabe Newell, had scored big over the years with hits such as *Half-Life* and (through a modified version of *Half-Life) Counter-Strike.* Valve was finishing up work on *Half-Life* 2 for the PC and had decided to do a version of that game for the Xbox. Now Newell wanted to know if Fries wanted a new Valve game for the Xbox 360.

Jay Wilbur, who ran business operations for Epic Games, had to do the negotiating, taking calls at all hours or at his kid's baseball game back in Raleigh. Microsoft wanted it as a launch title, but Epic knew it wouldn't be done in time for a 2005 debut, even with a year and a half to prepare and 30 people on the team.

John Kimmich, the trusty planner who signed up Bungie, came to Fries with both deals at about the same time. Fries remembered weighing the proposals from both companies. They were going to require expensive advances from Microsoft. And Fries didn't really have the political capital to do both deals. Valve was a tough company to work with, since it was developing its own online game distribution network dubbed Steam. Valve wanted the right to sell as many games as it wanted through Steam. It would compete with its own publisher for consumers in that sense. The deal was very difficult to swallow. Valve wanted the publisher to foot the bill for the game development, but take a small percentage of the profits. It was going to compete with the publisher's retail sales via Steam. And it was never clear when Valve would finish a game, given its track record.

Fries weighed both titles, holding stacks of contract papers in each hand at the same time. He looked at Epic on one hand, and Valve on the other. He decided, and he tossed the Valve deal in the garbage can. Those who heard about this decision later shook their heads and wondered why Fries didn't spend some of Microsoft's billions on both deals. It seemed like a case where Microsoft was Goliath, but it felt like it was David.

CHAPTER TWENTY-THREE

INDUSTRIAL DESIGN

*T*he design of the original Xbox didn't win Microsoft any awards. One blogger impolitely said that the design of the second Xbox would be like getting a chance to redesign the Titanic. At first crack, the design of Xenon wasn't breaking new ground. Jim Stewart, a former Apple designer and manager of design planning for the Xbox, had begun a bake-off to handle the industrial design of the project. He planned on searching through a number of American design firms to find the right one. The last Xbox had been created by a designer named Horace Luke, a former jewelry designer who had since moved on to design cell phones and handhelds at the company. The last project had been a mad rush. The Xbox had been criticized roundly by designers. It was big, the size of a video cassette recorder. The top of the box was rounded, so you couldn't stack another machine on top of it. Everything about it was bold, not subtle. It was an attempt to appeal to the macho crowd, not necessarily the masses. The controller was too big, especially for the smaller hands of Japanese gamers. This time, Microsoft had to do better.

Don Coyner, a former Nintendo marketer who had worked at Microsoft for years, had joined the Xbox team early on. He helped John O'Rourke to run marketing and was now looking for something different. Coyner joined J Allard's team to assist with planning for Xenon. Cameron Ferroni, who had stepped up to handle much of the Xbox 360 process for Allard, said, "We found that we had been under-utilizing Don. We decided to give him a broader role that brought together hardware, software, usability and planning."

Coyner took on a nebulous title as director of user experience. While he didn't supervise Stewart directly, he took charge of the design. He told Stewart that he wanted the search for a design firm to go worldwide. Coyner wanted design to be a higher-level position this time. He wanted the whole user experience to be consistent, like an Apple product, where everything from the screen to the package looked like it was designed by just one person. But Coyner and Stewart had to see where the state of design was before they started their work. They pulled together a design workshop involving designers throughout the company, and they keyed in on the important trends.

Microsoft's old way of designing products for geeks was no longer going to cut it. Geek was becoming chic. Apple had debuted its iPod with a minimalist white design. The small box with a black-and-white screen weighed 6.5 ounces and it was as thin as a wallet. Its software had been cleverly designed to automate the process of downloading songs into the player's hard disk drive. And it had a unique touch wheel that allowed its user scroll through menus and songs with one hand at very high speeds. The sales of the iPod started climbing, and Apple had once again changed attitudes – this time about the coolness of the color white. The iPod was iconic. It was instantly recognizable. If someone was walking down the street and they were wearing white earphones, you knew they had an iPod. The iPod's popularity underscored the importance of individualism, or being able to choose your own music, said Kathleen Gasparini, a market researcher at Label Networks.

But more important than the iPod itself, consumers were beginning to demand excellent design in everyday things. Design shops such as Ideo in Palo Alto, Calif., the creator of Apple's first mouse, were moving on to things like the stand-up toothpaste tube for Crest. They were now analyzing and reshaping retail store layouts, the position of seats in an airplane, and the interior of cars on Amtrak trains. [1] Stores such as the Sharper Image and Crate & Barrel built their businesses on clever redesigns of old products.

"Technology should almost be invisible at this point," said Ellen Glassman, general manager for brand design at Sony. [2]

For consumers, how something looked determined whether they bought it. Designers started going home with consumers, not just to hear what they said, but to see what they did. They shadowed people and built behavioral maps of how they moved around their homes and used things. They asked consumers to keep camera journals to document their daily activities. And they packed diverse people into focus groups to get a wide mix of ideas about consumer preferences.

As technology moved mainstream and cell phones became so cheap that one in six people in the world owned one, good design set them apart. At the annual Consumer Electronics Show, hundreds of companies started entering products in the best design category. Flat-screen TV sets started taking off not just because their images were sharper. They also looked good in the home, hanging on the wall. That gave them what Bruce Berkoff, then-executive vice president of marketing for flat-panel maker LG Philips, called "sofa," short for "significant other factor of acceptance." Lamps started incorporating colorful light-emitting diodes, which emanated neon-like colors.

"Technology was becoming an extension of personal style," said Mary Alice Stephenson, a contributing editor to Harper's Bazaar who offered advice to tech companies such as Intel. "There's a kind of show-off factor now."

But consumers also wanted something that matched their own lifestyles and fashion sense mattered more. The iPod was all about personalizing their song lists so they didn't have to listen to the songs that music companies chose to put on CDs. Personalization was evident in things like "skins" and ring tones for cell phones that showed to the world that a teenager's favorite band was Maroon 5. They were watching movies on their own time thanks to inventions like the Tivo digital video recorder.

Authenticity was another buzz word in design circles. Hartmut Esslinger, founder of industrial design firm frog design in Sunnyvale, Calif., said that painted plastic would no longer do when you wanted to create a metallic effect. Consumers wanted real metal, brushed or chromed, on something that suggested metal. That's why Hewlett-Packard included stainless steel in its digital cameras, said Sam Lucente, director of brand design and experience.

Don Coyner managed the industrial design and user experience

All of these trends made the design of the Xbox 360 more critical, and easier to screw up. After all, Microsoft had to learn the difference between a fad and a lasting design. Translucency, which Apple introduced with its iMac desktop computers in 1999, was no longer fashionable because it had inspired so many copycats that consumers were repulsed by it. The observational skills that companies needed were really akin to the skills that anthropologists developed in studying cultures, so the companies started hiring anthropologists, social scientists and psychologists. Microsoft had tried to do this with the first Xbox, but it had still missed on so many design points.

"There is a worry about making a technology too trendy and having it be so yesterday," said Genevieve Bell, a cultural anthropologist who studied technology and lifestyle for Intel. "There's a danger if you go down this road you get caught with the equivalent of a very wide tie." [3]

Soaking in all these trends, Coyner and Stewart got started on their work. Together, they set out to visit some of the best industrial designers in the world. They got the names of good Japanese and European designers from Microsoft's subsidiaries overseas. In December, 2002, they set out on a worldwide trip. Coyner talked to the designers at a high level. He wanted them to exercise their creativity, using only high-level guidance. He wanted them to design a box that was right for their region of the world, but the box had to be used in the rest of the world as well. Among the designers who made a prototype was Marc Newson, a London designer who had created a huge body of work, from Shiseido men's toiletries to Vidal Sassoon hair-care products.

By February, 2003, the designers submitted their first drafts. Six firms submitted seven ideas dubbed "gestures." Hers Experimental Laboratory, a design firm in Osaka, Japan, submitted two machines with handles, one with a white plastic strap and another with a solid metal loop for a handle. Microsoft took 3-D computer drawings from the group and used its own machine shop to carve out three-dimensional prototypes. They finished the models with the appropriate shiny metals, light-emitting diodes and made them into high-quality prototypes. It was an expensive process, but not outrageously so. Microsoft spent perhaps $100,000 on the models.

In May, 2003, Coyner hired Cheskin, a 60-year-old company in Redwood Shores, Calif., that specialized in design research. Its business was to understand people around the world and offer advice to product designers. The company founded by marketer Louis Cheskin was one of the first market research companies, offering advice and research on designs such as the ads for the Marlboro Man, the Gerber Baby, and the redesign of McDonald's restaurants with the "golden arches." Few people had ever heard of Cheskin, but people touched the products that it had researched just about every day. Cheskin had been working with different Microsoft divisions since 1990, and it had done more than 500 research projects for the company. Most of the work had been in software, but Cheskin had also done research for hardware companies such as Hewlett-Packard, Motorola, and Samsung.

"We brought a perspective about what works in design," said Darrell Rhea, CEO of Cheskin.

Rhea was well aware that Microsoft took a lot of heat from both consumers and the design community on the first Xbox. Coyner decided to do research and specified what the basic research would be and how Cheskin should tackle it. Rhea was stunned that Microsoft had engaged with so many industrial designers. In his experience, nobody had such massive bake-offs. Coyner decided to run the different design prototypes past a bunch of consumers. The idea wasn't to create a massive statistically valid study of what the entire world would think of the design.

Rather, Rhea's team of a few people suggested they try out the design among a variety of gamers in different cities around the world. They figured that about 100 consumers would be enough to get a qualitative idea of the range of opinions on designs. Microsoft used its own researchers to test the market in Japan.

"We needed a framework on how to think about design decisions," Rhea said. "We are trying to inform the intuition of the design team, like suggesting that the design needs to be softer or thinner."

Cheskin didn't do focus groups of a dozen or so people. Rhea felt that people in groups often said different things than they did when they were alone. In groups, people were bolder, and often wanted to show off to the others. On their own, they gave very different opinions. Cheskin wanted to get gut reactions. The point of the Xenon research wasn't just to get feedback on the prototypes. It was to find out about how consumers saw a product such as a game console and what they wanted from it. Each interview lasted an hour. Usually, after about 15 interviews, the subjects started giving the same answers.

"You run out of unique perspectives," Rhea said.

Based on earlier experience, Cheskin came up with a graphic of a quadrant that described the possibilities for the design style. On one line was a spectrum from organic – with softer, biometric designs with spheres and ovals that were hallmarks of Italian design. The other end of the spectrum was architectural, with rectilinear features such as a building or the PlayStation 2 design. On the vertical axis, Cheskin had a spectrum for taste that ran from mild to wild. The point was to find Microsoft's comfort zone. Xbox was more bold and wild.

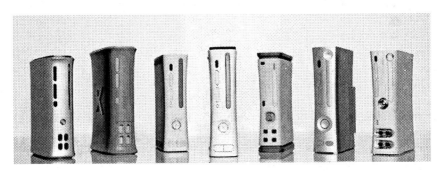

Seven early prototypes for Xenon design

The original Xbox was so beefy that it was like the "Incredible Hulk," said Paolo Malabuyo, who joined the User Interface group under Coyner. Even with the logo, with the green light bursting out, it was hardcore. The green orb was like the "Hulk's muscles busting through," he said. This new design had to appeal to a lot more people. It had to be more like Bruce Lee, strong yet graceful. In terms of mild and wild, Microsoft needed something more elegant, like a BMW, not a Ferrari.

"We needed to go for the mass market," Malabuyo said.

No design was perfect. Sparing no expense, Microsoft kept at it. Stewart decided to move to a different part of Microsoft. Then Coyner started interviewing for a new designer in the summer of 2003. He was nervous. The effort was running late. They were simply running out of time.

1. "Design Gets Real; How the Shifting Concept of Design is Changing the Way We Work and Live," *Newsweek*, Oct. 19, 2003.

2. "Geek Bling: From TVs to Cell Phones, Gadgets These Days Are More Than Functional; They Have To Look Good," by Dean Takahashi, *San Jose Mercury News*, Jan. 3, 2005.

3. "Geek Bling," by Dean Takahashi.

CHAPTER TWENTY-FOUR

MAKING DECISIONS, SIGNING CONTRACTS

Nvidia almost stole the graphics chip deal away from ATI Technologies in July, 2003. Jen-Hsun Huang, the CEO of Nvidia, was a shrewd negotiator. He stayed in the running for the graphics chip contract, in spite of the ill will over the first Xbox. One of the things Huang could offer was a discount on the current Xbox chips. He also noted how easy it would be to make the system backward compatible with the old system, and how Microsoft would likely have to pay a royalty to Nvidia if it intended on making old Xbox games run on the new Xbox, even if Nvidia's chip wasn't in the new one. Was Nvidia just a stalking horse?

"We went through a process with our criteria and ATI was at the top," said Microsoft negotiator Barry Spector. "We looked at another company that didn't have the capability to do it. As things stalled, Nvidia was back in the picture. We knew what happened in the past. We knew stuff happened. It was in the past. We wiped the slate clean and then tried to see if they could meet the criteria. It wasn't playing one against the other. It was keeping options open. You have to when there is so much at stake."

Spector knew they were running low on time in the summer of 2003. It was tricky to determine a price for a chip that didn't exist yet and didn't have a production history behind it that determined how cheap it would be to manufacture. Spector's boss, Bryan Lee, didn't want to do a deal that didn't meet all of Microsoft's long-term plans.

"Our people understood that getting the right deal was as important as getting it done soon," Spector said.

But the talks with ATI took a turn for the better. Todd Holmdahl, the vice president in charge of Xbox hardware, and Greg Gibson, the system designer, joined into the discussions. On ATI's side, sales and marketing chief Rick Bergman moved into the talks alongside engineering chief Bob Feldstein. Now there was a chance for each side to negotiate engineer to engineer, or sales to sales. They started to trust each other and compromise.

One day, Spector was talking on a call on a Saturday, just as he was about to embark on a fly-fishing vacation. He had been on the phone for hours. His wife came in and asked for his attention. She slipped him a note. Spector asked for a five-minute break on the call and said, "My 17-year-old daughter's friends are here and they want to take her on her first motorcycle ride." Everyone on the call laughed. They took the break and reconvened later.

"Every one of us had one of those moments," Spector said.

Fortunately, Feldstein believed that Todd Holmdahl was ethical and trustworthy.

"He was fair to both sides," Feldstein said. "That made it easier to work with Microsoft."

Robbie Bach also inspired the same warm and fuzzy feeling. Bach and Dave Orton, CEO of ATI, said they wanted to make the deal happen, but they left the negotiating to the team. ATI eventually got the deal back. Bach signed off on the contract, and so did Steve Ballmer. And Spector, who was actually a former elementary school teacher in another life, held a party for his legal team.

The contract had been very contentious, but ATI had been willing to bend. They gave the concessions Microsoft was looking for, with respect to owning ATI's chip design, leaving Microsoft free to shop the design to different manufacturers in an effort to lock in the lowest possible manufacturing costs. ATI committed to the launch date in 2005, with bonuses and penalties tied to making or missing that date.

"This was clearly make or break for Microsoft," said Bob Feldstein, vice president of engineering at ATI. "That's why the deal wasn't set up by engineers, but by the business people so that in the long run they knew they could make money. They had spreadsheets on how each part contributed to costs and cost reductions over time. A lot more thinking went into the business model this time."

They signed the deal on August 12, 2003, and ATI went to work on the chip it code-named C1. Under the deal, ATI would be paid engineering fees for its work and receive a royalty on each chip sold. But Microsoft wouldn't have to pay ATI the extra margin for actually fabricating the chips. Instead, they could cut out ATI as a middleman and take the chips directly to the contract manufacturers themselves. That lowered costs. And it gave Microsoft the right to set their own schedule for redesigning the chips to be less expensive. If someone sued Microsoft for patent infringement related to the design, ATI agreed that they would indemnify Microsoft. The deal had to spell out who was responsible for each step along the way in the design and manufacturing process.

Huang said that the deal didn't make good business sense for Nvidia and so his company had to walk away from it. While the negotiators such as Barry Spector were tough, the ATI executives got along well with Robbie Bach and Todd Holmdahl.

"They were both very fair when it came to business," said Dave Orton, the president of ATI. "Jen-Hsun said it wasn't a good deal. It was a good deal. We wouldn't have signed it otherwise. He just lost it."

Microsoft's chip experts, Nick Baker and Masoud Foudeh, had defined an impressive project for ATI. They had ordered a custom graphics chip with 232 million transistors, and a companion embedded memory chip with 100 million transistors. The graphics chip would have 48 unified shaders that could execute 24 billion shader instructions per second. Most graphics chips had separate shaders for vertex (locating a position) or pixel (giving it texture) processing.

The graphics chip would run at 500 megahertz, and process 500 million triangles per second. The chip would display images on both standard analog TV screens and on digital TVs with a resolution of 720P. That wasn't the highest possible quality target, but Microsoft figured it would the sweet spot of the market. ATI would also design a memory controller into the chip, and design the embedded memory chip that connected to the graphics chip at high speeds.

"ATI was thinking of this as a game console chip and not a PC chip," said Greg Gibson, the system designer.

On the technical side, that is what won ATI the design. The idea of putting embedded memory in the box made a great deal of sense to Gibson. If it wasn't there, the traffic on the main memory bus – the data highway between memory and both the CPU and the graphics chip – would have been too heavy. A shortage of memory bandwidth was the Achilles heel for systems such as the PlayStation 2, the original Xbox, and gaming PCs. Since the embedded DRAM was connected directly to the graphics chip, the graphics chip could fetch a great deal of what it needed from the embedded memory without needing to go across the bus to main memory. The game developers could have used more embedded memory, but its presence was a relief. It would allow the system to achieve more of its theoretical performance, in contrast to systems that could never come close to hitting their maximum theoretical performance.

"There's a huge amount of traffic that never touches the bus," Gibson said. "That was a huge thing that ATI brought to bear."

Feldstein had a team working since the spring on the project. Now he could kick into high gear, adding scores of engineers to the team. Larry Yang, the head of Microsoft's chip division in Mountain View, Calif., worked closely with Feldstein's team to set up the schedule. Microsoft would check progress on the work and then set up the fabrication schedule at its chip contract manufacturer, Taiwan Semiconductor Manufacturing Co. Meanwhile, Microsoft coordinated with NEC, which would make the embedded memory that would be coupled with the graphics chip. Foudeh was the program manager who stayed in constant contact at ATI's facilities.

Feldstein created solid walls so that the engineers working for Nintendo wouldn't be in contact with the engineers on Microsoft's project. He had to hold out some contingency plans, depending on whether ATI's graphics chip would be coupled with IBM's or Intel's microprocessors. The odds were strong that IBM would win the deal, but it wasn't signed yet. Microsoft still didn't know exactly what it would to make the old games compatible with the new machine, but it knew that it wanted to do so.

Feldstein didn't worry so much about the competition. He knew that the Cell microprocessor being designed by IBM, Sony and Toshiba was a complex multiprocessor. That would come with its own headaches for programmers. He knew that Sony was working on its own graphics chip, but didn't yet know that would fall apart.

Microsoft's hardware engineers and the ATI chip designers consulted each other constantly. On one of his trips to Redmond, Feldstein ran into Steve Ballmer in one of Microsoft's cafeterias. They shook hands. But he formed a business relationship with Robbie Bach, Todd Holmdahl, and Bryan Lee. ATI dispatched engineer Jason Mitchell to brief game developers on the architecture. Many were skeptical, but Mitchell kept at it. After a while, Microsoft's own people went out to do the briefings.

The schedule was going to be tough. ATI had to finish by the fall of 2004 in order to meet the timetable. It would take some time to fabricate prototypes. Then it would take months to debug the chip. Then a matter of weeks would pass before they entered full-scale production in the summer of 2005. Altogether, it was six to eight months less time to do the work than a typical PC graphics chip design.

"We were scared about that," said Feldstein. "We were afraid it would be a strain on the whole company."

The decision on the microprocessor came to a head in September, 2003.

Ever since it scored a deal to provide the microprocessor to the Nintendo GameCube, IBM was serious about games. John Kelly, the chief of IBM's semiconductor business, needed a big victory. Intel had beaten the PowerPC alliance of IBM, Apple and Motorola in the 1990s. The alliance was based at the Somerset Design Center, an Austin facility named after the fairness of King Arthur's round table. Apple's market share had fallen to all-time lows of about 2 percent. That wasn't going to be enough to finance the heavy-duty investment required to sustain the design of the highest-performance microprocessors. Motorola had already begun its retreat to embedded microprocessors – for cars and industrial machines. IBM had staked out networking for its PowerPC chips, but with the collapse of the dotcom and telecom bubbles, that was a shrinking business. To maintain its investments in the leading edge chip factories, IBM needed high-volume chip sales.

Jim Kahle, a senior architect at IBM, led a team of 450 engineers to conceive a new chip architecture from the ground up. They thought the video game market was the perfect launch pad for this chip. So did Sony. Hence came the Cell alliance of March, 2001. The Sony, Toshiba and IBM engineers gathered in Austin, the same city where the Somerset Design Center existed years earlier. IBM expected to win Nintendo's business again. It had the inside track, because Nintendo would likely consider IBM as the front-runner for its successor to the GameCube. This might be enough to garner sales of 100 million chips for the next-generation consoles. But IBM wanted more. All IBM needed was Microsoft to complete its coup de grace in the game chip market.

But the contract talks for the deal with Microsoft were bogging down. Microsoft wanted a second source for the IBM microprocessor. Since the microprocessor was extremely complex and was one of the most expensive components in the system, it was clear that it wasn't going to be easy to build. IBM had a lead in manufacturing process technology and it was in the process of licensing the technology to Chartered Semiconductor, a Singapore-based contract manufacturer. Chartered needed to catch up with rivals such as Taiwan Semiconductor Manufacturing Co. and United Microelectronics. Those companies were already moving forward with 300-millimeter factories, which made chips more efficiently by essentially baking bigger pizzas. They used 300-millimeter wafers of silicon as their starting point for chips, rather than the older, 200-millimeter wafers. That delivered cost and throughput advantages that Chartered needed to match. Since IBM had the technology already, it licensed it to Chartered. But Microsoft was going to use a special processing technique, dubbed Silicon on Insulator, or SOI, for its microprocessor, to give its chip power consumption advantages. Larry Yang said that Microsoft pushed IBM to license this technology to Chartered as well so that Chartered could truly serve as a second source for Xenon chips. It would take a lot of IBM engineers to help Chartered implement the technology. Once that deal was in place, Microsoft felt more comfortable. Now it wasn't going to be entirely captive to IBM, and it had an alternate source if IBM's yields were poor.

This side negotiation with Chartered delayed the final deal with IBM. At the rate that things were going, it was going to take longer to sign the dotted line on the contract than it would to design the chip. Microsoft had a very specific mission in mind so that it would make money on Xenon. The deal with IBM was going to be critical to that. IBM was willing to bend. Kelly was certain of one thing.

"Innovation is no longer centered around the PC," he said. "The computing and consumer electronics world are coming together."

But the decision involved a lot of politics. Bill Gates stepped in on behalf of Intel, asking whether the team could find a way to design Microsoft's longtime partner into the box. He pulled in Windows experts such as Rick Rashid, head of Microsoft Research, and Dave Cutler, who had crafted Microsoft's modern operating system. Gates listened in several meetings as Nick Baker and others defended their choice as the best one. They beat the drum on multicore, but outside the company the chatter was scarce. They had little validation they chose the right path. Game developers weren't that comfortable with it, but the tools experts believed that designing games for multicore, multithreaded machines was doable.

"In the end, IBM had a really powerful PowerPC core that was small and efficient," said Greg Gibson, the system designer. "It was the only one that could have given us three cores in one CPU in a small form factor, low cost, low power with the integrated cache memory."

Gates and Ballmer were ready to sign up to buy their first 18 months worth of chips from IBM. They cut a big check to IBM, and had a handshake agreement in place by September, 2003. In November, 2003, the company finally announced the deal. IBM had only about 13 months before it was supposed to finish that first design. Normally, such projects took about two years. This meant that Microsoft was not likely to have a console that was truly backward compatible. The ninjas had still not yet reported back on how much it would cost or even if it was possible. At the time, Robbie Bach was prepared to deal with the consequences.

Now that Microsoft had finally made its decision, Jon Thomason's software team could get started writing the operating system for the new machine. That job fell to both Dinarte Morais and Tracy Sharp, who had done the same work on the first console. The team was small and very compartmentalized. Thomason favored reducing the dependencies between components, so that teams didn't have to rely upon each other. The audio team could function without any help from the kernel team, and visa versa.

CHAPTER TWENTY-FIVE

SIGN OFF

y September, 2003, the Xe 30 team was done with its work. The schedule masters had decided this was the time to make a lot of big decisions. If Microsoft was going to launch worldwide in November, 2005, it needed two or three million consoles ready at that time. That meant that it would need to begin manufacturing 100,000 to 200,000 units a week as early as August, 2005. Since the factories needed lead time, they had to begin amassing finished components in July, 2005. Manufacturing of the graphics chip and microprocessor had to begin around June, 2005. Those chips needed about six months for proper prototype debugging, giving the companies two chances to fix major design problems and run them through the silicon factories. That meant the first prototypes had to be finished in December, 2004. Since it took two years to design the most difficult chips, Microsoft was already behind schedule. Sony had begun its chip development efforts in 2001 for a machine that would launch in 2005 or 2006. But Sony's work was on an untested, brand new kind of design. Microsoft's chips could be done in half the time because they weren't nearly so radical. In any case, Microsoft was already pushing the limit on timing. It had to set the project in motion.

In October, 2003, the Xe 30 group and all of the top Xbox executives scheduled a meeting with Bill Gates and Steve Ballmer. Although they had each spent time in small groups with the top dogs, this was the first time the entire team ran through the Xe 30 plan in detail. They had a lot of answers. As Robbie Bach had said, they would launch in the fall of 2005 in all major regions. They would use ATI's graphics chip and IBM's microprocessor. But Microsoft would own the design so it could bring down costs. Xbox Live would distinguish the console from its rivals. It would have a free version and a premium service. Everyone would be able to download games trailers, demos and promos. The system would have 256 megabytes of main memory, about four times as much as the

memory in the original Xbox. Players would activate the online service with a single push of the "Xenon button." The technical team was investigating whether they could use wireless controllers with Xenon, chasing the Wavebird controller that Nintendo used for the GameCube. Microsoft would have a version with a hard disk drive, as well as one without one. The box would be backward compatible, but it wasn't clear to what degree.

The job of summing it all up and making the actual pitch fell to J Allard. Allard had a lot of detractors inside Microsoft. Some were jealous of his successes and his favored status among Microsoft's brass. Even one of his best friends, Cam Ferroni, said that Allard had a big ego. But all the detractors envied Allard's experience and skill when it came to managing his bosses. He knew how to handle Bill Gates and Steve Ballmer. He had been in dozens of meetings with them over the years. They trusted Allard and his judgment. In pitching Xenon, Allard had been smart to keep the bosses informed of each decision. That way, final approval didn't require a massive leap of faith. It was just one more meeting.

"He just knew the right way to do those types of reviews," said Ferroni, who had been sitting in on Allard's meetings with the top brass since 1996.

"We've heard stories of Bill going crazy and yelling," Ferroni continued. "They were certainly contentious. But we had a solid plan with a solid team, and good answers to most of Bill's questions. We didn't get defensive. We didn't have an answer right now on some of his questions."

Gates and Ballmer had read and approved Robbie Bach's "3" memo. Gates was eager to read through the work of the XE 30 group and even got regular briefings from Greg Gibson, the system architect, and others in the XE 30 group about once a month. Even though Gates first saw a copy of their 80-page plan the night before the meeting, he had clearly analyzed and understood everything they wrote. His copy of the XE 30 had handwritten marks on every page. The team retrieved all the copies of the *News Time* article and later destroyed them. Both Gates and Ballmer gave the project the green light.

Gates pushed back in one area. He brought up "better together." The Xenon team, driven by the efforts of David Reid and Jeff Henshaw, made important concessions in this category by suggesting that the console include a Media Center Extender. Their idea was that Xenon was a digital entertainment amplifier, not a full-fledged stereo system. It would not include the full functionality of a TV set-top box or a digital video recorder. Such functions would drive up the cost and clutter the mission of focusing on a gaming appliance. Instead of including a full-fledged version of Windows for the living room (dubbed the Media Center Edition), it would work together with a Media Center PC. The Xenon console would "extend" the Media Center PC. Dave Alles' team in the eHome group were working on the extenders. Their first effort would be an experimental version. They would create an extender for the original Xbox first and learn from the experience. Then they would design it into Xenon itself.

"It was a dress rehearsal for Xenon," said Joe Belfiore, who took over the eHome group in 2003.

But the groups knew where to draw the line. Belfiore said that the idea to get Xenon to run Windows, and become a Media Center PC itself, never came up. For one thing, the choice of IBM as the chip vendor made it harder to achieve this goal. And for another, it just didn't make sense.

"It's a very complementary strategy," Belfiore said. "We feel our job is to make the PC the hub. Then the Xbox is a client connected to the hub. It's really two different things. It's one thing to architect a device to intrinsically be like a PC. It's another thing to say my device will be complementary to the PC."

Joe Belfiore's eHome group helped design the Xenon remote control.

The eHome group passed on some knowledge about remote controls to the Xbox group. They said that consumers should be able to turn on their device with a remote control, without having to get up from the couch or the bed. Maybe that wasn't the way that gamers behaved, but it certainly was in tune with the habits of couch potatoes. The groups agreed that Xenon would have a remote, and that the eHome team would design it. The Xbox team welcomed the 40 extra programmers and engineers. Belfiore generously funded the work, even though it didn't directly benefit the Windows team. What it did do is fulfill the mission of making Windows and the Xbox efforts fit better together. As long as a game box was in the home, the content on the PC could be used on a wider variety of devices, making the PC into a true home server. And that pleased Bill Gates.

Over time, a lot of people on the team came to believe that the presence of the extender, the ability to connect with video and music collections on the PC, would differentiate Microsoft's box from Sony's next machine.

"We all realized it would be a differentiator," Belfiore said. "The Xbox team embraced it more slowly. They had to strike a careful balance of nailing the world's best game device, and then consider adding non-gaming multimedia features."

But it wasn't clear that Gates saw things exactly the way Belfiore did. Gates liked the idea of the two separate versions, or SKUs. One machine would have a hard disk drive and sell for a higher price. That version would appeal to the hardcore gamers and those who liked playing online games on Xbox Live. But those who were on a budget might opt for the lesser machine.

Gates thought another category of user might want a third version. He was still clinging to the idea of getting Windows to run on the machine. That was why Intel was still a contender in the chip race, even though it was stubbornly resisting Microsoft's suggestions. If Microsoft could launch a high-end version of Xenon, it could offer the all-in-one experience. It could combine a Media Center PC with the game console. The machine would have Windows, so it would require a lot more memory in the system. Even if Microsoft chose IBM, it still had a way to run Windows. In February, 2003, Microsoft had acquired technology from a company called Connectix. The company made virtualization software. This enabled a Windows PC application program to run on a machine from Apple Computer with the Macintosh operating system. With that technology, Microsoft could adapt its Windows software to run on IBM's PowerPC chips. If this kind of technology worked properly, then Microsoft could make the shift to IBM without fear of losing the all-important Windows Xenon SKU.

Allard didn't have a definitive answer on the third SKU, though he had a team investigating the possibility of running Windows on Xenon. Belfiore in the eHome group said that there wasn't much need to get Windows on Xenon as long as Microsoft still had its separate approaches with the game console and the PC. Nobody insisted that the two groups had to eventually come together into the same business. But as a concession to Gates, he agreed to assign a team to go work on the project. If it paid off as Gates had schemed, it would be a brilliant maneuver. But changing events had made it less and less relevant. Gates still wanted to give it a try. The project's code name was Helium. Allard assigned Jon Thomason, his software chief, to choose someone to run the team for the project. Conceivably, students in a dorm room might want a combination Windows PC/Xenon machine to save on space. Insiders viewed it skeptically.

"We had code names for a lot of random Bill ideas," said one Xbox veteran. Another said, "It was a ridiculous idea that strayed from our core mission."

But Thomason noted in an e-mail after the meeting that Helium had graduated from an investigation to a development project. He picked Dwight Krossa, a veteran programmer who had once headed Microsoft's work with IBM in the 1980s, to lead Helium. With that angle being explored, Gates received assurance the team would explore his long-held dream of Windows running on Xenon. Krossa would coordinate with the hardware and software teams to see if he could make Helium come to life.

After they dealt with Gates' request and received their go ahead, the XE 30 team members breathed a sigh of relief.

"We got a glowing review," recalled one team member. "Bill only swore once. That was a special meeting. There were guys who had been there a long time who said that it was the best 'Bill meeting' ever. I thought we would get our asses handed do us."

Separately, A.J. Redmer presented the content plan for the first party division to Gates and Ballmer. The plan called for a total of 15 first-party and

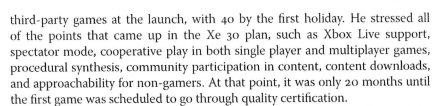

third-party games at the launch, with 40 by the first holiday. He stressed all of the points that came up in the Xe 30 plan, such as Xbox Live support, spectator mode, cooperative play in both single player and multiplayer games, procedural synthesis, community participation in content, content downloads, and approachability for non-gamers. At that point, it was only 20 months until the first game was scheduled to go through quality certification.

After those meetings in October, 2003, Microsoft had a plan. Some of the planners thought it had been watered down. But Allard declared that Xe 30 was done. Now it had to get a hundred trains moving on the tracks to execute.

"We had our marching orders at that point," Ferroni said. "That was a big deal. There were only 50 to 60 people who knew at that point what we were talking to Bill and Steve about. After that, we had to move."

J Allard's reward for another good Bill meeting was a sabbatical. He decided to take off a couple of months at the end of 2003 to ski and snowboard in Whistler, British Columbia. He didn't plan on coming back until March, 2004. Todd Holmdahl picked up his day-to-day duties of running the platform business, while Jon Thomason took charge of the Xenon planning initiatives.

"Now is the time to catch my breath," he said in a parting e-mail. "The current generation is running strong and the Xenon strategy/plan is tight."

Allard addressed rumors that he wouldn't be coming back. He said, "Those who know me well know how deeply committed to this project I am and how relentless I am about winning round two. In the immortal words of California's newly elected governor – I'll be back.... The Xenon plan kicks ass and is well underway.... The last month around here has a 'buzz' in the hallways and an energy level not seen since the beginning of the project."

CHAPTER TWENTY-SIX

ED FRIES'
LAST STAND

*E*d Fries had worries on his mind. He tried to stay abreast of the development of *Halo* 2, but it was just one of about 50 internal game projects that he was responsible for. Beyond that, he also had to oversee dozens more third-party games being made by outside developers and publishers. After the success of *Halo*, Bungie was off to a slow start on the sequel. Team members took breaks, but some of the sound team had to immediately work on localizing the game for different international audiences who were now demanding it.

Alex Seropian, co-founder of Bungie, had decided he had enough of the big company life and left Microsoft. He was starting a family and wanted to return to Chicago. Seropian was more of an entrepreneur, while Jones and Joe Staten were hands-on product guys who wanted to keep the *Halo* franchise going. Seropian eventually started a small game developer, Wideload Games, with six other Bungie veterans. But he didn't think that the "always crunching" work style at Bungie was healthy.

Most of the 68 people at Bungie were now considered the *Halo* team. Jones led the design team on *Halo* 2, while Staten took charge of the cinematics, or the movie-like cut scenes in between the levels of the game. With Seropian gone, the Bungie team needed a new studio chief, and they found it in Pete Parsons, a veteran Microsoft game marketer. Parsons had marketed *Halo* and the Bungie folks liked him. Parsons saw his job as "protecting Bungie." To him, it was "lightning in a bottle." It had a culture that he didn't want to change.

"We have to keep Bungie as Bungie," Parsons said.

Distractions surfaced immediately. *Halo* had turned into a cultural phenomenon. Fans were always asking what Bungie was up to next. Six months after the release of the game, agents from Hollywood came knocking on the door to make *Halo* into a movie. Parsons didn't want to distract the team, but he felt he had to investigate the opportunity.

He dispatched Staten to go to Los Angeles and feel out the studios. Staten was pleasantly shocked when film producers who claimed to be "big, big fans" of *Halo* actually described the parts of the game that they liked best.

"Though to be honest, when I say 'shocking' I really mean alluring," Staten later wrote in a post on Bungie's web site. "Here were a bunch of smart, talented folks eager to make a film that would be 'not just the first great video game movie, but one of the best science fiction movies ever made.' And I could see in their eyes they meant it."

Staten and Parsons regarded the visit to Hollywood as a "siren call" that would only distract them from making *Halo 2*. They told the producers "thanks but no thanks" and put the idea of licensing *Halo* to Hollywood on hold.

Fries decided to farm out the PC version of *Halo* to Gearbox Software, a game studio in Texas. He wanted the rest of Bungie to focus on exploiting the *Halo* franchise with a sequel. But Jones wanted to make another original game that involved Minotaurs, a topic that went back to Bungie's roots. He appointed others to run *Halo 2*, but it wasn't going well at first.

"No one was pulling them together, no one was pushing them," Fries said.

Bungie as a company was deep in the process of designing, writing and thinking. The high expectations were both confining and liberating. They wanted to offer more than just a version of the original *Halo* with Xbox Live enabled for online play. The team, and even the press, belittled that idea as *Halo 1.5*.

For Fries, the pressure was building to say something publicly about *Halo 2*. The marketing folks wanted Fries to reveal more about the game at the E3 trade show in May, 2002. Fries wanted the project be handled right, so he had several heated arguments with other executives about why he wanted to keep it quiet. He wanted the game to be done properly, with enough resources and time. If Bungie focused on the demo, it might be distracted from the game.

"There was a lot of pressure," said one Bungie veteran. "Some of it was dumb pressure."

Pressures to churn out sequels were common in the games industry. Electronic Arts was the perfect example of the kind of company that mobilized huge resources to exploit hits. The Sims became the best-selling PC game of all time because EA poured tons of resources into making sequel after sequel for the game on all platforms. Fries, however, felt he had something special in Bungie and that to follow EA's path would be to ruin the team. The Bungie team worked away from the bottom up.

"There was a fundamental difference between a top-down organization like EA," Seropian said. "Bungie was an extremely bottom-up company that focused on making a product as good as it could be."

Microsoft didn't force directives upon Bungie, with the exception that the original *Halo* had to be ready for the launch. That had its drawbacks. Without the pressure to ship something by Christmas in order to survive, Bungie could take its time. Yet it lacked a planning process that set timetables for future games such as *Halo 3*.

The thinking at Bungie was "good enough sucks." One of the biggest holdups was evaluating just how much the Xbox could handle. The team found they had to retrace their steps. They had created detailed graphics models with highly accurate shadows and lighting for the characters and vehicles in the game. But the graphics for those characters were so demanding that the Xbox couldn't handle them. Whenever a lot of characters crowded the scene, the Xbox came grinding to a halt. The team had to scale back those ambitions. Moreover, the artists had trouble with the new models because it gave them less control over how a scene looked. Everything in the scenes looked harsh.

For the Xbox executive team, it was important to get *Halo 2* out the door during 2003. The platform needed it. Microsoft was losing to Sony. Xbox Live had launched in November, 2002, and it was generating paying subscribers for online games. But Microsoft needed a game that could give Xbox Live a big boost. *Halo 2* was such a game, but it was falling further and further behind schedule. Fries pushed back and got more time. Microsoft said later that Fries didn't deserve the sole credit for securing this extra time. But it was clear that *Halo 2* was a disaster in cross-divisional communication, said one team member who had to fight the battle alongside Fries.

One Bungie veteran said, "I don't care about the platform. I don't care if we're with Microsoft or Sony. I care about the game. And Jason Jones, he's not a sequel guy."

It didn't help matters when Hamilton Chu, lead producer at Bungie, left the project and, ultimately, Microsoft altogether. At the beginning of 2003, Jones took back the reins. The work was hard on the Bungie staff, and at one point, Jones decided the missions had to be redone.

"It wasn't just about making new levels," Parsons said. "It's about rewriting the game from the ground up."

Everyone was nervous as they were rehearsing the *Halo 2* demo in the days leading up to E3 2003. In the final rehearsal, just 15 minutes before they opened the doors to the press, Ed Fries ran through his introduction. Joe Staten ran through the actual demo. A space ship came shooting through the atmosphere of earth and it crash landed. Master Chief, the main character of the game, turned and froze. And froze. And froze. Nothing was happening. The game had crashed. The technicians figured out quickly that the files on the Xbox had been corrupted. That was because the Xbox was sitting next to a big speaker for the whole day. The magnets in the speaker must have scrambled the magnetic hard disk in the Xbox. The team frantically copied the files to a new machine. In the actual demonstration, the demo worked fine. Fries breathed a sigh of relief. And the crowd roared its approval when Staten showed a new feature dubbed boarding, where a soldier could board the chassis of a moving hover Ghost, knock the alien off the machine, and then take over the flying vehicle. The crowd fawned over new features like the ability to hold two weapons at once and environments that could be damaged. That demo had been necessary from a marketing view, but creating it cost the programmers weeks of lost time. They felt the game still wasn't fun.

The team at Bungie was aware of the stakes. The game was more complicated because it had to work with 16 players on Xbox Live. The Bungie team wanted it to be just as fun playing online as it was sitting on a couch with friends. The scale of the game was huge, with 15 levels, each of which were many times larger than the levels in the original game. The script for the cinematic sequences ran 160 pages, and those sequences would run for more than two hours total in the game. *Halo* had 2,000 lines of combat dialogue, but there would be seven times as much in *Halo 2*.

"We don't spend a lot of time thinking about the pressure," Parsons said. "The enormity of the job we are trying to do and the high bar we set for ourselves is enough pressure. It doesn't help anything. This was a huge and enormously complex game. So we said when it's ready, it's ready."

And it wasn't ready for the fall of 2003. The revised schedule meant that Fries had to go back to the executives for a showdown. Fries knew that the delays on *Halo 2* meant that the team would be even farther behind on *Halo 3*. And without something like *Halo 3*, the launch titles for Xenon wouldn't be stellar. Now he had to push the launch date for *Halo 2* from the fall of 2003 to the spring of 2004. Even then, Bungie was falling further and further behind schedule. To make the new schedule, Jones decided to chop the story in half. The second part would become *Halo 3*. It would leave the game with a cliffhanger ending, but that was all they could accomplish.

Jones asked for even more time. He said his team could hit the April, 2004, ship date, but they would probably all quit once it was done. He even suggested that Microsoft hold the game for the Xenon launch in 2005, but nobody liked that idea.

"It's important to be ambitious," Jones later said. "Certainly you can go too far." [1] Yet again, Fries had to go back to the executive team. He asked if they would delay the game to the fall of 2004. That completely threw the development schedule for *Halo 3* and Xenon out of whack. It also meant that the Home and Entertainment division would miss its financial target for the fiscal year that ended June 30, 2004. Fries didn't really care about that because he could blow away the plan for the next fiscal year. But others didn't shake off that problem so lightly.

"We could wait until Christmas, 2004, and do the game right, screw the fiscal year and ship one of the best products ever made," Fries said.

Around July, 2003, Bach put the decision in front of the whole executive team. Fries didn't like that, since it was a product development decision. He had always run his business autonomously, and this was clearly a game decision within his division. But he went along with Bach's move. Bryan Lee, J Allard, Peter Moore, and Mitch Koch all weighed in. They wanted Bungie to finish the game by April, 2004, in spite of Fries' arguments that it would destroy the best franchise. Bach said that the needs of the platform outweighed the needs of any one game. When Fries left that contentious meeting, he thought for the first time that his career at Microsoft could come to an end.

He decided that he would always be under pressure to make the wrong

decision. To cut corners. Instead of making the decision in favor of the game, he would always have to sacrifice his principles for some greater good. That wasn't the way that he wanted to run a business, particularly one that involved artists. And even if he won the arguments on this game, he felt that the same issue would come up over and over again. The needs of the platform would go ahead of the needs of the product. That was all business. It had nothing to do with art.

"I walked out of that meeting and realized that I might wind up leaving the company," Fries said. "I had been there 18 years. I could see where the paths went. I could see the roads closing. It was inevitable. I had some hope that something would happen. That was when I was first surprised to discover the inevitability of me leaving. It was a shocking thing. I had never considered leaving before."

Fries considered the task he had to undertake within the games group. He now had to sort between Xbox and Xbox 360 titles. He looked at the top teams in the organization, the ones that were succeeding and the ones that were unraveling. Taking Bach's advice to cut back in other areas, Fries starting cutting back. Microsoft had bought Rare. But Nintendo was starting a new studio in Tokyo. Sony was buying key developers such as Naughty Dog, Eidetic, and Incognito. It was beefing up its development studios, and it had a hot studio in Polyphony, maker of the *Gran Turismo* games.

But Fries had a finite budget. He had to implement deep layoffs. The team of 1,200 developers and 1,000 contractors would suffer hundreds of jobs lost over time. Fries asked many of the studios to start cutbacks across the board. But what started out as small layoffs was almost like a Band-Aid approach, and it didn't really address many of the key problems. The moves hurt morale broadly. Microsoft was losing the battle in sports games against Electronic Arts, but Fries couldn't yet face the decision of bailing out of that war.

"Ed was a compassionate person," said Stuart Moulder, who ran the PC games studios for Fries. "He really struggled with the idea we need to close studios and lay off people. He is a super smart guy. But the reality of shutting down a studio was hard for Ed."

Moulder himself ran out of gas during the cutbacks. As chief of PC games, he had to help manage a half-dozen studios. He had gotten further and further from making games and served a purely managerial function. In the summer of 2002, he had asked Ed Fries if he could be assigned to manage a single studio. Fries asked Moulder to take over the studio in Japan from A.J. Redmer. He went overseas and checked out the schools for his kids. But he decided not to take the assignment because he didn't want to live the life of a Japanese "salaryman" who never saw his kids. He took off on a sabbatical, and when he came back he decided to resign in November, 2003.

Moulder later said that he has suffered a case of classic Microsoft burnout. Just after Moulder left, Fries sold off *Asheron's Call*, a massively multiplayer fantasy role-playing game for the PC, to its developer, Turbine Entertainment. Each of the shutdowns had its own tragedy. Internally, Fries canned a firefighting game. He canceled a platform game with a prehistoric setting called *Tork*, being

developed by a studio called Tiwak.

Among his outside developers, he also had to end longtime relationships. Lorne Lanning and Sherry McKenna had bet their Oddworld Inhabitants studio in San Luis Obispo on the Xbox. They were early critics of the PlayStation 2's complex technology and gave credibility to the notion that the Xbox was developer friendly.

Their *Oddworld* games focused on humorous characters with funny action-adventure titles with political subtexts. Their games appealed more to the mass market, not the hardcore gamers. But when the Xbox bombed in Europe and caught hold only with the hardcore gamers, Lanning knew that the writing was on the wall for his kind of game. *Munch's Oddysee*, Oddworld's launch title for the Xbox, sold about 500,000 units. It was a disappointment and a victim of over hype. Lanning tried another game.

He had pitched a Western style game dubbed *Oddworld: Stranger's Wrath*, once again a cute title with furry critters that one could shoot as "live ammo" at enemies in a game that carried a political message. A documentary by the Discovery Channel captured the pitch and Fries' initial reaction, "I think he really wants to do a Western." Fries liked the idea and thought it could be innovative. He gave it the green light in early 2002. But the game fell behind schedule. Fries honestly broke the news to Lanning and McKenna that the game was going to be canceled. Lanning felt that parting was a good thing, given the direction of the Xbox.

"We decided not to stay with the system that was losing the war," Lanning said. "Ed was supportive in making a healthy landing for Oddworld. We worked out an amicable parting. I appreciated Ed was honest and direct."

Other games fell apart. Tim Schafer had been working on *Psychonauts* for the Xbox since 2000. Fries had signed up Schafer because of his brilliant track record with games at LucasArts, working on award-winning original games with deep stories such as *Grim Fandango* and *Full Throttle*. Schafer set up a studio in a warehouse in San Francisco amid all the dotcoms and built a team that peaked at 45 people.

"We were inspired as Microserfs," he said. "The thing that got me to go with them was that Ed was passionate about expanding the potential for games as art. They talked a lot about that early on."

Schafer eventually got tired of the rats and the backed-up toilet so he moved to new digs that the dot bombs had left behind. But *Psychonauts* had gone over budget. It wasn't clear that gamers were going to understand and play the game, which created external cartoons of inner mental dramas. Fries supported the game, but eventually it got cut as well. Part of the reason was that *Psychonauts* was now going to ship in 2005, and Microsoft wasn't willing to support much of anything except Xbox 360 games. At least that was the way it was explained to Schafer. He couldn't really push back in part because he had the same problem that Lanning had.

"Adventure games don't really look good until the end when you pull it together," he said. "We got feedback where we went back and forth. They felt it was too hard, that they wanted more puzzles."

Schafer admitted that he had a hard time starting a company from scratch. He had some turnover. He hired an operations chief in 2003 so that he could concentrate on the game. He understood Microsoft's point of view on his late game. He still had kind words for Fries. But he worried about the industry that couldn't support original games.

"Licensed titles make the money," he said. "It's a really dangerous path. I like to make up stuff from scratch. Build worlds. Entertain people. Most stories are bad in games. They can make a game more challenging and be a great motivator. You interact on an emotional level." Shane Kim pulled the plug on *Psychonauts*.

John Tobias, the creator of *Mortal Kombat,* the ultimate fighting game, had tried to make a comeback with money from Fries. But his game *Tao Feng: Fist of the Lotus*, got some critical acclaim but didn't sell that well. Tobias had to shut his Studio Gigante down as well. When Fries looked at his portfolio, he had a hard time letting go of any of the studios that he had built up over time.

As Microsoft thinned out its ranks on its payroll and cut back on its independent contractors, it started to look for new ways to leverage its work force. The company turned to outsourcing of art in some situations to low-cost art teams overseas. In doing so, Microsoft was following Hollywood and other technology industries that were beginning to tap cheap talent in China and India. *The Simpsons*, for instance, relied upon animators in Vietnam for its art. Brokers like Mark Vange, who operated Ketsujin Studios out of Toronto, found game developers and matched them with Microsoft. As in the other industries, such shifts in jobs were controversial. But the economics made sense. If some could hire five artists in India for the cost of one in the U.S., or hire 10 programmers in China for one American coder, it made sense to do so.

But the outsourcing model only worked so far in games. You couldn't farm out a baseball game to Indian game designers who grew up playing Cricket. And it is hard for those who don't grow up playing games to understand them well enough to create them. Clearly, poor translation in games was a source of great comedy. One Japanese company created a game with the line, "All your base are belong to us." But Microsoft found that the artists at Dhruva Interactive, a Bangalore, India game outsourcing firm, were skilled enough to create the cars in *Forza Motorsport*, Microsoft's upcoming racing game. While the Forza team was small at just 27 people, Dhruva's artists were able to create 85 cars in the game. Microsoft's own developers concentrated on the fundamentals of game play and the style of the art, giving a roadmap for Dhruva to follow. Another company also helped create the cars. By a year after the work began, Microsoft had 230 cars and 18 tracks.

On *Halo 2*, Fries refused to go along with the executive team's decision to ship the game early. He threw a fit and threatened to quit. He didn't think that he was being a primadonna. He felt the franchises were what made the Xbox special. The creative people couldn't be expected to make artistic sacrifices for

the sake of the platform. The shortsightedness astounded him. He got them to reverse their decision and allow *Halo 2* to slip until the fall of 2004.

Both Robbie Bach and Peter Moore said they were never going to pressure an artistic team to compromise a game by shipping it before it was done. "There wasn't much debate about that," Bach said.

But Fries felt he had seen the practical reality of putting the platform first. It preserved autonomy for game decisions within the game development crews. But it removed autonomy from the top game executive and moved the decision-making power to a committee that included executives without enough detailed game knowledge.

"I knew I wasn't going to do that over and over again," Fries said. "I was in an impossible situation. I was emotionally upset because it was hard for me to leave a group that I had built."

After 18 years at the company, Fries was headed out the door. It turned out that Fries was the ultimate company man, but he wasn't one who would blindly follow the advice of his bosses or his peers. He left the company as a true individual. Fries had some good talks with Ballmer and Gates over his difficulties. He didn't want to run his contracts past Bryan Lee and preferred even more control over things such as marketing. But he couldn't say that his division was making lots of money and all of his games were hits. He wasn't in charge of the goose laying the golden eggs. Fries wasn't mad at J Allard, who had been a natural opponent in many of the executive sessions. Fries would have been happier if Peter Moore took control of all of marketing and marketed the games in Fries' group.

Late in the year, the executives threw a charity sing-along event in the cafeteria. All of the executives had to participate in a *karaoke* contest. Fries sang *Purple Rain* by Prince, and the words seemed particularly appropriate. Fries considered it to be his goodbye song to all of his compadres. Some of the words rang true, like "It's such a shame our friendship had to end" and "You say you want a leader, but you can't seem to make up your mind."

Fries' admin packed up his office for him, and over the Christmas holidays he didn't set foot on campus again. His staff threw him a going-away party. Friends from both the Xbox division and the Office division showed up. Robbie Bach delivered a nice parting message. The well wishers in the hardware group presented him with a special gray edition of the Xbox inscribed with the message, "Thanks for all you've done with MGS and Xbox." He also received a plaque that listed all of the 120 games that Microsoft had published during his tenure. Of those, it highlighted 18 games that sold over 1 million copies. Fries was sad during the festivities. In his going away, he remembered the words of his former Office boss, Chris Peters who had quit Microsoft five years earlier. Peters had gone back to school to study art. The best thing about working for Microsoft and then leaving, he said, "was that it gave me a chance for a second life." That's the way that Fries felt about leaving Microsoft as well.

Gates and Ballmer didn't do anything to dramatically change the organization. Fries officially resigned from the company in January, 2004. Robbie Bach appointed Shane Kim, who had been Fries' chief operating officer for eight years, as the acting general manager of Microsoft Game Studios.

"It's sad for us," Bach said in a phone call with a reporter on the day of the announcement. "Ed's a great guy. We're going to focus on great game content. Fewer games, but high quality. That's a change that Ed started 18 months ago."

Fries said at the time some things weren't right and that he needed them to be so if he was going to sign up for another five years of effort.

Bach later added, "Ed's departure was part of the process of Ed deciding what he wanted to do and how we wanted to run the project. Those things happen. Ed's a great person and we wanted him to be on the project. When someone decides to leave, or you have a hole in the organization, you have to be prepared to fill it. We have to structure the organization so that if someone gets hit by a bus, we move forward. In Ed's case, we changed the organization when he left. Those things have happened on every project I have worked on. People leave for personal reasons and you adjust and deal with it. Ed's tenure was critical. The first Xbox wouldn't have gotten done if it wasn't for him. "

Fries had built a world class game studio, and many of his decisions would play out and affect the fate of the Xbox 360. Kim, who was not a gamer, had some big shoes to fill. The Xbox executive team had lost the longest-serving leader of the games business. That made some outsiders stop and wonder about Microsoft's role in games.

But to say that Ed Fries was the gamer dude who fought a losing battle with the business suits and the Microsoft corporate warriors is a statement full of contradictions. As Bach points out, Fries had 18 years behind him and he was the ultimate Microsoft lifer. He started not as a game dude, but an Excel spreadsheet coder. He was hardcore Microsoft. Fries came to understand and know the people in the game business. But his departure didn't necessarily mean that suits had totally triumphed. After all, they gave *Halo* 2 the time to cook. At the same time, there was a big hole in the Xbox group.

A.J. Redmer told his friends at work, "You could call it a Greek tragedy. Ed was smart, and I really miss his presence."

The baton would pass to Shane Kim and to Peter Moore.

When Kevin Bachus, co-creator of the Xbox, heard that Fries was leaving, he said, "Ed was singularly responsible for the position Microsoft holds in PC and console games today. When Ed took over the reins, Microsoft was a joke in the game industry. Today, they have a very respectable position." [2]

1.   Behind the Scenes of *Halo* 2, Bonus Disk, *Halo* 2 Limited Collector's Edition.

2.   "Xbox Developer Resigns From Microsoft," by Dean Takahashi, *San Jose Mercury News*, business section page 1, Jan. 14, 2004.

CHAPTER TWENTY-SEVEN

SHANE TAKES OVER

At first blush, Shane Kim was as different as could be from Ed Fries. Kim got nauseous when he played fast-moving 3-D video games. The motion sickness is a common condition for those who can't adjust to the motion on the screen and the lack of motion in their bodies. It's more severe in games where the camera controls are poorly designed. But Kim's case was so bad he couldn't play games like *Halo* or *Halo 2* at all. Kim liked to keep that a secret as much as possible, given his job in Microsoft's Game Studios. But he kept a sense of humor about it when others found out that he couldn't play *Halo*.

"People tell me it's a good game," he joked.

As the acting general manager of the business, he was now the guy in charge of making sure that *Halo 2* made it into the market. He needed to have a personal rapport with the rock star talent among the game developers and be able to instill confidence in them about Microsoft's game effort. He had to woo the rock stars to Microsoft's platforms so that they could show the world the full power of the console and the PC.

After Fries left in January, 2004, Kim became the acting general manager of the studio, with nearly 1,000 people. The resignation surprised Kim. For a decade, Kim was the No. 2 executive at Microsoft Game Studios. He worked for Fries as the business guy. Fries said that over the years, Kim taught him a lot about business, while Fries tried to teach Kim about games. Together, they had the skills needed to run the business.

As much as Fries liked games and talking about it as an art form, the job at the top of Microsoft's game publishing arm was increasingly about big business. It was less about creative insights and more about managing a portfolio and setting a schedule.

Kim wasn't a hardcore gamer. But Kim's roots suggested he was both a good bean counter and an entertainment fan. His parents emigrated from Korea to go to college in the U.S. His mother was a

dietitian and his father worked for Southern California Edison. Kim grew up playing arcade games in Southern California. He played on the volleyball team at Stanford University, where he studied economics and international relations. He spent a lot of time in the arcade at the student union. He helped pay for an MBA at Harvard University by getting on the "Scrabble" TV game show and winning $14,000. He joined Microsoft in 1990 as a summer intern and worked in marketing. He was hired on and became a marketing manager in work group applications. He managed the Microsoft Mail for PC networks product. He said that after three years, "I decided I didn't want to work on enterprise software for the rest of my life." He ran marketing in the consumer division for a couple of years and then switched to the game division.

He made the move in 1995 because he "had a high propensity for goofing off." He was a huge sports fan and was delighted that Microsoft was dabbling in sports titles. He ran business development and spearheaded some of Fries' acquisitions. For a couple of years he ran a studio and scored a big hit. He struck a deal with Waltham, Massachusettes-based Blue Fang, hiring them to create a game called *Zoo Tycoon*. The children's zoo management game could have been an ill-conceived copycat title of *Rollercoaster Tycoon* and other spin-offs. But the game was well executed when it debuted in 2001, and its sequels sold more than 5 million copies. He was always the senior business guy behind Fries, the Harvard MBA to go with the savvy old programmer.

Being known as the *Zoo Tycoon* guy wasn't necessarily a good credential when it came to dealing with the rock stars of gaming, who had a predilection for hard-core, violent games. But Kim knew he had to maintain good relationships with the industry's elite developers and, now and then, cut them big checks to finance ambitious new games so they were willing to stay in Microsoft's camp. He said he wouldn't make convenient financial decisions if it meant Microsoft fell short on its broader goal of putting out the coolest games.

"We shared a passion for games," Kim said. "Ed has a development background and is more technical. I come from business and marketing. Ed has great business acumen. I believe I have pretty good product acumen. We shared the same philosophy about creating the best games with the best talent. It's dangerous to stereotype me and Ed. It wasn't just me talking spreadsheets at Ed."

Fries had started the cutbacks, but it would become clear later that Kim took a harsher attitude than Fries about business decisions. Kim built his credibility working with Microsoft's early development partners such as Ensemble Studios in Dallas. Tony Goodman, president of Dallas-based Ensemble Studios, met Kim in 1997. The two negotiated Microsoft's contracts with Ensemble, who made Microsoft's blockbuster *Age of Empires* series of PC games. Goodman said he felt like they were "two boxers who had gone the distance" after finishing their deals at the negotiating table.

"If you would have asked me then, I would not have expected that four years later Shane would be the Microsoft executive that I respect and enjoy working with most," Goodman said. "He is extremely bright and shows wisdom beyond his years. His best trait is his transparency."

But Kim's first job upon replacing Ed Fries was to follow through on the strategy of scaling back the game studios to focus on fewer titles. The process had started under Fries, and Kim had to execute on it. Shortly after Fries left, Kim and his general managers canceled *Mythica*, a massively multiplayer online game for the PC. As Microsoft cut back, rivals pounced on the opportunities the cutbacks created. The *Mythica* team formed a new company, "Fireant," with help from Ed Fries. Sony bought it and brought it into its online division. Sony thus gained a development foothold in Seattle. But Microsoft had a better MMO under development, dubbed *Vanguard.*

Shane Kim became the new head of Microsoft Game Studios

Kim also cut a small project called the Xbox Entertainment Network, which had been started by Eduardo Rossini. Ted Hase, one of the original Xbox co-creators, had joined Rossini and a small team that had proposed to do a different kind of entertainment for the console. They had ideas to do episodic games and entertainment, which were more akin to TV soap operas. They were talking to small game developers as well as Hollywood entertainers. This kind of lightweight content was the kind of casual fare that might draw in more consumers beyond the hardcore. But, while the ideas were fresh, it wasn't mainstream. Kim cut the program and Hase returned to Windows.

"I had to step up quickly," Kim recalled when he assumed the job. "I am a big believer in the just do it approach. You are dealt the cards you are dealt and you have to play them. It was not a shock, but it was a surprise. My focus was to make sure the organization kept humming and it didn't become a major distraction. Even though a guy who was fundamental to the growth of Microsoft

Game Studios was leaving, that wasn't going to change fact MGS was a leading publisher and we had a job to do."

Kim had to abide by a new management structure that limited his authority. He had to submit his contracts for approval by Bryan Lee's finance team. And he had to report to Peter Moore, who was elevated upon Fries' departure. Moore had control of international marketing, but now he was also put in charge of Microsoft's publishing efforts. He would oversee both Kim's first-party organization and the third-party game publishers who made games for the Xbox. This was the kind of supervision that Fries had felt would tie his hands when it came to independently managing the game studios. Game marketing was split between Mitch Koch and Peter Moore. It was much different than approach used by companies such as Electronic Arts, which had marketing people embedded directly in the product development groups. Those were the cards that Robbie Bach dealt to Kim.

"There are a set of people who think we should throw money at this," Kim said. "We didn't get to our position by doing dumb things as a company. Just because we have a lot of resources doesn't mean we will throw all caution to the wind."

Kim elevated Phil Spencer, a longtime studio manager, to be his No. 2 executive. Spencer oversaw studios such as Bungie, Ensemble, the racing studio, and the *Zoo Tycoon* team. Other studio executives included A.J. Redmer, who ran Asia; David Luehmann, who ran studios such as FASA and the simulations group; and Chris Early, who ran casual games. Kim backed many of the decisions that Fries had made, but he also tried to be true to his own style of management. He made some of the tough calls that Fries couldn't.

He backed up the cancellations of *Oddworld: Stranger's Wrath* and *Psychonauts*. One of the biggest was his decision to ax Microsoft's sports games like *NFL Fever*. Fries had already given the football team a pass for the year in 2004 as the team tried to redouble its efforts to beat Electronic Arts. But EA had the Madden brand that dominated the consciousness of the gamers and had the endorsements of the stars. Microsoft's sports teams were half the size of EA's.

"We liked to think that our teams worked smarter, but that was really just a kind of arrogance," said one former executive.

Kim backed up Fries' decision by giving all of the sports teams a pass for the season if they wanted it. The teams agreed that was the best chance for success. They were instructed to start working on next-generation games for Xenon, rather than just churn out slightly modified versions of their games each season. In the meantime, Robbie Bach had struck up a friendship with Don Mattrick, head of the worldwide studios for Electronic Arts. Mattrick had built EA's studios into the largest game development organization in the world. Every year, he held a fishing trip for his managers. He invited Bach along and the pair bonded. The men shared a lot of in common when it came to games. They believed in making wholesome games that met with the approval of parents and ratings boards. Edgy content made them uncomfortable, and they wouldn't approve games that pushed the limits on parental approval. That was one reason why Sony started stealing more of the mature gamers' market. It was happy to embrace edgy games such as *Grand Theft Auto III* that neither EA nor Microsoft would touch. *Halo* was a mature game, but it had been planned as a "teen" title until the September 11 bombings. After that, the Entertainment Software Ratings Board became more conservative and it changed the *Halo* rating to mature. EA was ready to support Microsoft now, and so the Cold War between the two big companies was starting to thaw.

It wasn't clear how long Microsoft's sports business was going to last. Inside the studios, morale cratered. The staff of the division fell from 1,200 developers to 1,000. But there were many more unseen cuts, with the contractor staff falling by many hundreds more. Recruiters were getting resumes from many of the people who kept their jobs.

The decisions were extremely painful for Kim, who helped put together the deals that brought the studios into Microsoft. It would have been easier to try to recoup the investment on games that were running over budget and behind schedule. The company could let them finish and see if the sales came in. But that wasn't always the right use for the team, if the team could be doing something that was much more promising.

"You can't be afraid to make decisions as difficult as they may be," Kim said. "I won't make a convenient financial decision."

As Kim cut back on the staff, he had to guard against creating the impression that the bottom line mattered more than creativity. Every step of the way, game industry observers wondered about Microsoft's commitment to the games business. Nothing would send the best talent over to Sony and Nintendo faster than if they created the impression that business was all that mattered. Kim kept saying in interviews with the press that Microsoft was still serious about investing heavily in its Xbox and PC games.

"I knew we would take a long term approach to winning in this space," Kim said. "Bill and Steve are committed and have committed significant resources. We try to make intelligent bets with our investments in titles and teams that make a difference. I think we can be significant contributors to profitability. Our primary focus isn't profitability. It's our mission to create great products. I'm confident that is the way to make money."

Kim and Bach said that they were committed to making "triple A" titles and were putting more resources behind fewer projects. Bungie was a good example of a studio that had expanded. Microsoft had also put a lot of money into Rare and was banking on a series of titles coming from the British studio. It continued to fund big games such as Epic's *Gears of War*. By now, CliffyB and his team had ramped up to more than 40 people. Tim Sweeney said he had a good relationship with Ed Fries and was sad to see him go. But he knew that Microsoft's operation had grown so massive that the departure of one person would no longer make a big difference in the organization. His team worked closely with Microsoft. Epic had spent so much time in pre-production, refining the concept and its technology, that *Gears of War* was no longer likely to be a launch title.

Kim said that Microsoft had to support a broad array of genres to get the Xbox off the ground. Now that third-party game developers and publishers were supporting the box, Microsoft itself didn't have to cover every genre. It could zero in on the games that showed off the platform and gave people a reason to buy Microsoft's console. Third party support was also symbolic. The original Xbox failed in part because the partners didn't fully trust Microsoft's intentions. They figured Microsoft wanted most of the market share for itself, and wasn't willing to share in the riches. By supporting third-party games, Microsoft would prove that wasn't the case.

Xenon was starting to loom large in the planning for games. But Kim wanted to make sure that Microsoft executed on the big games that were still in the works for the Xbox. Those games included Peter Molyneux's *Fable*, a role-playing game where players could control the ethical choices of the characters and see the consequences unfold in the game. Microsoft was also counting on getting a boost from its *Forza Motorsport* racing game, the *Jade Empire* role-playing game set in Asia from BioWare, and Rare's *Conker Live and Reloaded*, a sequel to a Nintendo title about a foul-mouthed squirrel. With such titles in the works, Kim insisted that the cutbacks at Microsoft shouldn't be interpreted as a retreat. He felt it was dangerous to make games in a genre just because it was a strategic genre. Microsoft had to have the right team and the right idea for the game as well, or the project would be a "me too" title.

"If you want to take a shallow look at it, you could say here is the Harvard MBA coming in and hacking stuff," Kim said. "But that is really not true. It's us growing up, making important and sometimes difficult decisions on prioritizing teams and titles. At the end of the day we will end up with titles with far more quality."

One of the studios that escaped the ax was Rare, which had not had a stellar beginning, with the weak showing of its first Microsoft game, *Grabbed by the Ghoulies*. Rare was working on a trio of big games, *Conker*, a role-playing game called *Kameo: Elements of Power*, and the shooting game *Perfect Dark Zero*. The studio had about four major teams working at any given time, with about 200 developers.

The conservatism in the business strategy was evident. By coming up with fewer titles with bigger budgets, Microsoft was becoming a lot like a Hollywood studio. Movie-makers were taking fewer risks as the budgets for movies soared. They were focusing on tried and true formulas. Everyone from Steve Ballmer on down praised the strategy. But Ed Fries' supporters felt that Microsoft was backing away from the commitment to find hits among the small companies who appeared out of nowhere.

Hank Howie, president of Blue Fang and one of Kim's fans, said he liked the fact that Microsoft was putting more resources behind big games. But he wanted to make sure that Microsoft kept an eye open to spotting the best new creative ideas in the industry.

"I wonder how innovative new ideas are going to get funded if everyone is being cautious and funding sequels," Howie said. "Start-up developers won't get the kind of shots that we did."

As Kim reported to Peter Moore, the former Sega executive contributed his two cents. Kim himself wasn't much of a schmoozer. He didn't wine and dine the rock star game developers and get them limos. "I never pretend to be something that I am not," he said. "I won't tell Peter Molyneux how to make *Fable* better than it is. Ed had capabilities there. I do understand what makes good games from a financial perspective and how to be a great partner. Once people realize that is my approach, and I'm not just the spreadsheet guy, the conversation goes well. I really haven't had to worry that the rock star developers don't have enough champagne."

But Moore certainly liked to wine and dine his talent, and he made sure that Microsoft tried harder in Japan. Ed Fries had looked at Japan as a lost cause. He had built a studio of 100 game developers in Tokyo and had funded titles such as *Kakuto Chojin*, a big fighting game that didn't do as well as anticipated. Microsoft had sold only a few hundred thousand titles in Japan, so the publishers and developers stopped making games for the Xbox. Square Enix, the merged software giant, had never even bothered to support the Xbox. It wasn't worth their time when the *Final Fantasy* games on the PlayStation 2 could clear ten million units in sales. Fries had wanted to scale back the efforts in Japan altogether.

But Moore and Kim worked with Norman Cheuk, hired by Fries, as the new chief of the game studio in Tokyo during 2003. Previously a chief in the sports studio, Cheuk had the charter to focus on Xenon titles.

"I sat down and looked at our issues in Japan," Moore said. "Top of the list has been relevant content for the Japanese gamer. If you look at what has made platforms successful, the ability to develop and own a certain genre is key."

In particular, Moore thought Microsoft needed role-playing games like the *Final Fantasy* series. That was the area where Microsoft was the weakest. Moore had his staff start pursuing the key developers in Japan who could breathe life into the Xbox.

Back home, the lateness of *Halo 2* clearly meant that Bungie was out of the running for creating a launch game for Xenon. But Kim still believed that Microsoft would have the innovative titles for the launch.

"We'll be the trailblazers," Kim promised.

But the contradiction was apparent in Microsoft's strategy, which focused a lot more on making the numbers than Ed Fries would have preferred. In May, 2004, Bryan Lee, the finance chief for the Xbox division, sent out a memo about driving cost efficiency deeper into the organization, hitting not only corporate overhead but marketing, sales and research and development.

1. "Microsoft Chief Is All Business On Gaming," by Dean Takahashi, *San Jose Mercury News*, May 3, 2004.

CHAPTER TWENTY-EIGHT

FINISHING THE INDUSTRIAL DESIGN

When J Allard and Don Coyner hired Jonathan Hayes as the director of design for Xenon in July, 2003, they were taking a risk. Hayes was not a gamer. He was a sculptor, which hardly seemed appropriate for designing a game console. He had "blond hair, blue eyes and beefy build, looks like a J. Crew model," according to the *Washington Post*. But he was a veteran designer who had been at Microsoft for seven years. [1]

"At Xbox, we're loaded with people who are off the charts in their technical understanding," Hayes said. "My job isn't to compete in that front. My job is to produce a counterweight to that. I'm never gonna understand enough about gaming. I'll always be an outsider looking in, almost like an anthropologist. That's a good thing to be."

He had at least come from the hardware side of the business. Hayes had worked with Coyner at Microsoft designing *Sidewinder* joysticks for flight simulator games. Hayes had also worked on "smart phones" and other mobile devices. He believed that Microsoft could design something as good as anything that Apple or Sony could create. And he was about to take the Xenon team through a process that was more like a trip down a rabbit hole of creativity.

Hayes was soaking in all of the industrial design trends that put more pressure on getting the design of a product right. He grew up in Boston and the coast of Maine. His mother is an abstract artist and his father taught manufacturing at Harvard University for 35 years.

"Industrial art is a union; I'm exactly a collision of my mom and dad," Hayes said. [2]

He attended the University of Amherst, where he wrote a thesis on wood as a material for sculpture. Some people thought that was crazy. He graduated from the Rhode Island School of Design, where he earned a Masters in Industrial Design. He favored works of art such as Pablo Picasso's *Guernica* and his favorite film was *The Fisher King* by director Terry Gilliam. His favorite album was *Rust Never Sleeps* by

Neil Young. He was anything but a technical guy. As Hayes puts it, he was "like sand in an oyster." Coyner liked him as a "fresh set of eyes." When Hayes came along, Coyner's work was well under way.

"We gave him a download, gave him direction," Coyner said.

Hayes' mission was to achieve a deep integration of hardware, software, and services and to deliver a cohesive message on all aspects of the Xbox brand. It would be a "choreographed" design that held together from many different points of view. This time around, Microsoft had the time and budget to build everything from scratch the way that Apple and Sony did. His inspiration for the Xbox 360 was a 1923 Constantin Brancusi sculpture called *Bird in Flight*. It was just a simple white sculpture of a wing balanced on a tiny cone atop a cylinder. He told his people that "technology needs poetry."

Jonathan Hayes led the Xbox 360 industrial design

Hayes based the "design values" of the project on the acronym OCCAM, inspired by the principle behind *Occam's Razor*. Named after a 14th century logician, William of Occam, the principle asserts that the simplest explanation for a problem is the best. If there's a burned tree, you could suppose that it was either hit by lightening or scorched by a dragon. The simplest explanation is the lightning strike. [3]

The acronym incorporated the principles that Hayes thought the Xbox 360 design should stand for. The "O" was for "open," where the gamer was the center of the experience and the machine allowed for customization. The "C" was for "clear," where it was easy to see what everything was used for, whether hardware, software or services. The second "C" was for "consistent," meaning the experience across all elements of the platform should be consistent: brand, design, hardware, software and services. The "A" stood for athletic, an emblem of the efficient use of power. And the "M" meant "mirai," a Japanese word for forward looking, or innovative. The design had to make a simple statement. It had to be memorable.

And it had to be authentic to gamers and unique to the Xbox. [4]

"It needed to pass the rear-view mirror test," Hayes said. "When you see certain cars coming up behind you in your mirror, they make a strong impression. A Hummer, or a Porsche 911, for example. This immediacy or impact also needed to be reconciled with the goal of creating a timeless design—because the console will be on the shelf for a number of years and can't look dated."

All of Hayes' instincts for design were about to come together with solid research about game consoles. He arrived on the scene in time for Cheskin's interviews with gamers. In August and September, 2003, the research company rounded up about 84 gamers from around the world to pass judgment on the prototypes. The gamers went into the interviews blind. They ranged in age from 12-year-old kids to 40-year-old gamers, with interests ranging from casual to hardcore. The teams went to Chicago, London, and Tokyo. In the U.S. and the United Kingdom, the team interviewed gamers in the 14 to 24-year-old bracket. About 80 percent were male, and the gamers were split into three categories of committed, time killers, and fun seekers based on the amount of time that they played. Some were digital media savvy, some not. The group represented both the target market and a cross section of consumers. The multiple regions offered a chance to see which design principles would hold up in all of the territories.

Rhea's team went to Europe alone. But Coyner and Hayes watched the interviews in both Chicago and Tokyo. The researchers showed the interviewees the boxes without telling them that they were Xenon designs, and the subjects didn't know they were talking to Microsoft. The researchers instructed the interviewees to think about their preferences for game consoles and react to the prototypes. The researchers asked their questions. Who is it good for? Is this powerful? Who would it attract? What do you like or dislike about the design? Would a sophisticated gamer like it? The answers that came back were opinionated.

"Everyone hated the ones with handles," Coyner said. "The young and hardcore gamers thought that the gray color was cool. They loved the attention to detail. They loved more subtle branding, rather than the big X at the center of the original."

They hated the Marc Newson design. The feedback was remarkably consistent from around the world. Coyner really wanted broad insights on whether the boxes could really be viewed and accepted as consoles. The consumers didn't want something that looked like a video-cassette-recorder, nor did they want something cutesy like the Nintendo GameCube, a purse-like, purple cube with a carrying handle. They knew what they liked when they saw it, and they didn't like any of the designs. One design looked like a pillow, while another gray model, dubbed the "Fisher Price Nuclear Reactor," had some nice concave edges around with some sci-fi green lights. Among the things they did like: the blue light-emitting diode, or LED, on the PlayStation 2. They also loved the fact that you could twist the red PlayStation logo on the machine so it was facing the right way, whether the box was horizontal or vertical.

Cheskin's researchers concluded that gamers wanted something small, with lighter colors. The dark colors appealed only to the hardcore games. They came up with design principles.

Hayes returned home and told his designers to create something that lived up to the design values, but he also gave them technical requirements that came from mechanical engineers like Jeff Reents. He didn't withhold information from them. Instead, he gave them some practical hints on how to move forward with the design. But all the work that had been done over a period of months was set aside. The process was supposed to be like a funnel, but it wasn't working out that way. The Cheskin research confirmed the direction that Microsoft needed to go, but Hayes had to blow the process out again.

Since things weren't going as planned, Hayes invited a pitch from Astro Studios. Astro was a small design shop in the Mission district of San Francisco. It was an inconspicuous place. No sign adorned the storefront, except an auto glass sign that belonged to its neighbors. Inside, the studio was mass of desks, computers, and motorcycles and bikes that the employees used for commuting. The founder of the studio was Brett Lovelady, a 42-year-old designer who cut his teeth at famed industrial design firm Frog Design, which designed the Apple IIc computer. Lovelady's aim was to blend technology, lifestyle and design into product development.

Over the years, Lovelady's team had worked on a lot of cool gear, posters of which hung on the walls of the office. They had done the first iPaq handheld computer for Compaq Computer. They had designed a raft of sleek gamer PCs for Alienware. Astro had created Hewlett-Packard's first digital TV projectors. In video games, they worked on the cover art for Electronic Arts' *SSX 3* and *NFL Street* games. And they worked with Nike for about nine years, designing a variety of products, such as Nike's first line of sports watches. The Alienware boxes in particular were hot rods for gaming die-hards. The boxes were irreverent and didn't care about how much attitude they exuded.

But Astro had never worked on a game console before. Lovelady played games on the Xbox such as *Project Gotham Racing*, but he admitted that his son kicked his butt most of the time. To Lovelady, consoles and PCs were very different beasts because consoles involved more compromises. They weren't as powerful as the fastest PCs, nor were they anywhere near as expensive. Quite often, Alienware customers spent more on their cases than someone would spend on an entire console. Astro started generating masses of green and white Xbox 360 art, but they didn't put any in the front room where just any visitor could see what they were working on.

"We are in stealth here," Lovelady told a visitor much later. "Two-thirds of our basement is covered in Xbox 360 stuff."

When Hayes first contacted Lovelady, Lovelady didn't know what the project was about. But within a month, Hayes had made up his mind. In September, 2003, he told Astro to start work on the Xenon design. He would give them the chance to engineer the entire look and feel of the Xbox 360.

Hayes gave Lovelady a brief with the design goals, a description of the target Xbox 360 user, the desired marketing attributes and some pointers on earlier attempts that didn't really work. [5]

Astro only had about 18 employees. So the team was going to be small. One of the people that Astro assigned to the job was Matt Day, a 31-year-old designer who had just graduated from the University of Cincinnati with a bachelor's degree in industrial design. He was on his fourth or fifth career choice, having already tried criminal justice, business administration, and ceramics. He had done a post-graduate internship at Nike's product test lab. When Lovelady came calling for some talent, the creative director recommended Day.

Day began sketching. For a solid two weeks, he and Mike Simonian gestured and conceptualized. Microsoft wanted the Xenon to be "the ultimate social magnet." It had to be as cool as it possibly could so that hardcore gamers around the world would embrace it. Yet it had to appeal beyond gamers to mainstream consumers and be used in a variety of rooms in the home. The second drawing that Day created had a unique look. It consisted of two concave lines. Hayes liked it. It had potential as an iconic design, or something that was easily recognizable. It looked like a metal box might look if it were a person who was inhaling fully, filling every inch of their lungs with air. Hayes referred to this design as an "inhale." It only mildly implied the letter X, stretching to the corners of the box and connecting them in a subtle way.

The team kept on going. Day and Simonian created 27 different concepts. The inhale design was just one of the pack they submitted. Day started at 50 or 60 hours a week and he just kept on going.

"I had a go get 'em attitude," he said.

Day believed in what Lovelady called the "Astro process." It included lots of brainstorming and freewheeling creativity, backed up with some heavy-duty technology. Astro wasn't a full-fledged design firm like the much larger Ideo in Palo Alto. Its goal was to remember that people are the ultimate clients.

"We want to give them as much as possible in the design -- as much function, fashion and fun as we feel is appropriate for the brand and marketplace at the time," Lovelady said. [6]

Astro moved to convert its sketches into the real thing. They recreated the images in three dimensions in a computer program called *Alias*. They then shipped the *Alias* computer files to a local machine shop. The computer-controlled tools carved a foam model. And the machine shop delivered the finished piece to Astro within a couple of days. Coyner once again brought in Cheskin so that it could again run the prototype ideas past consumer focus groups.

Working with Microsoft wasn't easy, since it shot down so many ideas.

"We didn't see eye to eye on lots of issues at first," Day said. "We proved to each other we all have visions that should be respected."

Lovelady had to convince Microsoft that it wanted to go in the direction of iconic. He wanted it to do something bold. He didn't want Microsoft to play it safe. He wanted it to embrace a design that showed it was a world leader. It had to inspire an instantaneous opinion from gamers, not a feeling of ambivalence. [7]

Astro had to figure out where Microsoft's comfort zone was, just where it wanted to be on the spectrum from mild to wild. The designers also had to pay attention to a lot of requirements. The first box was too big and it bombed in Japan. It was too heavy, the black X design with a green jewel was dubbed "unrefined." The original box could only be used horizontally, but Microsoft needed something like the PlayStation 2, which could stand vertically or horizontally. The original Xbox had high costs, manufacturing problems and usability issues.

This design had to work in all the regions. From the beginning, Microsoft was clear that this box had to be more broadly appealing. It had to embrace other kinds of entertainment beyond games. It had to be accessible. Microsoft wanted to "recraft the brand," Lovelady recalled. It wanted to stay true to the hardcore gamers, but it also wanted to go beyond the heat seekers who put up with a lot of hassles just to play their games. It had to have a certain authenticity, so that it resonated with gamers and wasn't just another consumer electronics box.

Don Coyner holds an early "inhale" design

From the start, the box had to embrace values that gamers loved, values like personalization, or the ability to take a piece of content and modify it to reflect the player's own personality. Astro proposed customizable face plates and Microsoft immediately jumped on the idea as a good one. Astro explored the idea of making the whole case removable and customizable, but that idea didn't work. So Microsoft focused on the face plates.

Gamers could snap face plates on the machine so that it reflected their own artistic preferences, much as they would their cell phone. It was a winning idea from the personalization point of view, and Microsoft could sell those face plates as an accessory that would help it cash in on all things Xbox 360. Microsoft could use the face plates for limited edition specials, co-branding, and upgrades. [8]

"People love to make things special to themselves, so this was just one way we could help," Lovelady said.

Microsoft wanted a lot more people to adopt Xbox Live. So it had the idea early on that a single button on the remote control should be able to take the gamer directly to the Xbox Live screen. This button, called the Xenon button early on, made Xbox Live into an instant experience, much like turning on or off the controller. And the thing couldn't weigh as much as a bag of bricks.

"We didn't want to overdo it, especially because of portability," Lovelady said. "Will people really carry these around? It's obvious these systems are going to go into cars, or be put in backpacks, so we need to suit those needs. People lug their consoles around, and even in the Japanese market, you've got to set them up, put them back, wire, rewire. It takes a lot of expert engineering and mechanical engineering to make things connect and disconnect and reconnect." [9]

These requirements added up to a long list of things that the designers had to balance.

"All of that was held out as 'let's not lose track of them,'" Lovelady said. "There were a lot of heat issues, power supply issues, how you were going to enable the consumer to access certain components. The technology was in evolution as we designed."

To keep the creative tension going, Coyner urged Hayes to pair Astro with another firm, Hers Experimental Design Laboratory, of Osaka, Japan. Hers had been part of the original group of companies that made pitches for the design. This company did not submit a winning design but Microsoft liked its perspective. Among its submissions was a silver machine with a unique-looking power button. It was caved in and had a ring at the center of it. Since everyone liked it, the teams decided to reinterpret it.

"Everyone liked the purity of the power button and its simplicity," Coyner said.

For two months, Hayes headed a collaboration between Hers and Astro. The companies traded e-mails, instant messages, phone calls and images with each other. But, by design, they never met in person. Hayes mediated, but he wanted the firms to work on their own. They were both competitors and collaborators.

Hers lent an international perspective, another set of eyes that could be on the watch for things that Japanese gamers liked. Lovelady thought he saw a difference in styles between the firms. His U.S. artists were bold and iconic. The Japanese firm emphasized subtlety, restraint, and craftsmanship.

"We brought those things together," Lovelady said. "They had some perspective on a feature, like turn this up or tone this down."

He said that Astro created the original concept and form language. Then his team reviewed and critiqued that design with Hers to get their input on how the

Japanese demographic would react to it.

"It is very much an Astro product, from beginning to end, but working with Hers helped us tune it for a broader market," Lovelady said. [10]

Microsoft always tested every idea. So it was no surprise that some of the designs leaked out. Some of the video game fan sites posted pictures that were obviously fakes, but some were concepts that were passed over in favor of Astro's design.

"A lot of people were poking around," Lovelady said.

Among the toughest things that Astro had to deal with were changes in the technology. Microsoft was having a tough time deciding whether it would put a hard disk drive into every box. Because of the cost, the company didn't want to put it in. But game developers wanted it. Microsoft floated the possibility of creating two versions of the Xbox 360, one with a hard drive and another without. So Astro had to assume that the hard disk would be an add-on device that was easily accessible to gamers who might snap it on or off as if it were something they could take to a friends house. That meant the hard disk had to go on the side of the box. Since it covered up some vents, Astro had to add more vents on the other side of the box.

Coyner had always wanted Microsoft to use wireless controllers. He hated the stupid ports and the cords sticking out of the middle of every console. Midway through the design process, the hardware group came back and said that it was going to use two wireless controllers as a standard feature on the box. That meant that the box could use just two controller ports on the front of the box instead of four. The wireless controllers would communicate with the box, but didn't need to connect to something on box itself. Since the controllers were now wireless, Astro had to accommodate a big battery pack on the controller.

But the wireless controllers also had to offer some kind of feedback to the player so that they knew which one was active at any given time. The team came up with a concept dubbed "The Ring of Light." This ring was separated into four quadrants, each of which was powered by a light-emitting diode and could light up independently of the others. Originally, the team thought that it would use different colors for each quadrant, red, blue, green and yellow. But they decided upon green, the cheapest and the most consistent with the rest of the colors on the machine. Better yet, the ring of light could flash red and communicate a couple of dozen different error messages to the user, giving it even more functionality. Remembering the PlayStation logo, they made sure that the ring of light would reorient itself whether the box was standing vertically or on its side.

Microsoft pulled in a lot of research to help with the design of controllers. Greg Martinez, a usability manager, started the research on the initial controller designs and how consumers responded to them. He tested the initial controller designs on 424 people in Japan, the U.S., and Europe. From that, he got feedback on where the buttons should be. That prompted him to move the black and white buttons on the original Xbox controllers to the shoulder above the left trigger, rather than near the other buttons. After Martinez moved on, Hugh

McLoone, a hardware engineer, took over the controller effort. McLoone studied ergonomics, or how humans interacted with devices from track balls to computer mice. He had training in physiology, anatomy, industrial hygiene, and occupational health. Just about everyone wanted a wireless controller. But McLoone had to make sure that the control buttons were in the right place, so people made few errors when they were in the heat of a game. He also had to make sure the controller would be comfortable to hold for a long time. He softened the edge of the thumb sticks to make them more comfortable, and also worked on a wired controller for both the console and the PC.

Because Astro had such a complete understanding of the design, Hayes put the team to work designing the game controllers, the memory units for storing saved games, the connectors and plugs, and a wireless Internet module that could be attached as an add-on. They used the ergonomic testing results to constrain their controller concepts. Microsoft defined the functions for the controller, but Astro had to figure where to put them in relation to the gamer's hands. The Xbox Live button was a new feature which activates Xbox Live wirelessly. But Astro had to obey the ergonomic requirements so that the controller would fit the hands of any player around the world.

Astro had to obey the laws of physics and economics. The physics in particular wasn't easy. Making a box that could stand vertically, for instance, might have threatened the durability of the two drives, Lovelady said. One thing that the team failed to consider would come back and haunt them. They put a DVD drive into the machine that could be either vertical or horizontal. But they didn't realize that if a consumer picked up the machine while it had a spinning disk in it and moved it from vertical to horizontal or visa versa, the disk would start grinding against the side of the drive. Microsoft would eventually discover the problem associated with this after the box shipped.

Some technologies had come a long way since the original Xbox. Microsoft's own hardware engineers and a mechanical design team at Flextronics pitched in to keep Astro anchored in the realities of costs and technical requirements. But, under the direction of Microsoft lead mechanical engineer Jeff Reents, Flextronics also added its own touches. The company pioneered a new way of molding plastic that allowed Microsoft to create the face plates, which the gamer could detach with a simple snap and fit a new, personalized face plate – a feature for which Microsoft could charge money.

The Astro team had to visit the San Jose offices of Flextronics to get the cost feedback and thoughts on how to improve the manufacturing time for the box. For a few things, Astro wanted higher quality plastics or different finishes, but it had to settle for less. Among the tips from Flextronics: blue LED lights cost twenty-five cents a piece at the time, while green LEDs were only two cents.

"I thought cost would be a bigger deal, but we were buffered," Lovelady said. "We would hear that this part can't be metal and has to be plastic instead."

Astro had some say in mechanical matters. But the mechanical engineers at Microsoft had their say as well. Jeff Reents said that the new machine would

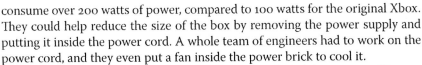
consume over 200 watts of power, compared to 100 watts for the original Xbox. They could help reduce the size of the box by removing the power supply and putting it inside the power cord. A whole team of engineers had to work on the power cord, and they even put a fan inside the power brick to cool it.

Still, the box needed a powerful fan. Reents concluded that an 80-millimeter fan was too big for the size of the machine. The smaller 60-millimeter fan didn't provide enough cooling so they had to put two 60-millimeter fans, in addition to a water-cooled heat sink for the IBM microprocessor. The patent-pending heat sink contained a heat pipe with water in it. When the water gets hot, it turns to steam. Then the steam moves to the aluminum fins, where cool air blowing from the fans takes the heat out of the box. To keep the fans from getting too loud, the microprocessor and graphics chip used sensors to either speed up or slow down the fans based on how much heat was being generated. [11] Once the second fan was added, Astro had to go back to the drawing board again on the design.

"It's a give and take," Lovelady said. "There are realistic things, like you can't put a heat-sensitive item near a super hot chip, but things like ergonomics, physical access, and elements like that have to communicate in a common sort of way as well. But then you're looking for a sense of design as well."

Everything had to be tested and cross-checked with other experts. The design had to tie in with the user interface. At the same time as he was searching for a design firm, Coyner looked worldwide for a user interface designer who would create the startup and menu screens for Xenon. After another worldwide bake-off, four design firms came in with final proposals.

"The driving idea was, don't expose the user to technological complexity," said Paolo Malabuyo on the User Interface team.

Last time, the user interface fit into 250 megabytes of space on the hard disk. But this time, Microsoft wanted the data for the UI stored inside the flash memory, which loaded as the machine booted up. That meant it had to fit within 4 megabytes of space. Hence, instead of a fancy 3-D UI, the company opted for a two-dimensional view. The four designs were dubbed *Loop, Concertina, Pilot,* and *Slice.*

The winner was *Concertina,* from the San Francisco web page/graphic design firm called AKQA. Microsoft initally worked with the London office of AKQA, but most of those AKQA team members moved to San Francisco to be in the same time zone as Microsoft. Their design fit with the overall look of the console. The design also had to fit the brand image, which was being created at JDK in Burlington, Vermont. JDK had done work with brands like Mountain Dew. They understood global youth culture and what gamers were interested in, fashion-wise. AKQA looked at Astro's design and came up with the concept of "blades." These were metallic menus within the screen that could be flipped through with a controller. The blades had the same iconic curved shape as the box itself, and the shape and look of the blades was the same as the external hard disk drive.

Coyner sought consistency in the packaging, the size of the manuals, the messages on the plastic bags, and common fonts in all of the lettering. Russ

Glaser, a manager of the User Interface team, said that the first thing that the user saw when they opened the package should *not* be a warranty card. The logos had to be visible in TV commercials, and when someone was sitting on a couch ten feet away. Cheskin ran the user interface – the screen layouts, typography and animations – past a last group of 24 consumers in San Francisco and London. Once all of these details came together, the branding folks ran with it.

"They wanted something that would be this gateway from the physical, tangible, real world to the voyeuristic world of gaming," Lovelady said. "So the idea is that we've got this box that's a containment device, that is containing some pretty amazing power. You just can't let anyone in or out of the portal, or access point."[12]

Once Microsoft chose the AKQA design for the user interface, the software team had to go to work creating the different screens. While the first Xbox had 45 different screens that the user could see, Xenon would have 450. That was because users could do so many more things with the box. Malabuyo and Glazer put every single screen shot on two hallway walls. Hundreds of pieces of white paper stuck on the wall, with the contents of some of them scribbled out. It changed every day. Consulting usability research, the team tested everything. Over 18 months, they ran 25 usability tests on the different parts of the user interface. The team tested some screens seven times.

Don Hall's brand marketing group came up with a redesigned logo, which featured a white orb with a nexus that was oozing green energy. It kept the theme of powerful energy from the first Xbox, but it dispensed with the menacing muscles and *Incredible Hulk* imagery in favor of lighter, more optimistic shades – without watering it down to the degree it alienated the hardcore gamers.

The brand team took the "ring of light" and used it in a series of concentric circles. Everything was interconnected, from the name to the design to the packaging and user interface.

"We wanted to brand not just the product but the experience," Hall said.

JDK and Astro collaborated on the E3 booth to make sure it carried the strong message of empowerment. Astro even participated in interviewing the teams that had to build the exhibition booth. To these branding folks, the "inhale" took on a new meaning. It now signified the "inhale of energy right before you explode into motion." Lovelady said, "The end caps are the place where the power is contained."

In the end, Hayes and the Microsoft team were most comfortable with the iconic, "inhale" design. The concavity suggested an "X" form from any viewing angle, Lovelady said. Once chosen, Astro went through four or five iterations. Hers also contributed its own changes. Some of the Hers contributions were reflected in the final design, such as the look of the power button on the console. It bore the most resemblance to the second drawing that Matt Day had created. After a year of roundabout, painstaking design work, the artists had all returned to the virtual beginning of their process to find the final look for the Xbox 360. To Lovelady and Day, and the rest of the team, it was satisfying, because the final design had "so much of our original intent."

Hayes saw the original Xbox design as "the Incredible Hulk," a big green monster that was all about raw power, raw energy, and showing the world that the Xbox was a gamer's machine. The Xbox 360, by contrast, was about restrained power, like Bruce Lee, Hayes said. [13]

Concentric rings in branding

Hayes and Coyner showed off the Xenon design to the executive team. Coyner was impressed that the executives were willing to let the design process run its course. J Allard and Robbie Bach thought it looked great, and offered no resistance. "It was more like, 'This is where we're going with the design' rather than asking our approval," Allard said. Bach said that he was quite happy that the team was making its own decision and simply needed to run the final idea by him.

"I am not a designer," Bach said. "You guys are the experts."

Bill Gates looked at the design and just smiled. The design was about six months late based on the original schedule. But nobody really cared, because they knew the machine was on the right track.

When people saw the light white and green color, they assumed that Microsoft was hopping on the iPod bandwagon. "There's a common product trend that people pay attention to," Lovelady said. "Familiarity kicks in."

White was the new black. Translucence, which Apple had pioneered with the first iMac, was tired and done. But it wasn't exactly the same kind of white as Apple used. It had more color in it.

Lovelady reasoned that the lighter color fit in with the grand plan. This wasn't a box that was supposed to stand out like a sore thumb in somebody's living room. That killed off the color blue, since so few other appliances were blue. It wasn't supposed to be a dark box that evoked the sci-fi themes of earlier consoles. It was supposed to match the broader environment of the household. Microsoft tested the color scheme on a global basis, and it confirmed Astro's initial impressions. Microsoft came back full circle on the design.

"This isn't something you shove aside in a cabinet when your relatives come to visit," Lovelady said. [14]

Coyner ran the completed design past gamers for a final feedback session. This time, he used Microsoft's own research team in Tokyo and their user interface vendor. The feedback validated the design. Japanese interviewees said that it looked like Sony's work. "There was one who said it was not a foolish American design," Coyner said.

It was clear that the box was sleek and much thinner and smaller than the original Xbox. The DVD component was flatter. The power supply was smaller (though it was now in the power cord). The fans were smaller, and the main circuit board itself was smaller. The final box was an inch shorter than the original concepts. Lovelady would have liked fewer vents and connectors. But it had to be functional.

"When people said this looked like something that Sony or Apple had designed, we knew it was right," said Peter Moore, corporate vice president of marketing and game publishing.

1. "Outside the Box," by Jose Antonio Vargas, *Washington Post*, Nov. 22, 2005.

2. "Outside the Xbox."

3. Jonathan Hayes interview with Xbox.com.

4. Jonathan Hayes interview with Xbox.com.

5. Brett Lovelady interview with GameDaily Biz June 14, 2005.

6. Brett Lovelady interview.

7. Brett Lovelady interview.

8. Brett Lovelady interview.

9. "Astro a Go-Go," Gamasutra, July 12, 2005, http://www.gamasutra.com/features/20050712/sheffield_01.shtml

10. Brett Lovelady interview.

11. "Xbox 360: the Guts," Xbox.com, http://www.xbox.com/en-US/hardware/xbox360/xbox360theguts.htm.

12. "Astro a Go-Go," Gamasutra.

13. "Outside the Box."

14. Brett Lovelady interview.

CHAPTER TWENTY-NINE

LEAKS AND
$10 MILLION BILLS

*T*he spring of 2004 brought new challenges. Microsoft held an Xfest conference for Xbox game developers in January, 2004. The company was getting ready to ship the first game development systems for the Xenon. These consisted of Apple Macintosh G5 computers with IBM PowerPC 970 dual-core microprocessors and ATI Radeon 9800 graphics cards. The G5s were powerful machines, but many Macintosh fans felt that the great unwashed masses had been brainwashed by Intel's marketing campaign which emphasized single-core microprocessors running at the highest megahertz possible. They believed the G5s could run circles around Intel's chips, but few people went to the trouble to understand the advantages of multiple cores. Not all the information was present in these development systems. The guidelines for making Xbox Live games, for instance, weren't included.

Since neither ATI nor IBM were finished with their chips yet, the game developers could use the G5s to simulate the kind of performance that they would get on Xenon. This could guide the artists so that they could determine the quality of their animations and the speed at which they could display them. It enabled them to get started with the process of making games. Game developers gathered at Microsoft's annual Xfest game developer conferences in Seattle to hear the latest about making games for the Xbox. At the event, Microsoft began telling wider groups of developers about the final specification of the box.

The timing of development kits had always been a sore point in the video game industry. Some developers hated how the console owners played favorites, releasing scarce kits to their favorite publishers or developers first. American developers had to wait in line behind the Japanese when the Japanese console makers released kits. The game developers needed kits as soon as possible because making games was taking so much more money and time. Getting the kits out at the last minute was a sure way to doom a console's appeal to gamers. But

getting the kits out too early could also be disastrous. The kits might include technology for making games that wasn't ready, was too raw, or might have to be changed later on. The only thing worse than getting a kit out late was to put out a kit that had to be corrected. Microsoft had much more time with its console preparations this go round, so it was able to deliver its initial kits early. It earmarked its earliest machines for those who were working on launch titles.

"There was a constant fear that something would go wrong, and the development kits wouldn't come out on schedule," said Cameron Ferroni. "You keep your fingers crossed."

The *San Jose Mercury News* and other Internet web sites reported the details of Xenon as it existed at the time, with the IBM triple-core microprocessor, the ATI graphics chip, and other details that Microsoft had revealed. Compatibility with the original Xbox wasn't guaranteed, prompting analyst Jon Peddie to call the plan "stupid" in the story. The article concluded that Microsoft was far more concerned about keeping the costs of the new Xbox down than keeping a technological edge over Sony. By that time, Microsoft had sold 13.7 million Xbox consoles, while Sony had sold more than 70 million PS2s worldwide. [1]

The *Mercury News* article quoted Tim Sweeney, CEO of Epic Games, as unhappy about the lack of a standard hard disk drive on all the machines. But Sweeney was happy the machine would be easy to program in keeping with the original. Other leaks followed. One was a diagram that Greg Williams had created for the Advanced Technology Group to give out to game developers. The slides had the name Pete Isensee on them, and they first surfaced in China. These leaks set expectations that Microsoft would reveal the details of the new Xbox at the Game Developers Conference in March in San Jose. Perhaps the only good thing for Microsoft was the actual industrial design by Astro Studios didn't leak.

"The leaks were a big deal and not a big deal," said Cam Ferroni, who had to warn his staff periodically to be discrete. "From a certain perspective, it's frustrating. You try so hard to keep things quiet. Whether intentional or not or by mistake, it leaks and it makes you mad. It puts upper management in a place where I don't want to talk about something at next team meeting, because it's going to leak. If we can't tell our own people, then we argue about getting stuff done. It's more of a process. More of an emotional issue. The fact that specs were out there, that didn't matter in long run. I'm sure Sony knew all of that or more already."

A week before the GDC, the top brass held another offsite retreat for the executive team at the Willows Lodge, a small resort in Woodinville along the Sammamish River about 20 minutes northeast of Seattle. It was a luxurious setting with spa, hot tubs, and fine wines. J Allard returned from his sabbatical in time for the retreat.

But Jon Thomason, who had run the Xenon program in Allard's absence and had been running Xbox software since 1999, decided to check out. His step-daughter had an illness that took him out of the decision-making for 12 weeks. When he came back, he decided to return to the Windows group where he worked before joining the Xbox team. Microsoft's new operating system, which would later be called "Windows Vista," was in big trouble. The Windows group was essentially restarting the project, and Thomason agreed to help out. Cam Ferroni took his place as head of software, expanding his responsibilities in other areas, while Chris Pirich stepped up to handle the operating system team. The irony was that Thomason was leaving a division where just one programmer, Tracy Sharp, wrote most of the operating system, and he was going to a division where thousands worked on a single operating system.

At this retreat, the team made big decisions. The paralysis that Ed Fries had complained about was gone. Steve Ballmer happened to have a retreat going on at the same time with another set of executives, but the urinal was the only place where the Xbox team ran into him.

"We had a clear plan and target from the CEO," recalled David Reid, the Xenon marketing head. "We went off to make the profit and loss statement work. We asked what can we do, given the target from our CEO. It is exciting to make these decisions. You can't be a leader by incrementally doing things."

Doug Hebenthal had printed a stack of $10 million bills for the occasion, with each one about three inches by five inches. On the board on the wall was a list of things that Microsoft could spend its money on. Based on Bryan Lee's spreadsheets and the overall plan to spend a total of $17 billion on the Xbox program over a decade, the executives had to decide where to spend their discretionary money. Most of the $17 billion had to be spend on components such as console parts, but Robbie Bach had decided that Microsoft could spend $770 million in discretionary money over the five-year life of Xenon. That was the amount they could spend and still hit the profit targets over the decade.

That wasn't the total amount of money they had to spend. That was simply the amount of money that they had not yet allocated but were free to spend. Under the long-term budget, they could still hit their profit targets – set by Steve Ballmer and Bryan Lee – even if they spent this money.

The scenario assumed that Microsoft would capture about 40 percent of the market, roughly equal to Sony's 40 percent share, while Nintendo would have 20 percent. But different plans and assumptions would kick in if Microsoft's market share grew to 60 percent, or it stagnated at the current 20 percent.

The categories on the wall included third party games, first party games, Xbox Live, software tools, marketing, the costs of goods, marketing, advertising, the effort in Japan, and a variety of other categories. Each of the executives and the few members of the Xenon Integration Team team present had to decide how to allocate their 77 bills. The voting was revealing, and it forced everyone to think about their budget as part of the whole.

"We did this wonderful exercise on where to make our investment," said one person who was present. "That was really managed well. Every meaningful decision was made there."

Cam Ferroni, who was now heading software, took what he called a "perverse pleasure" in seeing the territorial executives now faced with a zero-sum game.

The resources were finite.

"You have to make hard decisions, and you can't do everything," he said. "There was a lot of healthy discussion, and disagreement." As he held the $10 million bills in his hand, he didn't feel rich.

Separate from the $10 million bills exercise, each division chief from marketing to games had to make requests for budgets. They had to decide what they needed as a minimum investment, what was a reasonable middle ground, and what was their ultimate budget wish list. The upshot of the exercise was that almost everybody had put more weight for spending money on games. Third party could spend money on games. Another batch of money was set aside to eliminate exclusives, and another pile was set aside to steal away exclusive games from Sony and Nintendo. George Peckham, the head of third-party games, found that he had been allocated his top request.

"He got the maximum war chest," said one person who was there.

Shane Kim's first-party game group also got its maximum request. A.J. Redmer made a presentation about how to make another thrust into Japan, using about a quarter of first-party's overall budget. It was risky because role-playing games were extremely expensive. But Microsoft had potential launch titles with *Ninety-Nine* Nights and *Dead or Alive 4.* His list of potential partners included Yoshiharu Gotanda, Hironobu Sakaguchi, Akira Toriyama, Yoshiki Okamoto, Tetsuya Mizuguchi, and others. Redmer was convinced that Microsoft could crack open the market with the right handful of games, just as Sony dominated the current landscape with *Final Fantasy* and *Dragon Quest* titles. Everyone was on board with that plan at the retreat. A month later, Steve Ballmer approved the funding for the Japanese market. Content for Xbox Live was fully funded. "Everyone was around the table," said Reid. "George said we would improve third party attach rate by this much. Shane had so much. That was final."

Ferroni was happy because he had 50 new software positions authorized at the meeting, the rough equivalent to one $10 million bill for one year's time. The new staff, in addition to the 150 who were already there, would ensure that almost all of the team's major projects, from Xbox Live to the user interface, would ship in complete versions on the first day of the launch.

Bryan Lee, the finance chief, would take the numbers and plug them into a model, dubbed "divisional cost, regional margin," that would spit out the answers to financial questions. It put the entire Xbox business, from accessories to games to hardware to Xbox Live, all in the same simulation. The spreadsheet made people realize how their decisions had consequences that affected the businesses of others. If they hit 50 million units sold for Xenon, what kind of cost target would they have to hit? How many games would they have to sell if they were still losing a lot of money on hardware? What were the sources and the uses of funding? The DCRM looked out five fiscal years into the future.

Among the decisions that Bach continued to support were the worldwide launch, backward compatibility, and two different retail versions, one with a hard drive and one without. Bach had also decided that Microsoft wasn't going to lose money on hardware. In the first year, Microsoft would essentially break even on the whole business, while it would make money in the year that ended June 30, 2007. This meant that the price for the console would have to come in close to break-even with costs, something that console makers rarely did at the outset. These were decisions that were going to stick, recalled hardware chief Todd Holmdahl.

"Robbie was a new man when it came to laying down the law," said one person who attended the meeting.

One morning after the retreat at the Willows Lodge, J Allard went to Robbie Bach and told him he was quitting. He told Bach that he liked Donald Trump's *The Apprentice* show so much that he was going to quit so he could be on it. (The subject had come up at the Willows Lodge because the executives talked about a contestant who had been kicked off the show, and Allard had been a big fan of that contestant). Bach swallowed the practical joke. Allard let Bach stew on it overnight, and Bach sent a long email the next morning asking him to reconsider. Charlotte Stuyvenberg, leader of the PR team, was in on the joke. Then Allard told Bach it was an April Fool's joke. [1]

Indeed, after the retreat, it was no time to quit. The decisions the executives made had many consequences for the day-to-day work of hundreds of Xbox team members who were now toiling away on Xenon. The lower ranks were executing.

Jeff Simon, a program manager on the Xbox platform team, gathered the Xenon material and codified it in a document called *The Book of Xenon*. The idea was to give everyone a document with all the decisions that had been made up to that point in time.

"When you commit it to paper, it gives you a view you don't otherwise have," Cam Ferroni said.

The book's main contents included complete descriptions of the hardware in the box and the user scenarios that Microsoft envisioned. For instance, the digital photo experience would include screen shots of everything that a consumer would see on the user interface as they tried to attach a digital camera to a Xenon machine. It would walk them through the steps they take to upload the photos to the hard disk drive, and how the user would then access those photos and present them on the TV screen. The book also included scenarios for playing music from an iPod, playing a DVD movie, or what the user would see when they loaded a game into the DVD tray. It described the wired and the wireless controllers, as well as the versions of the machine with a hard disk, and another without one.

The document would grow, over time, to 147 pages. It would prove invaluable for the software team as it determined which screens it needed to create for the user interface, or which integration tasks had to be undertaken. The executives could read the document and ask hard questions about why the process for doing something wasn't easier.

"You have 20 program managers working on different parts of the system, but is anyone looking at it all together?" Ferroni said. "That was why we did

it." By the summer, there were printed, bound versions of the Book of Xenon floating around. It was a top secret document, and one that remained hidden from prying eyes.

The book was the Bible for anyone who had questions about what kind of experience users would have. By looking at the document, anyone on the team could discern how their piece of the plan would fit into the larger experience for the gamer.

Fortunately, most of these documents didn't leak out. The Xbox community clamored for news of any kind, and Microsoft's employees were getting frustrated that they couldn't comment. The company was developing ways to stay in close touch with its most avid members and to fuel their enthusiasm.

The gamers flocked to web sites that posted pictures of the alleged prototypes of Xenon made by the industrial designers. Many of them were fake, but some resembled the earliest mock-ups created by the various design competitors. Microsoft's marketing machine wanted to channel this enthusiasm for news into useful energy.

One of the willing tools in rumor control was Larry Hyrb. A former radio program director and on-air personality, Hyrb was an oddball hire for the Xbox Live team in December, 2003. He had been in Microsoft's MSN music group as the editor-in-chief. He talked with Ben Kilgore, the product unit manager in the Xbox Live group, about joining as the first programming director for the service. Xbox Live, which had its own gamer communications system, was a medium unto itself. Kilgore thought that Microsoft needed someone on the Xbox Live product team to communicate with gamers on a daily basis. Part of the job was public relations, part was marketing to enthusiasts, and part was to provide a channel for gamers to give their feedback directly to the product team.

"I was almost like an embedded fan boy," said Hyrb. "Not that I am a fan boy. I could influence the product group, but I was a tester. I could talk to people."

Hyrb thought about how he could use technology to reach the gadget-savvy hardcore gamers. He could read the user forums on Xbox.com and offer advice to people with questions there. But he felt it wasn't that easy to navigate through the site. So he decided to open his own blog, or web log, to offer his thoughts to the community. With the blog, gamers could instantly offer their feedback in a kind of running commentary on everything that Hyrb posted. But Hyrb needed a handle. He went home one day and watched *I Dream of Jeannie* on his Tivo. He decided his alter ego would be "Major Nelson," named after actor Larry Hagman's character on the show.

"When I grew up, being an astronaut was the coolest thing you could be," Hyrb said. "He lives on the beach. He's a single guy. He keeps a beautiful woman in a bottle. Who wouldn't want to be that guy?"

He created his gamertag and web site. His blog would be sanctioned by Microsoft, but the opinions on it would be his own and he paid for the hosting services out of his own pocket. He began blogging away, and then he started his own Internet radio show, dubbed a "blogcast," and started drawing crowds with a mix of humor and a peek into the Xbox organization.

"I tried to humanize the Xbox Live team," he said. "It was a chance to get the voice of developers, testers, operations guys. I knew at the end of the day that a lot of people wanted to have my job and work on the consumer electronics device."

Hyrb wasn't the biggest gamer. He grew up with the Atari 2600 playing *Pong*. But he saw gaming as the next avenue for Hollywood and entertainment. Traffic at his web site was doubling every week. He would throw up links to new game trailers and talk about new games coming out for the Xbox. He didn't comment on the rumors about Xenon at first, since he knew where the limits were. Within a year he was attracting 25,000 to 30,000 weekly listeners to his podcast, a respectable number for a fledgling medium. The good results in an early medium satisfied Hyrb's inner geek.

Through the feedback, Hyrb got some ideas to improve Xbox Live. Xbox gamers wanted to be able to have the same sign-on, or gamer tag, for Xbox Live on the console as they had on the Xbox.com site on the PC. They wanted to be able to move their Xbox Live account from one machine to another. With that information, the Xbox Live team could figure out what was most important to the biggest fans. Hyrb also suggested that the gamers be allowed to segment themselves into different groups so "they didn't get their asses kicked" by hardcore fans in online games. That led to the concept of "gamer zones," where people could classify themselves as "R&R" or "professional" gamers. When the Xbox Live matchmaking service put them into online duels, it would group the players in the right categories so they could all have an enjoyable experience.

Hyrb became aware of subcultures among the online players. One group called itself the "League of Amateur Gamers," or LAG, a joke about having slow connections. Another group called itself the "Gray Gamers."

During his day job, Hyrb would find a "mystery gamer." He would line up a match between fans and the mystery gamer, which would be someone like J Allard playing under his "HiroProtagonist" gamertag. If the fan won, Hyrb would send a T-shirt saying " I owned so and so at Microsoft." One employee kept bugging Hyrb to be the mystery gamer playing "*Halo 2*." In the match, he heard the high-level employee say, "Oh, wow, that is awfully useful." Hyrb was stunned to discover that his mystery gamer had finally figured out that he could hold two guns at the same time in the game. (That was one of the defining features of the game). Hyrb amused himself by looking at the gamer cards of players and figuring out if they really played as much as they said. But his true job was to keep Microsoft connected with gamers in a way that it never had been.

"I feel I'm a conduit between Xbox Live and the community," he said.

1. "Sony Chip To Transform Video Game Industry, by Dean Takahashi," *San Jose Mercury News*, March 4, 2003, pg. 1.

CHAPTER THIRTY

MAKING XBOX 360 GAMES

ow it was Shane Kim's turn to start getting worried. He didn't have enough teams working on games for Xenon. By and large, he had not been involved in the Xenon planning. The Rare teams were tied up on big Xbox titles such as *Conker: Live & Reloaded*, *Perfect Dark Zero*, and *Kameo: Elements of Power*. The latter two were originally aimed at the Nintendo GameCube. When Microsoft bought Rare in the fall of 2002, it quickly converted the titles for the Xbox. The games were well under way when Kim started to wonder if he would need them for Xenon instead.

Bungie's delays had pushed out *Halo 3*, killing any chance for a debut at the Xenon launch. Moreover, neither the *Perfect Dark Zero* nor the *Kameo* teams wanted to show up at the same time as *Halo 2*. BioWare was still working on *Jade Empire*, and Microsoft's own racing studio was toiling away at *Forza Motorsport*. Once those big Xbox games shipped, Microsoft could still have made more money milking the installed base of the current console. But Kim decided that the first-party teams had to play a different role. Once those teams rolled off the big games, he would reassign them to do Xenon games to kick start the platform. Epic Games wasn't scheduled to finish *Gears of War* until well after the Xenon launch in 2006.

Bizarre Creations was ready to undertake *Project Gotham Racing 3*, a new version of the racing title for Xenon. Roger Perkins, lead coder for PGR 3, was sold on the easier programming environment for Microsoft's console. [1]

Bizarre's games for the original Xbox had both topped 1 million units sold. Thanks to Bizarre, Microsoft was presenting a credible challenge to Sony's domination of the racing genre with its *Gran Turismo* title. Now the team wanted to up the ante with next-generation features. One of them was *Gotham TV*, a spectator mode where online onlookers could watch a championship race on Xbox Live. They would be able to choose from any number of angles, including sitting inside the car. The in-car view presented the art team with some huge challenges, but it would become a defining next-generation feature. To make the schedule on time, the team cut some other less-exciting features that had been done before, said Gareth Wilson, design manager at Bizarre.

Project Gotham Racing 3 featured an in-car view.

The schedule was going to be tough. *Project Gotham Racing 2* had shipped in November, 2003. The time was ideal for Bizarre to roll over onto a Xenon game. But the team knew that the hardware would be a moving target and that the software development tools would arrive in the middle of the project. Plus, the team would have to generate many more times the art, with detailed cities where gamers could race, thanks to the high-definition requirement. Wilson said the team's list of "core pillars" included the notion that you could race against anyone you wanted. That meant Xbox Live had to be fully enabled.

Some things moved slowly. The art team had a difficult time moving to a content creation software tool known as Maya. Wilson said the team had incurred "massive overtime" to hit the quality of art that it needed and to deal with last-minute changes. The company ordered catered food to keep the team working and "full of vegetables." The team outsourced the simpler art tasks to outside low-cost companies. Over time, Bizarre built up to a team of 67 people, including 20 artists, 15 programmers, 4 designers and a load of testers, sound engineers, and support staff.

Any games that were scheduled to ship in 2005 were now targeted for Xenon. Since the Bungie team didn't free up until the fall of 2004, they were formally off the hook for a launch title.

Ken Lobb, the manager in charge of the Rare studio, actually lobbied to move the Rare titles to Xenon. The teams had been at work on the titles for a long time. Both teams pushed back and wanted to just finish.

"The instant response was, 'You've got to be joking,'" said George Andreas, lead designer on *Kameo*. [2]

The teams had been at work since 2000 and were anxious to move on to new games. *Perfect Dark Zero*, known as PDZ, was less than a year from being finished, and *Kameo* itself was virtually done.

But Lobb and his executive producer talked the teams into it. By this time, hundreds of Xbox games were available. While PDZ and *Kameo* would sell well across the big installed base, they weren't needed as much on the current platform. Lobb argued that if they became launch titles, they could escape from the blast radius of *Halo 2* and garner big marketing budgets. If they didn't launch at the same time, the shapely forms of Joanna Dark, the heroine of PDZ, and the fairy princess *Kameo* would grace the covers of fan magazines.

Moreover, they could refashion their games and make them better. With the better graphics of the 360, the *Kameo* team realized that they could dust off the original description of what they wanted to do.

Andreas had originally hoped to link the different missions in the role-playing game through a single, common geographical space. It was a battlefield called the Badlands where a thousand trolls fought an army of a thousand elves. Kameo would ride her horse through the battlefield, at least on paper, as she moved to fulfill different quests at the edges of the Badlands. With the Xbox design, he had to jettison that part of the game.

"As we jumped from one platform to another, we refined elements," Andreas said. "We took out areas we didn't feel were working well, or couldn't be pushed forward with other elements of the game. Every platform jump is an effective start from scratch." [3]

But now that he had much more graphics horsepower, the team restored the Badlands. They were able to move from just dozens of characters on the screen to thousands, giving the game an epic feel.

"Putting the battlefield under the castle made it feel like one world," Lobb said.

And they found another way to make the gamer connect more closely with the main character. In the game, Kameo would morph into the bodies of "Elemental Warriors" that each had special powers. She could become a Yeti-like snow monster or a fire-breathing dragon. With the improved graphics, the Rare team could make those monsters appear translucent, so that the gamer could always see Kameo's image inside of them.

With these improvements, the team felt they could now make the game they had always wanted, Andreas said. They were on board. Likewise, Duncan Botwood, the multiplayer designer on *Perfect Dark Zero*, welcomed the delay. PDZ was a shooting game, but in the Xbox version, only 16 players could fight together on Xbox Live in online arenas with a limited number of weapons. With the added power of Xenon, Botwood saw that the team would be able to create a game with as many as 32 players at the same time, a level that was on par with some of the best PC games. They could also add more weapons, create much bigger environments for each mission, and allow players to go back into each mission and replay it with a wider group of weapons. Certain levels could be expanded 20-fold to give a much bigger sense of being in a virtual world. Moreover, the team was able to add cooperative play in online games, so that one character could offer cover for another character as they both tried to eliminate enemies.

Rare's Perfect Dark Zero became a launch title.

As such, both teams were among the first to realize the true power of the console, which was going to deliver performance that, on some measures, was 30 or more times more powerful than the original Xbox.

It wasn't a cheap decision. Kameo had 40 people working on it, and *Perfect Dark Zero* had 60. That meant about 40 percent of the staff at Rare in England was tied up on those two games. Between the two games, an extra year of work meant another $20 million in payroll costs alone.

The amount of work to be done, particularly in rewriting the games so they could take advantage of six hardware threads, wasn't easy. But there was still time. At the time of the decision in the spring of 2004, Microsoft had 20 months until it shipped Xenon.

"There is an awful lot of pressure and responsibility," Botwood acknowledged.

Added Chris Tiltson, project lead, "We just want to make a good game." [4]

Rare still had other big ideas in the works. One of them was *Viva Piñata*, a kids game that would expand Microsoft's reach beyond the hardcore gaming market. The idea came from the Rare team that made the zany *Banjo Kazooie* games for Nintendo. It started with a small team of about five people during

Ed Fries' watch, but it continued to thrive under Kim's leadership. The game consisted of a player building a variety of attractions to lure the enormously diverse piñata animals on an island to a safe zone where the player can protect them from being broken open. Ken Lobb, the general manager for Rare, said that the game didn't really hit its stride until the graphics team came up with a shader, or a graphics subprogram, that could render paper in an accurate and appealing way. The original Xbox didn't have the horsepower to do such a shader. But with it, the Rare team would be able to create simple cartoon characters in a visual style that had never been seen before.

Once one of the Rare teams finished *Grabbed by the Ghoulies* in the fall of 2003, work began on the *Viva Piñata* title. The title looked so good that Rare cut a deal with 4Kids Entertainment, the producer of Pokémon cartoons and other kids' franchises, to make a TV series based on the game characters. It promised to expand the audience for the Xbox 360, but the title still needed a lot of work and it wasn't expected to be a launch title. This was what Kim meant when he said he was still willing to take major bets. *Viva Piñata* stood a chance of being a hit Saturday morning cartoon, as well as the video game that kids played instead of watching Saturday morning cartoons.

Despite the big cutbacks at Microsoft's game studios, developers from all over the world were chomping at the chance to make Xenon games. Kim was flooded with requests for games. He listened most closely, however, to established companies. One of them was Silicon Knights, a former Nintendo developer that had made games such as *Eternal Darkness* for the GameCube. The team proposed, and Kim approved, a trilogy of sci-fi games dubbed *Too Human.*

BioWare, based in Edmonton, Canada, and run by two former medical doctors Ray Muzyka and Greg Zeschuk, proposed a series of their own that exploited their talent in role-playing games with deep stories. BioWare had done a blockbuster game for Microsoft and was finishing up *Jade Empire.* Now Muzyka and Zeschuk wanted to create an exclusive trilogy of games starting with *Mass Effect.* While many other developers created cross-platform games, BioWare's were always such massive undertakings – with thousands of non-player characters – that it was easier to do them on a single platform, Muzyka said. That was why the company allied itself closely with Microsoft. Mitch Koch's marketing team promised a lot of marketing dollars. BioWare decided to commit about 150 of its people to Xenon games.

One set of games was classified as the *Grand Theft Auto* killers. THQ had directed Volition, a studio in Champaign, Ill., to turn its attention to the gritty crime genre with *Saint's Row.* The urban setting resembled *GTA* in many ways, except it was immersed in a world that seemed much more real, with everything from weather effects like torrential downpours to lightning storms that occasionally zapped unlucky street thugs.

Another team that hit the radar was Real-Time Worlds, founded by Dave Jones, the creator of the original *Grand Theft Auto* series. Jones was proposing *Crackdown,* a virtual crime world that was as expansive as anything in the *GTA*

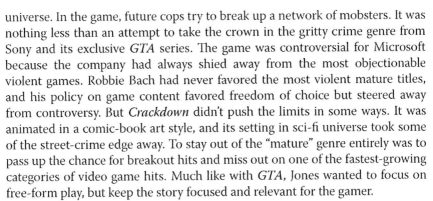

universe. In the game, future cops try to break up a network of mobsters. It was nothing less than an attempt to take the crown in the gritty crime genre from Sony and its exclusive *GTA* series. The game was controversial for Microsoft because the company had always shied away from the most objectionable violent games. Robbie Bach had never favored the most violent mature titles, and his policy on game content favored freedom of choice but steered away from controversy. But *Crackdown* didn't push the limits in some ways. It was animated in a comic-book art style, and its setting in sci-fi universe took some of the street-crime edge away. To stay out of the "mature" genre entirely was to pass up the chance for breakout hits and miss out on one of the fastest-growing categories of video game hits. Much like with *GTA*, Jones wanted to focus on free-form play, but keep the story focused and relevant for the gamer.

"This was more a chance to work with David Jones on an interesting new game than to have a *GTA* killer," said one team member.

Not every game had to be a gigantic enterprise. Greg Canessa, a 13-year game industry veteran, had been thinking about how to make online casual games more appealing for the mass market for years. He joined Microsoft in 1999 to work on the business strategy for games on the MSN entertainment portal. He helped start projects such as games for the MSN Messenger client for the PC, which enabled people to play small games while they were sending instant messages. He spent a few years studying the business opportunities for MSN and decided to pitch Xbox Live Arcade. He drew up a business plan in December, 2003. He pitched it to J Allard and Shane Kim.

The idea was to get gamers to use their Xbox Live broadband connections to download relatively simple games, from pinball to chess, and store them on the hard drives of their game consoles. They could play these games during breaks for 15 minutes or play them during parties.

With the Internet boom, casual game portals multiplied, with everyone from Yahoo! to Electronic Arts' **Pogo.com** offering downloadable games for the PC. At first, the simplest games ran on Internet servers and the players simply logged into the web site to play them. But the games could include richer graphics and faster play if the gamer downloaded them from the web site to his or her computer. Advertisers flocked to place ads on the portals because they liked the broader demographics of casual gamers. At least half of them were women, and many were older people who had money to spend.

Many of the games were free, but surprisingly large numbers were willing to pay for the games after downloading a free demo. This so-called conversion rate was respectable and it made the business of making casual games into a thriving business for smaller, independent developers such as PopCap Games in Seattle. John Vechey, Brian Fiete, and Jason Kapalka founded PopCap in 2000 and they quickly became the stars of casual games with hits such as *Bejeweled*, an addictive puzzle game that sold millions.

Canessa saw the industry shift from the Web-based games to downloads. Since a version of Xbox Live was going to be free with every Xbox 360 console,

Canessa thought it would become a great vehicle for downloadable games. The idea appealed to J Allard and Shane Kim because it offered a way for small developers to showcase their games to the public. Such developers could never get shelf space in retail stores. But they were already proving every day that a simple game, made by a few developers at a cost of around $150,000, could sell by the millions through Internet distribution. Using Microsoft's XNA tools, Canessa figured it would be easy to port MSN games to run on Xbox Live. At the same time, Canessa didn't want to open the flood gates. He felt some of the early downloadable game sites had diluted their appeal to consumers by offering seven versions of Blackjack or Poker, when only one was necessary.

Xbox Live Arcade could take the risk out of game development. And it fit in with Allard's plan to reach the broader market of people who didn't have the time or the dexterity to play the hardcore games. It was a low-risk project for Microsoft. Canessa only asked for 10 or 15 people in his proposal. They would take advantage of the existing Xbox Live software to quickly cobble together a user interface on Xbox Live. Then they would tap MSN game developers as well as external developers. Canessa had proposed a way for Microsoft to become the Miramax Studios of the game business, said Peter Moore. Allard was willing to give it a try as an experiment. It fit with his plan to broaden the appeal of Xenon to non-gamers. Canessa said he could offer a free disk for the Xbox that would allow people to begin downloading Xbox Live Arcade games for their original Xbox consoles. They could opt to buy them if they liked them.

Canessa's project got rolling in January, 2004. He pulled together his team to work on the software for downloading games and then sent his emissaries into the market. One of his stops was at PopCap in Seattle. James Gwertzman, director of business development, heard Canessa's pitch and opted to join. PopCap made three games available for downloading on the original Xbox Live Arcade for the Xbox.

PopCap was skeptical of the plan at first but decided to give it a try. They began work on making more sophisticated games for the Xbox 360. These games had to be able to run in high-definition formats, and Canessa wanted them to shine. He also wanted to tap the connected community of Xbox Live, offering points for every game that a player played so that they could see their rankings or become eligible to play in online tournaments against players all over the world.

"If they did it right, we thought it could be a great new channel that could be disruptive in the whole console market," Gwertzman said.

Canessa also tapped Alexy Pajitnov, creator of the original *Tetris* game that rocketed Nintendo to stardom in the 1980s, to create a high-definition version of his puzzle game dubbed *Hexic*. While the disk for the original Xbox was just an experiment, Canessa believed that building Xbox Live Arcade into every Xbox 360 could give the downloadable games market a huge boost. Every person who owned a console could download an arcade demo for free and buy it for $10 to $20 if they liked it.

"One click, and you are into arcade," he suggested.

The arcade games would also provide transitional entertainment in the early days after the console launch, when relatively few games would be available. And Microsoft's top executives believed that downloadable games would eventually catch on and become critical as a new source of revenue to supplement the razor and razor blades model.

Canessa had to make sure that the games weren't just retreads of what could be found on web sites. He didn't want to overload gamers with too many choices. But he thought the initial games should include a mix of original games, classic arcade games such as *Gauntlet*, and social games played against others. Above all, Canessa thought that downloadable games could return the game industry to its golden age and reclaim some older players who had drifted away from the hardcore fare. These were the kind of games that appealed to Nolan Bushnell, the founder of Atari, who was trying to recapture some of the innocent fun of arcade games in his new businesses. And better yet, these were the kind of games that Bill Gates loved to play.

1. "Developing on the Xbox 360," *Edge* magazine, December, 2005, p. 84.

2. "Kingdom Come," *Edge* magazine, November, 2005, p. 59.

3. "Kingdom Come."

4. "Miss Dynamite," *Edge* magazine, November, 2005, p. 47.

CHAPTER THIRTY-ONE

BIG EVENTS, LITTLE NEWS

*J*Allard and Robbie Bach delivered a keynote together at the 2004 Game Developers Conference, the first time that they had done so. But this wasn't the place to show off the new console. Bach had decided that Microsoft had tipped its hand too early in 2000. It needed to do so then because it had no credibility with gamers, developers or publishers. Now that Microsoft had a good following, it could release information as everyone needed it.

"One thing we learned on Xbox was that you don't have to tell everyone everything up front," Bach said. "You can say it a little bit at a time. Then there is always something for the community to talk about."

Still, Microsoft rolled out the top executives because it had to show the 10,000 game developers how important they were. But they disappointed the thousands of people who showed up for the keynote expecting that they would hear about the next-generation console. He started out with a historical review of Cinerama, a movie technology that used three 35 millimeter cameras to deliver a huge image on a curved screen. It was superior technology, but it was too cumbersome for both filmmakers and theater owners. Making a Cinerama film was the equivalent of making a game today, Bach said, where developers had to fight the technology.

Bach proceeded to raise concerns about the rising costs of game development. Gamers always wanted more from their games. Features, realism, freedom, and better graphics. But rapid improvements in hardware made it much harder to do detailed art work. Top titles cost $5 million and more to make, schedules were getting longer, and developers fretted that they spent 80 percent of their time getting technology to work and only 20 percent on the actual creation of the game.

Allard dug out Mike Abrash's old manifesto on how to use simple hardware and smart tools to produce the best games, and he delivered it to the audience as XNA. The audience was feeling the pain of game

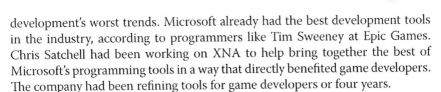

development's worst trends. Microsoft already had the best development tools in the industry, according to programmers like Tim Sweeney at Epic Games. Chris Satchell had been working on XNA to help bring together the best of Microsoft's programming tools in a way that directly benefited game developers. The company had been refining tools for game developers or four years.

"We had known that we invested tens of millions of dollars in programming tools," Satchell said. "We have all this complexity coming. Why don't we tailor those tools for games?"

Satchell and Boyd Multerer had helped round up an ecosystem of tools supporters for XNA. Part of the pitch was to create a common environment of XNA tools so that developers could use the same tools to make both PC games and console games. XNA would borrow tools from both environments. Gamers would notice the ease-of-use of Xbox Live's online game services, such as voice chat, on PC games in the future, while Microsoft would be able to use the same kind of game controller for both the PC and its next console. When gamers moved from one game to another, they would notice that certain things just worked the same way as they did on other games. Microsoft would build a whole ecosystem of middleware tool providers and graphics engine companies, from Criterion and its *RenderWare* software tools to Epic's *Unreal* engine and Valve's *Half-Life 2* engine. All would provide a range of tools that developers could use à la carte. They no longer had to spend so much of their own time on physics engines or artificial intelligence; they would be able to plug in a tool that would give them a basic capability in each area. Among the benefits were tools that would allow developers in different locations to synchronize their efforts, so that all the developers didn't have to be in the same location to be productive. This benefit would help grease the skids for trends such as outsourcing of programming and art to low-cost regions.

Beyond these headlines, a lot of game developers wondered what XNA was. Satchell knew it was mostly vision at this point. It would take a dedicated team of programmers and much more time to make the vision a reality. It was a classic case of announcing a product vision before work had really begun on the products.

Then Allard showed the three demos that Laura Fryer had commissioned. They were supposed to be demos of Xenon technology, but since Allard didn't have visuals to show off with the XNA speech, the events team commandeered the Xenon demos as examples of what someone could create with next-generation development tools.

Allard showed off Paul Steed's *Film Noir* demo of a woman named Eva. Steed's woman was in black-and-white, with a hat tipped over one eye. Her red lip stick was the only color in the scene. The effect was mesmerizing for an audience that only saw such characters in the movies. The point was to show off ambience from a highly-detailed, realistic environment. David Wu got up on stage to show off his *Crash* demo, which now looked totally polished as Wu rammed a blue Saleen S7 sports car – with reflective metallic paint and shiny windshield – into a wall at high speed. Allard laughed and was having so much fun that the camera showed the crash over and over again from different angles as the Saleen S7 went from 0 to 200 miles per hour in a few seconds and then exploded into flying debris. One web site described the *Crash* demo as "the most spectacular virtual car crash you'll ever see." Wu had labored all through the previous night to get the demo up and running. He had a beta version of a PC ATI graphics card that wasn't stable. And he had errors in the lighting on the car that looked really annoying. Wu gave a sigh of relief as the demo went off without a hitch. And it served his purpose of getting his company, Pseudo Interactive, noticed by publishers who were in search of a talented development team.

And finally, *Xenomorph*, developed by High Voltage, showed off the ability to morph a character from one animal form to another. It showed a running ape with white fur, changing into a spider-like creature, which in turn became a lizard and then a finally morphed back into the ape. These demos were the stuff of dreams that XNA would enable, once developers were freed from the chains of technology.

J Allard makes XNA promises at E3 2004.

To underscore its importance, Allard said that he was now the "chief XNA architect" at Microsoft. Allard said that the way Microsoft would beat Sony was not with hardware, but with software. Developer creativity, not technology, would set apart the next generation. Since Sony's hardware was widely expected to run circles around Microsoft's semi-custom hardware, Allard was setting the customers up for the expectation that Microsoft might not have the fastest machine the next time around. That was the unspoken part of Allard's message.

Just before the big game trade show, Intel made a surprise announcement. It had canceled "Tejas," the microprocessor that Microsoft considered putting into Xenon. The power and performance trade-offs just weren't working out with a

big single-core chip, and Intel said it would shift to multicore chips in the future. J Allard sighed with relief, feeling validated that his team foresaw the right trend and chose IBM instead. Intel had decided to switch its resources more quickly to dual-core chips, partly because Tejas wasn't working out, partly because its rival AMD was moving quickly to dual cores.

At E3 2004, Microsoft booked the Shrine Auditorium in Los Angeles for a briefing of 3,000 press, analysts, retailers and partners. In a note before E3, Bach had to remind his people to behave. Bach didn't drink, but he knew a lot of people on his team did. He had heard plenty of tales about raucous behavior at the various shows, many of which were recorded in the press, including a drunken revelry at the Game Developers Conference. During a dinner at Scott's Seafood restaurant, the Xbox crew, led by Seamus Blackley, got carried away with their shouting and drinking, infuriating the *maitre 'd*. Afterward, they packed 22 people into an elevator. The elevator fell a few floors to the bottom, sending the revelers tumbling. They pried the doors open and, after a brief debate about whether to tell anyone, ran off.

Bach pleaded, "We have a large group of people traveling to Los Angeles to attend E3 this year and I wanted to encourage everyone to work hard and have a good time. With that said, I want to remind everyone that you represent Microsoft, and what you say and do while you are at E3 can have a broad impact on our business. Please be conscious of your surroundings and remember that people are listening to what you say. Please be sensitive to conversations in elevators, restaurants, etc."

During the press conference, Bach noted that more than 14 million consoles had been sold and that Xbox Live had nearly 1 million members. Bach, Peter Moore and J Allard gave a glimpse of the games to come. The balcony full of Microsoft marketing people hooted and applauded with every big title. They showed off titles such as Peter Molyneux's long-delayed *Fable*, LucasArts' *Republic Commando*, Rare's *Conker: Live and Reloaded*, Microsoft's *Forza Motorsport*, and BioWare's *Jade Empire*. Allard touted Xbox Live and XNA. In demonstrating a new voice mail feature on Xbox Live, Allard had a chat with celebrity model Jenny McCarthy, who had agreed to rove the show floor as a pseudo-broadcast journalist interviewing fans about their favorite Xbox games.

"Hey J, Jenny McCarthy here. I had a great time at your place last night," McCarthy squealed. She went on, "I just lathered up Enzo and I'm ready for some PGR 2 baby." Peter Moore interrupted in a video feed from back stage where he was having a tattoo put on his bicep. Allard touted a new casual games initiative dubbed Xbox Live Arcade. With a disk from Microsoft, consumers would be able to download classic arcade titles such as *Dig Dug* and new puzzle games such as *Bejeweled* to their consoles. That was just the first of Greg Canessa's plans for downloadable games to debut. But he had much bigger plans still to come.

Allard brought up David Wu again to demonstrate *Crash*. By now, Wu had tapped the wonders of XNA tools to bring a second car into the demo so that he could crash them together. Allard concluded with the campy line, "You guys

have broken the wall between us and the future with XNA."

Peter Moore took the stage to introduce *Halo* 2. Joe Staten and Max Hogan of Bungie showed off a demo of multiplayer combat on Xbox Live.

As he closed the demo, Staten said, "The entire team is busting ass right now to finish *Halo2* and make it great. We're really excited to get it into your guys' hands. And the good news is we're pretty damn close."

Peter Moore tattoos Halo 2 launch date on his bicep.

Moore said that he finally had a street date for the *Halo* 2 launch. "I go out with the sales guys last Saturday night, you know how these things go, and after a few drinks – well, after a number of drinks I dropped the bomb on them, said, 'Guys, we've got a release date on *Halo* 2 and we weren't backing out.' They said they'd believe that the day I tattooed that on my arm; skeptical bunch. Well, fellas, I got your release date right here," showing off his tattooed bicep with the date on it. "November the 9th, the moment Xbox nation has been waiting for,

Halo 2. And yes, that is 2004."

No one knew just how much tension was behind that date.

Finally, Microsoft closed the night with its big bombshell of the night. Electronic Arts announced at the E3 show that it would produce 15 titles for the Xbox, including a number of Xbox Live-enabled sports games. Don Mattrick, head of EA's worldwide studios, appeared on stage to announce that Microsoft and EA had finally been able to work out an agreement about Xbox Live. EA had been impressed with how well Microsoft executed on its online business. Under the deal, EA was going to get a share of the revenues that Microsoft collected from Xbox Live subscriptions for the games that EA customers played. By holding out so long, EA got a better deal, Larry Probst, the CEO of Electronic Arts, said later. Beyond that, many suspected that the deal included a quid pro quo: that Microsoft would drop its sports titles if EA supported the Xbox and its online service.

Robbie Bach makes peace with Don Mattrick at E3 2004.

"There was no quid pro quo," said Probst. "They made a business decision on their own. They just decided they had better things to focus on and better ways to make money than to try to compete with us in the sports category."

Shane Kim also denied that he got any pressure to drop the sports titles because of EA. The conventional wisdom was that console makers had to do their own sports games. Sony had its line of sports games, so didn't Microsoft need one?

Kim would later throw in the towel altogether. He cut 76 jobs at the sports studio in Redmond and closed down the sports title. He shut the XSN sports online network, and put an end to Microsoft's football, hockey and baseball titles. For now, the Access Software studio in Salt Lake City was spared the shutdowns. It was making the *Links* golf and *Amped* snowboarding games. But Kim also decided that the Utah division was also going to go on the block.

"We weren't competitive enough with the EAs and Segas of the world," he said. "We don't want to disappoint our customers."

The entrance to Microsoft's booth at E3 2004.

Microsoft received respectable kudos at the show. The company had big cushioned Ikea chairs in the "*Halo* 2 Theater" in its booth that were always filled with awestruck gamers who had waited in line to play multiplayer *Halo* 2. Celebrities such as Billy Joe Armstrong, the lead singer from Green Day and Greg Grunberg, a star on the TV show *Alias*, visited the theater without having to wait in line. Jenny McCarthy captured the scene in her broadcast interviews, and she even managed to stage a fake ruckus by getting herself thrown out of the Sony booth. The Windows group had a separate booth that touted PC games. Michael Eisner, CEO of Disney, came through the booth and commented, "Movies are going to be harder to make now that games are so beautiful."

Sony and Nintendo slugged it out in the handheld arena as Sony announced the support behind its PlayStation Portable. It also said it would debut a slimmed down version of the PlayStation 2, using a single chip that combined the graphics chip and microprocessor into a single chip. Holding up a small 1.8-inch disk that could store movies, music or games, Sony's game chief Ken Kutaragi declared that the PSP would be the "Walkman of the 21st Century." No matter that Apple Computer had already claimed that title with the iPod. Sony was going to take the music handheld business back and steal some sales from Nintendo at the same time.

For its part, Nintendo's Satoru Iwata surprised everyone at his press conference at the Kodak Theater in Hollywood as he took the wraps off the Nintendo DS, a handheld with two screens, one of them a touch screen that could be tapped with a stylus. It used the simple stroke of a pen to create a new style of game play.

Halo 2 got top billing at E3 2004.

J Allard entertained a few important journalists at Morton's steak house during the show. N'gai Croal, a veteran from *Newsweek*, known for his dreadlocks and big-picture insights about games, bantered along with Geoff Keighley and others. Allard was skeptical of the PSP, while Croal thought it would ignite big sales.

"You can sell 500,000 units of anything," Allard said. "How fast they get beyond that is the question."

They made a bet. Croal wagered it would sell more than 10 million units quicker than the PlayStation 2 did, or about 18 months. If Allard won, Croal would have to get up on stage and shave his hair during a Microsoft E3 press conference. If Croal won, Allard would have to wear dreadlocks for a month, even on stage at E3. It was a bet that Allard would come to regret.

Allard's confidence masked concern at Microsoft. This wasn't something that Microsoft had counted on. By launching these new handheld machines, the Japanese console makers could build a bridge. Instead of seeing sales die off on their older consoles as they waited for sales to pick up on next-generation consoles, they could avoid a rocky transition. By launching the handhelds a year

or two before the next-generation consoles, the two companies could actually grow their market share of the games business. Microsoft would see its console sales wither at a time when the handheld businesses would pick up. It was as if the companies were playing musical chairs, and Microsoft was left standing.

But Sony was in the midst of making a rare tactical mistake in its console business. In March, 2004, Microsoft had cut the price of the Xbox by $30 to $149. It took until E3 for Sony to match the price cut. By that time, it had lost some market share. The price cut enabled Microsoft to double its Xbox sales in April, 2004. For one month, Microsoft even had the largest market share in North America. Sony had been caught trying to prepare the retailers for its smaller versions of the PS2. Sony would soon find that it couldn't make enough of the so-called "PS2 Slim" machines at a time when its older PS2s were out of stock. Microsoft sold a lot more units as a result.

Just after E3, J Allard held a meeting with Chris Satchell, Dean Lester, head of graphics in the Windows group; and Scott Henson from the Advanced Technology Group. Satchell said, "I have lived through these problems on game development again and again." They decided what they needed to do was drive Windows games and Xbox into a single development platform. It would take time and a lot of programmers. But the game developers would eventually see the benefits of XNA.

CHAPTER THIRTY-TWO

ONCE MOORE INTO THE BREACH

ince Microsoft was committed to launching Xenon worldwide, the company had to consider what to do in Japan. Ed Fries had felt that the company could never make much headway there and that it should stop trying. But Peter Moore was now calling the shots about what to do in Japan. A.J. Redmer had some big ideas on what to do about the Japanese market. Both men had extensive relationships among the Japanese developers and publishers, and they both wanted to an even bigger bet there. Microsoft wasn't going to meet either its market share or profit goals on a worldwide basis if it gave up Japan. Like Shakespeare's *Henry V*, Moore and Redmer charged once more into the breach.

After Redmer had cleaned up Microsoft's Japanese studio and cut back its staff, Stuart Moulder was supposed to take over the game studio. But Moulder resigned, leaving the studio without a chief again. Fries selected Norm Cheuk, one of the talented sports studio producers who had been left without a job after the cutbacks, to head the development effort in Japan. Moore and Shane Kim supported the decision. Yoshihiro Maruyama, a former executive from Japan's Square, agreed to head all of Microsoft's Xbox operations in Japan. He began crafting a strategy to gain share in the region, where Microsoft had about 1 percent of the market.

The smaller, better-designed Xenon was one answer. Another problem to address was the lack of unique games for Japan. Microsoft had only a couple of hundred titles on the original Xbox, with most of them being Western games. Very few games had been designed for the Japanese market by Japanese game developers. The number of titles was pitiful for a market that normally supported thousands of games. Most Japanese publishers had stayed away or published just a token title for the Xbox.

David Reid and the marketing team under Mitch Koch had been working away at what they called "Project Atlas," which was the global marketing plan. The group had decided that the marketing plan had to include elements that were global – such as the single name for the product worldwide, the consistent look and feel of the box, and games that would launch in all the regions. But the regions could also make decisions on their own. The Japanese team could decide where to spend marketing dollars and how to approach the retailers. In the U.S., about 80 percent of sales were concentrated in the hands of just eight retailers. In Japan, it was far more fragmented. Each region could set is own price, but Koch decided that prices would be roughly equal worldwide.

The marketing group's resources started pouring into the Xbox 360 project. Project Atlas was like a guide book. It addressed the details of the brand guidelines, the product positioning, the sales plan, the accessories outlook, the SKUs.

"To do it, we mobilized the entire organization," Koch said.

Meanwhile, Moore and Redmer set about pursuing external developers in Japan that Microsoft could recruit with big paychecks. The opportunity was ripe because the Japanese game market had been in a state of decline and old staples like arcades were in a tailspin. Worse, Japanese games, as Sega had discovered, were not selling well in the rest of the world. Big publishers were doing sequels, taking few risks.

"The top tier guys concluded that one problem holding them back was Sony," said Redmer. "They had 80 percent of the market and were the only game in town. They looked around and they didn't see Nintendo as the answer. So only Microsoft could create an alternative for better competition."

Some of the biggest names in Japanese video games started approaching Microsoft. Redmer started taking meetings with some of these developers in November, 2003, to start talking about Xenon games. Redmer had a lot of connections, not only from his Nintendo days but because he had once been a programmer himself who had shipped hit titles. The Japanese developers respected that kind of background.

"We couldn't get anyone to pay attention before," one team member said. "We had the opportunity to work with the first tier because of the climate in Japan."

Redmer had to meet with developers in secret during 2002 and 2003. Some were still working for publishers who were committed to making games for Sony. Some of the secret relationships extended for several years. Redmer established ties with Yoshiharu Gotanda, president of a studio called triACE, which made role-playing games such as *Star Ocean* for Square Enix, a key Sony ally. Gotanda agreed to make a title for the Xbox 360, but the relationship wasn't revealed until April 2005.

One meeting was with Hironobu Sakaguchi, the former creative chief at Square, the maker of the *Final Fantasy* series of role-playing games and the biggest independent game publisher in Japan. The series had sold more than 60 million titles worldwide and Square, one of the hold-outs that was still firmly in the PlayStation 2 camp, was on its 12th title. Early on, the company had ambitions of becoming the next great entertainment conglomerate, as it prepared to enter the movie business. Sakaguchi gambled big on *Final Fantasy: The Spirits Within,* a realistically animated film adaptation, that required a $167 million investment in production and advertising costs. The movie fizzled, drawing a worldwide box office of $85 million. Square had to dismantle a big animation studio that it created in Hawaii, and Sakaguchi resigned. Before it launched the Xbox, Microsoft had all but negotiated a deal to buy Square. But at the last minute, the Square executives asked for double the price. Microsoft balked and walked away from the deal. Much later, they were glad that they never bought Square for the inflated price.

When Microsoft came calling, it was clear that Sakaguchi still had a lot of stories in him. Microsoft had hired a lot of Sakaguchi's former team, and that made Sakaguchi more willing to work for Microsoft. Sakaguchi also knew Maruyama, who had also come from Square. Following up on the initial discussions with Redmer and Maruyama, Peter Moore met with Sakaguchi at the game creator's home in Hawaii to feel him out. Microsoft commissioned the 42-year-old, mustachioed Sakaguchi to collaborate with famed *manga* comic book artist, Akira Toriyama, and a development studio called Artoon. Toriyama would create the characters for the game. Together, they agreed to create a new role-playing franchise called *Blue Dragon*. Sakaguchi also wanted to create a fantasy title called *Lost Odyssey*, about a man who lives for 1,000 years. For *Lost Odyssey*, they decided to work with a Microsoft development team which made the sword-fighting game *Magatama*. That team had several former Square leaders. They pulled in Takehiko Inoue, another famous manga artist and author whose books sold more than 100 million copies.

Sakaguchi started his own development company, Tokyo-based Mistwalker, and Microsoft paid the bills. These titles were the kind of deep, story-based game that sold well in Japan. Role-playing games were the key genre that Microsoft had to nail if it was going to make any progress in Japan. *Blue Dragon* would debut in the fall of 2006.

One piece of good fortune from Sakaguchi's movie disaster was that Square had been shaken out of its exclusive focus on Japanese hardware. The company merged with Enix, another large game publisher, to form the biggest company in the region. Now that the "Final Fantasy" series had been damaged with the poor performance of the movie, Square Enix had decided that it ought to start publishing games on Microsoft's console. But its first offering wasn't that thrilling. It said it would publish *Final Fantasy XI*, an aging online game, on Xenon as its first title. It also began work on a first-person shooter, a rarity for a Japanese publisher, dubbed *Project Sylph*.

Tecmo was back on board with plans to create *Dead Or Alive 4* as an exclusive for Xenon. Tomonobu Itagaki and his Team Ninja had been loyal supporters of the Xbox, and the company had sold millions of fighting games as a result of the alliance. It wouldn't make or break the console, but it was a must-have. And Capcom had decided to create some new titles for Xenon, such as *Dead Rising*, a zombie-killing game.

Redmer, Moore and the team also met with Tetsuya Mizuguchi, the zany creator of Sega's *Space Channel 5* and *Rez*. Moore knew Mizuguchi well and exploited the personal relationship to get Mizuguchi to agree to make a series of Xenon games and open a studio called Q Entertainment. His first title would be *Ninety-Nine Nights*, a fantasy action title which Mizuguchi would produce and Korea's Phantagram would develop.

Redmer and Moore also talked with Yoshiki Okamoto, a former Capcom executive who had started a game studio called Game Republic. Okamoto had been instrumental in making hits such as *Street Fighter* and *Resident Evil*. He had a vision to make special games that could make the first-person shooter genre popular in Japan. They started several titles, including *Everyparty*, which was designated a launch title.

"All of this was work behind the scenes," Moore said. "We were constantly going over there to work with them. Between Robbie and I, we made five rounds of publisher tours. You jump in a minivan and go from headquarters to headquarters."

Moore said that many of the game developers and publishers felt that Sony had acquired too much power. They wanted a more competitive market. Moore also gave Cheuk leeway to create games for the rest of Asia as well, not just Japan. He also convinced Mike Fisher, a former Sega marketer, to take over marketing in the Japanese market. Overall, Moore invested a huge amount of energy in games for Japan.

"It's a shot across the bow that we are serious about the Japanese market," Moore said.

But Sony still had many more developers and publishers in its camp, and Nintendo had a lock on key franchises and development talent of its own. The plan was to make Xenon the dominant console for role-playing games. Microsoft had growing support in Japan, but it was razor thin. If anything went wrong with any of the games under production, Microsoft would feel the holes in its line-up.

CHAPTER THIRTY-THREE

THIRD PARTY TIME

ack in Redmond, Microsoft's third party chief, George Peckham, had no trouble lining up support from Western developers. The good thing was that Microsoft could turn to third-party game publishers and their developers to come up with launch titles. The company had enough clout to get its friends to show up at the party with high-profile, big-budget games.

Another console transition was coming, and for third party game publishers, that meant it was time to ante up for another round of billion-dollar poker. From the biggest of publishers to the smallest, a console transition was a time for daring moves. It was a chance to launch brand new titles in hopes of rising to the top. Peckham was doing his job. It looked like scores, if not hundreds of Xenon games were in the works.

Larry Probst, the CEO of Electronic Arts, the biggest of the independent publishers, liked what he was hearing with every quarterly briefing on Xenon. It still looked like Sony wasn't going to sell the PlayStation 3 until 2006. Microsoft planned on getting 8 million to 10 million consoles into the market before Sony launched.

"As a strategy, that made sense to me," Probst said. "It seemed they were committed for the long term."

EA and Microsoft had less to fight over now that EA had favorable revenue-sharing agreements on Xbox Live and the companies didn't compete in sports. Probst had come to trust Robbie Bach, in spite of concerns about Microsoft's ulterior motives. Microsoft had done a good job extending its lead in online games over Sony. Probst figured that Microsoft would gain ground on Sony with the next-generation, while Nintendo would likely lose share.

Scott Cronce, his chief technology officer, had his technical teams evaluating the technology, seeing what they could do with it. It looked like it would be easy to make games for the system. EA was creating prototype games and staffing up for the launch. EA had always invested heavily at the beginning of each new console generation. Probst believed that was the time to capture the market share and the mind share.

"If you start out with the losing market share on a console, it's very hard to get it back," Probst said. "Once we decided to support a platform, our goal is to be the leading company on that platform. We like to get out of the gate quickly, build up market share, and sustain that through the life of the console."

EA's management team drew up their plans. Through the end of March, 2007, they decided that they would do as many as 25 games for Xenon. That meant 25 teams with anywhere from 50 to 70 people per team. Altogether, EA would field an army of 1,000 game developers to create games for Microsoft's platform. That was just as many developers as Microsoft had itself, split between PC games and Xbox titles. For just one year of time, EA was prepared to spend an estimated $200 million on payroll costs alone for Xenon. That was more than what Microsoft was spending on its internal Xenon games. Development costs were expected to rise, so some teams might grow bigger still.

The Godfather: an offer gamers couldn't refuse?

Probst was happy to hear that Microsoft wouldn't have a *Halo* game ready for launch. That meant more opportunity for other games. The plan called for six titles at launch. One of them was a brand new game, *The Godfather*, based on the hit movie by Francis Ford Coppola. It would be one of EA's rare "mature" rated titles and an answer to the *Grand Theft Auto* series that had helped turn rival bad boy of the industry, Take-Two Interactive, into a billion dollar company. *The Godfather* would be available on other consoles such as the PS2 and the Xbox, but it would look best on the Xbox 360. In that sense, it would be a "virtual exclusive."

The Godfather would cost EA tens of millions to produce. Dave Demartini, the producer of the game, took a crew to interview actor Marlon Brando, the star of the original movie, for six hours to glean insights into the character and environment of the film. Demartini had watched the movie on a daily basis, and he wanted to recreate 1940s New York so that gamers could wander through a "living world" the same way they roamed through *Grand Theft Auto* settings. The gamers would be free to do just about anything.

EA would also make a version of its *Need for Speed* racing game, as well as a number of sports titles for the launch. It was the biggest bet that anyone was making on Microsoft's new video game console.

EA had to make those kinds of bets if it expected to hang on to or, perhaps, grow its share of 20 to 25 percent of the console market. Probst figured that Sony would still be the market leader. But because Microsoft was launching earlier, Probst could allocate a bigger share of resources to making Xenon games than if both companies launched at the same time. In that sense, Robbie Bach's strategy of going early paid off. He had figured out how to get more games out of EA.

EA wasn't the only third party that was coming through.

Xenon work was also under way at Visual Concepts, a rival sports game studio that would be acquired by Take-Two. Greg Thomas, head of the studio, had battled EA for years under the ownership of Sega. He needed to figure out ways to outdo EA, and he did so by focusing on fewer games for the Xenon launch. He started with realism. He knew that the graphics on the new machine would look good, but the overall improvements in realism would be much more subtle. The characters would have better facial details, bodies would glisten with sweat.

His team got to work on a new version of the 2K basketball line as well as a hockey game. Thomas and his team thought the development environment was fantastic for game production. The team decided to take advantage of the multiple cores to add some new special effects, namely a cloth simulation. In most games, the players' uniforms looked like they were painted on their bodies. Thomas wanted the uniforms to wrinkle and sway as the players moved, just like real cloth.

He assigned a couple of developers to work for a few months on the simulation of the cloth. They watched videos that showed how jerseys moved in action, and how the baggy fashion of the day made it even harder to duplicate in an animation. It was tasks such as that one that made Thomas estimate that he would have to increase the size of his team by about 30 percent. Developer support and the Advanced Technology Group helped on all the technical details so that Visual Concepts could exploit the new XNA tools as they became available. In truth, Thomas said that XNA wasn't ready for prime time just yet.

Many more publishers were stepping forward this time to create launch titles. THQ lined up several new titles on the hopes of establishing new franchises. Atari was cash-strapped but it also lined up a number of Xbox 360 titles. Activision had its staple properties ready. One of them in particular would prove to be particularly important to the Xbox 360.

At the end of 2003, Grant Collier had a runaway success on his hands. The 30-year-old president of Infinity Ward had just launched *Call of Duty*, a World War II shooting game on the PC that drew rave reviews in a tired genre. The game won best PC title of the year across a wide range of awards programs. It was selling like crazy, a big payoff for a team that took a lot of risks. Collier had started his company with partner Vince Zampella in 2002. They were grizzled veterans from companies such as Atari and 3DO. A few years earlier, they joined 2015 Studios to make a ground-breaking computer game, *Medal of Honor: Allied Assault*. Electronic Arts, the publisher, was scouting for a first-person shooter team to make games for the PC. Id Software's veterans pointed EA to 2015 Studios, which undertook the project. The game became famous for its attempt to repeat the visceral experience of Steven Spielberg's *Saving Private Ryan*, complete with a terrifying landing on Omaha Beach during the invasion of Normandy in World War II. But they didn't like to work in Tulsa, Okla., and they had their differences with the way that 2015 was run. So they made for the coast and struck out on their own. They founded Infinity Ward in Santa Monica, Calif., as far from Tulsa as they could possibly get and as close to the beach as possible.

A total of 22 members of the Medal of Honor team joined the company. Activision, a Santa Monica publisher, staked the team for its first World War II game. The team was full of history buffs who had maps of the D-Day landings and knew where to put all the trenches and foxholes in the games. Their first game, *Call of Duty*, resembled the intense, horrific battle scenes from movies such as *Enemy at the Gates, Band of Brothers*, and *Saving Private Ryan*. The point was to help gamers relive the experience and feel as if they were in the movie. They pulled it off with just 25 people. Activision decided to acquire the studio altogether so that it could keep the Call of Duty franchise exclusive. The team started work on the sequel for the PC. About three months into the work, in early 2004, Microsoft's third-party game planners contacted Activision. *Halo 2* had not yet shipped, *Halo 3* wouldn't be ready for the Xbox 360. Microsoft asked Activision if it would make *Call of Duty 2* into an Xbox 360 launch title.

"We were ecstatic about the request," said Collier. "We had been trying to get into console development. We were perceived as a PC developer."

Infinity Ward decided to proceed with the development of the PC game, but part way through the development the team would split off to create a version for the Xbox 360. The game could share the exact same art that the team had developed for the PC. But it was clear that Infinity Ward would have to grow dramatically. The launch was a little less than two years away. But the game development tools for the Xbox 360 were only beginning to be released. The team would have to start on Apple Macintosh G5 computers in order to simulate the kind of environment in which the games would run. The lead engineers went to Redmond to learn the system specifications and meet with the Advanced Technology Group. Mark Griffin, a Microsoft account manager, was in charge of cutting through any red tape to get the *Call of Duty 2* team whatever it needed.

Collier and his team wanted to make sure that they took advantage of the Xbox 360's processing power. The engineers figured that they could divide the workload of the game among the different cores. One core could handle the artificial intelligence processing; another could handle special effects, and the last one would handle everything else. They didn't want to port an exact copy of the PC game to the console. They tripled the size of the team to nearly 75 people, preparing to create the art assets that showed off all the console's power. They thought about the things they could create with the next-generation technology. One of the effects was smoke, which meant that soldiers could toss smoke grenades and use them for cover as they crossed dangerous streets.

Infinity Ward's Call of Duty 2

"We wanted to produce eye candy at 60 hertz," Collier said. "We wanted to get away from linear game play and open up the environment to the player so they wouldn't feel like they were on a rail or moving down a corridor."

That change would make the game more realistic. It meant that players could find multiple paths to an objective. If one route proved to be too dangerous with too much enemy firepower, the player could flank the position and go around it. That made the design of each level harder. The level designers had to account for just about any combination of maneuvers by the player. Collier's crew could also make the computer opponent even wilier by building artificial intelligence into the soldiers. If the player stayed too long in one position, the enemies would try to outflank and encircle the player. The gamer would also be constantly aided by non-player characters who served as fellow squad mates. They were cannon fodder that led the way to the enemy objectives.

In some ways, the nightmare of the next-generation was coming true. The game was costing more to make, with a budget of roughly $30 million in staffing costs alone. The team had to crunch to make its demo ready for the E3 show.

Collier gave the team a choice. They could either work six days with normal hours or do 12-hour days in a normal work-week. The team chose 12 hours for five days. They catered food for the team, brought in a physical therapist to give massages, and tried what they could to keep spirits up. As a joke, Collier asked if Infinity Ward could get an exclusive on World War II games.

In Toronto, the cold weather inspired David Wu to take another crack at making a game. His studio had been good at innovation, but the games were never big hits. Like his friend Seamus Blackley, Wu was built like a weightlifter with a boy's face. He looked tough but had a gentle demeanor. Wu was a pioneer, dedicated to bringing accurate physics into video games to enhance the play. When a car raced around a corner, he wanted it to slide in a way that resembled the way a real car would. It was his mission in life to make physics fun and to make game play emerge from the physics. For instance, if you shot out the sides of a building, you could make it fall on top of soldiers who were standing nearby. Taking advantage of the physics could be a winning strategy. He had quietly written papers on game physics for every GDC, and had managed to make *Cel Damage*, a cartoon car combat game where physics played a role. Microsoft canceled the game, but Electronic Arts picked it up. The game didn't sell well, but it was critically respected and eventually made its way onto the PlayStation 2 and the GameCube.

A car crash demo inspired Full Auto

With the *Crash* demo, Wu finally had the attention of the entire publishing community. His strategy of using the demo to revive his concept for a *Full Auto* car combat game had worked. He was able to get a deal with a PC game publisher. But, with the usual amount of bad luck, Wu's first deal fell through.

Then Japan's Sega came calling. Wu said, "No one has ever done vehicular combat in the way that it should be done." One of the coolest features in the game was something that started as a debugging tool. Wu had created for a feature, whereby the most recent few seconds of the game were recorded into memory. If something went wrong, he could just dial back the clock and unwind to the point where the flaw appeared. It turned out that this "unwreck" feature was a great way to rewind a race to the point where a gamer started to crash. The gamer could unwreck the game and pick up just before the crash rather than waste a lot of time restarting the race. Some games had used the concept of rewinding time before, such as *Blinx* and *The Prince of Persia: The Sands of Time*, but it had never been used in a racing game before. That one feature could be a defining point of the game's claim to be a next-generation title.

Scott Steinberg, vice president of marketing at Sega of America, felt that Wu's game was a "gotta have" for his company. Sega was still recovering from the collapse of the Dreamcast. It had an infusion of money thanks to its merger with Sammy Corp., a pachinko games company that was expanding into video games. But many of Sega's studios in Japan were still focused on the Japanese market. Sega of America needed to westernize its content, a need that Peter Moore had identified years before. It was time to start making some bets, and Steinberg and his boss, Simon Jeffery, decided that the next-generation Xbox was the prime opportunity to launch some new brands.

"There is this huge chess board out there that is like a game within a game," Steinberg said. "We had limited resources and saved our gun powder for the next generation. We had to put some pieces on the chess-board. We decided to tap external developers to bolster us in the West."

Working in Microsoft's favor was the fact that Sony didn't have any pieces on the chess-board yet. It wasn't talking about how to make games for the PS3, or any of the other details that game publishers had to know, said Simon Jeffery, president of Sega of America. In the absence of that information, Microsoft's business approach seemed solid and worth making a bet on, Jeffrey said.

Sega's team wanted to target games that worked well in any territory. Racing was popular across all the regions. The game reminded everyone of Sony's *Twisted Metal* franchise, which had been a blockbuster but didn't have physics that were anywhere near as spectacular with debris flying everywhere. So it made sense to partner with Wu's Pseudo Interactive.

Even though Wu had a head start on the work with the *Crash* demo, he still had a lot of work to do. His company had to double its size to about 50 people. They set a budget of about $8 million to $10 million. By comparison, a team of about 20 people had put together *Cel Damage* for about $1.5 million.

Throughout the industry, everyone was gearing up. Id Software had licensed Raven to make a new version of its *Quake* first-person shooter games for Activision. And, as with *Call of Duty 2*, Activision commissioned Raven to make both a PC version and a Xenon version at the same time. Todd Hollenshead, CEO of id, was impressed with the hardware because id's games always had to be scaled back to run on consoles. For the first time, the new *Quake 4* game would use the same art as a console game. For multiplayer, the game wouldn't have as

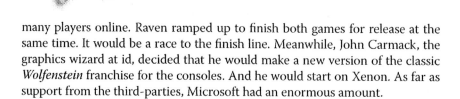

many players online. Raven ramped up to finish both games for release at the same time. It would be a race to the finish line. Meanwhile, John Carmack, the graphics wizard at id, decided that he would make a new version of the classic *Wolfenstein* franchise for the consoles. And he would start on Xenon. As far as support from the third-parties, Microsoft had an enormous amount.

CHAPTER THIRTY-FOUR

THE HARDWARE
HIGH TIDE

*I*n 2004, the hardware work on Xenon reached its high tide, and the Xbox business itself also hit its high tide. In early 2004, IBM, ATI Technologies and Silicon Integrated Systems were still hard at work on their chip designs. Putting a little scare in the Microsoft design teams, Sony announced that the first Cell microprocessors rolled out of the IBM chip factory in April, 2004. That clearly meant that, if it wanted to, Sony could have launched the PlayStation 3 as early as late 2004. But given the company's announcement of the PlayStation Portable, it seemed unlikely that Sony would launch two systems at the same time. Sony would take a swing at Nintendo, which held 97 percent of the portable gaming business, and then worry about Microsoft later. Meanwhile, it would drive the production costs of the PlayStation 3 lower by delaying the launch date and awaiting more cost-effective silicon. That delay would also give Sony time to pull together the right solution on the graphics chip. It was now talking with Nvidia, having failed to create a graphics chip with Sony's own technology. During the delay, Sony wouldn't be hurting. It was generating $1 billion a year in software royalties from the PlayStation 2, and it wasn't eager to end that revenue stream earlier than it had to. Sony had a good plan, but it gave Microsoft one of the lucky breaks that it needed. Microsoft was going to own the hardcore enthusiasts during the holiday seasons of 2005.

Most gamers had no clue how sophisticated their machines were. Chip design had become a great science, but it had its own share of black art. And when it came to the need for precision, it could be a terrifying enterprise. It was just as hard to predict whether a big game or a complicated chip would come in on schedule. The IBM microprocessor for the Xbox 360 had 165 million transistors, the basic on-off switches that controlled the flow of electrons through the chip and gave life to the game console. If any one of them contained a logical flaw or was wired incorrectly, the chip might not work right. If the task

of making the transistors was spread evenly across IBM's 450 project engineers, each one of them would be responsible for 366,000 transistors. Think of the task as akin to putting 165 million light bulbs in a gigantic marquee sign. If you didn't wire them all exactly right, row after row of bulbs would burst.

It was humanly impossible to hand craft such chips within a two-year design cycle, so chip designers had long relied upon automated tools to do their work. They broke the problem down into a hierarchy, with system architects focused on diagrams detailing the large functional blocks, while layout designers looked at specifics of the transistors and the wires that connected them. A complex semiconductor had an intricacy equivalent to a network of pathways winding through a city full of skyscrapers. To design a fast chip, the engineers had to make sure that someone could quickly move from one part of the city to another, whether it was down on the roadway or up in the elevators of a skyscraper. Using layers of abstraction helped make the problem manageable. Occasionally, the engineers needed to translate the digital wiring blueprints from a format used by one tool into the format used by another. Sometimes, something would go wrong with the translation, and an engineer would have to painstakingly run down the problem. Sometimes a small error made on one level of design abstraction wouldn't become visible to the engineers until two levels of abstraction lower in the hierarchy. That made hunting down such a bug into a monumental detective project.

Perhaps the most frightening thing about chip design occurred after the engineers finished their design, or "taped out," in engineering-speak. They would then ship the design to the factory and the manufacturing engineers would fabricate it, usually within 12 to 16 weeks. When the chip came back, it often didn't work the first time. The engineers would have to roll up their sleeves and find the problem. They would then fix the design and have to wait another 12 to 16 weeks to find out if they had made the right fix. Sometimes engineering teams got caught in an endless loop in search of killer bugs, and eventually had to make the extremely painful decision to cancel the chip altogether, at an excruciating cost to the company.

Ilan Spillinger, the head engineering manager on the Xenon microprocessor design team, had been moving in high gear since Microsoft and IBM signed their contract in September, 2003. His team had assembled a crew of 421 engineers in seven or eight locations to work on the Xenon chip on an accelerated schedule. One of the trickier tasks was to create the logic for the system bus, the data freeway that connected both the microprocessor and the graphics chip with main memory. Since IBM was crafting the bus, it had to bolt the interface onto its own microprocessor, but they also needed to work ATI's chip into the equation as well. That meant that IBM was actually working on the design of ATI's chip, something that other vendors, such as Intel and Nvidia, would likely have never done.

From the outside, observers wondered if Microsoft was merely getting IBM to make some minor changes to a chip that it planned to sell to someone else.

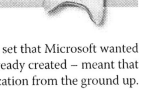

But Spillinger said that the changes to the instruction set that Microsoft wanted – which meant changes in the cores that IBM had already created – meant that the entire design had to go through a complete verification from the ground up. Some of the instructions were not compliant with the PowerPC architecture and were owned by Microsoft itself. But IBM had the rights to the pieces of the chip that it was designing for Microsoft, and it had the right to use those again if it wanted.

"It's truly a custom microprocessor," Spillinger said.

On a day to day basis, Spillinger and his engineers stayed in touch with Jeff Andrews, the Microsoft CPU architect who worked in Mountain View. They argued about many things, but on a technical level. Given the legacy of battles between IBM and Microsoft, everyone knew that they had to be extra careful, and diplomatic, on this project. Microsoft stayed in touch with IBM every step of the way.

"We made the trade-offs together," Spillinger said. "It started with communication between two teams, and then it expanded so that they talked to any of our engineers."

A couple of the trade-offs were big ones. During 2003, IBM realized it had to scale back. Instead of hitting 3.5 gigahertz, IBM decided that it could only target 3.2 gigahertz speeds. (Sony had the same problem; it said its Cell chips would run at 4 gigahertz, but had to settle for 3.2 gigahertz). Otherwise, the yields on its chips might be too low, driving the costs up for both IBM and Microsoft.

Another setback was that IBM had also decided that it couldn't do out-of-order execution. This was a modern technique that enabled microprocessors to dispatch a number of tasks in parallel. A sequence of instructions was broken into parallel paths without regard to order so they could be executed quickly, and then put back into the proper sequence upon completion.

Instead, IBM had to make the cores execute with the simpler, but more primitive, in-order execution. Out-of-order consumed more space on the chip, potentially driving up the costs and raising the risks. When Microsoft's Jeff Andrews went to Jon Thomason and told him the news, it was like a bombshell. One by one, many of the Mountain View group's biggest technological dreams were falling by the wayside.

"You always shoot for the best you can do, and then reality kicks in," said Nick Baker. "You go through iterations and sometimes you get nasty surprises."

"The schedule was a constant worry," said Bob Feldstein, the ATI engineering vice president on the project. "2005 doesn't move."

Early on in the cycle, the two companies were running simulations to work the bugs out of the design. They took advantage of industry tools, as well as proprietary IBM technology, that allowed them to simulate each module of the design and debug it in software. This process of running parallel tests on individual subsystems of the chip had its limitations and risks, since such tests couldn't ferret out the most complicated bugs that involved multiple modules within the CPU.

"It wasn't the normal way to do things," Spillinger said. "But it was the way that we were going to be able to make the schedule. We couldn't wait to do verification at the end when everything was done. By doing it this way, we got toward the end and there were a lot fewer surprises."

Work on the graphics chip was also going well. That was encouraging, since the graphics chip was even more complex than the CPU, with a total of 232 million transistors. Working for Baker, Masoud Foudeh touched base with ATI on a daily basis, checking their progress on hitting their contract milestones. To his friends and relatives, Foudeh had one of the coolest jobs in technology. But to him, it was a pressure cooker.

"The magnitude of the project was huge," he said. "There were engineers at several locations with ATI, working with the manufacturer in Asia."

Foudeh and Nick Baker got some relief in August, 2003, when the team hired Peter Birch, a 34-year-old graphics wizard who had spent a decade working for Silicon Graphics, the computer graphics pioneer that had fallen on hard times as the PC surpassed the older workstations that SGI made. At SGI, Birch worked for Dave Orton, who was now the top executive at ATI Technologies, and Birch knew a lot of other ATI engineers. Birch became Microsoft's technical lead on the graphics chip. As he did so, everyone laughed at the idea of the old Silicon Graphics group getting back together. Where once the graphics supercomputer doing complex weather calculations was the coolest thing in Silicon Valley to work on, now it was the video game console.

Birch believed firmly that the embedded DRAM solution, which meant putting extra memory next to the graphics chip, was an idea whose time had come for the game console. Sony had used the idea on the PlayStation 2, but now the amount of memory that someone could put in such a solution was much more meaningful. For ATI's Bob Feldstein, having engineers like Birch and Foudeh on board was a blessing. When Microsoft and Nvidia talked about hardware and software, it was like mixing oil and water. Now ATI and Microsoft had the people in place so that they could speak the same language as they completed the design.

"At some point, you would have a group of people in the room and you couldn't tell who was from Microsoft or ATI," Foudeh said.

By going with a semi-custom chip, Microsoft got the benefit of using blocks of the design that had been used before and battle tested under a variety of conditions. But the time to do the tough work was short. By 2004, ATI had 180 engineers working on the project, code-named C1, in three different locations.

Fortunately, the team was making great strides finding and fixing engineering bugs. Engineers could now tap software programs and hardware from companies such as Mentor Graphics to simulate their systems. They could find flaws in the design of the system before the designers were finished. They could then direct the designers, helping them correct the designs to get around the flaws.

Larry Yang directed Nick Baker to come up with a plan to verify as much of the work on parallel tracks, rather than waiting to test everything at the end.

Microsoft's Xenon hardware team had now grown to more than 200 people.

"We hit what we called high tide in the summer," said Leslie Leland, director of hardware evaluation in Mountain View, Calif. "It was the time when we had to finish all of our work to make the launch happen."

Greg Gibson put his people to work on engineering validation. The industrial design from Jonathan Hayes' team was done. Don Coyner's team had moved on to testing the user interface software, getting reaction from Cheskin Research's random consumers. But the look and feel of the hardware was done, and that meant that Gibson's team could finally zero in on a single design and a single set of parts to test.

Gibson wanted to test whatever subsystems he could before the chips were finished. The first task was to take an early development machine, an Apple Macintosh G5, tear it apart and remove the motherboard. The team hacked into the board so that they could run some of the hardware that was ready. They tested the DVD drive, the wireless game pad module, and a version of the operating system software being created by a team headed by Tracy Sharp and Dinarte Morais. By integrating the subsystem together and testing it, Gibson's team was able to drive some of the risk out of schedule. They didn't have to wait for everything to be finished before they could start testing parts of it.

The first test version of the IBM CPU came out of the factory in August, 2004. Not all of the features were working on this test chip. It was called version 0.9, as opposed to the 1.0 traditionally used to name the first chip. Andrews worked with the board engineers, going through a couple of hundred steps just so that they could produce one or two working boards a day. Bill Gates visited the labs in Mountain View where the engineers were looking at a chip. When he heard the description of what it could and couldn't do, he remarked, "So you really mean it's version 0.1?" But it was enough to boot the operating system. All of the systems that were dependent on the microprocessor could now be tested.

In September, 2003, just a month after IBM finished its test chip, ATI taped out the graphics chip. It was an astonishing accomplishment because the team had signed the agreement only a year earlier. The engineers pushed the button and sent the design on its 12-week journey through the Taiwan Semiconductor Manufacturing Co. factory.

While the graphics chip and the CPU were the most time-sensitive, there was a lot of unsung work on the rest of the components. Taiwan's Silicon Integrated Systems was designing the "south bridge," or the input-output communications chip that allowed the major chips to communicate with the outside world or the hard disk drive. Adamec said the chip stayed on schedule and never rose high on the radar. That was thanks to an engineer named Yahbin Sim. He had visited Taiwan so often that the manager of the Ambassador Hotel in Taipei took him out to dinner. One of his counterparts at SiS invited Sim over so frequently that the man's children called him "Uncle Yahbin."

Meanwhile, the logistics staff installed a new version of the software for tracking each of the parts through the supply chain. Microsoft's parts buyers would use the system to keep track of all 1,700 parts and make sure plenty of parts flowed through the pipeline to the factory. Microsoft started picking more and more of the vendors who would supply the less important, but still critical, commodity parts. Todd Holmdahl knew that a shortage of any single part could create a severe bottleneck. He wanted everyone to plan ahead. Larry Yang's team helped install a new enterprise resource planning software program that tracked everything, from the cheapest passive components coming from On Semiconductor to the inventories at IBM.

Seagate was building the capacity to start manufacturing its 2.5-inch disk drives for Microsoft. While it had not yet signed an Xbox 360 contract on the dotted line in 2004, it still expected to win the business. Pat O'Malley, senior vice president of finance at the Scotts Valley disk drive maker, and his team had been in close touch with the design team about the kind of drives they needed to supply. The personal computer business was moving down the cost curve. It wasn't uncommon to find $200 or $300 computers in places such as China. Those computers needed the same kind of low-cost drive that Seagate planned to make for Microsoft. That meant that Seagate could count on taking the drives it made for Microsoft and finding other homes for them. O'Malley was confident that Seagate could make the drives for Microsoft at a cost of $30 or $40, far lower than the $50 cost of the initial Xbox disk drives. That – along with Microsoft's plans for two SKUs, one with a drive, one without – would definitely help the business model.

By the fall of 2004, the competition was exceedingly quiet. Sony had made a major misstep as it transitioned to the slimmer PS2s. It couldn't make enough of the machines, which combined microprocessor and graphics functions on one chip. Microsoft seized the opportunity to make a million more of the original Xbox machines in 2004. Flextronics and Wistron cranked up their factories. Microsoft could have sold more, but it didn't want to flush money down the drain, because it still lost money on every console.

It was also becoming clear to Microsoft that neither Sony nor Nintendo had any intention of launching consoles in 2005. The Japanese companies were obsessed with their handheld competition. They were tying up game developers and publishers in their effort to produce games for the PlayStation Portable and the Nintendo DS. There was no bandwidth left over to get the developers to make PlayStation 3 games as well. Larry Probst, the CEO of Electronic Arts, decided to pour more resources into making Xenon games because he still didn't need to allocate anyone to make PS3 games. If both systems were coming at the same time, Probst said he would have allocated more resources to the PS3. Since EA had thousands of game developers who could make or break the launch of Microsoft's new console, Bach's decision to go with the early rush strategy seemed to be paying off.

One technology still lay at a crossroads. Sony was now saying that it wanted to include the Blu-ray high-definition disk players on its PlayStation 3. The thinking at Sony was that the company saw HD as a chain of technologies. It

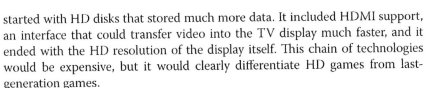

started with HD disks that stored much more data. It included HDMI support, an interface that could transfer video into the TV display much faster, and it ended with the HD resolution of the display itself. This chain of technologies would be expensive, but it would clearly differentiate HD games from last-generation games.

The problem was that Blu-ray would raise the cost of the PS3 by hundreds of dollars at the outset if the Blu-ray drives weren't ready for prime time. That would likely delay its production yet again. Meanwhile, Sony's own partner on the PS3 chips, Toshiba, had proposed a different format for HD disks. Its HD DVD format used a blue laser technology to store anywhere from 15 to 30 gigabytes per disk. Sony had also adopted blue laser technology, but theirs started at 25 gigabytes and could extend to 50 gigabytes. Both formats could store a lot of data, but it started to look as if Blu-ray would have higher costs. Sony collected its allies into the Blu-Ray camp. While Toshiba was a partner on the Cell chip, it was a rival as the chief proponent of HD DVD. All of a sudden, the battle over the standard threatened to boil over into a civil war that resembled the Betamax-VHS battle of the 1980s. The differences between the sides weren't huge, but if both standards launched into the market, everyone could lose from the resulting consumer confusion and hesitation to adopt any new technology that might become obsolete.

Amir Majidimehr, vice president of Windows digital media at Microsoft, took notice when Sony started making technical choices related to Blu-ray. Microsoft and Toshiba developed iHD, a technology for adding interactive features to HD DVDs, and Microsoft decided to use it in its upcoming Windows Vista operating system, which was now scheduled for launch in 2006. Sony had adopted a Java program instead. The Blu-ray group also adopted an encryption technology called BD+, which Majidimehr didn't want. Microsoft wanted to support an idea floated by Toshiba dubbed "managed copy," which allowed a consumer to make personal copies of disks without running the risk of rampant piracy. Majidimehr took a deeper look at how expensive the Blu-ray technology would be. He and his assistant Jordi Ribas talked with everyone in the supply chain to determine the costs. Word filtered back that Sony wasn't meeting its cost targets for making the technologies. Consequently, the tide was turning against support for Blu-ray. [1] This strategy would eventually line up with Microsoft's grand plans for the Xbox 360.

Meanwhile, the Xenon team was free to make its own decisions. J Allard's team once again consulted the game developers and noted that few of them had ever used the majority of the space on the original, 4.7 gigabyte DVD disks. They also wanted faster access times so they could spin data off the disks quickly. The new 12X drives promised to be faster. Moreover, the dual-layer DVD-9 disks could store twice as much data. And Microsoft could apply compression technology to the data as well. No game developers were anxious to fill 50 gigabytes of data. Microsoft monitored the situation, but it had decided that it could add HD DVD later as an accessory device if the market really required it for movie playback.

But for game disks, it would rely on DVDs. After all, if game companies wanted to, they could always ship multiple disks with a game.

"None of the game developers said this was important to them," Allard said.

Microsoft's engineers were glad they chose to sit out the format battle. They had chosen a standard DVD-9 disk because it was faster and because it could hold more than enough data to make game developers happy. They ran the risk that pirates would make illegal copies of Microsoft's games, since it would likely be easier to crack the copy-protection scheme behind the DVDs than the new-generation disks. Still, the Microsoft team couldn't believe its good fortune. The Blu-ray delay was beginning to slow the PS3 down. Microsoft could beat Sony to market by more than a year if everything went well.

ATI started producing its embedded memory chip in the fall of 2004. The graphics chip was more complex and took longer. The first graphics chips emerged from the TSMC factory in Taiwan in Nov. 9, 2004. It was the same day that *Halo 2* launched worldwide, but the engineers at ATI had other things on their minds. An ATI engineer picked up the chips and hopped on a plane. The engineers in Toronto tracked his progress. One of them was Rick Hagen, director of engineering and the manager in charge of debugging. About 30 engineers waited alongside him. They went out to dinner at a Chinese buffet restaurant. They ate for a couple of hours. The engineer's plane touched down and he caught a taxi to ATI's campus. The engineers were munching on sushi. As the courier arrived, everyone dropped the food and opened the boxes of chips. They stayed through the night. The team followed a 12-hour script to get the chips working. At 5 am, someone made a run to the nearby Tim Horton's donut shop. Everyone was excited, but the work was boring. They had put the chips into boards in the nearby assembly line.

Hagen was there when the engineers plugged in the first chip. They ran some electrical tests on a PC. They connected the graphics chip to the microprocessor. The electrical tests worked. They then connected it to memory. Again, it worked. And they connected it to the south bridge, or communications chip. Then they fired up a crude graphics test. When images of a dolphin swimming through waves came up on screen, they let out a cheer, Hagen recalled.

"Was it nerve-racking?" Hagen said. "No, we do this all the time. You make sure the simple things are working first."

Getting the dolphin up and running quickly was a good sign. It meant, Hagen said, that about 95 percent of work was done. But the team of 40 verification engineers had planned for about six months of debugging. The IBM microprocessors started coming out of the IBM factory on Dec. 8, 2004. Within 48 hours of getting the first microprocessor back, the IBM chip was running code for the dolphin program. The IBM team was ecstatic.

"We had pizza parties in a number of locations," Spillinger said.

The graphics chip and the microprocessor were the biggest risks in the schedule. So everybody sighed with relief. Within six days, the IBM engineers had the code for *Quake* running on the game console prototypes. IBM had gone from contract signing to working chip in 14 months on a project that could have taken two years to complete. ATI had also done its first chip in 14 months. Microsoft had bet on an aggressive schedule for the chips, and so far it was paying off.

Once the main chips came back, Gibson's team was able to build the first prototypes of Xenon. The chips ran at slower speeds than the final ones would. But it was enough to start producing chips by the thousands. Microsoft started seeding the game developers in December with game development systems that for the first time included the prototypes of the real chips. These systems made a big leap forward because they would allow developers to properly assess how their games would run and look on the real system. While the Apple-based development systems were good, they couldn't give any more than rough approximation of the real system.

Greg Thomas, the head of Visual Concepts, said that the prototypes did operate slightly differently in some respects. That forced his game developers to toss out some code and rewrite it. That was a normal part of the console game development process, especially for new consoles. Each month, however, Microsoft rolled out the changes on a regular timetable, with either hardware or software updates. Brian Farrell, the CEO of THQ, was pleased Microsoft was meeting all of their targets for delivering game development kits early.

"That was almost unheard of in the game industry," he said. "But they're a software company."

The game developers had no clue that it was touch-and-go at times. IBM ran into a bump in the road on the schedule for delivering prototypes. Some developers, as a result, might have missed out on scheduled deliveries. But both Microsoft and IBM engineers put their heads together to come up with a solution.

"It was a slip, but it was not significant," Bill Adamec said. "It's the normal thing that happens in any chip program. We worked out a way to mitigate the problem."

Scott Henson and the technology experts at Microsoft's Advanced Technology Group worked closely with the game developers. They assigned account managers to work with major third-party developers, such as the *Call of Duty 2* team. Grant Collier, president of Infinity Ward, said that his account manager always acted quickly to get whatever his team needed, whether it was advanced development systems or technical data. It was another example of Microsoft's tactical advantage because it was a software company foremost, said Rick Rashid, head of Microsoft Research.

But it wasn't time to coast. Although the graphics chip worked in the initial tests, it had some bugs. The team had created emulator software to see how older Xbox games would run on the new console. Every so often, one of the games would freeze for no particular reason. It brought the system to a halt. The problem wasn't easy to diagnose.

ATI had planned to recast the design a couple of times to debug the chip and bring it up to the full speed that Microsoft had promised game developers.

Falling short would have meant that the game developers would have had to scale back their designs. By making small changes to metal layers on the chip, ATI hoped that it would fix the problems without having to back into the core part of the design. Six weeks had gone by and the same game kept crashing. Because it took 12 weeks of waiting as the revised chips went through the factory, the engineers had to wait, not knowing if they had fixed all the problems or not. They knew they only had three shots – or three 12-week cycles -- to get it right before the delays would start driving the whole project off schedule.

"Bug hunting is so touch and go," said Bob Feldstein at ATI. "That was terrifying."

Microsoft engineers consulted with ATI on a daily basis. The bug was so worrisome that it now had a large team of people working on it. They would keep on working on it well into the new year.

At Microsoft, Nick Baker and his pals were on pins and needles. While his job as a chip architect had long been done, he was also responsible for the system wide product bring-up. He had to coordinate the testing and participate in the initial debugging of the chips in the labs and the final systems when they came out of the factories. He was an architect who had to get his hands dirty, and his big job was approaching.

At one point, Leslie Leland was prepared to take on her role as director of hardware evaluation, replacing Glade Bacon. But in October, 2004, she was sidetracked for a time to deal with the voluntary recall of power cords for the original Xbox. She had to travel to China to investigate the problem and report regularly on what to do about it. Robbie Bach, the chief Xbox officer, quizzed her about the safety issues. He said that if hazards were possible, Microsoft would recall the power cords. Her team concluded that it was dangerous enough for a recall. The team had to redesign 15 different power cords for all the different countries, and then it had to get them approved by regulatory agencies. When she got back to doing the evaluation job on the Xenon hardware, she noted there were more than 10,000 bugs to fix in the entire system. When engineers fretted about the task ahead of them, Bill Adamec would say, "I'm going to get really drunk on launch day." It was a sentiment shared by many.

1.　"In Sony's Stumble, the Ghost of Betamax," by Ken Belson, *New York Times*, Feb. 26, 2006.

CHAPTER THIRTY-FIVE

ILOVEBEES

As the launch date for *Halo 2* neared, Peter Moore encouraged the marketing team to think creatively about the community of fans for the game. Chris Di Cesare, group product marketing manager for Xbox, wanted to create a big marketing event without spending the kind of money that Sony did for films such as *Spider-Man 2*. He called upon Jordan Weisman, a former Microsoft game developer and founder of Fasa Interactive, the maker of the *MechWarrior* series of games. Weisman had been the creative director for Microsoft Game Studios under Ed Fries. He left at the end of 2002 to tend to Whiz Kids, a toy company that he had created on the side. Weisman had cooked up a new way to combine marketing and games, and Di Cesare tapped him to promote *Halo 2*.

While still at Microsoft, Weisman had to deal with a tough task. He had gone to the Consumer Electronics Show with Robbie Bach and Ed Fries to meet with movie director Steven Spielberg, who had been working on a new DreamWorks film called *A.I.* The movie was a sci-fi retelling of Pinocchio, only with a robot boy who dreams of becoming human. Microsoft's brass cut a licensing deal and needed to make five games based on the movie. Weisman felt it was a touching story, but he had no clue how to turn it into a game because it didn't have a lot of action. But he was toying with ideas for different kinds of entertainment media in the age of the Internet. Then he got a weird call, which he dubbed a "Hollywood moment." It seemed that Spielberg's own film marketer didn't have access to the director. Since Weisman did, the marketer wanted to know what Weisman could do to help pitch the film. He stole some resources to get started.

To create an interactive marketing campaign, Weisman commandeered a game designer, Elan Lee, and a writer named Sean Stewart. Stewart came via a recommendation from sci-fi novelist Neal Stephenson, who liked Weisman's ideas but didn't have time to work on the project. Together they all wanted to create a game akin to a treasure hunt that tapped into the concept of the "hive mind." Weisman figured that a single motivated audience could pool its collective resources to solve a gigantic puzzle.

"This hive mind with 200,000 people would be able to solve anything because it would have someone from every type of skill," Weisman said.

They essentially wrote a mystery story and then broke it up into parts. As soon as the audience solved one clue and posted the answer on the message boards, they would unlock the next clue. Because the game was fictitious but involved using clues in the real world, fans called it an "alternative reality game." The game, if it could be called that, was entitled *The Beast* and it helped launch *A.I.* in the summer of 2000. In the film, they left what they called a "rabbit hole." The clue was a fictitious credit for a "sentient machine therapist" named Janine Salla. The clue led to another, and Weisman bet correctly that someone would notice.

Jordan Weisman specializes in immersive entertainment

The game was a big viral hit that broke new ground by pulling groups of fans together to solve a mystery. The game directed fans on a murder-mystery treasure hunt through e-mails, web sites, fax numbers and other things that they had to track down. It made fans feel like they were part of the movie's world and could participate in it before its release. The game didn't cost a lot, but it was so innovative it generated stories in the *Wall Street Journal, Time, USA Today, CNN, Wired,* and *Slashdot.* An estimated 3 million people followed the campaign, which created about 350 million exposures for the film on a shoestring marketing budget. Still, the film didn't do well in the U.S., and Microsoft canceled its other games.

Weisman left Microsoft, worked at Whiz Kids for a time and sold it to Topps. Then he and started a company called 42 Entertainment, which designed "immersive entertainment" marketing campaigns. Di Cesare directed Weisman's team to create another alternative reality campaign that could run

for months before the release of *Halo 2*. Di Cesare wanted to create fervor in the Halo community, an excitement akin to Orson Welles' *War of the Worlds* radio broadcast. It would be an alternate reality game that mixed fiction with the real world.

With roughly 10 people, they created a campaign called *ilovebees*. It kicked off in July with a "rabbit hole," or a secret path into the story, embedded in the film credits of *I, Robot*. A single web site address, **www.ilovebees.com**, flashed across the screen at the end of the *Halo 2* game trailer that accompanied the movie. A few people noticed it. But more paid attention when the trailer was released on the Internet. The site described a beekeeper named Dana in Napa Valley whose web site was attacked by a virus and taken over by a rogue A.I. A countdown started ticking down at the site. The story, set in the *Halo* universe, unfolded slowly over time. The goal of the game was to track down pay phones by their global positioning system coordinates. Players had to coordinate by the thousands to get to the phones at the exact times so they could listen to snippets of a five-hour radio broadcast. Each snippet would lead to another clue. In essence, the broadcast explained why the enemy of the human race, the Covenant, had located the planet Earth at the beginning of *Halo 2*.

The lucky few who did the legwork were invited to *Halo 2* launch events, while 1.5 million fans followed the updates. The enthusiasts endured hardships to get to the phones, with one fan braving a hurricane to listen to the snippet and another having a difficult conversation with Canadian border police about why he was crossing the border. At a debate between presidential candidates George Bush and John Kerry, someone held up a sign that said, "I love bees." For the amount of investment, the campaign paid off handsomely, with an estimated 300 million impressions created.

"It spilled over into pop culture," Di Cesare said. "It worked for us because the community drove it."

When it was all over, the marketing campaign drew creative accolades, taking prizes such as the International Game Developers Association innovation award, as well as a *Webby* award.

The Bungie team shipped *Halo 2* in time to make the final launch date of Nov. 9, 2004. It wasn't on schedule by any means, but it matched the date on Peter Moore's arm. Estimates for the cost of developing the game ran around $30 million to $40 million. Marketing and advertising costs were even more. In the end, it came together. Jason Jones referred to the process as "assembling a cathedral out of a hurricane."

The game shipped simultaneously in 27 countries and eight languages. *Halo 2* shipped in the fall of 2004 and sold $125 million worth of units in 24 hours. It became the best-selling Microsoft hit of all time, making back its investment many times over. Gaming hours on Xbox Live skyrocketed as a million new people began fragging each other in *Halo 2* matches. And in the fourth quarter of 2004, for the first time, the Home and Entertainment Division that included the Xbox division made a small $55 million profit. Ed Fries, who had left many

months earlier, would have finally blown away his revenue targets. *Grand Theft Auto: San Andreas* for the PS 2 outsold *Halo* 2, but a greater percentage of Xbox owners bought *Halo* 2. That was the last act in Ed Fries' Greek tragedy.

The toll on Bungie was high. Hamilton Chu, who had been producer on *Halo* and *Halo* 2, left some time before the game shipped. Michael Evans, engineering lead on *Halo* 2, moved over to work on *Perfect Dark Zero* and later left Microsoft. Pete Parsons, the general manager of Bungie, also eventually went on a sabbatical. Those who knew him didn't expect him to return. The industry insiders knew that many at Bungie had burned out on *Halo* 2, but to the public at large, all seemed well.

"If you noticed a lot of people left, that was because of burnout," said one veteran Bungie insider.

For the first time, Microsoft beat Sony in consoles sold during the holiday season in the U.S. For the year, Sony saw its U.S. sales of PS 2 consoles drop 28 percent from 2003, thanks to a shortage. GameCube sales were flat, but Xbox console sales were up 27 percent for the year. Electronic Arts had moved its games to Xbox Live. In the U.S., the tie ratio of game sales per console had hit 7.5. Some cross-platform games were selling higher on the Xbox. Microsoft finally had some momentum.

"Microsoft gained tremendous credibility with retailers, consumers and publishers in 2004, because of better execution, a solid title release schedule, and pricing leadership," wrote John Taylor, an analyst at Arcadia Investment.

Taylor estimated that Sony lost 1.5 million in console sales, worth hundreds of millions of dollars, due to the shortage. The Nintendo DS, launched in November in the U.S., also had a stellar debut, as Nintendo was able to beat Sony to market with a new handheld game player. The negative turn of events for Sony would trigger changes at the Japanese company. Taylor raised an interesting thought: "It is difficult to quantify the cost of Sony's mistakes in 2004. Microsoft might actually have a chance to displace Sony as leader in the next console cycle."

CHAPTER THIRTY-SIX

WELCOME TO LAUNCH YEAR

At the start of 2005, Bill Gates delivered a keynote at the Consumer Electronics Show. While he highlighted some Xbox games, he didn't say a word about the new console. He did say that Microsoft expected to move 20 million consoles by July.

The Xbox team showed a demo of *Forza Motorsport* during the keynote. But in the middle of the demo, the game froze. Conan O'Brien, the talk show host who joined Gates on stage, cracked, "Who's in charge of Microsoft anyway?" The speech reminded everyone of the buggy software that Microsoft had produced over the years. Gates did note that Microsoft and MTV had struck a strategic partnership, but the significance of that announcement wasn't clear to Xbox fans at the time.

Gates did announce a series of "portable media centers" aimed at taking some of Apple's iPod customers. But the announcement was received with considerable consumer skepticism. Apple had taken the music player market by storm in less than two years.

At a silicon review meeting, Todd Holmdahl opened with, "Happy New Year everyone. Welcome to launch year." There were groans around the table. The statement's gravity sunk in with Bill Adamec.

Fortunately, IBM had completed its final tape-out on the PowerPC microprocessor on Jan. 31. IBM was ready to start debugging its factories and the chip itself in preparation for high-volume manufacturing. It was just 17 months after IBM signed its contract. The chip program was in good shape, but it had little room for error. After "Waternoose" went off to the factory, the IBM engineers started working on the cost reduction of the silicon design for the second year of production. Jeff Andrews had some scary moments, but he breathed a sigh of relief when his chip was done. The final IBM chip would come back just before E3 in May.

The ATI graphics chip, however, wasn't finished yet. Hagen's team made changes to fix the known bugs in the graphics chip. They sent it back to the Taiwan Semiconductor Manufacturing Co. factory and they got the chip back in January. They had to run a huge suite of tests, using a few hundred computers, to make sure they didn't introduce a new bug. But they had not yet found a solution for the most difficult bug. The chip locked up and failed to work under certain conditions. Although the ATI team could extract data about every piece of the chip at the instant that it froze, the information didn't help them. They had to start writing tests to zero in on the problem. On daily calls with Microsoft, they referred to the problem as a "phenomenon."

Then the engineers isolated the bug. Two logical functions happened in sequence, one after another. Most of the time, they worked fine. But once in a while, the clock in the chip fell victim to electrical noise. It would "jitter," or pause long enough to cause a delay. That delay was long enough to insert itself between the two logical functions. When that happened, the chip failed. Hagen said it was hard to find because the jitter was an analog problem, occurring a couple of levels of abstraction below where the digital engineers were looking for it. In about February, ATI submitted the solution for the flaw. They revised the logical data in the design and drew up plans for another chip. TSMC began working on it.

"This was not something that showed up in the tests," Hagen said. "We had to noodle it out."

If the ATI engineers had been caught in an endless search for the bug, the consequences could have affected the entire program. The game developers needed a new set of development kits to make further progress on developing their launch titles. Instead of getting a final chip in the spring, Microsoft was going to get another prototype. To make sure that Microsoft could use those prototypes in machines for developers, the team in Mountain View had to figure out a way to fix the problem. Neil McCarthy, Microsoft engineer, figured out that he could create a one-time "metal spin." That is, he would alter the top layers of electrical wiring on the chip for the next prototype only. By doing so, he could make the chips functional enough for the game developers.

"He single-handedly saved the program," said Bill Adamec, the Microsoft graphics chip program manager.

At the Dice Summit in Las Vegas that year, Sony's U.S. sales chief, Jack Tretton, warned about the rising costs of next-generation games. Console game costs had gone from $2 million to $7 million from 1995 to 2000 to roughly $10 million to $25 million in 2006. At the same time, the price of software had fallen from $47 in 1995 to $32. He said 91 console software publishers were actively making games, but the top 20 accounted for 93 percent of retail game sales. Publisher would face tough calls about developing games for three current consoles, three next-generation consoles, two new portables, and the PC.

"It's a world of choices, but you have to place your bets," Tretton said.

About this time, Electronic Arts had decided upon its launch portfolio. Of the 25 games in the works, at least six titles would be ready for the launch. One of them would be *The Godfather*, another would be *Need for Speed: Most Wanted*, and the balance would be sports titles. Larry Probst and his teams were

betting equally on the Microsoft console as they were on the Sony PlayStation 3. The costs of creating games was escalating, but EA knew it had to invest.

Looking at the budgets, something had to give. For Nintendo, Probst had decided that the company was satisfied in its niche of appealing to kids. EA would make games for the Revolution, but they would be fewer in number, and they would be more targeted at Nintendo's niche.

"Sony and Microsoft are looking at each other as formidable competitors," Probst said. "It's a battle to the death. They both care about market share. I don't think Nintendo cares much about market share."

He wasn't counting Nintendo out. "Every time people do that," he added, "They show up with something clever and innovative."

Sony took the wraps off the design of the Cell microprocessor at a chip conference in San Francisco on Feb. 7, 2005. After years of silence, IBM, Sony and Toshiba disclosed that the performance of the Cell chips would be about 256 gigaflops, or, put another way, 10 times the power of the fastest Intel chips for personal computers. As the patents suggested, the chips consisted of one PowerPC core with eight subprocessors for handling floating point processing. The chips were modular in design, so that bunches of them could be ganged together in a supercomputer, or a slimmed down version could run in a handheld.

Richard Doherty, an analyst at the Envisioneering Group, said, "This is a shot across the bow for Intel." [1]

Intel itself didn't feel threatened. Pat Gelsinger, then-chief technology officer at Intel, remembered that Sony's PlayStation 2 microprocessor, the Emotion Engine, was also supposed to be used in a wide variety of consumer electronics devices. That prediction never came true. Analysts raised the prospect that Apple might use the Cell chips in future Macintosh computers. In fact, the opposite was happening. Apple had been disappointed that IBM had diverted so much engineering effort to Sony's chips and neglected the PowerPC for computers. So it was planning to migrate its entire product line from the PowerPC to Intel's microprocessors. The reverberations of all the big alliances were still cascading downstream.

J Allard was having lunch with Wired magazine writer Josh McHugh on the outdoor deck of the Ramp on San Francisco's waterfront. His phone started buzzing and he looked at the text message. He ran out to the parking lot to make a few "frantic calls" to verify the text. Ken Kutaragi, father of the PlayStation, had been demoted at Sony. Allard thought it was an early April Fool's joke and asked McHugh if he was in on it. He wondered if Robbie Bach was getting him back for "The Apprentice" joke a year earlier. [2]

It was no joke. Just before the Game Developers Conference in March, 2005, Sony's public relations staff started dropping hints that reporters should be prepared to travel to Japan for a premiere announcement. It looked like Sony was going to tip its hand on the details of the PlayStation 3. It had already described the Cell microprocessor – jointly designed as the PlayStation 3's brain by Sony, IBM and Toshiba – at a chip conference in February. Ken Kutaragi was expecting to be named CEO of Sony within a short period, and he was planning the coming out of his new baby. It would be like a triumphant unveiling of his masterpiece just as he became the top executive. But the announcement that took place wasn't at all what anyone was anticipating.

On March 6, Sony announced in Japan that Chairman and CEO Nobuyuki Idei and Chief Operating Officer Kunitake Ando resigned from their jobs. Taking the CEO job was Sir Howard Stringer, a Welsh-born executive who ran Sony's U.S. entertainment operations. He was the first non-Japanese to run the consumer electronics conglomerate in its history, and he didn't even speak Japanese.

Kutaragi, the father of the PlayStation and vice chairman of the company, was demoted. He had been in charge of the games, semiconductor and electronics businesses. His mission was to roll out the Cell processor and figure out how each of Sony's different divisions could make use of it. Sony would design the Cell into everything from handheld computers to advanced digital TV sets.

That was the original plan. But now he was leaving Sony's board and returning to his job as president of the games business, Sony Computer Entertainment. Ryoji Chubachi was named president of all Sony, leapfrogging Kutaragi.

Microsoft had been gaining market share ever since Sony had a shortage of the newly redesigned PlayStation 2 consoles. But this wasn't just about the Xbox. The threats to Sony came from a multitude of directions. Among them were Apple's iPod digital music player, Samsung's ascent in consumer electronics as well as China's production of low-cost DVD players and other gadgets. Sony responded by striking a joint venture with Samsung to make video displays and by shifting much of its manufacturing to China. But the strategy seemed so last minute. Dell and Hewlett-Packard were making inroads into consumer electronics, launching their own flat-panel TV businesses, as they were already selling the displays as computer monitors. Those companies sourced their TVs from low-cost Chinese players.

"All of these companies are taking share and that is creating a crisis," said Rob Enderle, an analyst at the Enderle Group in San Jose. [3]

The low-margin electronics businesses accounted for 70 percent of Sony's revenues, but only 36 percent of the operating profit. The game division was still the cash cow. It generated 13 percent of revenue and 32 percent of operating profit.

Kutaragi had been considered the favorite to succeed Idei as CEO. A Sony spokeswoman said that the change in position wasn't necessarily viewed as a demotion; rather, it reflected the need to focus on a critical business unit. Kutaragi was still in charge of the crown jewels. But in the press conference announcing the changes, Idei publicly berated Kutaragi, saying that he didn't listen very well. That was easy to imagine, since Kutaragi had a temper and didn't come off as particularly friendly in his public appearances. Analysts didn't view this spin as a positive.

After such a public tongue-lashing, some thought that Kutaragi might even resign. J Allard at Microsoft had said that he woke up every morning thinking

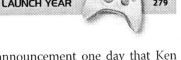

about his goal in life. That was to read an announcement one day that Ken Kutaragi had resigned. This wasn't quite there, but it was a rare public setback for the man who had been known as the golden boy of Sony.

"The Cell is the next big strike that Sony has against its rivals," said P.J. McNealy, an analyst at American Technology Research. "It's a surprise that they would do this now. It shows a lack of patience for the plan they have outlined."

For sure, the games business had a long way to go. In March, Sony was launching its PlayStation Portable in the U.S. market. Kutaragi had to focus on catching up with Nintendo, which was ahead of the PSP with sales of its dual-screen Nintendo DS handheld. Meanwhile, Stringer, who had run the company's movie studio and Sony BMG music business, had to figure out how to unite the company's entertainment strategy with the electronics business. In music players, Sony had lost the dominant share that it held in handheld music players for 25 years. The Walkman had given way to Apple's iPod, which had united the music labels behind a business model where songs were sold for 99 cents apiece.

Some analysts say Sony's failure to recognize the digital music revolution is classic big-company myopia. As the leading manufacturer of portable CD players and boom boxes, it's easy to see how it could reflexively dismiss MP3 players as a passing fad.

"Lots of big companies miss those shifts," said Stephen Baker, director of industry analysis for market researcher NPD TechWorld. [4]

Sony also was guilty of a not-invented-here mentality, said Baker. It remained committed to its own digital music format, called ATRAC, and refused to make devices that played popular MP3 digital music files. Even its most recent generation of MiniDisc players, released late last year, required music to be converted to Sony's proprietary format.

"The market rejected them," said Michael Gartenberg of Jupiter Research in New York. "Even if they were beautifully designed, relative to other players on the market at the time." [5]

Apple exploited that void in the market with the iPod. The portable music player not only played music in the most common format but was seamlessly integrated with Apple's iTunes music software and iTunes Music Store.

"The world is not the same place it was just a few years ago," Stringer wrote in a memo to Sony employees the day after he was promoted. "The needs and expectations of our customers have changed. The dynamics of the competitive landscape have changed. The pace of innovation across all of the businesses in which we compete has changed. Sony, too, must change."

One thing Sony had to worry about was cash. Microsoft had been leading price cuts in the console business, because it knew it could stand to lose more money than Sony. In the spring of 2005, Microsoft had $60 billion in cash compared to Sony's $3.7 billion. That meant that Sony had to handle the PlayStation 3 launch perfectly.

"It's clear the Sony brand no longer demands a premium price," said John

Yang, an analyst at Standard & Poor's. "It started with flat-panel TV sets, and now they can no longer justify high prices. The competition from the Chinese and others is hurting. Their savior is the PlayStation 3 and the Cell." [6]

The Xbox team had convened to rethink another big decision: how much main memory to put into Xenon. The financial model and the current plan called for 256 megabytes of a special kind of fast graphics memory, dubbed graphics double data rate 3, or GDDR3. Over the years, that item alone was costing Microsoft an estimated $900 million based on its estimate of how many consoles it would sell over time.

At the time that Greg Williams and other engineers specified the amount in 2003, that seemed like a lot, Allard said. They maintained some flexibility, designing the box so that it could use anywhere from 128 megabytes to 1 gigabyte of memory. The 1-gigabyte number was clearly out of reach, but with prices coming down, 512 megabytes was reasonable.

"Competitive intelligence suggested that we needed to be flexible on the amount of memory," said Greg Gibson.

The game developers wanted more. The average amount of main memory in a PC was rising. They argued that Microsoft had scrimped in other ways, making the hard disk drive optional and including a DVD drive instead of an HD DVD or Blu-ray drive. Tim Sweeney, the graphics wizard at Epic Games, lobbied hard. He created a series of screen shots for what Epic's game, *Gears of War*, would look like with 256 megabytes of memory, and what it would look like with 512 megabytes. Clearly, the 512-megabyte solution looked far better. With it, Epic could implement "high dynamic range" images. These were images that improved the realistic feel of games because they could show both low-light and bright-light images in the same picture. The effect could create images such as the rays of the sun shining through some dark clouds.

Robbie Bach said that he wasn't going to just make a decision based on the best guesses that the team punted upward to him. He wanted the team to provide its own answer. The team worked through its process and came back with the recommendation.

"There were enough zeroes on the cost of it that I ultimately had to decide," Bach said. "We decided to go ahead."

It was a $900 million decision. Microsoft would have to make arrangements with both Samsung and Infineon Technologies, two of the biggest memory-chip makers, to produce more GDDR3 chips. When the crew at Epic Games heard the decision, they hooted in celebration. But again, rather than spend more money over the life of the program, Microsoft decided to find cuts in other parts of the program. It scaled back some of its other plans in the spreadsheets, and then moved to make more decisions. Nobody knew it at the time, but by doubling the amount of memory, Microsoft had made one of the most fateful decisions on the entire Xbox 360 program.

The company finally cut a deal with the hard disk drive suppliers, which included Seagate Technology. Holmdahl never had much doubt about which

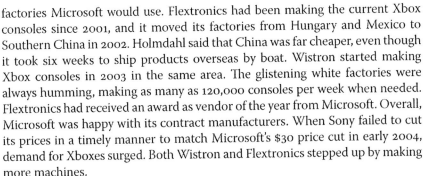

factories Microsoft would use. Flextronics had been making the current Xbox consoles since 2001, and it moved its factories from Hungary and Mexico to Southern China in 2002. Holmdahl said that China was far cheaper, even though it took six weeks to ship products overseas by boat. Wistron started making Xbox consoles in 2003 in the same area. The glistening white factories were always humming, making as many as 120,000 consoles per week when needed. Flextronics had received an award as vendor of the year from Microsoft. Overall, Microsoft was happy with its contract manufacturers. When Sony failed to cut its prices in a timely manner to match Microsoft's $30 price cut in early 2004, demand for Xboxes surged. Both Wistron and Flextronics stepped up by making more machines.

Flextronics planned how to cut over from making original Xbox consoles to making Xbox 360s in its 70,000-square foot factory, which was part of a campus that employed as many as 25,000 workers. Though it wasn't working under a specific contract yet, Flextronics would periodically fabricate prototypes of the Xbox 360. Its mechanical engineers on staff in San Jose would review the industrial design of the new machine and offer advice about which parts would be most cost effective in the console. Jim McCusker, a senior vice president at Flextronics, said his team provided information on the generic parts such as voltage regulators, bezels, electromagnetic interference shields, and power supplies. Unfortunately, the power supply was going to be huge. Flextronics made suggestions on how to build the wireless controllers that Microsoft wanted. The controllers would use the same kind of wireless signals that wireless land line phones used.

Flextronics also had to prepare Microsoft for a big change in Europe. The European Commission declared that all machines manufactured and sold in Europe after the middle of 2006 would have to be compliant with a new environmental regulation. The machines couldn't use lead in the solder or any other part of the system, nor could they use several other hazardous chemicals. The entire base of suppliers had to deal with the changes part by part. Leslie Leland, the director of hardware evaluation at Microsoft in Mountain View, had to assign some specialists to make sure the suppliers complied.

McCusker knew this product was going to be a lot more complicated to build. The worldwide launch also meant Microsoft couldn't stage its factories to begin one at a time. This time, Flextronics and Wistron had to start their factories simultaneously. They would have to be able to make machines for the different regions, including the different countries in Europe with all their language differences, in flexible factory regions. Moreover, Microsoft wanted two different versions, one with the hard disk drive and the other without. The packaging and contents for both would be different. Each of these factors added risk, so Holmdahl decided that the company needed to sign up yet another contract manufacturer. It started talking to Celestica, a Canadian contract manufacturer, which could also build machines in the same region in China.

Bringing on a third factory was a big bet. The volumes it produced could certainly be useful for the launch, when scarcity of consoles would be the main thing holding back sales. But the chip makers didn't have enough lead time to build millions of chips by the launch time, so a third factory might have nothing to do. Also, the contract manufacturers weren't really interested in a business that required them to build millions of consoles at launch and then just a trickle for the remainder of the year.

Holmdahl decided that the company could manage the launch with just two factories. Microsoft had only needed two factories for the volumes associated with the original Xbox. And there weren't enough engineers to bring up three factories at once.

1. "New Chip Called Threat To Intel," by Dean Takahashi, *San Jose Mercury News*, front page, Feb. 8, 2005.

2. "The Xbox Reloaded," by Josh McHugh, June 2005, *Wired* magazine.

3. "New Chip Call Threat To Intel."

4. "New Chip Call Threat To Intel."

5. "New Chip Call Threat To Intel."

6. "New Chip Call Threat To Intel."

CHAPTER THIRTY-SEVEN

GDC 2005

At the Game Developers Conference in March, 2005, J Allard had returned for a second act. Tantalized by the possibility of a real console announcement this time, Jamil Moledina, executive director of the GDC, and his board were happy to give Allard one of the precious keynote spots. Some board members were bummed out by the previous year's false alarm. Sony still wasn't ready to talk, but Satoru Iwata, CEO of Nintendo, had also agreed to give a keynote. This time, Allard's crew promised something more newsworthy for the crowd of thousands of developers – a tough promise to keep without giving the game away to their rivals.

"There was a need for Microsoft marketing to remain mum on critical details," Moledina said. "They didn't want to tip their hand too much, but they needed to communicate to the development community what the new playing field was."

Moledina enjoyed hanging out with Allard in rehearsals. He found Allard to be down to earth, personable, and very bright. This time the speech was in a cavernous hall at the Moscone West convention center in San Francisco. The night before the speech, Allard had a chance to meet with Nolan Bushnell, who, along with Nintendo's Shigeru Miyamoto, was inducted into the Walk of Games at Sony's Metreon entertainment mall. The honor was akin to getting a star in front of Mann's Chinese Theater in Hollywood. Hidden from mobs of journalists and game developers, Allard and Bushnell chatted at a small table not far from Sony's PlayStation store. Allard later said, "There's a little bit of Nolan in every Xbox."[1] The store was the flagship of Sony's presence on the West Coast of the United States, where it had launched the PlayStation 2 in October, 2000, and where it would again debut a new gadget, the PlayStation Portable, later in the month.

David Wu attended the same reception and was happy to finally drop some hints about his work on *Full Auto*. Once again his team supplied a demo to show off the power of Xenon. It was a repeat of last year's demo, but this time with two speeding race cars. Wu set them up so they could smash into each other.

Allard showed up, in one writer's sarcastic prose, looking "as fit as any upscale professional with a personal trainer."[2] At the beginning of his speech the next morning, Allard said, "Meeting Nolan for me was a special thrill because when I was growing up my heroes didn't come from movies, they didn't come from sports or music; my heroes, Evel Knievel and Nolan Bushnell."

He continued, "Now, it might seem like a strange pair but if you think about it, they both took incredibly big risks and really changed a generation. Now, the nature of the risks might be a little bit different, right; I mean, Nolan didn't break quite as many bones as Evel did but he did launch Chuck E. Cheese. But despite that and despite the success of the XGames, in my view, Nolan made the more lasting impression for our industry, the bigger contribution to our society."

Allard noted how he grew up with a game controller in hand in the 1970s.

"There is one TV commercial from that era that I'll never forget. It starts out with the two kids on the couch and they're playing a game and they're having a great time. It cuts away to the requisite screen graphics and there's Breakout. It cuts back on the couch and now dad is playing with the kids, switches back to Space Invaders and goes on and on."

He added, "And eventually the grandparents are playing on the couch, playing some game on the couch, holding the joysticks and it was a crowd of like 20 people around the couch all screaming and cheering at the TV and having a great time. And it ends with one of the most profound statements that I can recall from that era of gaming: It asks, "Have you played Atari today?" And the thing about the statement for me, the thing was, it was an open invitation to the world to come and join this new medium."

He talked about how, when he was 10 years old 25 years earlier, that the world changed when he shifted from board games to video games. He said three new trends were just as fundamental. One of them was the "HD era," which would be just as big as the shift to 3D in video game history.

Inside Microsoft, the company could finally start talking about the trend that it built Xenon to exploit. Allard said that the digital entertainment lifestyle was another driver of new gadgets like Tivo, digital music, and digital cameras. Consumers wanted to control their own content from these gadgets and view them in the living room. Allard scrunched all of this behavior into a trend he called "high def connectivity." Lastly, he mentioned the trend toward personalization, in everything from tattoos and nose rings to tricked-out car stereos. He referred to kids today as the "remix generation." In doing so, he was going down the checklist that Xenon marketing director David Reid and his marketers had come up with in so many of the Xe 30 meetings.

"Today we have the opportunity to make videogames the center of the HD era," Allard said, coming to his big point. "We have the opportunity to establish ourselves as the cultural force that other media looks to when they're looking

for cues to the future. We have the opportunity to dramatically expand our audience. If we're smart and we really capitalize on the HD era, I'm confident that we can double the size of our audience this decade."

It was an outlandish claim, given the trends that showed a modest gain for video game ownership in the last console cycle. Schelley Olhava, an analyst at International Data Corp., noted that console ownership in the U.S. had gone up from 40 percent to 45 percent in the past five years. If there had been much progress, it was more common now to see homes with multiple game consoles. But it was classic J Allard, shooting for the stars. Then Allard shifted into his pitch for XNA, Windows gaming, and the blending of hardware, software and services in an integrated approach to the console business.

Then he mentioned the new console for the first time, starting out with the kind of software that it would have. He reiterated how hard it was to develop games and how developers and publishers often became enemies in the development process. He announced that Microsoft would create a set of tools called XNA Studio in the next year. He also noted that that Microsoft had shipped 3,000 Xenon software development kits.

"In the HD era the volume of content is going to go way up, and when that volume goes up that means teams are going to go way up, it means the interactions between these teams are going to go way up, the relationship is going to shift between you and your QA department and your publisher and we're even going to see the introduction of offshore development," he said, recapitulating the rant of his first XE 30 document. "These are the realities in the next generation, we all see it coming."

Indeed, game developers were not in a happy state over game costs. "Ten million dollars is just the ante to get in the game. The risks are going up and it is very scary for game developers," said Gordon Walton, a veteran game developer who had made online games for Electronic Arts and Sony. [3]

The concern about the toll that making games was taking on the quality of life for developers was a front and center issue at GDC. In November, 2004, the spouse of an Electronic Arts worker posted an anonymous letter on a blog complaining about the horrendous work hours and unreasonable crunch times her husband had to endure.

She had closed her diatribe with the words: "If I could get EA CEO Larry Probst on the phone, there are a few things I would ask him. 'What's your salary?' would be merely a point of curiosity. The main thing I want to know is, Larry: you do realize what you're doing to your people, right? And you do realize that they *are* people, with physical limits, emotional lives, and families, right? Voices and talents and senses of humor and all that? That when you keep our husbands and wives and children in the office for ninety hours a week, sending them home exhausted and numb and frustrated with their lives, it's not just them you're hurting, but everyone around them, everyone who loves them? When you make your profit calculations and your cost analyses, you know that a great measure of that cost is being paid in raw human dignity, right?"

The posting circulated throughout the game industry, and journalists finally took note of several lawsuits filed against EA for overtime law violations. The issue became a storm and it landed on the front pages of many newspapers, which noted that not all was paradise in the industry where elves could work on their favorite games. As programmers and artists moved from one project to another at EA and other big studios, they lived in a perpetual crunch time. Something had to be done, said Jason Della Rocca, executive director of the International Game Developers Association. While Allard didn't bring up this issue specifically, XNA nibbled around the edges of it.

Allard said that he wasn't going to reveal the console details until E3 in May. But he talked about the approach to designing hardware. In a backhanded insult at Sony, he said that "you could design hardware to win at science fairs." Referring to Cell, he said, "Forget the fact that it's hard to program, it's cool. It becomes apparent because after you launch a system like that it takes a year before anything worth playing comes out. That's a crime, that's a crime; there are too many good ideas in this room to go that approach. The science fair approach turns game programmers into hardware schedulers and the only emotion that approach can elicit from you is frustration."

Making Microsoft's pitch to developers in a nutshell, Allard said, "We designed the hardware with the software in mind, software that maps back to your needs, the needs of content creators. The better the marriage between hardware and software the closer you're going to get to achieving that theoretical performance of the hardware."

Having just said that, he still touted the unannounced console's performance, which would top 1 teraflop, or a trillion floating point operations per second. It was the product of 1,000 engineers working over the last three years – an accurate statement, if you consider that most of those engineers were at IBM and ATI.

Filmmaker James Cameron appeared in a video played during the speech. He said next-generation games will be more movie-like, where "it will feel like you are inside a movie and interacting with it," and he said his next film would be launched simultaneously with a related game, presumably for Xenon.

Once again, GDC was just a big tease. He said that Microsoft would have high-performance, multicore silicon that was hand-coded "just like the other guys." Pulling out one of the team's "sparklers," he said, "Our approach here was Bruce Lee. It wasn't brute force."

The few details that he did disclose were revealed earlier by Raymond Padilla, a writer at <u>GameSpy.com</u>, a gamer's web site.[4] Padilla noted that game developers were being asked to develop games for 720P, or 1280 pixels by 720 pixels, a level above most of the Xbox games.

Allard said that Microsoft would distinguish itself from the others with its high-quality services on Xbox Live, from authentication to micro-transactions on Marketplace, and that it would try to drive subscribership from 2 million paying customers – each with an average of 20 friends on Xbox Live – to 20 million. It would add more female gamers and broaden the age reach. He

showed off the user interface for Xenon, the concept of the gamer card that Larry Hyrb suggested, the process of adding custom soundtracks, and a demo of Marketplace. With the gamer cards, he noted that friends could look at the kinds of achievements someone has earned.

Playing to the crowd's heart, Allard said, "In 2004, the best selling game was 5 million units, give or take. In the HD era we're designing the platform to sell the first title that does 20 million units."

Then, to show that Microsoft's love for video game developers was bigger than Sony's, Allard gave away 1,000 Samsung high-definition television sets to those who had the right yellow-coded badge. Whether the stunt earned any allegiance among game developers wasn't clear.

"Bribery," said Sony's Dominic Mallinson, director of research and development for Sony's U.S. game division, as he walked out of the Microsoft event.

He soon fired back by giving a talk with Mark DeLoura, Sony's head of developer relations, about how it would be easier to program the PlayStation 3 and its Cell microprocessor than it was for the PlayStation 2. They made a convincing case, noting that game developers could program without assembly coding. They could instead use a high-level programming language that was easier to understand. But a number of developers still said the Cell was a nightmare because it required them to keep track of so many different threads being processed, said Kevin Krewell, then editor-in-chief of the *Microprocessor Report*.

Nintendo's chief gave a speech about his own passion for games. Satoru Iwata, who had been appointed CEO three years earlier, had more credibility with the crowd than J Allard because he was a game developer, not just a fan. He had the perfect opening to please the crowd.

"On my business card, I am a corporate president," Iwata said. "In my mind, I am a game developer. But in my heart – I am a gamer. Today, I'd like to speak to you from my heart."

Like Allard, he too was a *Pong* fan. When he was young, he programmed games on his Hewlett-Packard calculator, including a baseball game that had no graphics. When he became a game developer, he said, "And when I told my father this, you can imagine it was not the happiest moment in the history of my family."

He talked about the need to innovate.

"Think about this," he continued. "Someday our games won't look any better. What will we do then?"

Iwata said that Nintendo had a responsibility to make games for all skill levels, including those who were intimidated by games.

Echoing Allard's concerns, Iwata said, "Of course, the games themselves have become much bigger in several ways. They are bigger in a technical sense … occupying more digital space. That, in turn, requires bigger teams… bigger budgets…and bigger challenges in meeting deadlines. This also means that big game companies are getting bigger – by consuming smaller ones. We know that in the next generation, budgets for AAA console games will regularly move into

eight digits – and that's before any marketing money is spent. Only the biggest companies can afford such costs. Not surprisingly, the success of our industry – and the profit margins for hit games – has again drawn big interest from larger entertainment companies. But we may not be compatible."

Pointing to games such as *Geist* and an upcoming *Zelda* title for the GameCube, he said Nintendo had not turned its backs on the hardcore gamer. He showed off games for the DS handheld such as *Nintendogs* and *Electroplankton*. He demoed WiFi gaming on the DS. Then he said the next-generation console, the Revolution, would be backward compatible with the GameCube, support WiFi and offer an entire library of Nintendo titles. He confirmed that the Revolution would have a chip code-named "Broadway" from IBM and a graphics chip code-named "Hollywood" from ATI Technologies. Iwata mentioned that casual gamers were intimidated by game controllers, dropping a hint about Nintendo's as-yet-unannounced secret innovation in controllers. He closed by fondly recalling the moment of success, when gamers started playing his first Smash Bros. game, which became a franchise that sold more than 10 million copies.

Moledina, the GDC chief, said later that Iwata set the standard for a keynote speech. While the speech was well received, it was clear that Nintendo wasn't anywhere near shipping a game console. In contrast to Microsoft, it had still not shipped any development kits for making games, nor had it briefed anyone on its hardware. His presentation shared many common threads with Allard's, but the messengers were so different.

In an interview, J Allard was intrigued to hear speculation about the management shuffle at Sony that left Kutaragi without the CEO job. He reiterated again that Sony had produced a science project that was nice on paper but would never live up to the theoretical performance.

Away from all the speeches, Epic Games was entertaining a lot of traffic at its demo room. Since Electronic Arts had purchased Criterion, a maker of the *Renderware* game production tools, a lot of developers were getting worried that they wouldn't be able to use *Renderware* anymore. Looking around at their options, they had to consider Epic's *Unreal Engine 3*. That explained part of the traffic. But Epic was also showing its Xenon title behind closed doors. In the demo, a group of heavily armored, beefy human soldiers were walking through a ruined city at night. The graphics were breathtakingly realistic, with no rough edges around the characters. Then a group of enemies unleashed an ambush on the humans and the firing started. At the end of the intense experience, the viewers walked out of the room stunned at what they had seen. It was the same sort of reaction that gamers had when they walked out of the original *Halo* demo at E3 years earlier. Tim Sweeney and Mark Rein smiled at the reactions as people walked past. Sweeney mentioned that Microsoft wasn't happy that he went public with his criticism of the Xenon design. But he said he was pleased with the direction everything else was going.

In classic tradition, Moledina invited a bunch of elite guests to a hotel suite party, away from the crowds of journalists. The party at the Argent Hotel wasn't as crazy as in years past when Alan Yu, the former head of the GDC, defied the security teams sent to quiet the party. The rich tradition of game developers partying side by side – whether they were from Sony, Nintendo or Microsoft's camps – continued into the wee hours. Moledina's party drew its share of complaints from hotel guests and was eventually broken up by the security staff.

"Everyone told me they had a good time," Moledina said.

Just after the GDC, rumors surfaced that Cam Ferroni had left Microsoft. Everyone wondered why now. It seemed an odd time to make such a change. Microsoft didn't address it at the time, and no one in the press wrote about the departure. He had been in charge of about 250 people at the time, having taken over the software team from Jon Thomason. Ferroni had still been managing Xbox Live, Jeff Henshaw's alternative entertainment team, Scott Henson's Advanced Technology Group, and Don Coyner's planning team. Ferroni said later that he couldn't point at any one reason.

"I had known for a while I wasn't going to stick around at Xbox beyond Xbox 360 shipping. I had been there almost 13 years. Two rounds of Xbox. I had two or three strong leads working for me, ready to step up. At the end of the day, my strength was never in the final push. There are guys far better at it. I was much more on the vision side, getting us on the right path. It's hard to believe. When you look at it, that's where we were. We were on cusp of defining the next holiday. How do we get it out the door?"

He added, "We were about to start planning. So we decided it was a fine time to take a break. I was ready for a change. I started hanging out at the house and building my wife a jewelry box for her birthday."

The tough part was that Ferroni and J Allard were so close.

"It's tough to lose a partner," Allard said. "We were co-founders."

This was not strictly true, since Allard and Ferroni joined an existing Xbox team in 1999. But it was the way that Allard thought about the beginning.

Allard added, "We had 20 of us in the beginning. Half of us are here."

Ferroni said, "There were some tears shed on both sides. It was a tough time. It's business. Things change. We are still friends, which is great. Maybe our paths will cross again. It was good for both of us. I worked for him for eight years. It was good for me to get a change. We complemented each other well. We were a great team."

1. "The Vision of Microsoft's J Allard," Tom's Hardware Guide, http://www.tgdaily.com/2005/03/19/gdc_2005/page5.html.

2. "SmartBomb: The Quest for Art, Entertainment, and Big Bucks in the Video Game Revolution," by Heather Chaplin and Aaron Ruby, Algonquin Books, 2005, p. 254.

3. *San Jose Mercury News*, by Dean Takahashi, March 25, 2005.

4. "We Got Next," by Raymond Padilla, http://xbox.gamespy.com/xbox/microsoft-xbox/594331p1.html.

CHAPTER THIRTY-EIGHT

MTV

*P*eter Moore and Mitch Koch decided that MTV was the right network to loop into the biggest marketing bash for the Xbox 360. The affinity of MTV fans and video game players was high. Moore had taken on the global marketing role for the Xbox 360, while Koch concentrated on the regional marketing.

"Instead of unveiling the console for the chosen few at E3, for the lucky few, Peter thought that we should do something different for real gamers," Koch said. "MTV was a good alignment with us on demographics, lifestyle, with everything from the hardcore audience to the mass market. For this, we needed a broad estimate, not a narrow one."

They pulled together the show quickly, a bit too quickly, according to Reggie Fils-Aime, the top marketer at Nintendo and a former MTV executive.

The Xbox marketing team negotiated a half-hour special on MTV to air on May 12, 2005. By launching the Xbox 360 earlier than the big E3 trade show, Microsoft could garner a worldwide stage and preempt the announcements by the other companies. That was important, because Sony had managed to book its E3 press conference on a Monday afternoon, before Microsoft's Monday evening event.

The special was taped in advance in Los Angeles, where a number of B-List celebrities such as Tony Hawk were invited to attend. Among the attendees was Kevin Bachus, co-creator of the original Xbox. The show opened with a pretty model walking up on the stage and pulling an Xbox 360 out of a shoulder bag. She put the box on a podium and pressed the "Ring of Light," starting up a cool video montage. The huge power supply on the power cord was conveniently hidden underneath the podium.

Elijah Wood, the actor who starred as "Frodo" in the *Lord of the Rings* movies, was the host of the show. He promised an exclusive peak at a game console that was going to "change digital entertainment forever." Then he introduced the band, *The Killers*, which sang their smash hit, "Mr. Brightside." In San Francisco, Peter Moore and Shane Kim played host to a number of journalists who showed up in a bar in a part of town next to a bunch of tourist strip joints. Then the special described the console and showed videos of various games. The stars of MTV's *Pimp My Ride* car modification TV show created a tricked out version of the original Xbox. Meanwhile, industrial designers Jonathan Hayes and Matt Day described the evolution of the industrial design. The video highlighted games such as *Perfect Dark Zero, Gears of War, Tom Clancy's Ghost Recon 3: Advanced Warfighter, Quake 4,* and others.

Fans got to play *PDZ* in death match mode, offering proof that Microsoft had working consoles. No one noticed that the games were really running on prototype hardware, not the real thing. The video followed a group of gamers on a trip to visit Rare's headquarters in Twycross, England.

At the bar in San Francisco, Moore acknowledged that some of the leaks about the industrial design were planned, while some weren't. After the show aired, opinions about its effectiveness varied. Many complained about the lack of emphasis on the games themselves, or what was in the console. Moore said that the show was aimed at capturing the broader mass market that had eluded Microsoft the first time around.

Elijah Wood, better known as Frodo, hosted the MTV Xbox 360 show

Meanwhile, Moore also noted that Microsoft didn't entirely abandon the hardcore gamers that were its most loyal fans. On March 14, 2005, someone going by the moniker "Gamem8ker" sent e-mails to a number of Xbox fans. It showed an image and asked fans to respond by sending 36 different images. Once they did that, the mysterious e-mailer said "the real game begins." The game distributed some codes to the players, who quickly figured out they were the call letters for international airports. The game also asked fans to create colonies of at least five people who would play the game together and solve the various puzzles. The game was a product of Microsoft PR man David Hufford, the marketing department and Edelman Public Relations. They wanted to stoke fan anticipation of the Xbox 360. The "alternate reality game" resembled the *ilovebees* promotion that stoked the fans of *Halo 2*. One of the puzzles included one of the last lines of the book, *Opening the Xbox: Inside Microsoft's Plan to Unleash an Entertainment Revolution* as well as the bookseller's code number for the book. The whole game was a test of how much trouble fans would go to in order to find out something about the Xbox 360 that their friends didn't know. The end of *OurColony* showed off a video of J Allard demonstrating the Xbox 360 console.

"Not a lot of people knew about the game at first," Moore said. "But we didn't abandon our most loyal fans. We did something special for them."

At the end of the month, Sony launched its PlayStation Portable in the U.S. The $250 device sold out quickly. At places such as the Metreon entertainment complex, hundreds of fans waited in line for more than a day to secure their boxes. Sony had another hot seller on its hands, and it had found a way to keep dollars from going into the pockets of Bill Gates before the launch of the PlayStation 3. J Allard had lost his bet with N'Gai Croal at *Newsweek*.

CHAPTER THIRTY-NINE

A TRIP TO REDMOND

*D*uring the spring of 2005, Microsoft's PR machine started inviting journalists to visit the Millennium campus in Redmond for their first taste of the Xbox 360. Microsoft asked the journalists to sign non-disclosure agreements, but some of them balked. The company had to compromise in order to get some journalists there.

The campus was ready for the outsiders. Acid-green signs adorned the hallways of the Xbox building. One sign read, "Xenon Secret Lab: Move along, there's nothing to see here." Another said, " Xenon: This is not your father's inert gas" and yet another said "Xenon Lab: High Voltage." [1]

By this time, no one was allowed to talk about the console as Xenon. Now it was the Xbox 360. J Allard made the mistake of saying Xenon in one of the planning meetings and the group fined him a dollar. He pulled out a ten-dollar bill and said, "There, I've prepaid my next nine fines."

Among the earliest of journalists invited was Lev Grossman, a writer at *Time* magazine who was hard at work on exactly the kind of article that J Allard had hoped would be written when he included the fake *News Time* article in the original Xe 30 document in 2003.

Peter Moore met one journalist in the big conference room where the XIG group had met so many times to plan the console. At one end was a 63-inch Samsung digital TV set. He rattled off the specifications, noting the machine had 512 megabytes so it could be "future proofed." He said the off-white color of the machine is called "chill."

"We're delighted with the design," he said. "It's indicative of where we are going with the brand. We have a top 20 aspirational brand, but it needs to broaden and to brighten."

He said that the HD era was nigh and that the Xbox 360 would give people a reason to buy one. He predicted that digital TV prices would fall as low as $400 by the holidays. He said that Microsoft hoped to get 10 million paying subscribers for the premium version of Xbox Live in this generation and to have more than 50 percent of users on the free version of Xbox Live. Moore said the company would launch in all three major regions.

"It's never been done before," he quipped. "We'll find out why." Shipping six months late to Europe, he said, is disrespectful. He noted that *Perfect Dark Zero* would have as many as 64 players in online games, a figure that would be cut in half later. Then he fired up the demos running on an Apple Macintosh G5 system, the game development system of which Microsoft had now shipped 4,000 units to developers. The Samsung TV came to life and Moore showed a series of demos. The volume was turned up to thunderous levels. "Our partnership with Samsung," Moore shouted over the noise. "It's a match made in heaven. We both share a competitor."

The troll army in Kameo showed off the graphics power of the Xbox 360.

Moore showed off Rare's *Kameo: Elements of Power*. He showed a fairy princess flying through a brilliantly colored field of grass. In a scene that became familiar to journalists for months, he zoomed in on a little bit of mildew on an urn. Then he panned over to the Badlands and zoomed out to show a thousand green trolls on the march. Next he showed a scene from Activision's *Call of Duty 2* where a British soldier kicks down a door, only to get mowed down by a German machine gun. He showed Epic's *Gears of War*. He said, "There's the poster child for *Unreal 3*."

Next he moved into Ubisoft's *Tom Clancy's Ghost Recon 3: Advanced Warfighter*. As soldiers fired weapons, shells flew out of their guns and clattered on the ground. And, lastly, he showed a demo of basketball star LeBron James bouncing a ball in a scene from Visual Concepts' *NBA 2K6*. "Look at the sweat on his body," Moore said. "The spectral highlighting, the fabric moving, the muscles."

He noted that both Kameo and Perfect Dark Zero would be available in the

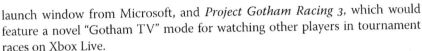

launch window from Microsoft, and *Project Gotham Racing 3*, which would feature a novel "Gotham TV" mode for watching other players in tournament races on Xbox Live.

Asked if this system was Microsoft's "Trojan horse," which gets into the living room as a game system and becomes a portal for all entertainment, he said, "Trojan horse sounds like someone forcing something down someone's throat for an ulterior motive. That's not the case. The consumer wants something that fits with their digital lifestyle. Think of it as a digital entertainment amplifier, not a full stereo system. It has a Media Center Extender for seamless integration with the Media Center."

Of the benefits of going first, Moore said, "The first one to ten million units could be anointed the winner." And as for quality, he said, "It's going to be close to what we've all talked about, interactive movies."

Moore handed his visitor off to J Allard, who talked in a design room where there were lots of prototype drawings on the wall. He talked about framing the transition to high-definition gaming to his team as a big discontinuity, like the shift from 2D side scrolling games to 3D "Tomb Raider" polygonal images and finally, with HD, being able to see the feathers on birds. He said that the online experience would be more compelling, allowing kids to buy new race tracks for 25 cents. And he laid out the economics for game publishers.

"Say you have $50 million and games cost $10 million to make in the HD era," he said. "You can do one big game that costs $30 million. You can do another one for $10 million. With the last $10 million, maybe you do five $2 million pilots. In the HD era, we've got a system where you can make more bets."

Without mentioning that a camera would cost $100 extra, Allard said that gamers could take pictures of themselves and post it on their gamer cards for everyone to see. "You can take a picture of your opponent being taken down," he said. "You can leave video messages for friends." Explaining the meaning behind the name, Allard said that we shift the focus to the gamer, "the gamer at the center." Going through the design process, he gave his magical product speech that his team had heard before. "We inventoried magical products," he said. "Disney World. The Mini Cooper. Wonka Chocolate. They feel like they were created by one person. People want to believe that Steve Jobs created the iPod. With Xbox 360, we knew 20,000 people would be involved. How do you make it feel like it was designed by one person?" The team created the Book of Xenon, he said, and then boiled it down to one sentence: "Living entertainment experiences powered by human energy." He repeated it for emphasis. "That's what we want to create."

Allard talked about making gamers creators, so they could race through the streets of Tokyo and then create their own track from the path they followed. Each customizable game would be infinitely replayable. With the HD era, he said, the goal was to reach a billion gamers. That compared to the current base of around 150 million gamers. It was a classic "out there" goal for Allard. This was his 28th product at Microsoft, he said.

"I want to make a magical product that has cultural impact," he said. "I want to get to a billion gamers. Our job isn't done yet."

Chris Satchell, meanwhile, sat in a faux living room and showed off the non-gaming features of the Xbox 360. He ran through a demo of the dashboard and the gamercard where Xbox Live users could look up the profile of a gamer. He talked about the digital entertainment lifestyle, and showed how someone could take their own picture with a webcam and upload it into their own gamercard profile. Then he showed how the Xbox 360 could serve as a Media Center Extender. All of the plans of David Reid, Jeff Henshaw, and Joe Belfiore were now reflected in a working prototype.

1. "Microsoft Previews A New Breed of Xbox," by Dean Takahashi *San Jose Mercury News*, May 13, 2005.

CHAPTER FORTY

E3 2005: THE BATTLE OF THE DUELING PRESS CONFERENCES

While GDC drew 10,000 game developers, the Electronic Entertainment Expo in Los Angeles would draw seven times that number in May, 2005. It was the place where years of bets would come to fruition, with competitors showing technologies that would either upstage the rivals or go down in defeat. Gamers, publishers, developers and the press would be able to judge whether Microsoft had really learned anything in four years. Staged in the gigantic convention center in downtown L.A., it was the place where developers, publishers, the press, and other industry participants came to see the best video game products for the year.

Going first with its press conference, Sony picked up busloads of journalists and analysts at area hotels and took them to a gigantic Sony Pictures Studios sound stage in Culver City. The event started on "Japanese time," or later than it was supposed to. The 2,000 members of the press, analyst, and industry executives lingered about, eating the sumptuous buffet under tables with big umbrellas. The food included a giant table of tuna, beef, chicken and vegetarian wraps; a pile of mini cheeseburgers, garlic fries and pigs in a blanket; Chinese chicken salad; trays of desserts such as wrapped fudge; and huge bins of Coke, Sprite and Red Bull. The press corps included everyone from cub reporters at game web sites to three reporters from the *Wall Street Journal*. Vivendi Universal's North American chief, Phil O'Neil, anxiously waited in line with everyone else to hear how much, or how little, Sony would say about the PlayStation 3.

The crowd filed into the soundstage, which was flooded in blue neon light. The photographers rushed for the best seats up front. Kaz Hirai, looking much thinner thanks to his Atkins diet, took the stage and pumped up the crowd.

"All of us at Sony Computer Entertainment have been waiting a long time to get to this point today," he said.

He reviewed the history of Sony's accomplishments, including the

March 2005 U.S. launch of the PlayStation Portable. Sony had sold more than 87 million PlayStation 2 consoles and 9.8 games for each one of them. Sony's PS2 had outsold its combined console competitors by more than two to one. Then he introduced Ken Kutaragi, the father of the PlayStation business.

"We are proud to introduce our third-generation PlayStation system, PlayStation 3," he said. He went over the details of the PS3, including the Cell microprocessor. He said the system would include Blu-ray high-capacity high-definition disks. Blu-ray disks stored 25 gigabytes to 50 gigabytes, far more than the 9-gigabytes in Microsoft's dual-layer DVD disks in the Xbox 360.

"We want to accelerate this transition," he said.

Taking another jab at the Xbox 360, Kutaragi said that the system would also be backward compatible with the 5,200 titles on the PlayStation 2 and 7,700 titles on the original PlayStation. The announcement drew loud applause. He described the Cell microprocessor, which had 234 million transistors, more than the 165 million in the Microsoft's PowerPC chip.

Kutaragi and IBM's Jim Kahle, who spoke on a video, said that the Cell chip had supercomputer performance. Kutaragi said that the Cell processor had twice as much floating point performance as the Xbox 360 and was 35 times as fast as the PlayStation 2. The PS3 also had eight times faster memory bandwidth – the critical highway that moved data within the system – than the PS2 and slightly faster bandwidth than the Xbox 360. The PS3 would have two teraflops of floating point performance, again twice as fast as the Xbox 360. That compared to 36 teraflops for IBM's BlueGene, the fastest supercomputer in the world. Sony neglected to include a hard disk drive as a base feature on every PS3, but the machine would come with Blu-ray disks for storing HD movies and games.

Kutaragi was playing the technology card. The Cell would have eight sub processors, but only seven would be operational. The reason, analysts later observed, was to improve the yields on chips and bring down the costs of the PS3. Then he described the RSX, the graphics chip from Nvidia, as "the world's most advanced GPU that can synthesize movie-like graphics." The graphics would be so good that it would drive two full screens of high-definition at 1080P resolution, about twice the resolution of Microsoft's 720P. Moreover, instead of just one bus linking memory, CPU and graphics chip, the PlayStation 3 would have two, one linking 256 megabytes of Rambus XDR memory and another linking 256 megabytes of graphics memory. Game developers would later say this helped avoid the traffic that Microsoft created on its single bus.

Sony's definition of HD wasn't just vertical resolution on the TV. It was HD from beginning to end, from the high-capacity storage disks to the HDMI interfaces for transferring video to the TV to the highest 1080P resolution. It was a gargantuan level of technology, but likely a very expensive one as well. PS3 would also have Bluetooth connections for seven wireless controllers and built-in WiFi (which was optional on Microsoft's machine). Just about every spec Kutaragi mentioned drew hoots and applause. Even while playing games, the PS3 would be able to serve up digital photos and videos, or surf the Internet at the same time.

Kutaragi yielded the stage to a promo video on a 2,300-square-feet screen that showed movies of what you might be able to do with the PlayStation 3, such as deconstructing a car into its parts. Jen-Hsun Huang, CEO of Nvidia, took the stage and said he was honored to be part of the "most important consumer device to be unveiled this decade." He said that Kutaragi had invited Nvidia to create a chip to synthesize movie-like graphics. It was the culmination of three years of talks. He showed a demo of a character, Luna, and noted how the light danced off her lips and light penetrated underneath her skin to show her rosy cheeks. The still image of the beautiful Asian woman with "hair that was so incredibly soft" was evidence of what Nvidia's programmable pixel shaders could do, Huang said. With the RSX, the PS3 would be able to achieve two teraflops, or two trillion floating point operations per second. That was 120 times the capability of an Intel Pentium 4 microprocessor for the fastest PCs.

Using Nvidia's designs, Sony would manufacture the chip, dubbed the RSX "Reality Synthesizer." Analysts soon estimated that Nvidia could generate $1 billion in license revenues from the deal. Suddenly, losing out on the Xbox 360 didn't seem so bad. Nick Baker was watching the details unfold. He immediately saw that Sony's engineers had made a much different choice about moving graphics data within the system.

Sony had chosen a relatively expensive Rambus-based 256 megabytes of high-speed XDR main memory to feed data to the CPU. But it had a separate data pathway connecting the graphics chip with 256 megabytes of GDDR3 graphics memory. It was the exact opposite of the unified memory architecture that Nick Andrews and Jeff Baker created, and that meant it wasn't going to be easy to program. But while the Cell architecture was going to be a difficult beast to master, the presence of Nvidia's graphics chip eased the mind of many game artists. The RSX had more than 300 million transistors, considerably more than Microsoft's ATI-based graphics chip, and it could outdo twin graphics cards on a PC that cost $1,000.

Tim Sweeney, the CEO of Epic Games, had been one of Microsoft's big supporters. But Huang invited Sweeney on stage to show off a stunning battle scene from *Unreal Tournament 2007*. He praised the PlayStation 3 as a machine that was easy to program, allowing his team to create the demo in just two months. Sweeney's presence gave some at Microsoft a foreboding sense that Sony was upstaging Redmond. Huang asked Sweeney to prove the demo was in real time, not a canned animation, so Sweeney's demo guy froze the screen and moved the point of view in mid-demo. Huang closed by saying, in words that were loud enough to be heard in Redmond, that the PS3 was the "most important digital entertainment platform in this decade."

Mas Chatani, chief technology officer at Sony's game unit, said that gamers could connect an EyeToy visual control interface or a PlayStation Portable to control the PS3. He talked about how consumers could upload their own HD videos to the network via the PS3. He said every aspect of the system was designed to be always on, always connected to the Internet via broadband to the PlayStation Network. It was the Trojan Horse of the living room that the PlayStation 2 never became.

Phil Harrison, head of Sony's worldwide game studios, showed off the PS3 rendering ducks swimming around in water, and hundreds of thousands of leaves swirling in the wind. Demo after demo followed. Harrison wowed the crowd with a demo that showed how cars from the upcoming *Gran Turismo* game could be spliced into the movie footage of *Spider-Man 2* seamlessly so that no one could tell which part was game and which was movie. Harrison said it showed what happened when you took two billion-dollar franchises, one from the game industry and one from film, and collided them together. He showed how Cell could play 12 HD videos simultaneously.

Kaz Hirai came back on stage to introduce a series of game demos. He said game developers had been working for some time. Then he invited Larry Probst, the CEO of Electronic Arts, to show off his company's *Fight Night 3 Round 3* demo. Probst talked about making the huge bet that EA made with the PS2, showing up with six launch titles. EA sold more than 220 million units on the PlayStation consoles.

"With the PlayStation 3, we're making another big bet," Probst said.

Yoichi Wada, CEO of Square Enix, followed Probst to show off the newest *Final Fantasy XII* game on the PS3. While the demo was pure animated film, it once again showed how far a company could shoot with the PS3 hardware. A video clip of CEOs followed, including former Nintendo supporter Julian Eggebrecht of Factor 5, praising the potential of the PS3 to revolutionize games. Sam Houser of RockStar games, creator of the *Grand Theft Auto* series, felt the PS3 could unlock a "living, breathing world." Overall, it was a performance meant to impress games and intimidate competitors. Finally, Hirai introduced the final aces up Sony's sleeve. The company showed a series of incredible demos from partners. The one that truly stunned everyone in the audience came from Sony itself. The *Killzone 2* demo depicted an aerial assault landing of a combat team that immediately became engaged in a heated firefight. The intensity of the experience echoed through the cavernous room, and Microsoft felt the reverberations.

Ken Kutaragi took the stage again. He introduced the PlayStation 3, which stood on a pedestal. It was sleek with soft curves, standing vertically or horizontally, and came in white, silver or black. Then the words appeared on the screen, "Coming Spring, 2006." Sony left a lot of questions unanswered, such as the cost of the console, which markets would debut first, and what games would accompany the machine at launch.

The press conference ended. Journalists struggled to file their stories. As they waited in the valet parking line, they talked about what they had seen and fretted about whether they could make it on time to Microsoft's press conference. Some drove like crazy to get to the Shrine Auditorium near the University of Southern California campus in downtown Los Angeles. Shane Kim, the chief of Microsoft Game Studios, passed by a journalist and offered him a ride in his SUV. He asked how Sony had done, and the journalist was very impressed. "What did they say about online?" Kim asked with a smile. "What did they say about services?" They drove the last few hundred feet and joined the crowd. The event started late.

When the lights came up on the stage, the arrangement was interesting. Microsoft had a bunch of gamers sitting up on the stage in seats so they could watch the press conference up close. A model named Kim came out and brought out an Xbox 360. She put in on a pedestal, plugged it into an unseen power supply below the stage, and turned it on. She was mimicking the opening on the MTV special. By that time, most of the print newspaper reporters had written their stories for the next day about Sony.

Robbie Bach was a little worried he was going to slide off the slanted stage. He faced the crowd with a sense of excitement and relief. "Here we are, at the end of the beginning," he thought.

Bach had done press conferences like these a million times before. He came out with J Allard and Peter Moore. Bach welcomed the audience to the future of gaming. They talked about how far they had come with Xbox. Bach announced that the Xbox 360 would be compatible with the "top selling Xbox games." At each moment, the PR folks in the balcony and the fans on stage cheered at the news.

The audience waited for him to say more about backward compatibility, but that was all he mentioned. While *Halo* and *Halo 2* were working, Microsoft had no clue how many games would be ready by the launch. Drew Solomon and his ninjas were still locked away converting as many

Kim marched out with the Xbox 360 in a bag and then placed it on a pedestal, which conveniently hid the huge power supply.

games as possible. One publication, 1Up.com, revealed later that Nvidia would receive a license payment from Microsoft in order to make the machine partially backward compatible. Marv Burkett, chief financial officer at Nvidia, said the payments would add up to a rounding error for Nvidia. But it was still painful for Microsoft to pay money to its former partner.

"We built Xbox 360 based on a mission, a dream if you will," Bach said. "That dream is to inspire people to think about entertainment in new ways, to revolutionize the way people think about having fun." He said that the company would stick to its initial plan to launch Xbox 360 in three regions worldwide at the same time. Bach promised the best launch line-up in history.

Then he broke into a long demo of *Dead Or Alive 4*, the Tecmo game that would once again be exclusive to the Microsoft console launch. It had plenty of female characters with jiggling flesh and fighting arena environments that could be smashed. Allard said 25 to 40 titles would launch for the Xbox 360 in 2005, and that 160 titles were in development. He gave his spiel about the HD era, and promised to reach 1 billion people. A number of people in the audience rolled their eyes at that claim. Allard went into his rant about how games needed to reach more people beyond the hardcore.

"The essence of our vision is reflected in the name: Xbox 360," Allard said. "It's the product that delivers experiences where the player is always at center stage." He had articulated the words that Don Hall and his team had dreamed up so long ago. He walked the audience through the user interface, the gamer card, Xbox Live, and then sat down with *Kameo: Elements of Power*. He described some of the scenarios for users who defined gamer types. He showed off Xbox Live Arcade and Xbox Live Marketplace. The vision of Greg Canessa was finally unfolding before the world.

J Allard, Robbie Bach and Peter Moore greeted journalists at E3 2005

A video with Bill Gates and Steve Ballmer playing chess on Xbox Live provided some comic relief. It was high camp, but not one of their funniest.

"That's an interesting demographic, two billionaire software moguls attempting to be funny," Allard said.

More telling was what Microsoft didn't mention. It didn't talk about having more than one version of the Xbox 360, and some journalists left with the impression that the machine had a hard disk in every machine.

Allard praised the vision of integrating hardware, software and services. Allard closed out his pitch to reach a billion gamers, while Peter Moore took over and promised, "In the HD era, we will deliver the Zen of gaming."

Moore went on to talk about the games. He showed a demo of Hironobu Sakaguchi's *Lost Odyssey*, but he didn't note when it would debut. He noted how *Project Gotham Racing 3* would offer a spectator mode for competitive races on Xbox Live, where gamers could watch *Gotham TV* as they sat in the passenger seats of the champion racers as they played in tournaments. He proceeded to show demos of *Tom Clancy's Ghost Recon 3: Advanced Warfighter*, *NBA 2K6*, and *Perfect Dark Zero*. In contrast to Sony, Moore set up each title with a description of the game, before the video rolled. He moved on to *Call of Duty 2*, *Elder Scrolls 4: Oblivion*, and *Gears of War*. He didn't mention which ones would be launch titles. During the demos, the sound was loud enough to shake the knees of the people in the audience.

Don Mattrick, executive vice president at Electronic Arts, came on stage to say that EA would make 25 games for the Xbox 360, including six launch titles. One of them was *The Godfather*. Robbie Bach's decision to join Mattrick's fishing trip had paid off dividends. Mattrick's appearance, however, once again told journalists, such as Steven Kent, that Sony had upstaged Microsoft by getting the CEO, Larry Probst, to show up at Sony's press conference while Microsoft could only manage Mattrick.

Bach then introduced Yoichi Wada, CEO of Square Enix, who had finally decided to support Microsoft by making games for the Xbox 360. But the journalists knew that Wada had already showed *Final Fantasy XII* for the PS3. Microsoft could only manage to get Square Enix's online game, *Final Fantasy XI*, for the Xbox 360.

Bach closed with a speech on the Xbox 360 and its appeal to the mainstream masses.

"With Xbox 360, video games will become a true mainstream entertainment medium, a medium where bestsellers are measured not in the millions of units but in the tens of millions," he said.

He adjourned the press conference and invited everyone to join the after-party. Big white domes were set up in the parking lot with food (that was not as good as Sony's) and lots of consoles in front of inviting white couches. Microsoft entertained the guests with performance from such bands as *The Killers*. It also gave away personalized "face plates" for Xbox 360s. The limited edition face plates turned out to be valuable. In the subsequent days, they sold on eBay for hundreds of dollars.

Soon after the event, the journalists racked up the score. One journalist said he felt like he had been stained green in Microsoft's press conference. But on sober reflection, it seemed Microsoft's bets had all fallen short. Microsoft had shown off real working games, but Sony's technology looked so much better. It looked like Microsoft had shown up with a knife to a gun fight, and a number of gamer web sites said so.

One former Xbox veteran said, "Microsoft showed up with an entertainment server. Sony showed up with a game console." Another former Xbox team member said, "I was afraid this was going to happen" when Microsoft launched early. [1]

Game retailers in particular were worried about the worldwide launch. They had counseled Bach and Mitch Koch not to try it. Why waste a lot of good units in Japan when they would be starving the huge fan base in the United States?

The next morning it was Nintendo's turn. Anticipation built up inside the Kodak theater ballroom in Hollywood. Tetsuya Inamoto, a Japanese freelance journalist, didn't mind the delay. He was using his Nintendo DS handheld to chat with dozens of other Nintendo fans, sending hand-drawn picture messages wireless to others in the crowd.

Satoru Iwata, CEO of Nintendo, welcomed the crowd with a story about how he beat Nintendo Executive Vice President Reggie Fils-Aime, nicknamed the "Reginator" for his booming voice, in a game of *Super Smash Brothers.*

"Who's your daddy?" Iwata said, as he introduced the Reginator.

Fils-Aime said that he had one number for the competition: two. As in 2 billion games sold to date. He said Nintendo was on its way to the next billion. "Our mission has not been to just play the game, but to change the game," he said.

He dropped a small surprise as he announced the GameBoy Micro, a palm-size game player that was only two-thirds the weight of an iPod. Fils-Aime said it was aimed at "image conscious" consumers, and it would "fit in your pocket no matter how tight your jeans are." Fils-Aime said Nintendo would launch free WiFi service for the Nintendo DS and that 25 companies were working on games to exploit WiFi.

Tina Wood, a host on G4TV, shared the stage with Nintendo star game designer Shigeru Miyamoto to show off her new Nintendog virtual pet. She invited Miyamoto's puppy to join hers, and Miyamoto's showed up with a Mario hat. In what was surely a joke that he didn't write, Miyamoto turned to Wood and said, "Would you like to learn a few more tricks? Please follow me back stage."

Iwata came out again. "You say you want a Revolution?" he asked the crowd. Then he showed off a prototype of the new console, a small machine that would be the height of just three DVD cases. He said it would debut in 2006, but offered no further details on the timing or territories for the launch.

The details he shared: it would play DVD movies, have built-in WiFi, it would have 512 megabytes of flash memory, and could download just about any game from Nintendo's 23-year-old library.

Nintendo closed by talking about the new Zelda game for the GameCube and it noted 60 GameCube games would arrive in 2005. That would pale versus the 200 coming out on the Xbox. For Nintendo, it was quality over quantity. But it wasn't clear if that was really going to be enough.

The buzz about the press conferences started to accumulate. Sony's barrage of information and demos had completely overwhelmed interest in Microsoft's press conference, and Nintendo's scant details left everyone guessing about its role in the next generation. Sony was the one beating its chest with fresh information.

Sony was making the "jump from partial reality to the illusion of complete reality," wrote Mike Antonucci, a veteran game columnist for the *San Jose Mercury News.*

"As always, this was largely a demonstration of the potential that lies in the technical specifications," Antonucci said. "It was also about reclaiming the highest ground in the marketing and image wars for all devices vying to become the hub of digital entertainment in the home."

Larry Hyrb, the Xbox Live podcaster, pulled some reactions out of a couple of technical experts from Microsoft's Advanced Technology Group. They were of course critical in a technical way. Analyst Jon Peddie, the graphics expert who helped Nick Baker guess what the PS3 would do, said, "Based on what I've seen, Sony's performance numbers look accurate. Is it right to compare to the Xbox 360 just by looking at a chart of numbers? That's not right. But it's very impressive. It's all 'faster, better, louder,' but I'd still like to see them show a kind of game that's never been done before."

Time magazine had put Bill Gates on its cover that week. A home run for Microsoft public relations, it was the incarnation of J Allard's dream for the "*News Time* article." Lev Grossman's piece credited J Allard with "hiring a sculptor" for the industrial design, but it also created a headache for the PR team. Bill Gates said that he thought Microsoft had to fund some high risk games to break out of the hardcore market, and he wondered when Sony would get its act together on online games. Gates was "radiant with bloodlust" as he said that Microsoft would release *Halo 3* the same day as the PlayStation 3 launch. "It's perfect," Gates said. "The day Sony launches, and they walk right into *Halo 3*." [2]

In interviews that day, Robbie Bach tried some damage control. He said that Bill had spoken out of turn and that it was really up to Bungie as to when it would be ready to release *Halo 3*. Bach also contended that Sony's press conference was all smoke and mirrors.

"Our hardware will be the best, but we're also going to beat Sony on hardware and software," he said. "Things have gone the way we scripted. There weren't any surprises. Sony didn't have anything to compete with Xbox Live," though it did mention the PlayStation Network.

"That's a material omission," Bach continued. He picked up some lines from the technical team, adding, "They picked the floating point spec sheet to talk about. But we have three times better performance on integer operations. The CPU spends 80 percent of the time on integer. Whose is fastest? They're both incredible. The story is the same on the GPU. Their architecture may be memory bandwidth constrained. We'll have embedded memory. From our view, the performance will be a draw."

Asked about the *Killzone 2* demo, Bach said, "You can always do something on a rail. Don't worry about interactivity. When you show some real game footage, you get the kind of things that we produced. They have a demo running on rails. They are trying to argue superior technology. I won't concede that point at all."

Richard Doherty, analyst at market researcher Envisioneering Group, said he doubted Microsoft would have the most powerful box. He said, "It will be true, but only for a matter of months."

Bach said, "Our strategy is not rocket science. We went early with a powerful system. In the battle of the dueling press conferences, I feel confident in how we came out. How much technology can you put in the box at a certain cost is the same for them as us."

Bach predicted that Blu-ray would be a double-edged sword for Sony, since it wasn't clear if Blu-ray would become the standard.

Bach said that game developers had had development kits for a long time. He added, "Our tool set, which is an advantage, is 95 percent the same set of tools as those for the Xbox."

Gamers tried out the first Xbox 360 games at Microsoft's Xbox 360 booth, but the games ran on Apple Macintosh G5 development systems.

As for the key chips, Bach said, "Our stuff is in production. The chip set is done. The platform is way ahead of where we were on Xbox 1. They didn't use working systems here at the show because developers haven't had chance to transfer to beta hardware. We learned last time that people didn't want to see games running poorly on beta hardware." (The IBM chip was in production, but the ATI graphics chip still wasn't in its final form). As for the lessons Microsoft learned, Bach said, "The difference is, we're prepared. We've been working on this for three years."

Robbie Bach wasn't the sort to engage in too much trash talk. But, asked if the graphics chip would be ready on time, Peter Moore said, "There's a reason we're working with ATI."

Moore predicted that prices for HDTV sets would fall to as little as $400 by the fall launch. And he reiterated his claim that Microsoft could get to 10 million units sold before Sony sold one. At that point, he said, it could have an insurmountable lead.

Inside the quiet conference room within the noisy Sony booth, Kaz Hirai took a chair and smiled. The president of Sony's U.S. game unit exuded confidence.

"I think we were able to present a very solid vision of what we wanted to do with our technology, where we want to take the consumer electronics experience with Playstation 3," he said. "We are well positioned to keep leadership for the next 10 years."

He confidently said Blu-ray was the right medium for a "future-proofed console."

"More than 50 gigs is the kind of capacity for the kind of game play that consumers will come to expect," he added. "If we are talking high definition, we want to take advantage of high-definition Blu-ray blue laser disks and put it out at 1080P."

Asked about the Xbox 360 games, he said he was pleased to hear journalists refer to the Microsoft effort as "Xbox 1.5," a phrase used in the *Time* magazine article that was starting to spread fast.

"I was pleased to hear that, and maybe we're PS3.5." He added that backward compatibility was important.

"When you go with the familiar architecture, that works to our advantage," he said. "We know what we want to do. Exclusives will be in play and matter. For the PlayStation Portable, we won't just cut off production and let it twist in the wind," a reference to the expectation that Microsoft would end production of original Xbox consoles.

"This going first thing," he said with an amused look. "We've never gone first. Saturn, Dreamcast were before us. Content drives whether a console is successful or not. The logic of going first doesn't hold water."

Meanwhile, Satoru Iwata sipped water from a bottle in a private room in the Nintendo booth. He spoke through a translator. Asked about Sony and Microsoft, he said, "The direction we are heading is completely different from the directions the others are going. They are spending enormous energies on specifications so they can claim an edge in computer graphics. But the result so far is the media and game fans are still not quite satisfied with the resulting graphics. I believe we need to refrain from announcing anything specific about performance right now. They graphics they can generate now are not to be trusted to be the real thing."

Iwata said that Nintendo had unique ideas for the Revolution's controller, but he didn't want to reveal them for fear that the others would copy it. Asked what were the lessons from the GameCube, he said, "We should not be too late starting to sell. Immediately after the launch date of the hardware, we need to constantly provide the market with new games. As far as getting games out at the launch, we were OK. But within six months of launching the GameCube, we were unable to supply quality software at a continuous pace. People talk about the size of their game library. I don't think quantity is important. Quality is important."

Iwata didn't think that the first company to approach game developers would win. Rather, the developers would support the company with a good proposal that wasn't too late. [3]

(Left) E3 takes place every year in the cavernous Los Angeles Convention Center. (Right) Booth babe, a rich tradition at E3.

"I thought 2005's E3 was somewhat disappointing," said Chris Morris, a columnist for CNN.com. "Who won the battle of the press conferences? From an information point, I don't think anyone did. But from a PR perspective, I have to give Sony the nod. Their presentation was the thing that had people talking during the show – and for weeks afterward."

1. "The Buzz: Sony Upstaged Microsoft With A Better-Looking Console," by Dean Takahashi, Dean & Nooch on Gaming blog, http://blogs.mercurynews.com/aei/2005/05/dean_stays_up_l.html.

2. "Out of the Xbox," by Lev Grossman, *Time*, May 23, 2005.

3. "Nintendo Chief Discusses the Future and Strategy For Games," by Dean Takahashi, *San Jose Mercury News*, May 28, 2005.

CHAPTER FORTY-ONE

THE BATTLE OF THE DUELING PARTIES

E3 was a great place for everyone in the game industry to catch up. Jonathan Hayes held a dinner where the staffs of Hers Experimental Design Laboratory and Astro Studios met for the first time, after their successful collaboration on the Xbox 360 design.

Nintendo held its E3 party at The Highlands nightclub at the Hollywood & Highland entertainment complex. Guests were packed into a tight space and had to elbow their way to the decadent food trays, which included chocolate truffles and drink-pouring ice sculptures. Nintendo was the oldest gaming company, but it had to prove to the elite crowd that it could party just like any of the youngsters.

The hired band was *Maroon 5*, a pop rock group that had hit the charts with the song "This Love." The lead singer, Adam Levine, bantered with the audience, telling fans not to grab his legs. Scoring a point for Nintendo on the pop culture war, he said, "I grew up playing Nintendo games. I can't remember them all. *Super Mario Bros. 3*, that was great." The crowd roared its approval. He added, "But if you died on one level, you had to go back and start again. That's bullshit. Whoever is responsible for that, if you're in this room, that's very uncool."

The set went on and closed with a retooling of AC/DC's *Highway to Hell*. Satoru Iwata walked through the crowd alone but avoided having any conversations because of the deafening noise. [1]

At the party, one game developer lamented Nintendo's failure to focus on technology in the graphics arms race. He said he was switching from the Nintendo platform to the PlayStation 3 because it was such a leap forward. Despite rumors that Sony's demos were fake animated movies and not real games, he said that Sony used a real prototype to show off the *Unreal Tournament 2007* demo at the press conference, but it was a huge prototype. (The demo reel, however, was mostly cinematics). He noted that Sony was on its second set of Cell microprocessor prototypes, a good sign for game development purposes.

He worried, however, that he would have to triple his human resources. With that kind of demand on his resources, he had nothing left over for Nintendo. Asked what he was doing at the party, he said, "It's a small industry. We all understand that." As he said so, a member of the Xbox team cruised by. Perrin Kaplan, vice president of corporate marketing at Nintendo of America, showed off a GameBoy Micro hanging on a necklace.

Asked about the technology for the Revolution, she said, "People will assume that you've got the worst technology of the three. People will think you're doing the GameCube strategy over again, and that didn't work. All three of the consoles are going to be Ferraris. Technology does matter. But at a certain point, do you need something that goes 170 miles per hour when the top speed is 70?"

Sony's parties at E3 were legendary spectacles that showed off the combination of Sony's Hollywood muscle and its technological prowess. Dozens of buses converged on the party across from Dodger stadium, on a hilltop in L.A.'s Elysian Park. On the way, the buses approached a dozen searchlights piercing the night sky along with the green beams of a laser. Funny, it wasn't blue. Stretch limos were everywhere.

The sunset skyline of downtown Los Angeles burned orange in the background as guards checked for orange wrist bands. Among the crowd were aspiring actors, actresses, models and Hollywood suits. One of the architects of the PlayStation was there, remarking that Sony seemed to have the best technology, while Microsoft had the cheapest.

The hilltop was ringed by a dozen white canvas circus tents, each with a concert stage, a food line and a bar. This was all part of the political statement that Sony had to make: it throws the best parties, it treats its followers like VIP guests, and it was the right company to have as a partner.

David Kirk, the chief scientist at Nvidia, cruised through the crowd and chatted with Ken Kutaragi. Kirk was happy that the buzz favored Sony. Others present in the conversation expressed sympathy for Microsoft's plight. Microsoft came into the show thinking it would capture the leading market share. Now an Electronic Arts executive said, "Now we think they will only gain market share. We're going to go back and reallocate our resources toward Sony." EA executives, including CEO Larry Probst, would later deny that they changed their level of support for Microsoft after E3. But EA amended its language in subtle ways. They had first said they were doing 25 Xbox 360 games. But later they would change it to say they were working on 25 "next-generation games."

One journalist said that he had a fake horse head in his bed at his hotel. It told him to check out *The Godfather* game from Electronic Arts.

Kaz Hirai stepped out on a stage.

"Are you ready to rock?" he asked. "Are you ready for PlayStation 3? What time is it? It's party time!" One of the night's many bands took over the stage. At another stage, a dozen women in bikini tops and skimpy pants danced like strippers. But at the next stage, there really were strippers, with swinging tassles and all. Back at the main stage, Liz Phair was singing, *Feel like Makin' Love.*

Celebrities showed up in force at the various E3 booths and parties. Snoop Dogg, Fergie, and Wilmer Valderrama (Left to Right).

Ray Muzyka, co-CEO of Canada's BioWare game development house, was a big Microsoft supporter. But he said he felt Sony beat Microsoft on the technology front, while Microsoft did better marketing to non-gamers. Todd Hollenshead, CEO of id Software, also thought that Sony had outwitted Microsoft. Even so, both men said they would still develop games for the Xbox 360. [2]

Throughout the rest of E3, the game publishers expressed their reactions to the dueling press conferences. The chatter was consistent. Sony won on better technology, but Microsoft showed a better integration of hardware, software and services. Microsoft's online story was better, but that was a place where Sony could catch up. There was no catching up on technology now that Microsoft had locked on its box.

"It's almost as if they switched positions this time around, with Microsoft going first with current technology," said Brian Farrell, CEO of game publisher THQ. "Last time around, Microsoft had superior technology, but it didn't win."

Phil O'Neil, president of Vivendi Universal Games, said, "We're agnostic on consoles. But if I had to choose a religion, I'd think very seriously about Sony."

Behind closed doors, publishers were showing some spectacular Xbox 360 titles. But that didn't help Microsoft win the publicity battle. Jack Sorenson, an executive vice president at THQ, said that until Sony showed working games on final hardware, it wouldn't be clear if it really had an edge.

"There's a huge difference between closely controlled demos and working games," he said.

Microsoft was in a far better position than four years earlier, and it had key publishers on its side like Square Enix. Billy Pidgeon, an analyst at the Zelos Group, said that Microsoft would likely reap more revenues than Sony in online gaming. But no one walked out of the show thinking that Microsoft would have a larger market share than Sony in the next generation. Nintendo could have said more to get developers on its side, and its supporters worried that it would be late again. [3]

Back at home, Greg Gibson wasn't worried. He calculated that the Xbox 360 had more useful performance than Sony's box could deliver.

"E3 was culmination," he said. "When you cut through marketing and PR of what we and they are doing, my analysis was we hit 2005, beat Sony to market, have a better performing computer, and a cost of goods advantage."

A. J. Redmer, who had put so much effort into the planning, didn't think that the press would be fooled by suspicious demos. He came back from E3 convinced that Microsoft would still be able to steal Sony's thunder on HD gaming.

Jeff Andrews couldn't make it to the press conference at E3. The IBM chip came back from the factory the week before the show. He stayed in the lab to make sure it worked. Fortunately, it did. IBM started production.

1. "At E3, Dean Parties With Maroon 5," by Dean Takahashi, Dean & Nooch on Gaming blog, http://blogs.mercurynews.com/aei/2005/05/at_e3_dean_part.html.

2. "An Inside Look At Sony's E3 Party," by Dean Takahashi, Dean & Nooch on Gaming blog, http://blogs.mercurynews.com/aei/2005/05/an_inside_look_.html.

3. "E3 Scorecard: Who Won, Who Lost," by Dean Takahashi, Dean & Nooch on Gaming blog, http://blogs.mercurynews.com/aei/2005/05/e3_scorecard_wh.html.

CHAPTER FORTY-TWO

SUDDENLY THE LAST SUMMER

After E3, the high tide kept building for everyone. The Xbox 360 hardware team was busy at work, redesigning the chips for the first major cost reduction. This was a new version of the Xbox 360 that would be cheaper to manufacture and debut about a year after the launch. If they hit their targets, then Microsoft would be able to cut the costs of its console in the fall of 2006. Microsoft would then have the option of slashing the price of its console, just as its rivals came out with their first consoles. That would put a lot of pressure on both Sony and Nintendo.

The ATI engineers were still finishing up the final version of the graphics chip. The tough bug was out of the way, but the company needed to refine the designs so that they could improve their yields, bring down the costs, and produce the chips in high volumes. Masoud Foudeh and Peter Birch, the top Microsoft engineers on the graphics chip, were in daily contact with ATI, checking on its progress. Microsoft engineers helped with the verification process. A bank of 400 computers was up night and day, running tests to ensure that the chip would have no showstopper flaws.

"There were surprisingly few big problems," said Bob Feldstein at ATI. "There were lots of small ones."

They submitted the final design in July. Twelve weeks later, the final chips started coming out of the TSMC factory in Taiwan. They worked. And everyone celebrated. ATI's engineers then got to work on their own cost-reduction tasks for Microsoft.

For the game makers, the tide of work kept rising. XNA tools weren't ready, but Microsoft had modified its tools to make some tasks easier. Microsoft now had to make the final calls on its launch titles. Based on observations at E3, it was clear that *Call of Duty* 2 had won the hearts of the gaming press and the enthusiasts. Major publications from *Time* to *USA Today* gave the game a lot of ink.

As Microsoft's third-party account managers voted for their

favorites, the Infinity Ward game came out on top. That meant it would get first crack at the resources that Microsoft had lined up for the launch. The Advanced Technology Group and developer support team offered the programmers whatever technical help they needed. They would get the development kits as soon as they were ready.

Electronic Arts had six titles lined up, including *The Godfather*. UbiSoft had *Peter Jackson's King Kong*, timed to come out with the remake of the movie for the fall. But both games had received mixed press at the show. Both companies had to start thinking about making tweaks to the game that would please the gamers and critics.

Besides *Call of Duty 2*, Activision's launch titles included *Gun*, a Western shooter, *Quake 4*, and *Tony Hawk's American Wasteland*. Take-Two Interactive had a couple of sports titles and *Amped 3*. Tecmo was working on *Dead Or Alive 4*, UbiSoft had *Ghost Recon: Advanced Warfighter*. Microsoft also had *Kameo: Elements of Power*, and *Perfect Dark Zero* slated for the launch. Bethesda lined up its role-playing epic *Elder Scrolls IV: Oblivion*. THQ was hard at work on *The Outfit* and *Saint's Row*.

The mix had something for everybody. Dozens of other titles also looked good, but some didn't make the cut for the launch window. David Wu's *Full Auto* game, for instance, still needed some polishing. Three other racing games were in final stages: Microsoft's *Project Gotham Racing 3*, Electronic Arts' *Need for Speed: Most Wanted*, and Namco's *Ridge Racer 6*. In that line-up, gamers would likely gravitate to the well-known brands first. Sega of America President Simon Jeffery decided it would be best to delay the launch of *Full Auto* into the new year. Sega still had a launch title from Monolith, dubbed *Condemned: Criminal Origins*.

The Infinity Ward team came out of the show ecstatic that their title was so well received. Grant Collier had negotiated with his staff, which had grown to about 75 people, how much work they would do on "crunch time." They managed to keep to the schedule they had set.

On June 25, Microsoft shipped the final game development kits to the teams working on the launch titles. The graphics chip still wasn't done, but the prototypes were working well enough for the kits to ship. These kits were gray boxes that looked just like the final consoles would look, with giant power bricks and humming fans. By mid-August, Microsoft had shipped 5,000 of the final game development kits.

The teams took the kits, revised their games to accommodate the changes, and began their home stretch to the finish line. Despite their best efforts, many of them would not hit the finish line for the launch. Teams such as Rare's *Perfect Dark Zero* were ready for the final march. With the finish line in mind, the Rare teams had parallel efforts. One team was perfecting game play on the Alpha kits, while the graphics team was pushing the limit on the final development kits.

Greg Canessa's plans for Xbox Live Arcade were coming through better than he expected. With barely 15 people in his division, he was preparing to open a whole new revenue stream for Microsoft. His team had lined up enough independent publishers and developers to post as many as 40 games on Xbox Live Arcade for download. So many small game developers liked the idea that the team had to screen out games. They didn't want seven versions of *Hearts*, and concentrated on delivering a mix of puzzle games, old classic arcade games such as *Gauntlet*, and some remakes of hit titles such as Alexy Pajitnov's *Hexic HD*.

The games would offer free demos which were advertised on the dashboard, or the user interface of the console that the user saw when there was no game playing. With just a click, a user could download the demo and try it. Since Xbox Live Silver was going to be available for free to all Xbox 360 owners, Microsoft hoped that more than half of console owners would be able to download games. If just a small percentage of those turned around and purchased the games they had tried out, Xbox Live Arcade could be a home run. Meanwhile, J Allard said that the investment didn't carry a lot of risk. "It would be a contributor to the bottom line, but we didn't have to count on it," he said.

James Gwertzman, director of business development at Seattle's PopCap Games, now believed that Microsoft was serious about downloadable games. When Canessa fully disclosed the plans to build Xbox Live Arcade directly into the console dashboard, Gwertzman realized what that could mean.

"It's going to have an impact on the traditional games industry, and that's exciting," said Gwertzman, whose earlier console game business had failed because of the difficulty raising money for big games. "It creates a cool new channel for distribution and could be a disruptive move in the console space. Everyone loves to complain about the lack of creativity, but this opens up a new avenue for taking creative risks."

Bill Gates was a big fan of casual games such as PopCap's *Zuma* and *Bejeweled*, and he wanted to hear more. In a meeting in June, Canessa filled Microsoft's Chairman and Chief Software Architect in on the plan. Gates loved the idea, particularly because the casual games were linked to the overall gamer card, where players could rack up points based on how many games they had played. Those points could be exploited for rewards and promotions.

"This is the type of thing I've been waiting for," Gates said.

In Japan, Gates' arch rival was talking smugly. In an interview with Nikkei Electronics magazine, Sony's Ken Kutaragi said that Cell chips would be useful in a range of applications from home servers to high-end computers. Asked if the two next-generation DVD camps could strike a compromise on standards, he said a deal could no longer happen.

"E3 was the last chance," Kutaragi said. "The PS3 is the console of the future, so I wanted an extreme amount of capacity. But for that, we need cutting-edge technology, and not technology that is currently available. My suggestion was to come to an agreement with a physical format that is as close to Blu-ray as possible. But the PS3 launches in spring 2006. If we had continued to wait for a unified standard, we wouldn't be able to release the PS3. We no longer have any more time. It's game over."

During the summer, the game developers cut over en masse to the final development kits. Every month, Microsoft would update the software on the kits and the game developers would slowly see new features materialize.

The operations team in Mountain View started using their automated supply-tracking software to order some of the 1,700 parts. They had to make sure that enough inventory was on hand at every critical point in the supply chain, from the factories to the ports to the warehouses to the distribution centers and, finally, the stores.

ATI got its final silicon back on its graphics chip in July, just in the nick of time to begin volume manufacturing. At that point in the cycle, there was still plenty of time to begin manufacturing the 2 million or so consoles needed at launch. In July, Flextronics built its last Xbox at the factory in the city of Doumen in Southern China. That factory and its predecessors in Mexico and Hungary had made more than 13 million consoles. By this time, manufacturing chief Rick Vingerelli left and was replaced by Marc Whitten. Leslie Leland saw the last one move off the line. Full told, Microsoft had sold more than 22 million Xbox consoles by the end of June, 2005. It had sold 14.6 million in North America, 5.5 million in Europe, and 1.8 million in Asia. For the fiscal year, Microsoft had lost $391 million. But the company said it would make money by the middle of 2007. Xbox Live now had 2 million subscribers. Sony had sold 87 million PS2s.

As Leland watched that last machine roll by, she realized it was the end of the Xbox era unfolding before her eyes, though it would be a long time before Microsoft completely sold out of the old machines. She then toured the Wistron and Flextronics factories where the new machines were built.

At the moment, the 70,000-square-feet buildings stood empty. The complex had more than 150,000-square-feet of factory space. With more than 25,000 workers, it was like its own little city. Soon enough, the company would bring in line after line of automated factory tools for molding about 30 different plastic parts. There were eight full lines of surface mount machines, which mounted the chips on the motherboards.

Nick Baker and his whole team had to be on hand to assist the Flextronics assembly workers with the process of debugging the first consoles. When he went to work on the line in China, it was his first trip to Asia. If a machine failed a test, he had to stop the whole line. Then he had to figure out what happened. In one case, the line stalled because someone put the wrong disk into a test machine. Leland admired Baker's acumen.

"No one was better at debugging," she said. "Nick was awesome."

Here and there, problems cropped up. An operator would kick a power cord and bring down a testing machine. The power in the fast-growing region was unreliable. One day, lightening struck a factory building. Microsoft lost about five hours worth of manufacturing data. For the whole summer, the factory ran two 12-hour shifts, 24 hours a day. Leland had three meals a day in the factory. The cafeteria served food on shiny silver metal trays. One morning at 7 am, Todd Holmdahl called her to tell her the line was down. She had to drop everything

and go to work.

"That was death," she said. "I got that pit in my stomach. It was down for hours, and it seemed like years."

Once Flextronics hit its stride in manufacturing, the team moved over to the Wistron factory. The teams held conference calls, one at 9 am, and another at 9 pm, when the shifts changed over. Sometimes dozens of people were on the line. Bill Adamec, the program manager on the major chips, also made the trip to China.

"I would joke with people that I was an adrenaline junkie," he said.

Ideally, Microsoft needed about 2 million consoles shipped into stores by the end of the year. A total of 3 million would have been a home run. No console maker had ever been able to sell so many consoles in its first season. That was because every company had to deal with "ramping" a factory. In Microsoft's case, it had two factories in place and planned to start a third as soon as it could. But it couldn't start all three at once because the initial parts would be in short supply, and the hardware test engineers such as Nick Baker were a scarce commodity. They couldn't be everywhere at once.

IBM had started manufacturing its chips earliest. It had an advantage because it had its own factory as well as Chartered's new plant that could make the initial chips. Jim Comfort, the IBM vice president, said that each factory could discover flaws in the chip or the manufacturing process on its own and then tell the other factory what it had found. The factories were thus able to learn from each other and ramp production faster.

"Having two factories was a big advantage," said Kevin Krewell, then editor-in-chief at the Microprocessor Report.

But chip factories don't just stamp out chips overnight. It takes 14 weeks or so to run a raw silicon wafer through the factory, where dozens of processes are applied for laying down layers of metal and insulator to create chip circuitry on the wafers. At the end of the process, the wafers are tested and then sliced into chips. Then they are shipped to assembly houses where they are put into packages.

To get 3 million units by the end of December, Microsoft had to allow six weeks for consoles to reach their end markets by boat, which was the cheapest form of delivery. For the launch itself, Microsoft planned on air freight as much as a year in advance. It hired BAX Global, an air shipper and supply chain management company, to handle the air freight. BAX Global booked 90 Boeing 747 air cargo charter flights between mid-October, 2005, and February, 2006. Those planes would transport Xbox 360s from Hong Kong to a hub in Toledo, Ohio, in the U.S., or to Cologne, Germany, in Europe. [1]

Even with the air freight, getting millions of consoles into the market was tough. But Peter Moore still hoped that the first console maker to get to 10 million units would be unbeatable. The company had to allow weeks for Flextronics and Wistron to reach full capacity. Each factory was capable of about 120,000 machines a week. These factories had to start production slowly. They would make 100 machines or so and pull them off the line. Then some lucky engineers would spend hours playing games in a room, complete with couch, to see how well the machines worked.

Once they had a good batch, they would load them into a truck. The journey to Hong Kong on the crowded roads took more than three hours. There, they could be put on an airplane bound for San Jose, California, where they were once again loaded into trucks bound for Microsoft's hardware evaluation labs in Mountain View. There, Leslie Leland and her teams tore the machines apart and examined them. They baked them in heated chambers and left them running for days to test their limits. This process took weeks as well. Once the machines started regularly passing these tests right off the line, the workers could speed the lines. The engineers stayed late, as they communicated by instant messenger with their colleagues on the front lines in China.

In mid-August, Microsoft unveiled some long-secret plans. At an event in Leipzig, Germany, Larry Hyrb, AKA Major Nelson, was feeding information back to his fans as fast as he could. He found that his persona was becoming famous among gamers. At Leipzig and everywhere else he traveled, gamers took pictures with him and asked for his autograph. He had the job inside Microsoft that everybody else wanted.

Microsoft finally announced that it was going to do two versions of the Xbox 360. The enthusiast version would have a hard disk drive, a wireless controller, a wireless remote control, a built-in Media Center Extender, and an Xbox Live headset. It would sell for $399 and come with preloaded music and movie content. That box packed a lot of technology into one machine.

Meanwhile, it would sell the Xbox 360 Core version without a hard drive for $299. Games would likely sell for as much as $60. The reaction was mixed. Many enthusiasts realized that the game developers would scale back their games so they ran on the lowest common denominator, a machine without hard disk storage. They felt the games would be underwhelming as a result.

But Robbie Bach had favored the two-SKU plan all along because he didn't want to convince Wal-Mart that it should sell a $400 game console. Those on budgets and people who weren't as crazed about games might appreciate the lower price. It would allow Microsoft to reach larger numbers of consumers faster.

"The point here is about choice," he said. "In the past, game consoles didn't offer much choice. You got what they said you got.

Taking a visitor on a tour through the Mountain View labs in mid-August, Leland was feeling confident. Half the offices were empty because so many engineers were in China. But behind white doors with coded door locks, the remaining engineers were testing the final machines. Dozens of final Xbox 360 consoles lay with their guts torn out. Cables were plugged into them as if they were on life support machines. The boxes were "chill white," the final color that Astro Studios had chose. The air was thick with the humming of fans and air conditioners, which blew air through the racks of machines. Rings of light glowed bright green. The lab engineers would overclock the machines so

they ran at speeds faster than normal just to see where the machine would hit its breaking point. One man was literally roasting his Xbox 360 at 70 degrees Celsius. The engineers would get the swimming dolphin application running first, then they would run *Halo 2* in emulation mode.

Rich Lee, one of the Mountain View engineers, showed off a big chamber where he would take 120 machines down to zero degrees Celsius and then back up to 45 degrees for up to 72 hours at a time. Behind a locked door in the EMC lab, the team tested the machines to see what would happen if they were subjected to power surges or lightening strikes. They would see what would happen if there was radio interference or voltage dips. Seeing all this, Leland could claim the Xbox 360 as her own. The original Xbox was a product she did not create. But she was with the 360 from the beginning. This was why the Mountain View crew had tripled in size. They had to decipher every bug, every failed machine.

"There's something emotional seeing it at this stage," Leland said, pausing for a moment. "We're well on our way to having a successful launch. We have to hit the Christmas window."

Backing up that schedule, Todd Holmdahl knew that production had to get going several months ahead of the worldwide launch. The teams had calculated that volume production had to start in August in order to ship enough consoles to each market. Jim McCusker, the Flextronics executive said, "You could say you're going to build 5 million units with enough time. But Microsoft products always push the edge, with the chips getting done just in time. You don't have time to build up a buffer of inventory."

"On top of that, it's a business," he added. "What contract manufacturer wants to build 5 million units in two months and then 1 million units for the remaining 10 months? It's a balancing act because no customer has the appetite to pay for unused equipment. You have to have the right amount of capacity so you don't have leftover inventory, and you have to build inventory gradually. These are almost unachievable goals."

This time around, the production job was harder because the factory had to produce different products, with distinct packaging and a variety of languages, for the different regional markets. It had to make the right mix for each market. And Microsoft had a version with a hard drive and one without. It was a complicated process to bring all the parts together at once. Flextronics had calculated that it needed to start building production volumes in August. But McKusker said the production really got going in September. The manufacturing started behind schedule.

At that point, the Xbox 360 was out of the hands of the executives. It was time for execution, and all 25,000 people associated with making the Xbox 360 now had to step up and get the products to market. To Greg Gibson, Microsoft had done all that it could to drive the risk out of the schedule. Now it was up to fate. Absorbing all of the reports, Robbie Bach said, "I felt we were in good shape."

In mid-September, Mitch Koch told reporters in calls that Microsoft would launch in North America on Nov. 22, in Europe on Dec. 2, and in Japan on Dec. 10. As Robbie Bach had ordered, no regions would be second class. He expected 25 to 40 games to be available by the end of the year. He estimated that Xbox division sales would grow 50 percent in the coming fiscal year, from $3.2 billion to more than $4.8 billion. By the end of June, 2006, Microsoft would sell 4.5 million to 5.5 million Xbox 360s.

"It's unprecedented what they're trying to do," said David Cole, analyst at DFC Intelligence in San Diego. "No one has been able to do it before."

1. "Xbox 360 Launch Logistics Detailed," by Cesar Berardini, Xbox365.com, March 14, 2006, http://news.teamxbox.com/xbox/10456/Xbox-360-Launch-Logistics-Disclosed/

CHAPTER FORTY-THREE

THE TOKYO GAME SHOW

On Sept. 15, 2005, Microsoft held a press conference in Tokyo's trendy Shibuya district on the eve of the Tokyo Game Show. More than 500 journalists, some carting digital cameras with big lenses, crowded into a ballroom filled with acid green lights.

It was an eventful day. The company had disclosed it would sell the Xbox 360 in Japan for 37,900 yen, or about $345. That version would include a removable 20-gigabyte hard drive, a wireless controller, a media remote control, and an Xbox Live headset. In effect, Microsoft was going to make the $399 version from the U.S. available in Japan at a lower price. But it wouldn't sell the low-cost version without the hard drive at all. Mitch Koch, corporate vice president for global retail sales, said that research showed that the Japanese gamers didn't care for the low-cost version. So while Microsoft would sell two versions in Europe and in North America, the Japanese would get one.

Robbie Bach and Peter Moore were in the crowd, but they left the press conference in the hands of Yoshihiro Maruyama, general manager of the Xbox division in Japan, who spoke entirely in Japanese. He stood at a white podium with an Xbox 360 and said that seven games would launch in Japan on Dec. 10. By the end of January in 2006, he promised 20 more games. As an incentive to buy early, he said that those who picked up the Xbox 360 at launch would be guaranteed a spot in the beta test of the system's version of *Final Fantasy XI Online*.

Maruyama showed a video montage of games, highlighting titles such as *Biohazard 5*, *Project Gotham Racing 3*, and *Dead or Alive 4* from Japan's own Tecmo. Cliff Blezinski of Epic Games showed off *Gears of War*, and Phantagram's San Youn Lee showed off *Ninety-Nine Nights*. He also said that Microsoft would promote the Xbox 360 by opening up a huge multi-story "Xbox 360 lounge" in Tokyo where gamers could go to try out the games for free.

Maruyama said that as much as Maruyama emphasized online

games, he didn't have much to show. *Final Fantasy XI Online* wasn't ready. Roughly half the games that Microsoft had planned for the launch weren't finished. Some of the big titles were falling off track. Inside Microsoft, the debate focused on whether to postpone the Japanese launch.

Sam Kennedy, editor-in-chief of 1Up.com, the Ziff Davis video game web site, sat in the audience. He listened to the translations of questions from the Japanese press corps. They were skeptical. They joked about the size of the first Xbox and wondered what Microsoft was doing better this time. Maruyama was polite in his answers, but Kennedy felt the hostility to Microsoft and how much resistance it had to overcome in Japan. A couple of reporters pressed Maruyama about the price: why was it even higher in yen than the last time, if Microsoft truly wanted to sell more consoles in Japan.

Asked about the mistakes, Maruyama said that the first console was rushed and so was its marketing plan. Microsoft didn't get the games in the hands of actual gamers early enough. Given polls that showed demand for the Xbox 360 in Japan was low, Maruyama said that Microsoft had challenges in Japan and needed to get the games in the hands of gamers. It seemed no amount of atonement was enough for the Japanese press.

Kennedy said it seemed as if the journalists weren't that impressed with *Gears of War*, which seemed more like an American title than a Japanese one. But he still thought that Maruyama did a good job politely answering questions.

"Maybe it would have been better to highlight Hironobu Sakaguchi's *Blue Dragon*," Kennedy said. "The demo reel was not really focused on the Japanese market as well. They had *Final Fantasy XI Online*, but it's already on the PS2. They didn't impress the Japanese press. If they set out to do that, they failed."

The next day, the Tokyo Game Show opened at a venue an hour's train ride away in a local suburb. At the first day, game industry attendees got to go inside. But outside, the fans had come dressed as their favorite game characters, a tradition that had given the show its quirky charm. Fans could slip into their costumes in a big dressing room. The fans, which included everyone from *Sailor Moon* school girls to a kid walking with a full-size boy mannequin, posed for photographers.

Inside the vast hall, the Xbox booth was one of the largest. It was in the shape of a huge circle, with green signs everywhere. In the center was a theater and a set of kiosks. An entire living room had been outfitted to show off the digital lifestyle. About 20 games were playable, including *Ninety-Nine Nights*. There were big HDTV sets and flat panels hanging over the game kiosks so a lot of people could view the playable games. Pretty women in white and green outfits greeted the crowds. Fans were waiting a half hour at a time just to get their hands on a game.

Robbie Bach welcomed the crowd to a big assembly room for his keynote speech.

"*Konichi wa*," he said. "I am honored to be speaking at the Tokyo Game Show, one of the world's greatest events in gaming, at one of the most exciting times for our industry."

"If there is one thing I would like you to remember from my remarks today, it is this. We are now entering a new high definition era in digital entertainment, a global revolution that transcends national boundaries and is poised to completely rewrite the rules and change the reality of the video game industry."

"Ladies and gentlemen, let me be clear. Xbox 360 is the world's first next generation console and world's first and most powerful high-def gaming and entertainment platform. So the next generation in the history of our industry starts here and now. And I mean that literally. Tokyo Game Show is the first time anywhere in the world that consumers can see the Xbox 360 and its high-def entertainment in action. And I invite you to experience it today."

Bach went on to describe his own entry into the computer software industry a couple of decades ago and how the digitalization of the office was a parallel for the coming digitalization of the home.

"Microsoft played a significant role in this transformation. And I was fortunate enough to play a role as marketing leader for Microsoft office," he said.

He described some usage scenarios for music and video in the home. He said Microsoft's consumer strategy was to make everything work together, including Windows PCs, Xbox 360, digital cameras, MP3 players and other consumer electronics devices. The Xbox 360's role was to be "the ultimate digital amplifier" for all the content connected to a PC.

"The devices will work together regardless of the brand name of the devices," he said.

Then he talked about the important trends in consumer technology, including the delivery of mind-blowing, high definition entertainment. Gamers, he said, are expecting high-def content to make a big leap forward. He predicted 100 million homes would have HDTV by 2008, including 8 million in Japan by 2009. By 2011, all Japanese terrestrial broadcasting was scheduled to shift to digital.

"We must lead the way with innovation or be left behind," he said. "Now let's keep in mind that while it's a red hot trend, high-def is not the end. It's the means people need to enjoy the mind-blowing games that the latest technology enables. Everyone in this room knows that games will be at the cutting edge of this high-def revolution."

So Bach called out CliffyB from Epic Games. He ran through a live demo of *Gears of War*. He introduced the jarhead character Marcus Fenix and his friend Dominick in a sequence where they get caught in a war-ravaged city after dark. He showed how the soldiers had to make use of cover to survive in their missions, so *Gears of War* was not a "run and gun game."

After the demo, Bach returned to his speech. He said watching the game as a group reminded him of the days of arcades when gaming was a social activity. Microsoft wanted to bring that era back with online games via Xbox Live on the Xbox 360. He introduced Shinichi Minaka to show off the entertainment features of the Xbox. He spoke in Japanese, talking about the console's ability to connect to MP3 players and digital cameras and play media files stored on a Windows Media Center PC.

After that lengthy demo, Bach continued his speech to talk about personalization trends. He noted how Japan led the world personalizing cell phones with ring tones, sounds and face plates. He even praised Nintendo's *Nintendogs* game because it let players control the experience.

"In a way, it's kind of ironic. The more millions of people share things in common and do them together, the more they want to express their individuality," he said. "This personalization trend is here, and Xbox 360 has been designed with an unsurpassed capability to give people the power to customize their own games and entertainment content, putting people at the center of the experience that they helped create themselves."

Bach mentioned that Microsoft had achieved "thought leadership" with the Xbox. That, no doubt, was the consolation prize in the console market. But he promised the 360 would be in a position to achieve "global market leadership in the next generation."

He noted the Xbox's humble beginnings just four years earlier, when Microsoft had no experience. Then it went on to sell over 22 million consoles and sign up 2 million Xbox Live subscribers. He said *Halo 2* sold $125 million in units in one day. The portfolio was now only getting stronger. He said that compared to Sony's next-generation console, the net result on hardware performance was going to be "jump ball," which was a very strange way of putting it for a Japanese audience. He said that it would be easier to develop games for than the PS3, though it wasn't clear how he knew how easy or hard it would be to make games for the PS3. Xbox Live would also give Microsoft an advantage, and Microsoft's game lineup was "stronger than any launch set of games in history," spanning everything from casual games to the *Halo* series.

He added another mea culpa. "As you know, the first generation of Xbox has done very well in the U.S. and Europe but not so well here in Japan. As we move to market leadership, we are absolutely committed to build on our successes and perform and do better in Japan. To put us on the right path, we have listened carefully to consumers and partners here and we have learned many valuable lessons."

He added, "Now take, for example, the console design. As you know, our first Xbox console didn't exactly win any design awards. It was kind of big, kind of bulky. We've certainly learned from that and we have changed our approach to design. When we created Xbox 360, we wanted to create a physical presence that would be truly international. We collaborated with two of the best and most innovative design firms in the world, Hers Experimental Design Laboratory in Osaka, and Astro Studios in San Francisco. What they created is a product that distills our vision to its very essence."

Then Bach spoke about the games that Japanese game publishers were working on, with every major third-party company accounted for this time.

"Four years ago we were newcomers to the business," he said, in closing.

"Four years later we will be the first company to do a three-territory launch of a next generation console this holiday season in Japan, Europe and the United States. We are right on track. Yesterday we announced we are manufacturing product. Here's a picture of the first Xbox 360 rolling off the line, heading for retail and on sale in Japan on December 10.

"We have steeled our reserve to succeed," Bach said, and Microsoft was prepared to make the investment it takes to succeed worldwide.

As sincere as Bach's speech was, almost no one wound up writing much about it. That's because Satoru Iwata, CEO of Nintendo, unveiled Nintendo's new controller for the Revolution console in his speech. The controller resembled a remote control and had sensors in it to detect where on the screen it was being pointed. It was totally different from any other console controller and showed how Nintendo was still willing to take risks. Iwata said that Nintendo wanted to draw in more non-gamers who were intimidated by game controllers. This controller was more intuitive, since everyone knew how to use a remote control. Iwata demonstrated how it could be used as a fishing rod for a fishing game. In a video, Nintendo showed it could be used as a sword, a gun, a nunchaku and any other variety of game that would have gamers off their couches and on their feet.

The U.S. game blog, **Joystiq.com**, dedicated exactly one sentence to Bach's speech and then devoted the rest of the story entirely to a discussion of Nintendo's game controller. By no means did Nintendo's controller steal the show, for it wasn't even on display at the Nintendo booth. But if anyone emerged from the Tokyo Game Show with "thought leadership," it was Nintendo.

Robbie Bach wasn't going to admit that Microsoft was headed for another failure in Japan. Speaking at a Tokyo Reuters event, he dismissed a recent survey by Enterbrain's *Famitsu Weekly* that showed interest among Japanese was low for the Xbox 360, with only 6 percent saying before the Tokyo Game Show that they wanted to buy the Microsoft console. "None of that is worth anything," he said.

He acknowledged the weak software last time was the reason the Xbox didn't take off.

"Ultimately, if we had great games, people would have put a big, black box in the living room. We learned a lot from the first launch of Xbox in Japan. People didn't get excited about the games."

But the analysts were naysayers. "There is no way it will come close to the PlayStation," said Deutsche Securities analyst Takashi Oya. "Microsoft will have done well if it gets 10 percent market share in Japan."

On October 14, just after the Tokyo Game Show, Microsoft's Xbox 360 showed some gains among Japanese gamers. It was still third in the polls behind Nintendo's Revolution and Sony's PlayStation 3. Enterbrain said that 23.9 percent of the gamers surveyed said they wanted to buy an Xbox 360, a much bigger percentage than before the show. But about 40.4 percent remained unsure, while 35 percent didn't want to buy it. The negatives included both the weak line-up of games and the higher price. [1]

Enterbrain later did another market study, compiling the list of the top ten pre-ordered video games for the holiday season. At the top were several PlayStation 2 games and the Mario Kart DS game for Nintendo's DS. No Xbox 360 games, original Xbox games, or Nintendo GameCube games were on the list at all. [2]

"I worry that people will see these 360 games and not realize they are next-generation games," Kennedy said. "Ridge Racer 6 looked good. But some of the titles don't make that quantum leap." At the end of the Tokyo Game Show, the success or failure of the Xbox 360 in the Japanese video game market remained a toss-up.

---

1. "Survey says: Japanese Gamers Want More Info On Next-Gen Systems," Gamespot news article, posted Oct. 14, 2005.

2. "Japanese Retailers Share Top Holiday Picks," Oct. 17, 2005, www.gamasutra.com.

CHAPTER FORTY-FOUR

AND NOW FOR OUR NEXT TRICK

As the hardware team wrapped up its work, Microsoft had to consider what to do with its talented team of 200 engineers. Many of the engineers would be tied up on the cost reductions for the Xbox 360 for years to come. They would redesign the parts so they could be simpler and cheaper to build. They would combine the graphics chip and the microprocessor into a single chip at some point.

But some engineers needed work to do before the next console had to be designed. Microsoft's executives hatched a plan to keep them busy. They dusted off the old scheme to create a portable game player. It was about time. Bill Gates and Steve Ballmer decided to realign Microsoft's top executives so that the company could move faster to deal with its new rivals. It had to start thinking beyond Sony and Nintendo. Microsoft had to compete faster against companies such as Google, Yahoo!, eBay, Amazon.com, Apple Computer, and a host of fleet start-ups.

On September 20, 2005, the company split itself into three divisions. The core Windows group would be called the Microsoft Platform Products & Services Division, led by Kevin Johnson and Jim Allchin as co-presidents; Jeff Raikes was named president of the Microsoft Business Division; and Robbie Bach was named president of the Microsoft Entertainment & Devices Division. Bach would no longer be the chief Xbox officer. He would step up beyond the Xbox. His Home and Entertainment Division would be combined with Mobile and Embedded Devices, including gadgets such as smart phones, MSN, music services, and Internet TV. With this portfolio of businesses under his control, Bach could end some internecine warfare within the company and launch a counterattack against rivals in portable gadgets. He now had everything within his control to launch a so-called "iPod killer" that played games.

For a long time, Microsoft had watched Apple's resurgence with frustration. The iPod had become a cultural phenomenon, selling well

over 10 million units a quarter. Everything that Microsoft did in music services had fallen short. It created PocketPC software that enabled people to play music on their handheld organizers. It had SmartPhone software that was just starting to break into the cell phone business. It licensed its software to makers of Portable Media Players, but even though it won over dozens of licensees, none of the companies could break Apple's hold on the market. The smaller players didn't have enough advertising money to establish a brand, and they didn't have control of hardware, software, and services the way that Apple did. Apple was so well integrated that it could design a product and everything to go with it. It was time for Microsoft to step up and take on Apple directly, in the same way as it took on Sony with the Xbox and Xbox 360.

Different parts of Microsoft had tried to take a stab at Apple. Otto Berkes, the co-creator of the original Xbox, had left the project early in its inception to return to Windows products. He was a right wing hawk when it came to supporting the PC and Windows. Berkes began research to try to make a handheld Windows computer. He didn't know or care what it would be used for. But he knew if Microsoft could pull it off, people would find wonderful uses for it the way they had done with the ever-evolving PC. He teamed up with Horace Luke to create various prototypes. But the Intel-compatible chips of the time had not been designed with extreme low power in mind. Even Transmeta, which made low-power microprocessors, couldn't make chips that enabled the tiniest handheld computers that Berkes had in mind. He persevered, even as Luke shifted over to designing SmartPhones. Bill Mitchell, the head of Windows mobile devices, encouraged Berkes to keep at it. Bill Gates held up an early non-working prototype, which Berkes had dubbed "Haiku," at a Windows Hardware Engineering Conference in April, 2005. But that version proved too hard to make, so Berkes started work on a successor, dubbed "Origami." This system got traction as Samsung and other computer makers in the Far East decided to launch versions of it in the spring of 2006.

But nobody expected the *Origami* machines, which had 7-inch diagonal touch-screens and couldn't fit in a pocket, to do any damage whatsoever against the iPod or the Sony gadget. Microsoft needed a game machine that was small. Bach assigned J Allard to take on this "next big thing." Doing so would make a huge statement that Microsoft was going to ship this iPod-killer and that it would do it with the same precision planning that it had done with the Xbox 360. Allard would run the platform, handling the hardware, software, and services for the handheld. Bryan Lee, meanwhile, would become the chief financial officer for the entire Entertainment and Devices Group and run the handheld's business side. Peter Moore would take charge of the Xbox 360 and Windows games businesses, effectively replacing Bach in his old job. These promotions set in motion another series of promotions. Todd Holmdahl replaced Allard as the head of the Xbox platform. Larry Yang in Mountain View took Holmdahl's old job, while Bill Adamec eventually stepped up to replace Yang as the semiconductor chief.

Allard picked Greg Gibson to be the project director on the handheld.

Gibson had a proven track record for managing a complex design. He would be able to spearhead the core team as it tackled difficult technical challenges, such as cramming a powerful microprocessor into a handheld device that couldn't consume a lot of power because of battery life requirements. Microsoft hired Transmeta, the low-power chip company, so that it could use 30 of Transmeta's engineers on a secret project, and the press began speculating about a connection between a handheld project and the Transmeta team. After all, Transmeta was helping Sony create low-power versions of the Cell microprocessor for handheld applications. The Microsoft project would operate in secret until, once again, the media blew the lid off the story in the spring of 2006.

The project reminded Microsoft veterans of other times when the team had considered handheld game players. Back in 2001, Margaret Johnson explored the idea of doing the Xboy handheld with technology from R.J. Mical's Red Jade project. But that project got scuttled. And the Xe 30 team contemplated handhelds again, but they decided to wait until the Xbox 360 shipped.

The hardware gang had moved on to bigger and better things. The handheld seemed like the logical next step for Microsoft in games, but by no means was the Xbox 360 finished.

At the end of September, both Microsoft and Intel publicly threw their support behind HD DVD, the next-generation HD storage disks being created by Toshiba and its allies. The companies threw down a gauntlet because they had a common enemy in Sony. Both Microsoft and Intel said the technology from Toshiba was more flexible, cost-effective and friendly to consumers than Sony's Blu-ray technology. But a format war could very well benefit the Xbox 360, which used only a standard DVD drive. If HD DVD systems became the standard, then Sony's PlayStation 3 would be saddled with an expensive loser. Intel could also benefit from Sony's setback. Intel was preparing its Viiv brand of home computers for launch in January, 2006. If the PS3 and Blu-ray prevailed, then no one would need home computers anymore. The PS3 could crush them. The good thing about HD DVD was that it was cheaper than Sony's Blu-ray. All it needed was more support, and the endorsement of Microsoft and Intel saved it.

CHAPTER FORTY-FIVE

XO5 IN AMSTERDAM

icrosoft was getting better at entertaining journalists. It knew that goodwill, good times, good food and entertainment were the path to good reviews. The gaming enthusiast press was still loyal to its readers and its favorite games. But they liked to be wined and dined. One of the biggest soirees that the Xbox team threw for the press was its series of X events in Europe. These started with the launch of the original Xbox in Europe in 2002. The company would occasionally reveal some news at these events. Microsoft had skipped Xo4 as it had little to say about the upcoming Xbox 360.

For Xo5, the event took on greater significance. The company was about to launch the Xbox 360 in the fall of 2005 on a worldwide basis. It needed something special. So the European team headed by Chris Lewis decided to hold the event in the Las Vegas of Europe, the city of Amsterdam in the Netherlands. In Amsterdam, the Xbox folks knew they wouldn't have trouble attracting the press from all over the world. The city was known for its wild, hippie-inspired culture and political tolerance. At coffeehouses, you could order hash or marijuana to smoke in sidewalk cafes. You could tell which places offered weed because they had potted marijuana plants in the window. The Hemp Hash Marijuana Museum honored the hallucinogenic weed. As a joke, the public relations teamed booked Peter Moore in the famous suite at the Amsterdam Hilton where John Lennon and Yoko Ono held a peace-inspired "love in" against the Vietnam War.

At the center of the city was the Red Light district, where prostitution was legal. Encircled near the very center of the horseshoe-shaped city, the Red Light district was hundreds of years old, but it recently had made prostitution legal. A lot of signs said photography was forbidden, but not much else was. Microsoft even printed a translation of "Do you know the way to the Red Light district?" on its press badges.

Journalists came by the boatload to Microsoft's Amsterdam venue.

Of course, officially, this was not the kind of activity that Robbie Bach, chief Xbox officer, was about to endorse. So the actual event was held miles away, in an old gas factory dubbed *Westergasfabriek*. The place was a huge brick building in a spacious green park. The building's ornate design made it seem more like a museum than a factory. Behind it was a huge round cylindrical building that once served as an oil storage tank. The press had no idea of the entertainment in store for them and made their way from the hotels through a circuitous route. Their friendly Xo5 hosts and hostesses in white outfits walked them down to canals where they boarded tour boats. The journalists, many of the sleepy and hungry after long flights, were herded aboard where they sat at tables and grumbled about the lack of beer and food. The ancient captain of one boat told jokes, "A herring a day keeps the doctor away. Two herrings a day keeps everyone away." The boats took off and went through a number of the 88 canals that ringed Amsterdam. The captain pointed out landmarks like the Cat Museum and the Anne Frank House, where a young Jewish girl and her family hid from the Nazis during World War II until they were betrayed and sent to Auschwitz.. Houseboats were everywhere. Brick buildings lined the canals, many with storefronts on the bottom and apartments on top. At the tops of many of the narrow but tall houses, the old captain said, were hooks for the pulleys that workers would use to raise furniture to the upper floors. He remarked that the streets were so narrow, one or two cars drove into the canals each month. That's why so many residents rode bikes to work. There were supposedly 600,000 bikes in the city of 750,000 residents. Upon arriving, the guests on the boats walked up the gangways to a growing crowd of people inside the big white and green tents that filled *Westergasfabriek*.

Walking inside, the 1,000 journalists checked in and were herded through a

walkway through a circular hallway. Around the edges was a list of every person attending the event. The names included Seth Schiesel of the *New York Times,* Geoff Keighley and Tom Russo of *G4 TV,* a 24-hour cable network in the U.S. just for video gamers. Analysts such as P.J. McNealy of American Technology Research, independent analyst Billy Pidgeon, and Schelley Olhava of International Data Corp. were present. From the U.S. gaming press were Mark McDonald of *Electronic Gaming Monthly,* Andy McNamara of *Game Informer,* Rob Smith of the *Official Xbox Magazine,* and seven writers from the GameSpy gamers news web site. It was a subset of the usual U.S. crowd, since not all of the press that attended E3 could afford the trip to Amsterdam or accept free accommodations from Microsoft at the 400-euro-a-night Hotel Okura. But it was a key group of opinion makers that Microsoft had to win over.

Microsoft displayed the name of every attendee on the welcome screen.

Everyone could see their names on the big screen in the front of the room, in a tip of the hat to personalization, one of the marketing themes of the console. The Japanese press showed up in force, even though the Tokyo Game Show was just a few weeks earlier. Gamers around the world awaited the Amsterdam event news, which would be broadcast live in video feeds over the Internet. At the end of the long corridor was a big theater, only about 30 seats across but hundreds of rows deep. A signature green video screen framed the stage. After everyone filed in, the heat started to build to stifling levels. Chris Lewis welcomed the crowd and spoke about some of the lessons Microsoft had learned since the first console. That including coming out at a price that was right for the market. It seemed that a game console maker had finally realized how important Europe had become in the world's gaming market, and that, at last, it was getting its due with a launch simultaneous with the other major markets. He felt that would go a long way toward winning the hearts of the gamers in Europe.

Lewis told the crowd, "You're the first people in the world who will get to play games on the Xbox 360." He said that Microsoft raised the bar on what games could and should be. About 200 games were in the works, coming from almost every major game publishers and developer. He went through the list of titles launching for the current Xbox. Then he introduced a video of Joanna Dark, the heroine of *Perfect Dark Zero*, the prequel to the original *Perfect Dark* that debuted on the Nintendo 64 console in 2000. The live action video was a commercial that Microsoft would use to promote the game. Then a Microsoft employee showed the game in playable cooperative mode on Xbox Live. In the "rooftops level" of the game he showed how one player could snipe at shooters at the top of the building, while one on the street could take out the enemies on the ground. In one nice touch, as the Dark character rounded a corner, a bunch of pigeons flew off.

The game didn't draw much applause. Maybe it was because a lot of the public relations people were sitting in an overflow room watching the press conference on TV monitors. Then Robbie Bach, chief Xbox officer, stepped out on stage. He talked about various scenarios for the digital lifestyle, whether on the go, at the PC, watching TV or listening to a stereo, and the fact that Microsoft was addressing them all, with the Xbox 360 a big part of this picture. Microsoft used the technology in the original Xbox to gain "thought leadership" in the game industry. He talked about all the successes of the first console: *Halo*, *Fable*, being No. 1 over Sony in console sales for the 2004 holidays, and getting 2 million subscribers to Xbox Live. He said that Microsoft had learned lessons from their last go round.

"We have a plan in the Xbox 360 to drive to the next level," Bach said.

The goals, he said, were to drive creativity in the industry, open the market for new audiences, and drive social experiences through integration of technologies, and to make the 360 No. 1. He said Microsoft would do some things differently, like not treating Europe as a secondary market. He said the Xbox 360 had the best lineup for a launch in video game history, and he proceeded to show off the titles.

J Allard came out again to demonstrate what you could do with the improved digital lifestyle features. Going over the same ground he covered at the GDC and E3, he talked about expanding the market with things like video chat, personalization of media such as music, and the ability to play DVD movies.

With the stifling heat and long trips, journalists were nodding off during Allard's speech and one noted as much in a blog. Allard went up to him the next day and said, "Hey, we go back a long time. Why couldn't you say you fell asleep in Robbie's speech or Peter's speech?" He chuckled as he said it. But that evening, a few things woke everybody up. Until this point, Microsoft had been very quiet about its games. Deliberately so. After the embarrassment at E3, it had decided not to show much more until it was really ready to display the games on final hardware at their best. For more than an hour, it showed demo after demo on stage.

CliffyB of Epic was once again ready to show off *Gears of War*. It was still getting good press as the best original for the Xbox 360 since its debut at E3 2005. He repeated his presentation from the Tokyo Game Show, showing off a heavily scripted level that showed off the horror elements of the story-driven shooter. CliffyB didn't show it, but he was worried. The wireless controllers were randomly failing. And of the two boxes he brought to show off *Gears of War*, one wasn't working.

He talked about the theme of "destroyed beauty" in the game. He introduced the main characters, two jarhead soldiers Marcus and Dominick, as they arrived with two other squad mates in a Batmobile-like vehicle dubbed an Armadillo. They were sent to scout an abandoned refinery in the pouring rain. Water glistened off the soldier's body armor and CliffyB noted how the flashes of lightning showed off the high dynamic range of the Xbox 360 hardware. This meant that both extremely low-light shadowed areas and extremely bright areas could be rendered in detail at the same time, adding a richness to the realism the same way that high-quality cameras captured mixed light images on film. The soldiers moved forward in pitch dark, staying alert for WretchHorde monsters who had attacked the human world from subterranean depths. As the soldiers shined lights on areas, they could see four-legged beasts scurrying away. With each strike of lightning, they could see shapes moving in the darkness. Upon entering the refinery, the camera focused on the bodies of humans decaying in pools of blood. CliffyB had to stop there and tell the crowd to await "emergence day," which would kick off *Gears of War*, in 2006.

Grant Collier of Infinity Ward also took the stage to show off *Call of Duty 2*, which was in the final stages of completion in preparation for launch day. Many had singled it out as the best game in the launch line-up. Collier took the controller himself as he played the game on final hardware. He led a squad of British soldiers and one British tank against defending Germans in a town. A Tiger tank crossed the approach of the British, but the lightly armored British tank was no match for the German Tiger. Shells bounced off the Tiger, which turned its turret and sent the British tank into flames. The squad fled the road for a stone wall and hopped over it, only to find German soldiers shooting at them from a stone house.

The highlight of the event was when Peter Moore mentioned *Halo*. He didn't say a word about the long-awaited *Halo 3*. Rather, he told the crowd that Microsoft had signed up Peter Jackson and Fran Walsh as the executive producers of the *Halo* movie. Jackson said in a video clip that Universal Studios and 20th Century Fox would participate in the project. Jackson, notably thinner than when he accepted Oscars for Best Picture and Best Director at the Academy Awards, said in a video that he was a big *Halo* fan and played *Halo 2* through to the end while he was making *King Kong*. This immediately led to murmurs in the crowd about whether the *Halo* movie would be released at the same time as the

Halo 3 game. But Microsoft didn't say what Bungie Studio would do next. Asked what the big news was afterward, Billy Pidgeon said, "It's the *Halo* movie."

As the lights came on, the media were ushered into the big cylindrical building that used to store oil. Inside were open bars serving drinks and servers with French Fries and Hollandaise sauce. Everyone stood around, snacking on food, waiting for the next part of the show.

The seating was narrow and deep at XO5

A big screen showed a slick animated commercial starring Joanna Dark, the heroine of *Perfect Dark Zero*. A series of dancers swinging on ropes descended from the ceiling. They had automatic pistols and were dressed as various characters from the *Perfect Dark Zero* cast. Clearly, Microsoft was dropping some strong hints about what would be the biggest game on the Xbox 360. Yet, as the lights came up and journalists munched on the French fries with mayonnaise, it was clear that other games were getting a lot of attention. *Call of Duty 2* in particular was drawing crowds. Grant Collier wandered through the crowd, taking congratulations from the journalists there.

The next day, the bleary-eyed press showed up for a round of small group briefings on each of the games and half-hour sessions with the executive team. For whatever reason, most of them said they had only a few hours of sleep. This was Amsterdam at work. The *GameSpy* guys said they got one or two hours of sleep because they were diligently filing stories all night to their round-the-clock web site. Such was the curse of the Internet, where gamers would scurry to the site which got the news first, no matter what time of day or night.

Shane Kim, the general manager of Microsoft Game Studios, was eager to hear what journalists thought about his line-up. One journalist said he liked *Call of Duty 2*, but then Kim asked, "What about *my* games?" The journalist said he had reserved his opinion about whether *Perfect Dark Zero* or *Kameo: Elements of Power* would really be that fun.

As Kim talked about the expansion of the market, Schelley Olhava listened politely. But she remarked, "I've heard this all before. I went back and looked in my notes last time and saw that J was saying the same thing about the first Xbox." She remembered the predictions about how the game industry was doubling in size with every five-year cycle, about how household penetration in the U.S. would go from 40 percent to 70 percent. It had, in fact, grown to 45 percent. Kim was aware of these naysaying arguments and said that the market was probably getting close to topping out for the traditional kind of game console. But because Microsoft's was linked to a digital entertainment lifestyle, its aim was to broaden the whole experience to non-gamers. He noted how his kids never played much with their cousins in Los Angeles. But with a connected Xbox 360, they could talk to each other with video chat and get to know each other. Then he said that there would be other kinds of interactive game experiences as well. Developers were making 45 to 50 Xbox Live Arcade games, including simple games for casual players who didn't buy many video games, but far outnumbered the hardcore.

Ken Lobb was looking around at the machines. He firmly believed that *Kameo* would become the next *Legend of Zelda* franchise. It had everything that Nintendo's legendary role-playing franchise had, and it was aimed at kids. He also thought that *Perfect Dark Zero* was the killer application for the Xbox 360. He thought that it would shine in multiplayer and that array of weaponry would give it a lot of replayability.

CliffyB showed off some real game play for *Gears of War* in his room. In the demo, a squad of rag-tag defenders of Earth arrive in an "Armadillo" car that looks like the Batmobile. The Marine Jarhead buddies, Marcus and Dom, arrive at an abandoned refinery in the middle of the pouring rain with two other soldiers. They slink through the rain and as the lightning strikes, they can see shapes WretchHorde monsters moving in the shadows. They open the doors and the camera cuts to a cinematic of decaying human bodies. CliffyB says you can see sweat running down the side of the face of the characters with the second-person view.

"Game's probably for kids, by the way," CliffyB quipped. Inside, the lights blinked because the power for the facility was going on and off. Marcus and Dom picked off a few monsters hanging in the rafters and walkways above them. Every time the monsters appear, the jarheads had only a second or two to dispatch them. If a monster tangled with the soldier, CliffyB shook the joystick and the character shook off the enemy. "Gonna hitch a ride, huh?" CliffyB said as he blasted with a gun that's a cross between a rocket and a shotgun. The horde kept coming in the darkness, where only failing lights and light flashes gave the humans a chance to shoot back. They moved into some rail cars that coasted through the factory. "I call this Space Mountain with guns," CliffyB says. He said the cooperative mode with another player, where one character played Marcus

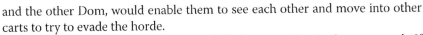

and the other Dom, would enable them to see each other and move into other carts to try to evade the horde.

"I love horror games," CliffyB says. "I find protagonists in them are weak. If you have a strong protagonist, you need enemies that take cover." [1]

Robbie Bach was squeezed into a small conference room for the whole day, talking to a small crowd of journalists in half-hour slots. At the end of the day, he sat down with the last group. It was a very stuffy room that Robbie had been locked in all day. "I'm having fun but it's hot," Bach said. Keighley asked Bach about Microsoft's decision to support the HD DVD format for next-generation high-definition video disks instead of Sony's Blu-ray rival technology.

Bach noted that Paramount was supporting both formats and, like other studios, would likely want to see which hardware gets to the market faster and at the right price. "So prove it, they're saying," Bach said. "See what gets to the market. See what they cost to manufacture. See what they cost to produce." Bach said it was an uncertain environment and he said Microsoft chose to side with HD DVD because it wasn't comfortable with the direction that Blu-ray was heading in terms of a copy-protection scheme. He would not say whether Microsoft would eventually start shipping Xbox 360 consoles with HD DVD drives instead of the current planned DVD drives.

One journalist asked Bach about the toughest console-related decisions Microsoft had to make this time around. He said that early on, selecting the chip vendors was tough because moving away from Intel and Nvidia meant that the company would have a tough time with backward compatibility. But he said that the advantages of going with IBM and ATI outweighed the obstacles. Microsoft chose them because of their better ability to customize their hardware, the move to multiple cores on a chip, and overall performance.

Bach also said that launching in all three major regions at the same time was also a decision that taxed the resources of the team. It was difficult to decide it was going to happen on time in every territory no matter what.

Later he said that it wouldn't be easy to keep supplies from running out in all the territories. Microsoft plans to resupply them more quickly than Sony typically does. But he said that demand will likely outstrip Microsoft's ability to ship units, at least until more factory capacity comes online in January and February. He said the actual supplies would be dependent on chip yields and needs of each market.

Bach said that groups made decisions at levels lower than when Microsoft began planning the original Xbox, which debuted in 2001. That reflected the growing experience of the team, he said.

Asked about backward compatibility, Bach said he couldn't answer yet. He said that in two to four weeks, Microsoft would announce which games from the old Xbox would run on the new console. He said Microsoft created an "engine" to make some of the old games work. But he said that the list of games would be based on popularity, whether it has a big Xbox Live component and therefore was still being played, and whether the game had a sequel coming soon.

Bach also declined to comment on how many units Microsoft would supply to all the territories and what the sales forecasts were for each region. Why do that, he said, when critics would simply use the number to hold Bach accountable to them later. Brian Lee would step onto that slippery slope later on.

Asked if Microsoft had to sacrifice certain functions because they were too expensive, Bach said Microsoft included most of the use scenarios" that it envisioned for the box, ranging from doing massively multiplayer online games on the box to not requiring a credit card for Xbox Live online subscriptions. He said that he wished that Microsoft could have allowed songs from the iPod in Apple's own formats to play on the Xbox 360, but that decision was out of Microsoft's hands. (The Xbox 360 can play songs in Windows Media and MP3 formats).

Bach said that there were never any plans to show a planned Marvel comic book heroes online game at Xo5. He said that Microsoft would decide in the next few days what titles would be available on the first day of the launch. That, he said, was dependent on the certification process which wasn't done yet.

A pesky journalist asked a few questions about making money. Was it possible to make money if Microsoft came in second place? Was Microsoft trying for an "early rush," beating the other guys with speed to market, and were making money and gaining market share mutually exclusive?

Bach said that Nintendo makes money on smaller volumes of console sales, so it was possible to make money without being in first place. "Selling more consoles helps, but it's not the only thing in our business model," he said. "If you're silly, you can be a high-volume company that is unprofitable." He said Microsoft designed the box in a different way this time and that it would allow for better cost reduction over time.

Sans *Halo*, Keighley asked whether Microsoft had a killer application this time. Bach said many more titles could be potential killer titles this time around because of the wider selection. He said that third-party game publishers were happier that their games would have a better chance to gain attention. He took a little jab at Sony and said that it never produced a game like *Halo* in its own studios at all. He didn't consider Sony's *Gran Turismo* to be such a game, and he said it was really more the *Grand Theft Auto* series that made the PlayStation 2 successful. He noted that Ubisoft's *Tom Clancy's Splinter Cell* was key to the first Xbox's sales because it showed that the Xbox was more than just a *Halo* console.

He said that launching without *Halo 3* was good for the Xbox 360, since the *Halo* title will sell well whenever it launches and that it's good for the console to emerge as something more than a *Halo* machine. It's a chance, he said, for original titles to shine. He said that Microsoft would not tie *Halo 3*'s launch to Sony's launch of the PS3. Even though Microsoft Chairman Bill Gates said just that, Bach said that Bungie would finish when it decided it was done. Releasing the *Halo* movie at the same time would be nice, but he said that either would be strong enough to launch on their own, if necessary.

As for its share of developers, Bach said that Microsoft's allies were growing, as evidenced by how many more Xbox 360 development kits had shipped

compared to its rivals. "We have a lot more mindshare in Japan," he said. And he noted the additions of Epic Games, id Software, BioWare, and Infinity Ward with major new commitments to the Xbox 360.

Upon walking out of the group interview with Robbie Bach, Seth Schiesel at the *New York Times* said, "They're totally backed off" from identifying *Perfect Dark Zero* as the killer game of the launch line-up. Maybe the rope dancers from the night before weren't worth the money after all?

At the Schipol airport, the security guards were well aware that many journalists had been flying in for XO5. Jamie Church, 24, was one of them. "I wish I got to go to that," he said as he grilled a journalist about why he had been in the country. "I'm going to take a week off work when it comes out. My friend is going to take two weeks off work.'" He had already pre-ordered his console and had picked games such as *Perfect Dark Zero* and *Project Gotham Racing 3* as part of his bundle. He wanted to hear what the best game at the show was. Then it was time to move on to grill the next passenger. "It's great that it's coming early for Europe this time," he said.

1. "XO5: So What's the Game to Watch?" Dean & Nooch on Gaming, Oct. 5, 2005, http://blogs.mercurynews.com/aei/2005/10/xo5_so_whats_th.html.

CHAPTER FORTY-SIX

COMING UP FOR AIR

Todd Holmdahl hadn't had much time to enjoy himself during the Xbox 360 project. But on a trip to Wistron's Xbox 360 factory in China, he and his team took a break to play some basketball at a court just outside the factory. The Microsoft engineers challenged some of the Wistron workers to a friendly match. They took off their shirts and enjoyed the little break. Holmdahl remembered that his team dominated the games. But Leslie Leland, who videotaped the game, said, "The short guys won."

"My body ached the next day," Holmdahl said. "But it was a good feeling."

More than 4,500 stores across North America planned to open at midnight on Nov. 22 to begin sales. Target and Wal-Mart stores put up kiosks to demonstrate games running on 360 machines.

Meanwhile, with just six weeks to go before launch, Microsoft still had to locate an appropriate venue for the Xbox 360's debut. Peter Moore, David Reid and Chris Di Cesare had something special in mind for gamers once again. They would stage a "Burning Man" style event where the most faithful fans would congregate. John Ellard in Xbox PR scouted around for places with the staff of Zedink, an events company. Finally, they found a place to stage their gigantic launch event, dubbed "Zero Hour." The event would be at a gigantic aircraft hangar in the town of Palmdale, in the middle of California's Mojave Desert. Reid said they chose the spot because it took a real journey to get there and could be an ideal setting for an "Area-51" style theme. Microsoft announced that Zero Hour would start on Nov. 20, just a day before the launch.

Every now and then, Larry "Major Nelson" Hyrb would have to beat down a rumor. Someone posted speculation that the face plate that Microsoft gave away at E3 would never fit the actual console. Hyrb went to industrial designer Jonathan Hayes and asked him if it was true. He took one of the face plates, snapped it into a console and posted the

picture.

Microsoft started some speculation and gossip of its own. David Reid and Chris Di Cesare had launched yet another viral marketing campaign, dubbed *Hex168*. At Peter Moore's direction, they wanted to stage another event for the most loyal fans. This campaign was once again masterminded by Jordon Weisman's 42 Entertainment in Emeryville, California. The firm, which handled *ilovebees*, aimed this time for a cross of the *Weekly World News* tabloid and the Internet site *Hot or Not*. This time, they had to move fast. Di Cesare approached them in August, 2005, leaving them a short time to prepare.

"We didn't have time to do our traditional story," Weisman said. "But we did create a light fictional skin for our audience to create the content."

In this campaign, a wacky professor Lutz implored fans to take notice of *Hex168*, the prime force of the universe which was behind anomalies such as the Biblical story of the falling walls of Jericho. Lutz thought that if people harnessed the "transformative power" of *Hex168*, they would unleash the power. In the hexadecimal numbering system used in computer programs, the number 168 actually translated to 360. As part of the campaign, Weisman's firm hired an English man who specialized in creating "crop circles." They hired him to create *Hex168* images in corn fields in the Midwest, and they got others to build *Hex168* sand carvings on beaches. They also had eight marching bands create *Hex168* patterns during half time shows at college sports games Fans picked up on the reference quickly, and they complied with Lutz's request to submit videos that depicted the power of *Hex168*. A few thousand submissions came in. Microsoft enlisted Marden-Kane, a promotional marketing operator, to evaluate the videos and choose 360 winners.

"In all of these cases, the most exciting thing is to watch the creativity of the audience," Weisman said. "You inspire them and then they blow you away."

The team would select the winners of that event and other enthusiasts as the chosen few. Microsoft invited the lucky gamers from the *Hex168* campaign, and thousands more, to pay their own way to go to the *Zero Hour* event and be among the first to play Xbox 360 games and buy the consoles on the spot. The marketing events team got to work transforming the hangar into a gigantic green monster.

Just after X05, J Allard made a stop in San Francisco to show off the Xbox 360 to another group of gamers and journalists. Gamers and journalists played all day long on a couple of dozen Xbox 360 machines on several floors of a multistory building in a warehouse district in the city. Allard stepped out to speak to the crowd and said, "Tonight there will be less rhetoric and more game play." He said that things were moving along well for the launch plans. "Tell us where we could be better," he said. "We're by no means done. We're going to be pushing it. We aren't complacent. We're taking this to the next level."

Then he told the crowd to go play some games. Among the guests in the group were a handful of the engineers from Mountain View. It was one of their first chances to mingle in public with the finished boxes. Leslie Leland

was beaming as she stood next to Allard. Peter Birch and Masoud Foudeh, the Microsoft engineers who supervised the graphics chip with ATI, were laughing as they watched one of the games in action. Jeff Andrews wasn't there because he was on a trip to visit IBM in Rochester, N.Y. Nick Baker, now 38 years old, held a drink in his hand and sat down for his first interview with a journalist. He said he was excited to be able to play games with his kids. Typically, he said, he played about one game per generation because he didn't have enough time. Last time, it was *Halo*. This time, he figured *Kameo: Elements of Power*, would be the one he would play with the little ones. He noted that 15 people from the original 3DO had worked on the console and were still at Microsoft in Mountain View. One of 3DO's founders, R.J. Mical, was now over at Sony working in the research labs in Foster City, Calif., just a short drive away.

Birch looked at the games and noted that the learning curve was just beginning for the developers. Developers had to skip so many tricks due to deadlines. He was convinced that the second-generation games would look far better. He was skeptical of the performance claims that Sony made about the PlayStation 3.

"Whatever we put in this box, it has to have legs for a long time," he said. "We lock it down and don't change it for years. I'm proud of what we've done. We made huge strides with this box."

Foudeh, 42, was relaxed. He said, "This team is great. Brilliant. Flexible. We work well together. We play well together. It didn't hit me how big this was until I went to E3 and saw all the hype about it. Everyone I meet says that I have one of the coolest jobs." Allard sat down with a journalist and sang the praises of the Mountain View team.

"They were there from the inception as the advance scouts," he said. "It's their baby. Their sense of pride is close to mine. Without Nick Baker and Jeff Andrews, there was no way we could have done the Xbox 360. I'm a co-creator. But we pushed our decision deep down into the team this time."

Allard said that Amsterdam gave him a lot of confidence since more than 1,100 people got hands-on experience with the box. It was a risky move to show so much so early, he said, but Microsoft was convinced that seeing and playing was believing. Those who were wowed could spread the good word, generating authentic viral marketing. He said he truly didn't mind showing up without another *Halo*.

"There have been 69 game console launches and 68 of them didn't have a *Halo*," he said. "We'd love to repeat the magic. Maybe we don't have Michael Jordan at the beginning here. Most console launches suck. We have breadth and depth in our line-up. Remember the PlayStation 2 with *Fantavision*, *Tekken*, and *Ridge Racer*? *SSX* saved them on the games. Remember *The Bouncer* video? More people bought the PS2 to watch *The Matrix* on DVD."

He said that the console had some real potential to start new revenue streams with Xbox Live Arcade and Marketplace.

"Xbox Live Marketplace?" he said. "It's like interviewing Meg Whitman

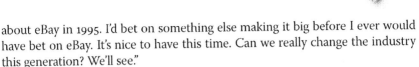
about eBay in 1995. I'd bet on something else making it big before I ever would have bet on eBay. It's nice to have this time. Can we really change the industry this generation? We'll see."

Allard promised that because of the edge that the Mountain View team delivered, this time Microsoft could afford to be the leader on console pricing. And he added, "We aren't finished with this yet. I feel more convinced than ever that we made the right bets."

Microsoft's confidence was building by the day. Bryan Lee, the chief financial officer of the Home and Entertainment Division, predicted that Microsoft would sell 2.75 million to 3 million Xbox 360 consoles in the first 90 days. That was roughly by the end of February. For the fiscal year ended June 30, 2006, or just over seven months, he predicted Microsoft would sell 4.5 million to 5.5 million units. That meant that Microsoft's rate of sales growth would slow dramatically after the initial surge of holiday sales. It was a conservative forecast, and it wouldn't give Microsoft much of a lead of Sony and Nintendo launched their consoles in the spring of 2006. David Cole, an analyst at DFC Intelligence, said the wild card was whether consumers would really come out in the holidays for the Xbox 360. Both Nintendo and Sony were particularly quiet during the holidays, but Nintendo marketing chief Reggie Fils-Aime promised that Nintendo's console would be the cheapest. Nintendo kicked off its free WiFi service for the Nintendo DS at a variety of locations. Retail surveys suggested that the Xbox 360 and Apple's video iPod would be the hottest gifts of the season. But both Sony and Nintendo were gearing up to produce large volumes of their gaming handhelds in the hopes of blunting Microsoft's launch.

Gamers started taking sides. Rudy Seidl, a 29-year-old systems analyst in Streamwood, Ill., reserved a system. But he was worried that the Xbox 360 games wouldn't look much better than the current Xbox games.

"My initial feelings on the Xbox 360 are that it's too early to be introduced," he said. [1]

Josh Sattler, a 28-year-old student at a video game school in Winter Park, Fla., said, "I'm ecstatic to see what things the 360 holds for us. I know that Microsoft has put forth their best effort as well as a no-holds barred approach in order to capture the global market. If they stick to their word, keep their customers updated with the latest info, and provide the best online services, I don't see anything stopping them from being the top team at the end of this next generation." [2]

1. Dean & Nooch on Gaming, Nov. 14, 2005, http://blogs.mercurynews.com/aei/2005/11/microsofts_xbox_2.html.

2. Dean & Nooch on Gaming, Nov. 14, 2005, http://blogs.mercurynews.com/aei/2005/11/microsofts_xbox_1.html.

CHAPTER FORTY-SEVEN

SHORT TERM MEMORY LOSS

It turned out the celebration at Microsoft was a little premature. As November approached, game reviewers were getting nervous. They sent messages to each other, asking if anyone had received final hardware from Microsoft. Microsoft was planning to have about 18 titles available for the U.S. launch. The game reviewers wanted to have deep reviews ready for the first day of sales on Nov. 22. But because each game took hours to evaluate, they wanted to get hands-on game time as soon as they could. When Microsoft started rationing out the machines, some suspected something was wrong. And for some of those who received their machines early, Microsoft asked them to return the machines so that they could receive replacement units.

P.J. McNealy, an analyst at American technology research, stayed in close touch with the retailers. They began telling him that they did not expect to receive anywhere near the allocation of consoles that they had pre-sold in the previous six months. Worldwide, analysts estimated that Microsoft would only be able to sell about 1.5 million to 2 million units during the holidays. Split between three territories instead of just one, that was a pitiful number of consoles. Perhaps demand in Japan wouldn't be that large, but Microsoft was likely to frustrate a lot of consumers. Microsoft contended that it never promised specific numbers to retailers, and that the retailers took the orders based on their own assumptions about what they would receive.

Something was clearly going wrong with the supplies. If Microsoft's two factories started manufacturing in September and hit full capacity in the beginning of October, it should have been able to produce almost 3 million units by the end of December. The last six weeks of production would still have been in transit and would not have arrived in stores by the end of the holidays, as long as Microsoft did not ship them by air. The machines that Microsoft had time to ship by boat would have amounted to about 1.5 million units.

But on Nov. 8, Bryan Lee, the finance chief, told industry analysts that Microsoft had plans to ship 2.75 million to 3 million consoles in the first 90 days of sales, or around the end of February. To analysts, that seemed like it was about half of what Microsoft could have made during that time, particularly if a third factory from Celestica came on board. Lee was being conservative, the analysts hoped.

Where was the weak link in the supply chain? The IBM and ATI chips were in full-scale production. Flextronics and Wistron had started somewhat late, losing a few weeks time. But their factories were operational. Even so, Microsoft was suffering an unexpected component shortage. The memory chips in the box were in short supply. The *Project Gotham Racing 3* team at Bizarre Creations in England had stumbled upon the problem. Their game wasn't working perfectly. Every now and then, it would misfire. The programmers traced it back. Only two months before launch, they isolated the problem to the memory chips in the system.

Normally, the main memory chips for computers, dubbed dynamic random access memory, were commodities. DRAM chip prices fluctuated by the week and suppliers were constantly overproducing and cutting prices. But Microsoft's engineers had specified a very fast memory for the 512 megabytes of main memory chips in each Xbox 360. The type of memory was called graphics double-data rate 3, or GDDR3. It operated at a higher speed than most graphics memory chips and was often used as the dedicated memory, dubbed a frame buffer, in a PC graphics card. Most high-end gaming computers used the fast GDDR memory.

But the GDDR3 flavor had only begun production in the second half of 2005. Samsung was the first to get its chips to market and was cranking out GDDR3 chips that ran at a speed of 700 megahertz. Mueez-Ud Deen, a graphics and mobile DRAM marketing director for Samsung, noted that these chips weren't just commodities.

"These are tough memories to make," he said. "They're running at three times the data rates of most memories."

They were the cream of the crop when it came to memory. Microsoft had taken the risk of using the fast memory chips because it needed them to keep up with the speeds of its fast IBM CPU and its ATI graphics chip. In fact, because Microsoft used a unified memory architecture, where the CPU and the graphics chip sent traffic over the same data pathway to main memory, it needed the fast chips to avoid bottlenecks.

Samsung wasn't expected to be a sole supplier. Infineon Technologies and Hynix were preparing to produce the GDDR3 chips too. But Hynix was behind, and Infineon, a German chip maker, hit a big snag. In August, 2005, Infineon announced it had won a contract to supply security chips to Microsoft as well as flash memory chips for storing games in memory units. Infineon would also supply a wireless game controller chip and GDDR3 memory chips. Those game controller chips were important because they would prevent peripheral makers from making their own compatible game controllers without paying

Microsoft. On the surface, Microsoft said that it wanted the security chips to ensure a quality experience by allowing only licensed and certified products to work with the machine. Of course, this time, Microsoft wanted to get its fair share of the revenues from accessories. Indeed, Microsoft would sell the wireless controllers for $50 a piece, while their cost was about $12, based on an estimate by Portelligent, an analysis firm which specialized in estimating costs. The deal was important for Infineon at the time because it was near a decision to spin off its memory chip division as a separate company.

Some of the Infineon chips ran at speeds below the 700-megahertz required by Microsoft. As a result, Flextronics had to set up a separate line to sort the good parts from the bad. The good parts were used in the machines, but the bad ones had to be passed over. The suppliers were producing as quickly as they could, but increasing capacity wasn't an easy thing to do. It could take half a year to increase capacity sufficiently to meet unexpected demand. Microsoft had doubled the amount of the memory in the machine in the spring. But the chip makers had not been able to adjust their production. On top of that, the high-end graphics cards for the PC also required a lot of memory. But Microsoft was making so many consoles so quickly – each with eight GDDR3 chips in them – that it was commanding a huge percentage of the available chips. Nam Hyung Kim, an analyst at market researcher iSuppli, estimated that Microsoft consumed 20 percent of the available GDDR3 chips in the fourth quarter. If it had made every box it wanted to, it might have commanded 40 percent of the market.

"This was a very aggressive plan by Microsoft," Kim said. "To me, it was risky to go ahead with it."

Infineon was just one of 200 suppliers making 1,700 parts for the Xbox 360. Who would have predicted that an $8 memory chip would derail Microsoft's ambitions for its game console? Microsoft declined to point a finger at anyone. Certainly, the supply chain had other shortages and complications, Jim McCusker at Flextronics said. Microsoft didn't say anything specific about the shortage for some time. Many people dismissed the shortage as something that always happened in a console launch. To others, it was like watching a train wreck in slow motion. And it would cost Microsoft a lot of goodwill with consumers, game publishers, and its retail partners.

"It was high excitement, high stress," McKusker said.

CHAPTER FORTY-EIGHT

COUNTDOWN TO LAUNCH

*E*ven as the production was progressing slower than expected, the launch line-up went through its final changes. Under the direction of Chris Satchell, Microsoft had prepared the game developers in advance. As early as January, 2005, it had told the developers what they needed to do to pass certification. While the final hardware development kits didn't go out until June, software kits prepared the developers for what they needed to know.

The certification division under Doug Hebenthal was prepared to handle a crushing work load. Since Microsoft also used independent contractors to test games, it could swell the ranks of the game testers at the last minute as 20 games came in all at once. The Advanced Technology Group under Scott Henson spent hours of time with developers on the fine points of bringing in their games.

"Some of the teams thought they could go bigger as they learned about more features," Satchell said. "But those who really needed to ship locked down on the features in the game and spent their last hours on game balance, game play, and making sure that they everything worked right."

Call of Duty 2 met its schedule and it was the first to go into the certification process in September. At Microsoft, Doug Hebenthal's dozens of testers in England and Redmond would attack the game and see if it had any flaws. Within a week after submitting the game, Infinity Ward learned it had passed inspection on first pass. On average, the certification added two more weeks to the development cycle for a game. *Perfect Dark Zero* was also ready early enough to get review copies in the hands of journalists. Five years in the making, it was finally done. *Kameo: Elements of Power*, followed shortly thereafter. And Bizarre Creations wrapped up *Project Gotham Racing 3* on time.

Not everything was smooth sailing at the end. Raven Software's *Quake 4* team had to remove full-scene antialiasing – which removed

jagged lines from images on the screen – because the software update never arrived to enable it. Todd Hollenshead, CEO of id Software, fretted that Microsoft had promised it early on. But when the team ran the game, they had to rejigger it and remove the antialiasing to hit the full 60 frames per second that they needed for an ultra-fast play experience. They still managed to make their target for a launch title. *Quake 4* debuted on the PC a few weeks earlier, but the Xbox 360 game was ready at launch. Half the titles that came in for certification made it through on their first pass. Most of these developers had about two years to work on their games, about one year to work with prototype development kits, and about four or five months to work with the final development hardware.

Peter Moore had to make the calls about what games would make the launch window. At some point, Microsoft had to declare the final list so that retailers could start taking pre-orders for the games. In some cases, he made decisions that hurt Microsoft but benefited the Xbox 360 platform. In Japan, for instance, Microsoft delayed the launch of *Project Gotham Racing 3* so that Namco's *Ridge Racer 6* could be the marquee racing title. That was the kind of pro-platform decision that Robbie Bach had favored, but Ed Fries did not. By this time, many titles such as *Gears of War* had been pushed back. But late in the game, more big games fell out of the launch line-up. In Japan, the curse hit Microsoft again. Tetsuya Mizuguchi's *Ninety-Nine Nights* delayed into the new year, and Tecmo's *Dead or Alive 4* missed its target as well. Sega had voluntarily delayed *Full Auto*. Bethesda Softworks delayed its role-playing game, *Elder Scrolls IV: Oblivion*. Atari pushed back *TimeShifters*.

Electronic Arts took such a pounding on the early previews of *The Godfather* that it decided to delay the game at least another six months. Since EA had more than 100 people working on the game, the decision cost EA an estimated $10 million in extra payroll costs alone. The game was already two years in the works, so analysts estimated its costs would to $30 million to $40 million. With the loss of *The Godfather*, many journalists wondered if the line up was going to be too weak. About a quarter of the big projects slipped beyond the launch window. But a total of 18 games were still slated to show up for day one. That wasn't as good as the 19 for the original Xbox launch, but it was far better than rival launches in the past.

Not only would Microsoft have the 18 marquee titles, it also had 12 Xbox Live Arcade games ready, including *Geometry Wars Retro Evolved*. It would make *Hexic HD* available for free, while players could download demos of the other games and pay for the full versions if they wanted.

Electronic Arts, Activision, Take-Two Interactive, Sega, Ubisoft, and Namco all joined Microsoft with launch titles. Another 20 titles could be out by the end of the year, including *Dead or Alive 4*. About 160 games were in the works. The pipeline looked healthy.

But the supply picture seemed to be worsening. Colin Sebastian, then an analyst at Thomas Weisel Partners, checked with retailers and estimated only 1.5 million units would ship worldwide by the end of the year, with 1.2 million

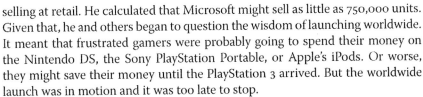

selling at retail. He calculated that Microsoft might sell as little as 750,000 units. Given that, he and others began to question the wisdom of launching worldwide. It meant that frustrated gamers were probably going to spend their money on the Nintendo DS, the Sony PlayStation Portable, or Apple's iPods. Or worse, they might save their money until the PlayStation 3 arrived. But the worldwide launch was in motion and it was too late to stop.

GameSpot Trax kept tabs on the buzz in the hardcore gamer community be monitoring the interests of the 20 million monthly visitors to its game web sites. It found that the most-anticipated titles were *Madden NFL 06* from Electronic Arts, *Perfect Dark Zero*, *Project Gotham Racing 3*, *Call of Duty 2*, and Sega's *Condemned: Criminal Origins*. But GameSpot found no title was emerging as the *Halo* of the launch. CliffyB, who wanted to make that game, was still hard at work on *Gears of War* and it would be months before he was done.

"The wild card is whether consumers are really going to come out in the holidays for the Xbox 360 or just wait for Sony next year," said David Cole an analyst at market researcher DFC Intelligence.[1]

Just a few days before the launch, Robbie Bach stopped in for a visit at the Mountain View campus. He reiterated his guidance on the launch, but admitted that forecasting sales was challenging.

"What you have to recognize is, nobody has done what we are doing," he said. "This is the first time anyone has done a three-territory launch in the same holiday. We are well-prepared for it. Everything is going exactly as we planned it. But, the first time is the first time. That makes forecasting a little bit challenging."[2]

Bach said he had decided to avoid the Zero Hour launch event in the California desert. "I'm nowhere near cool enough to go," he said. Instead, he would accompany Bill Gates and attend a midnight launch at a Best Buy store in Bellevue, Washington.

1. Dean & Nooch on Gaming, Nov. 14, 2005, http://blogs.mercurynews.com/aei/2005/11/feature_story_m.html.

2. Dean & Nooch on Gaming, Nov. 26, 2005, http://blogs.mercurynews.com/aei/2005/11/an_interview_wi.html.

CHAPTER FORTY-NINE

ZERO HOUR

Mahdi Ashktorab, a freshman at De Anza College in Cupertino, California, signed up for the "Zero Hour" contest on **Xbox.com**. When he checked his e-mail, the 18-year-old from San Jose was shocked to discover that he had won a free Xbox 360 and two tickets to attend the event in the desert. He called up his friend, Shayan Khales, another 18-year-old San Jose resident attending Santa Clara University. They fit squarely in the hardcore gamer demographic that would jump at the chance to spend money on the Xbox 360.

"I got two tickets to Zero Hour and you're going," Ashktorab said. Khales dropped the pizza he was eating and said, "Wow!" Khales told all his friends. They didn't believe him until he showed them the invitation.

They had a tough time convincing their parents that it would be okay to drive five hours to attend an event that their parents just couldn't grasp. It was even worth skipping a couple of days of college. The generation gap had never been wider.

"An experience like this is once in a lifetime," Ashktorab. "They didn't understand why we would drive 40 miles to go to a gaming event. We're going to stay up for the entire 30 hours."

The young men were so eager that they drove the long trek and arrived two hours early for the event and about 32 hours before the consoles went on sale at midnight, eastern time, on Nov. 22. As they arrived at the edge of Palmdale, they headed west into the Mojave Desert. Five miles later, they could see the giant twin aircraft hangars rising in the distance, looking like ancient Greek temples from afar. Rows of search lights were mounted around the 200,000-square-feet buildings, which were both bigger than the factory where Flextronics was building the Xbox 360. As Microsoft marketing guy David Reid had planned, it was a place that was hard to get to. Only the craziest of fans would make this journey.

The acid green sign out front said, "U R Here." It was classic UFO-style speak. Security was tight. They passed three guard checkpoints on the way in. A K-9 dog was sniffing backpacks. Rows of portable bathrooms bore signs that warned visitors to beware of snakes and other hazards in the high desert. At 6 pm, the guards allowed the crowd into the compound, but the doors of the hangars remained closed. As the sky dimmed, the search lights came on, bathing the buildings in an eerie green light. The glow could be seen from miles around. Inside, the gamers found all the conveniences they could ask for: sweatshirts to keep them warm in the cold desert air, a cafeteria, a bar where those 18 and older could buy alcohol, and blaring loud rock and hip-hop music. Microsoft had built a couple of white dome tents where it was handing out memory cards for Xbox Live accounts. That way, the gamers could play online games that evening and keep the same accounts once they went home.

Shayan Khales, left, and Mahdi Ashktorab waiting for the Zero Hour hangar door to open.

The crowd of gamers looked small compared to the giant buildings. They sat on white bean bags that Microsoft handed out. Sitting on his bag, Ashktorab said he had put $300 down on a console pre-order in June, and he planned to spend $650 altogether. He had been a big fan of *Halo 2* and *Project Gotham Racing 2*. Of the Xbox 360, he said, "I like how it's more geared to the community. Bigger hard drive. You can choose your music. It's meant for you." It was like the words tossed about in the Xe 30 planning meetings from 2003.

The crowd hailed from 20 different countries, showing the vast cross section of humanity that was dedicated to games. Sure, it was mostly young men. But some of these folks were out of the ordinary. Zachary Jones, a 23-year-old genetic engineering student from Edwardsville, Ill., sported red-and-black dyed hair. Jones had been drinking Mountain Dew like crazy just to get a chance to enter a contest to win a free Xbox 360. He was even looking through garbage for old cans. But he won his ticket through the Hex168 contest after he submitted a picture of himself in a clown outfit. Jones got an Xbox 360 in the mail and had already played through a test version of *Kameo* in just 16 hours. Now he wanted to get his hands on *Perfect Dark Zero*.

As the beginning of Zero Hour approached, a Taiko drummer group marched to the front of the huge sliding door of the hangar. The drummers banged away and the gamers cheered. They started throwing around huge white bean bags they had been sitting on. Peter Moore and J Allard, the Microsoft bigwigs at the event, climbed up on the steps of a big lighting rig and preached to the gathering.

"Who is ready for Xbox 360?" said Allard, his voice booming from the speakers. The crowd cheered. "Who is ready for free bean bags?" More cheers. Moore said, "This is the culmination of three years of work by thousands of people." Then the big doors opened and bright green and white lights beamed out of the hangar. The sign revealed said, "Jump in." A banner with a giant Xbox 360 standing vertically hung from the ceiling.

The glowing Zero Hour hangar was visible from miles away.

The crowd rushed in like the Greeks rushing into Troy. But some of them took the time to shake the hands of the Microsoft executives. They even posed for pictures with them and asked for autographs. Like water rushing to fill an empty space, the gamers dispersed through the hangar to all of the hundreds of waiting Xbox 360 machines, each attached to a monitor or flat-panel TV. The glare of green lights was everywhere. Huge screens hung from scaffolds. At the far end was a stage, surrounded by silver metal bleachers. The music from the ubiquitous speakers was deafening, but most of the gamers only paid attention to the sounds coming from their own TVs as they played their games to exhaustion.

Microsoft's PR team was busy matching journalists up with gamers. They led one off to a guarded hallway, which led into a place called "The Green Room." Inside, it was incredibly silent compared to the noisy floor. Peter Moore was dressed in jeans and a T-shirt that said, "I'm a legend in Japan." He was pleased with the venue, which he said was "accessible but required a journey that was like a pilgrimage." The event was a cross between the X-Files and Burning Man, a present for gamers.

"We thought about doing a celebrity event," he said. "But this is giving back to the community. The return on investment is out of whack here, but the good will isn't something you can measure."

Moore said Zero Hour was the reward of the Hex168 campaign in the U.S. Those who played had to figure out trivia questions such as what was the last line of the book *Opening the Xbox*. Winners included fans of the <u>OrigenXbox360.com</u> viral marketing campaign, which AKQA staged. In that European campaign, fans tuned into a web site show that featured talking rabbits Boss and Didier. Those who played the campaign and answered its trivia questions enjoyed an inside joke. At Zero Hour, they were the only ones who understood why live bunnies nibbled at grass at a tree inside the hall.

(Left) Peter Moore in the Green Room. (Right) J Allard was the man of Zero Hour.

The gamers at the event would be among the first to buy boxes because Best Buy had moved a temporary store with cash registers into the hangar. Moore said the execution was "flawless." But he was sorry about the console shortage and denied that it was deliberately planned to raise the hype around the Xbox 360 to a fever pitch.

"We're attempting to go global in 18 days instead of 18 months," he said. "The pain of that is familiar to our employees who are working days and nights."

Despite the shortage, Moore said he expected to get to 10 million consoles sold before the next holiday, though he wasn't sure if it would be before Sony sold its first machine. For the moment, Moore was perfectly happy to remember the surge of humanity that heaved through the doors at the opening of Zero Hour.

Outside, volunteers such as Bill Adamec got to mill with the crowd and watch the fruits of their labor unfold. Jeff Henshaw, now the executive producer of Xbox Digital Entertainment, talked about how Microsoft had him assigned to make the Xbox 360 appeal to much broader audiences. Atop one of the scaffolds, he surveyed the crowd below and said he was a casual gamer himself. He could afford a broader look.

Henshaw had inaugurated projects that helped around the edges. J Allard suggested they go after Jeff Minter, a veteran creator of zany "light synthesizers." Barry Steinglass, a member of Allard's team, got Minter to create a new visualizer, dubbed *Neon*, for the Xbox 360. The software created 3-D animations that pulsated to the beat of the music, and it was intended to create disco-like effects for parties.

A sea of humanity jumps in.

This time, he was glad that Xbox Live Arcade was integrated into the system, as were a bunch of other functions. He said that it would have been nice to add wireless WiFi connectivity but it was just too expensive. Asked if it made sense to put all of Windows or the Windows Media Player into it this time, he said only the things relevant to entertainment were considered. "If it was productivity, it stays on the PC," he said.

Would the presence of other entertainment on the platform make gaming more acceptable itself as an entertainment art form? He said, "That perception of gaming is happening naturally in the industry. *Halo* 2 has eclipsed the revenues of film hits. It brings credibility to the game industry. It helps us convince the critics that gaming is an art form, and it's tier one."

Cortland Klein, 18, of San Jose, and his friend Ben Daviela, 20, of Tracy, showed up late on Monday to check out the scene. They drove hundreds of miles to get to the event. "My parents know I'm on a road trip, but they didn't know it was for video games," Daviela said. Klein, a student at De Anza College, said that he was a huge *Halo* 2 fan and manages to squeeze out about five hours of gaming per week. He was looking at titles like *Gun* and *Quake 4*, but he didn't plan on buying a console yet. His friend, Daviela, was trying to get Klein to take the plunge. But neither of them had the money to plunge in just yet. "If they were selling *Halo 3* today, it would be flying off the shelf," Daviela said. "I don't make enough money." They weren't happy that each game would cost $59.99, instead of the usual $49.99.

Mahdi Ashktorab and Shayan Khales were still going strong more than 24 hours into the event. Carrying bean bags, they cheerfully noted they had about four hours of sleep in the car. The music kept them up, but it quieted down around 4 am, only to start up again at 6 am. Shayan said he had set the world record for a race in *Project Gotham Racing 3*. For a day, he said, his record would stand. "I spent more than $730," Ashktorab said. "Now I'm broke." Zachary Jones from Illinois said that he hadn't slept at all.

Saul Augustine, 21, of Union City, and his brother, Eric Augustine, 18, of Modesto, were briefly in the limelight. They both got to go up on the big stage and play in the finals of *Call of Duty 2* multiplayer. They fragged each other and fought fiercely. Saul came in fourth and Eric took second. They slept on the floor and had about one or two hours of sleep. Eric said he was going to buy an Xbox 360, but Saul needed to save up more money for it.

Everyone in line had a good story about their trip. Chelsea Clapper, 21, a nursing student from Orange, California, was the first woman in line. She came with her boyfriend and was running on four hours of sleep. She said she wasn't a big game fan but was willing to wait in line to buy her cousin a box. But she said she liked the various fighting and shooting games that she played with her boyfriend during the 30-hour event. Microsoft's hope is that the Xbox 360 will appeal to consumers beyond the typical young male stereotype. That's why it put in the music and photo features that appealed to Clapper. She was glad, for instance, that her boyfriend would be able to get rid of the DVD player since the Xbox 360 had one built in.

"This is a fun experience," she said. "I've been sending camera phone pictures home."

Rob and Mindy Cassingham came from Moab, Utah. They own a video game center where kids can play on networked machines. They carried "Xbox" license plates around their necks. They were picking up two machines and then were going back to get four more in nearby Grand Junction.

"We're going to have a corner on the market in our town, ha ha ha," said Rob Cassingham, 41. "Kaching!"

"Yeah," said Mindy Cassingham, 38. "We're here doing our market research." The reason they said they were so excited about gaming, despite being older gamers, was that they see games as a great social bridge. "You get kids that play together who would never otherwise make friendships," Mindy Cassingham said.

As the appointed hour for sales approached, the gamers began lining up. The line snaked all the way to the door. A phalanx of security lined the route to the cash registers. The first two guys in line were told that a couple of special guests would get the first machines. But these "special guests" weren't celebrities. They were just two guys from Mississippi who drove for 35 hours straight to get there.

A rapper named Tommy the Clown brought the two men up on the nearby stage. The lucky men were Edgar Bounds and Mike Dedwiler of Senatobia, Mississippi. Bounds, 20, and Dedwiler, 19, drove 1,800 miles to get to the event, only to get there 24 hours early. They killed time by driving out to the ocean to see it for 20 minutes. For their enthusiasm, the Best Buy manager agreed to let them get the first boxes. Tommy the Clown asked them who was the better gamer, and the pair bickered on stage. Then a big clock appeared and started counting down the time with 354 seconds to go. The big hangar doors opened and three Best Buy trucks drove in with a police escort. The green lights start flashing and the crowd was chanting. The security force cleared everyone out of the way. "Can we get the media out of here?" asked one security officer. TV cameras started rolling and cheers went up wherever they focused. Music was blasting out of the speakers the entire time.

Gamers looked in awe when the truck doors opened.

The Best Buy employees flung open the doors of the trucks, revealing the first of the 3,000 consoles. At 9 pm Pacific Time, Tom Narr, the district manager for Best Buy, handed over the consoles to the two men.

"We're going to play it right away," said Bounds, who said he'd figure out how to do that even though home was 35 hours away. "It was crazy."

It wasn't exactly a flawless launch. One worker untied the ropes securing the boxes and a bunch of machines fell down and hit the floor. Norm Edwards, a 33-

year-old electrician from Brentwood in Northern California, was the third to get his machine. Narr apologized for allowing the two guys from Mississippi to cut in line. Edwards had staked out a spot in line eight hours earlier. He spent a week's worth of pay on his console, and he already had six games waiting at home.

"I was all played out," said Edwards, who came at the invitation of his friend Mike Henriquez, a 36-year-old student at the Academy of Art College in San Francisco. Henriquez, an Antioch resident who wanted to be a game designer, said he enjoyed waiting in line and making friends. Both men were bleary-eyed after about 90 minutes of sleep inside the loud hangar.

"This is about being the first on your block to have one," Henriquez said. "We wanted to have the new toy, the first on our block so we could have everybody over. We have high-definition TVs and we want to show them off."

Most of the people who came to the event didn't really care that it was a staged marketing event from start to finish, even down to the point where the first two purchasers were allowed to cut in line ahead of hundreds of others. To the gamers, it was *the* cultural event, *the* place to be recognized as the coolest person with the hottest gadget.

Norm Edwards gets an Xbox 360 from Best Buy's Tom Narr.

Mahdi Asktorab of San Jose grabbed his machine and games, for which he paid $730. Asked how it felt after nearly 30 hours of waiting, he said, "Heavy," referring to the weight of the box. His friend, Shayan Khales added, "I didn't think it would be this heavy." Asked if he was tired, Khales said, "I do this all the time." The two young men picked up their white bean bags and dragged them outside for the 400-mile trek home. They didn't have anything more philosophical to say. It was, after all, just a console launch. Oddly enough, 500 extra boxes remained. Some of the Zero Hour gamers didn't show up, some didn't have the cash, and

some just couldn't make it to the finish line. The Best Buy employees asked if they could buy some of the leftovers, as did the journalists and the PR people attending the event. If only the happiness that Microsoft created within that hangar could be repeated across the rest of the world, the 360 would rule.

Shayan Khales & Mahdi Ashktorab show off their reward for spending 30 hours at Zero Hour.

CHAPTER FIFTY

EXECUTION

*R*obbie Bach went to the Best Buy store in Bellevue, Washington, on the night of the Xbox 360 launch. He watched Bill Gates banter with gamers and hand over the first box at the stroke of 9 pm Pacific Time.

Gates gave the first box to Dan Friedman, a 26-year-old programmer from Microsoft's server & tools division. He had waited almost four days. One journalist said that Friedman "hammed it up for the media" as if he were a prize fighter.

"I just want my Xbox!" he yelled upon entering the store. [1]

Gates played a round of *Project Gotham Racing 3* against 26-year-old Isaias Formacio of Bellevue.

"I felt it was like the end of the beginning," Bach said. "It was a feeling of excitement, relief. I felt we were in very good shape. Now we were ready to go. To me, it is super personally satisfying."

The Best Buy store sold more than 275 boxes, many of them to Microsoft employees such as Friedman.

Bach went to an after-party and then called it a night at midnight. He had TV appearances and media phone calls scheduled, starting at 8 am the next morning. That night, Reuters reported that gamers camped out in front of stores. They endured dense fog in Seattle and rain in Manhattan. [2]

"I feel amazing," said Peter Gonzalez, a 19-year-old from Manhattan who waited 30 hours at a Best Buy store. He said he would go home and play games until he had to attend classes the next morning.

But across North America, a big shortage was brewing. Gamers lined up by the dozens at every store that advertised a midnight launch. Best Buy was Microsoft's key retail partner, but even some of its stores didn't have many boxes on hand. Many Circuit City stores had scores of people camping out overnight, even though they only had about 25 boxes each. A Wal-Mart in Lynnwood, Washington, had 14 boxes. These stores sold out instantaneously. [3]

Felix Dalldorf, a 49-year-old San Jose resident, went to a Wal-Mart store in the morning of the launch, only to find the consoles sold out. He visited store after store.

"It's certainly not the way I want to spend the holidays, but when you have kids you have no choice," Dalldorf said.

Although Microsoft had first promised them regular shipments, retailers had no clue when they would get their next supplies. BAX Global was sending dozens of loaded 747 cargo planes with Xbox 360s. Some of the flights had to be scheduled at the last minute, costing Microsoft a fortune in air freight. Stories began to surface accusing Microsoft of intentionally creating an artificial shortage so that it could stoke demand hysteria. John Taylor, an analyst at Arcadia Investment Corp. in Portland, estimated Microsoft might sell about 800,000 units. He didn't think it was intentional.

Bill Gates played some Project Gotham Racing 3 before the countdown.

Some store managers handed out vouchers so that the customers could go home and arrive the next morning to claim their machines. Best Buy managers in some cities handed out notices to those lined up that said customers had to buy at least $700 worth of non-returnable merchandise to get a machine, even though the chain's advertising had not mentioned any such requirement. The chain eventually had to issue an apology to those who felt cheated.

Within a week or so, eBay CEO Meg Whitman said that more than 40,000 Xbox 360s sold on eBay. Many machines went for over $1,000. One market research firm got its hands on an Xbox 360 via eBay and proceeded to tear it apart. Chris Crotty, an analyst at iSuppli, said the firm concluded that Microsoft was spending about $553 for fully assembled Xbox 360s. That meant it was losing

$153 on each machine with a hard disk, without factoring in marketing costs. That compared to an estimated $168 a box over the life of the Xbox. Microsoft insiders said the estimate was high, since there was no way, as iSuppli had estimated, that ATI was getting $141 for its graphics chip and IBM was getting $106 for its microprocessor.

The Xbox 360 had indeed become a part of pop culture, but not always in the light that Microsoft wanted. One Internet troubadour even wrote a song, to the tune of *Arthur's Song*, about the Xbox 360 shortage. The song included a satirical threat to kill a Microsoft executive. In Toronto, an art house opened an exhibit entitled *Play: The Art of the Xbox 360*. National Public Radio said the Xbox 360 was worth the $400, if you were a hardcore gamer. An Xbox 360 TV ad that Microsoft decided not to release made its way around the Internet. In the ad, strangers in a subway station point their trigger fingers at each other and pretend to fire, igniting a fake massacre. In an age of terrorist attacks, Microsoft decided it wasn't funny.

The first machines were like status symbols.

Some of the customers lucky enough to get their hands on a console found, when they got home, that their machines didn't work. The blinking red lights on the "ring of light" helped to decode some of the error messages. But numerous examples of overheated consoles surfaced. Molly O'Donnell, a spokeswoman for Microsoft, said the company had received isolated reports. Microsoft said the "vast majority of Xbox 360 owners are having an outstanding experience with their new systems," and the return rate was within the industry average of 3 percent to 5 percent. The company directed people to its 800-number and noted on its support site that owners shouldn't put the console on a plush rug or keep it in a tight compartment without air circulation. Microsoft paid for shipping on both ends and said that each incident would be handled case-by-case.

Microsoft also got some bad press because of the size of the power brick. It had never highlighted the size of the brick, literally the size of a real brick, in any press before the launch. Hence, consumers went on and on about the "rude surprise".

Quality problems surfaced. Some gamers reported that some games, such as *Perfect Dark Zero* or *Project Gotham Racing 3*, would crash. While the problems may have been small, they were amplified in the age of blogging and the Internet. Even as Microsoft denied the reports, dozens of people would post their troubles on **Xbox.com** forums and other places. These reports may well have scared off buyers who were reluctant to brave the crowds in the first place. To the Japanese gamers, the problems sounded as horrifying as "scratch gate" did, so many years ago. In fact, if someone turned an Xbox 360 while it was on, it could scratch the spinning disks with a grinding noise. Microsoft's engineers had not considered the fact that the DVD was spinning at a much faster speed than the previous Xbox. They had to start working on a fix.

Chris Szarek, a 37-year-old imaging specialist in Chicopee, Mass., ordered his Xbox 360 in August, 2005, from EB Games. He wasn't able to pick up the unit until Dec. 23, a full month after the launch. He thought it was an awesome machine. It worked until 28 days later, when the "ring of light" turned into "the three red lights of death."

He returned it to Microsoft and received a replacement, only to discover his new Xbox 360 wouldn't connect to Xbox Live. He complained and said he received poor service from Microsoft, including a two-week gap with no response at all. He eventually received both a free copy of *Kameo: Elements of Power*, and a promise of a quick repair turnaround. He read an interview with Peter Moore about the company's great customer service and that the launch problems were being "blown out of proportion by about 12 people on the Internet." Steamed, Szarek sent messages to Mike Snider, a reporter at *USA Today*, and Matthew Yi, a reporter at the *San Francisco Chronicle*. That prompted a quick reply from Microsoft's PR people, who said that customer satisfaction was their highest priority. Szarek complained of Microsoft's "lousy, horrible, disgusting" service, and even got in an argument on the forums with Larry "Major Nelson" Hyrb. The company told him it had a problem with its repair center in Texas. It sent him a free wireless controller and gave him a free month of Xbox Live service.

"It really pained me to see my favorite gaming company act like this," he said. "But I had no intention of being taken for a ride by any company that I have supported with literally thousands of dollars in purchases over the years."

Hyrb tried to be the friendly face of Microsoft. He was tracking the problems with the returns and reporting what he found. There were "small numbers of units being returned," he said. "I monitored and shared that. If a person was having a problem, we would get them support. Every person who is at home and

playing games – you don't hear from them."

Despite the shortage and the quality problems, the launch was a cultural event of the digital age. Most of those who took their consoles home were happy with the games for a while. But even with 18 games on the market at launch and many more by the end of the holidays, the hardcore gamers inevitably blazed through their games and wondered what was next. Some of them started turning to Xbox Live Arcade as they waited for more games to come out.

Microsoft tried to counter the bad press with its own good news. Most people seemed happy with the games, particularly *Call of Duty 2*. But with the basketball games, they saw flaws. While the players looked real, they didn't move realistically. Loyd Case, editor-in-chief of ExtremeTech.com, said, "As graphics get better, a person's eyes move to the next area that doesn't look right."

Microsoft said more than half of those who bought early machines were plugging them into the free Xbox Live Silver Edition. And more than 90 percent of those who bought one said that they wanted to buy a high-definition TV set.

Even though it couldn't supply enough consoles for the U.S. market, Microsoft followed through with its December 2 launch in Europe. Mitch Koch, head of sales and marketing at the Xbox division, said that it was important, for the long term, to make sure no one felt like a second-class citizen. As a result, Microsoft's shortage was doomed to disappoint consumers in all the regions. The company managed to get an estimated 300,000 units over to stores in Europe for the launch. It shipped another 200,000 units by the end of the holidays.

The launch in Europe went off well in 16 different countries. Chart Track reported that the 360 was the fastest-selling home console ever in the United Kingdom. Premium editions outsold the core version 2 to 1. Of the 15 launch titles for the region, 10 were on the top 40 list for UK sales for all formats. [4]

Kevin Sage, 33, of London, stayed in line from early afternoon the night before at a GAME store. "I will remember this for the rest of my life," he said. [5]

Japan was another story, as sales began on December 10. Microsoft primed the launch with the opening of an Xbox 360 lounge in Tokyo. The three-story building was the place where fans could go to see the launch titles and play them before buying.

The launch began on a Saturday morning, 18 days after the North American debut. It took place on the same spot where the original Xbox debuted: the first floor of the Tsutaya store in the Shibuya district of Tokyo, a central nexus of the region's subway system. About 250 devoted fans showed up the night before. They wore Xbox Live hats and game gear. They cheered Peter Moore and Yoshihiro Maruyama as they arrived. The store started a counter at 360 seconds before launch and the crowd counted down. A 22-year-old film maker scored the first box, handed to him by one of the "hot babes" that the IGN reporter was admiring.

Some people lined up at some stores in Tokyo overnight. But bloggers and journalists on site took numerous pictures of Xbox 360s sitting piled up in a lot of stores. IGN reported that one Shinjuku store drew only 65 fans, compared to

1,200 people for the PSP launch in December, 2004. *Famitsu* magazine reported in a survey that Microsoft sold only 62,000 consoles over two days in Japan, less than half of the 159,000 consoles it had in stock. It was less than half the 123,000 original Xbox units Microsoft sold over three days in February, 2002. Microsoft had only six Xbox 360 titles ready the week of the release, compared with twelve for the original Xbox.

"There is just one reasons for the slow sales – the postponement of the launch of the *Dead or Alive 4* game," said Munetatsu Matsui, editor-in-chief of *Famitsu Xbox 360*. [6] The magazine's survey said that 61.5 percent of readers surveyed said they would buy that game. The most popular titles in Japan were Namco's *Ridge Racer 6* and Microsoft's *Perfect Dark Zero*. But the bad launch was what the media focused on. Despite all of the care it took in the industrial design process, the heavy investment it had made into the Japanese games, the care toward regional fairness in the worldwide launch, Japan was an unmitigated disaster once again.

Reggie Fils-Aime, Nintendo's executive vice president of marketing, said he didn't wish to offend his friends at Microsoft. But he said that the shortage of units worldwide was a "massive miscalculation." He said the lack of games for the Japanese market was unforgivable. And he said that it made no sense to have units piling up in Japan while gamers elsewhere were screaming for boxes.

Peter Moore said, "In a perfect world, *Ninety-Nine Nights* and *DOA4* would have showed up at launch. They didn't quite make it. We won't force something to meet a date. In the case of *DOA4*, it was 19 days later. That hurt us quite a bit. It's a marathon, not a sprint over there. There are good games in the pipeline."

But as sales slowed and Microsoft's consoles started piling up in stores, Japanese game publishers started to worry. An executive at one major Japanese game publisher said, "Maybe we won't do any more games for it. They should have waited to launch when better games were ready. Everything was fine except the launch strategy. Now, no one wants to buy the machine."

It wasn't that Japanese gamers were fickle. They came out in force to buy the Nintendo DS and the Sony PlayStation Portable. Nintendo had huge hits with games such as *Brain Age* and *Nintendogs*. Thanks to the growth in the portable game devices, Japan's game market grew for the first time in years. Hardware sales rose 47 percent in Japan in 2005, according to *Famitsu* magazine. The DS sold more than 4 million units in Japan, taking 40 percent of total hardware unit sales. DS games accounted for six of the top ten games of 2005. The Sony PSP, meanwhile, sold 2 million units. By the end of the year, Microsoft sold an estimated 107,800 Xbox 360s, with less than a game per box sold. The top-selling 360 game, *Ridge Racer 6*, sold a pitiful 29,891 units.

Most of Microsoft's brass refused to acknowledge that anything was going wrong. Greg Gibson, the system designer, said that a shortage was a good problem to have considering all the other things that could go wrong. Todd Holmdahl said there were component shortages but overall the launch went more smoothly than last time.

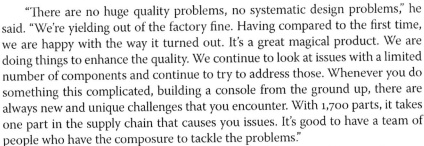

"There are no huge quality problems, no systematic design problems," he said. "We're yielding out of the factory fine. Having compared to the first time, we are happy with the way it turned out. It's a great magical product. We are doing things to enhance the quality. We continue to look at issues with a limited number of components and continue to try to address those. Whenever you do something this complicated, building a console from the ground up, there are always new and unique challenges that you encounter. With 1,700 parts, it takes one part in the supply chain that causes you issues. It's good to have a team of people who have the composure to tackle the problems."

But Leslie Leland, the director of hardware evaluation, said she wept because of the shortage.

"People stood in line for hours and couldn't get their boxes," she said. "One saw my name on a blog and called me. I thought the overall quality was good. But then one person stands in the snow, brings it home and it doesn't work. I stood with Todd one day and I said, 'I feel terrible.' He said, 'Yeah, I feel terrible.'"

She said, "We would dwell on the one person who couldn't get it. We didn't realize the demand would be like that, in the millions. People got tickets to get one. That disappointment is real."

Stepping back, Leland said, "We're perfectionists, me and Todd and Greg. Super-critical. It's never good enough. You always want to do better. You look at yields and want to get them up. It took people showing me the good press and good reviews. We wanted this out in August with so many million units. We had expectations of making it work, making trade-offs, setting up the factories. We're still working to get optimum yields. You are so close to the product, but I'm now appreciating what we've done. November and December were tough."

In December, Robbie Bach announced the series of executive reassignments that followed his own promotion in September. He made Xbox finance chief Bryan Lee into the leader of a new non-gaming entertainment business, including video. J Allard was promoted to what could be described as a chief technology officer for the broader Entertainment and Devices Group. Mitch Koch would run retail for the whole group. And Peter Moore was put in charge of the Xbox business and Windows games. Todd Holmdahl assumed J Allard's role as the head of the Xbox platform. Larry Yang stepped into Holmdahl's job as head of hardware. Bill Adamec moved into the job as head of the semiconductor group in Mountain View, California. Many of the team members took long-needed vacations. Yang left for a sabbatical. Nick Baker took off for a skiing vacation up in the Sierra Nevada Mountains.

Bach explained the set of moves. "Peter is not chief Xbox officer because his business is bigger than the Xbox, with games for Windows and casual games on MSN. We had our last meeting in December, and now we'll meet once a month instead of once a week. That's now Peter's weekly Xbox meeting, and I don't attend. Peter has been in games for a long time. He has the right blend of gaming, marketing, sales, and business management aptitude."

Retailers were furious about the shortage, but they didn't point fingers at

Microsoft publicly. Still, Hal Halpin, then-president of the game retail group, the Interactive Entertainment Merchants Association, said that the shortage caused a big strain between retailers and Microsoft. David Reid, director of Xbox 360 marketing, tried to put the "failure" in perspective.

"We still have the fastest-selling console ever," Reid said. Peter Moore acknowledged, "If we knew how hard the global launch might be, we might not have done it." But he had no regrets about trying.

The last shoe to drop from the launch shortage was worse-than-expected financial results for video game publishers. Electronic Arts was the first to declare in December that its sales were tanking. Larry Probst said that sales of current-generation titles were drying up as gamers saved their money to buy an Xbox 360. But because the new console wasn't available, the gamers just sat on the sidelines during the holidays. The rest of the game companies, from Midway to Activision, would suffer similarly poor financial results. And they would lay off hundreds of employees collectively.

"If history teaches us anything, there are always glitches," said Probst. "None of the companies ever satisfy initial demand."

1. "Todd Bishop's Microsoft blog," Seattle Post-Intelligencer, http://blog.seattlepi. nwsource.com/microsoft/archives/100596.asp

2. "Microsoft's Xbox 360 Debuts In North America," by Nicole Maestri and Reed Stevenson, Reuters, Nov. 22, 2005.

3. "Musical Chairs For the Xbox 360 Will Leave Many Standing," by Kristen Millares and Todd Bishop, Seattle Post-Intelligencer, Nov. 22, 2005.

4. "360 Blitzes Europe," by Brendan Sinclair, GameSpot, Dec. 6, 2005, http://www. gamespot.com/xbox360/driving/projectgothamracing3/news.html?sid=6140803

5. "Xbox 360 Takes Europe by Storm," Xbox365.com, Dec. 6, 2005, http://www.xbox365. com/news.cgi?id=GGPPLLiddi12060836

6. http://news.com.com/2102-1043_3-5992548.html?tag=st.util.print

CHAPTER FIFTY-ONE

THE CONSUMER ELECTRONICS SHOW

On the eve of the 2006 International Consumer Electronics Show in Las Vegas, Microsoft Chairman Bill Gates delivered his annual keynote address. Peter Moore was there to rehearse his role in the keynote.

The crowd of 5,000 line up early outside the theater of the Las Vegas Hilton, the same stage where Robbie Bach spoke about the Xbox launch in January, 2001. They moved past the noisy rattle of the slot machines as they filed into the theater. Microsoft entertained some VIP guests and journalists in the bar next to the theater. As the lights came down, Gates mentioned that he was proud to be named, along with his wife and U2 lead singer Bono, as *Time* magazine's Persons of the Year. He painted a vision of computing in the future, bringing up familiar themes from his previous "digital decade" speeches. He gave a preview of Microsoft's Windows Vista operating system, the new version of Windows that had been years in the making.

"There are a lot of themes there," he said. "Themes of personalization, themes of empowerment, themes of everything moving to the Internet."

His demos went off without any glitches. His aide showed how he could navigate through Windows Vista with an Xbox 360 controller. The president of MTV Networks and Justin Timberlake came out to lend a little star power and talk about MTV's upcoming "Urge" music downloading service. Gates spoke about the idea of connecting a Windows Media PC to an Xbox 360. Taking a little stab at Sony, Gates noted that a Toshiba HD DVD drive would debut in March for just $499, far cheaper than the expected prices for Sony's Blu-ray drives. Then Gates said that he had spent an awful lot of time using his Xbox 360. He invited Peter Moore out on stage under the bright lights. The baton had clearly passed. Five years earlier, Robbie Bach stood on the stage with Gates. Moore spoke about all of the achievements since that time, 22 million Xboxes sold, 2 million Xbox Live subscribers, and the launch of *Halo* 2. Moore said Microsoft was moving from thought leadership

to market leadership. But he didn't mention how many Xbox 360s had sold. He simply said the console was on track to sell 4.5 million to 5.5 million units by June 30. Gamers were buying four games and three accessories for every console.

"Now, it's no secret to anybody in this room that our biggest challenge has been meeting the high consumer demand for the console," Moore said. "We are working to deliver consoles as quickly as we can manufacture them. To further bolster our capacity for output, I'm happy to announce that next month Celestica will join both Flextronics and Wistron as our third manufacturing partner. We need to meet the consumer demand worldwide, and having this ability now to do that with three manufacturing partners helps us do that."

Moore noted that more than 50 percent of console owners were connecting online. Consumers had downloaded more than 4 million items on Xbox Live Marketplace, from Xbox Live Arcade games to movie trailers. Roughly one in five people who downloaded an arcade game demo was paying money for the full game. Microsoft had staged some debut events such as downloading the trailer for the film *Mission Impossible 3*. By March, the roster of Xbox Live Arcade games would grow from 12 to 20. Then Moore said that the Xbox 360 would have an HD DVD accessory drive by the holidays. The external drive would be for movie playback only, not for storing games.

Moore closed out the appearance with a classic Las Vegas spectacle. He called on Al Bernstein, an ESPN commentator, to introduce the fighters who were about to take the stage in a demo of *Fight Night Round 3* from Electronic Arts.

"Now, I've announced a lot of fighters in my day, but none exactly like the two that I'm going to talk about right now," Bernstein said. "First of all, in this corner, playing the role of Mohammed Ali, he floats like an MSN butterfly and he stings like a bee, let's welcome back a true heavyweight, Bill Gates. Can't wait to see your style, Bill."

Then Bernstein bellowed, "Now, in this corner, playing the role of Joe Frasier, he's the sultan of security, and he's the prince of productivity, the Motor City hit man, Steve Ballmer."

Ballmer boomed, "You've got it, you've got it. C'mon, Bill, 30 years I've been training for this opportunity."

"You've got the weight on me, I give you that," Gates said.

Ballmer yelled back, "Heavyweight division!"

Bernstein interjected, "Can we have a heavyweight against a middleweight, is that possible?"

Ballmer said, "He could be a lightweight with all this weight he's been losing."

Bernstein added, "Oh, ooh, a lot of trash-talking up here."

In front of the laughing crowd, the men re-enacted the classic fight between Joe Frazier and Muhammad Ali. It was a staged fight. Gates knocked out Ballmer's fighter in the first round. The camera caught the final blow in slow motion as Frazier's face sprayed blood and hit the canvas. Ballmer threw down his controller in mock disgust.

Peter Moore stepped back to center stage and said, "Don't throw your controllers at home, please, thank you."

Gates and Ballmer retired for the evening. In an interview with reporters, they talked about how much they had been playing the Xbox 360. Giving a boost to Greg Canessa's team, Gates said he and his wife had played Xbox Live Arcade games like *Zuma* for hours and racked up loads of gamer points.

Bill Gates and Steve Ballmer slugged it out.

Talking with **News.com** reporters, the two men said they had known the console would be in short supply. Gates said, "We are shipping faster than any videogame has ever shipped. The thing is just hot, and I spent over 100 hours playing with it over Christmas. It's fantastic. And it really draws you in because you get these awards, you meet people, you get into the contests. It's something."[1]

Ballmer added, "It's accomplishing a lot of what we'd hoped to in terms of appealing to a broader demographic. We've got to make a bunch. We knew we would be in short supply, but we also knew we could build a lot. We've built a lot. We've sold a lot. We've got to keep building more and, as Bill says, we're on target for our roughly 5 million by the end of the financial year. I feel like everything is great guns on Xbox. I mean, yeah, every one we can make we're going to ship, but everything is great guns. I couldn't have laid out a much better place to be than where we are today."

Gates said, "We know what it's like to go second. We've tried that. And that was last time. Last time was very different in that, if I bought a PS2 and you bought an Xbox, we'd go to your house and play PS2, we'd go to my house and play Xbox.

"So it works, when it becomes this 'Live' thing, that you're accumulating your achievements and all that, and anybody can play with anybody. If I bought an Xbox, when you go to buy a machine – whether it's 2006, 2007 – if you want to play with me in Live, which is what the thing is all about, then you need to buy that same machine.

"So we've got that leading-edge group, most of whom won't buy two machines--some will, but they're telling their friends, look, connect up to me, and that's done with Xbox. So going first was more important in this generation than in any generation there has ever been."

Ballmer said, "The Live advantage is... there's no Sony announcement for a Live equivalent type deal. We had, if anything, a cost disadvantage last generation. If anything, depending on what they do with [Blu-Ray disc support], we're not going to have a cost disadvantage this time."

Gates added, "Have you seen the basketball game? I think it's great."

Ballmer replied, "Oh, have I seen it? Shall we say it's quite hot in the Ballmer house. My son comes up to me the other night, 'Dad, the guys start perspiring in a few minutes...just the way they're supposed to; that is really awesome, Dad.' I've got three boys, 13 on down, and unlike Xbox 1, my wife thinks it's a good addition to the house."

The next day, Howard Stringer, CEO of Sony, fired back with his own keynote speech. He invited Kaz Hirai, president of Sony's U.S. games unit, on stage. Hirai said the PlayStation 2 had topped 100 million units. He said that the PS2 had outsold the Xbox 360 during the holidays, and so did the PlayStation Portable.

"The next generation of games?" Hirai asked the crowd. "It doesn't really start until we launch it." He said the PlayStation 3 would be worth waiting for. Sony was committing billions of dollars to its launch. But he didn't mention when the PS3 would go on sale.

During the show, Peter Moore held meetings with the press. "That's the last time they can make that claim," Moore said, responding to Hirai's comment about outselling the Xbox 360. He noted that Sony was hiring network engineers in an apparent attempt to duplicate Xbox Live.

"We have a very clear strategy," Moore said. "With more social gaming, we are squarely hitting the mark." Moore said 50 games would be out by June on the Xbox 360. He said E3 would bring a half-dozen more key announcements. He said Microsoft was doing everything he could to ship more consoles.

At a luncheon at "The House of Blues" restaurant at the top the Mandalay Bay hotel, Moore insisted that everything was on track and that the Xbox 360 would be in 30 countries by the beginning of March.

"Demand is monstrous," he said. "We created a cultural phenomenon. The preorder situation at retail got ahead of itself versus what the actual allocation was. Some overstepped their allocations in accepting more preorders than they had units. We didn't tell retailers a number and then chop it back. The retailers were told a number, and it was less than what they hoped for."

This comment would upset some retailers, since they felt Microsoft had let them down and was blaming them. The same pesky reporters kept asking the same questions. Asked about overheating, Moore said, "There is no overheating." By this time, Robert Byers, a Chicago resident, had filed a class-action lawsuit

alleging that Microsoft shipped consoles that overheated and had obvious quality problems.

Asked if he found it satisfying to get up on stage with Bill and Steve, Moore smiled and said, "It's good to be on stage and talk about success, rather than promise success. When I think about success, I also think about where we will be a year from now."

Moore noted that Bach had passed on responsibility for the Xbox business. "We have rearranged the deck chairs," he said. Moore said Sony was too quiet about its own plans for launching the PlayStation 3. "They're awfully quiet about details if they are truly going to launch in the spring as they said," Moore said.

Ken Kutaragi made a rare appearance at a chip conference in San Francisco, the same place where he talked about the Emotion Engine for the PlayStation 2 in 1999. There, he talked about how the Cell microprocessor would be used in a wide array of supercomputing applications, from medical imaging machines to stock market computers. "The goal is real-time computer entertainment," he said.

But as a pack of reporters closed in, he declined to say when the PlayStation 3 would launch.

1. "Microsoft: We're in Fighting Shape," by Ina Fried and Michael Kanellos, News. com, Jan. 5, 2006, http://news.com.com/Microsoft+Were+in+fighting+shape+-+page+3/2008-1082_3-6020157-3.html?tag=st.num

CHAPTER FIFTY-TWO

WHO WILL WIN THE CONSOLE WAR?

ithin the grand console war, there were small victories. Grant Collier, the head of Infinity Ward, was ecstatic to learn that 85 percent of the early console buyers were taking home *Call of Duty 2*. He said, "We had some bets and I picked the high side of 35 percent. At 85 percent, it was beyond my wildest dreams." His company staged some parties and Collier did interviews with loads of mainstream press, including *Entertainment Tonight*, *Time*, and *Newsweek*. It was like having the *Halo* of the Xbox 360 launch. But every developer, retailer and publisher was disappointed in Microsoft's inability to make enough hardware. This lost good will would make a difference in terms of loyalty later on. How fickle would Microsoft's allies become, once Sony and Nintendo arrived?

Despite promises that the supplies would loosen up, Microsoft didn't ship as many consoles as it hoped. On January, 26, 2006, the company reported its earnings and finally disclosed just how many Xbox 360s it sold. Chris Liddell, the chief financial officer, said that Microsoft sold 1.5 million consoles by Dec. 31, 2005. In North America, Microsoft sold 900,000 units; 500,000 in Europe, and just 100,000 in Japan. In six weeks of sales, Microsoft had been able to move 300,000 consoles a week across three regions. The NPD Group calculated that Microsoft sold 607,000 Xbox 360 consoles in the U.S.

"With their brand awareness and brand equity, they could have sold much more," said Anita Frazier, an analyst at the NPD Group.

By comparison, Sony sold 1.4 million PlayStation 2s and Nintendo sold 606,000 GameCubes. It was, said analyst Michael Pachter at Wedbush Morgan, an "abysmal" number. The Home and Entertainment Division, which included the console business, lost $293 million on sales of $1.5 billion. Liddell blamed the shortage on component scarcity and said that Microsoft expected to hit 4.5 million to 5.5 million by June 30.

Even worse, the retailers said that the shortage was going to last until late spring. In January and February, sales continued to trickle in.

Retailers still couldn't keep the boxes in stock. Each store would get a few boxes a week. It wasn't until the Game Developers Conference in March that Microsoft said it finally had an inventory surge, with two or three times as many units coming out.

Fortunately for Microsoft, Sony came to the rescue with a blunder of its own. The week before the GDC in March 2006, Ken Kutaragi held an event for game developers in Japan. He announced that the PlayStation 2 had finally crossed the 100 million unit mark in sales after six years. It held an average 60 percent market share, had sold 1 billion pieces of software, and had a total of 6,732 game titles. About 41 percent of homes in Japan, and 32 percent in the U.S. had PS2 consoles. Kutaragi announced that the PlayStation Portable would get accessories such as the EyeToy camera and the Flash multimedia player. It would also cut the price for the PSP from $249 to $199.

But then Kutaragi dropped the bombshell. He apologized that the PlayStation 3 wouldn't ship in the spring of 2006. The industry ran into delays finalizing the copy protection standards for the Blu-ray high-definition storage drives. Since Blu-ray was a critical feature of the PS3, the game console was now off track. Kutaragi tried to soften the blow by saying Sony would launch worldwide in November, 2006, and begin shipping 1 million units a month. Game developers and most people in the industry weren't surprised. Larry Probst had always bet that the PlayStation 3 wouldn't debut in North America until the fall of 2006. After all, he knew that EA wasn't planning to ship games in the spring.

All of a sudden, Microsoft looked like it had a reprieve. Everybody in Redmond took a deep breath at Sony's fumble. "We've got a chance to take the lead again," said one team member. Microsoft announced that it would double or triple the number of Xbox 360s in the pipeline at the end of March. Coincidentally, that was when there was a renewed surge of interest in games coming out for the Xbox 360, said Josh Larson, director of GameSpot Trax, which tracked the "buzz" among hardcore gamers.

While Sony put the best face on the news, it was a PR disaster and it disappointed consumers. Analysts at Merrill Lynch estimated that the PlayStation 3 would cost Sony $900 to manufacture, mainly because of the high costs of the Blu-ray drives. David Carey, an analyst at Portelligent who specialized in hardware cost estimates, doubted that the Merrill Lynch figure was accurate. It was too high, he thought. Still, Sony would have a tough time knocking out costs. Kutaragi said that a hard disk drive would be required. But the next week, at the Game Developers Conference, Phil Harrison, executive vice president at Sony's worldwide studios, declined to confirm that. Later, a Sony engineer said that they weren't sure a hard disk would be on every machine because Sony was trying to cost reduce the box. Delaying the launch until the fall gave Sony a chance to cut the costs further, but the reality was that Blu-ray was a colossal risk.

Consider this calculation. If Sony lost $400 per machine at the outset, and it lost an average of, say, $200 per machine over the life of the product, then the losses on 100 million consoles sold would be $20 billion before marketing costs. If Sony sold 1 billion games, and made $10 per game, then it would make $10 billion in revenues. The net loss on such a product would climb above $10 billion. That is more than Sony's cash hoard. No one can afford to make such a mistake, not even an electronics giant.

There was also some doubt about Sony's HD strategy. Bob O'Donnell, an analyst at International Data Corp., really wondered if Sony needed to target the highest HD resolution with the PlayStation 3 and include the Blu-ray on every machine.

"If you have a 42-inch TV and you watch it from ten feet away on the resolution that Microsoft used, you wouldn't be able to tell the difference from the resolution that Sony targeted," he said. "And would you buy a $600 console just because it had a Blu-ray drive? I don't think so."

At the GDC, it was apparent that Sony was chasing Microsoft's leadership in at least one respect. It announced the PlayStation Network, an online gaming service that would enable consumers to shop online, browse trailers, download demos, or enjoy episodic content. The plan was a clone of the Xbox Live service, except for the part where Sony said it would not charge for multiplayer gaming. In fact, Sony executives sat in on a session at the GDC where James Miller described the initial success with Xbox Live Marketplace. Miller said that there were more than 10 million downloads, including 3 million downloads of Xbox Live Arcade games. About 20 percent of those gamers were actually buying the games for about $3 a piece. That added up to about $1.8 million in revenue for Microsoft. Overall, that cut the loss per console by maybe a dollar. It wasn't much, but it was at least the beginning of an important new revenue source.

Phil Harrison appreciated that as he sat in on Miller's presentation. Later, he said, "With all due respect to our friends in Redmond, they didn't invent the online market place either. To say that we're copying them is like saying that one racing game copies another because they're both racing games." Sony was indeed following Microsoft's lead. But Harrison had one good point. It was easier to duplicate a software service such as Xbox Live than it was to launch a leading edge console with the best games. If Sony preserved its advantage on the latter two, then it would still win the war.

While no one was really surprised at Sony's delay, consumers weren't happy. The risk for Sony was that some might conclude that it wasn't worth the wait. The temptation was high for gamers to buy the bird-in-the-hand instead of waiting for the PS3.

In the first quarter, Microsoft's second wave of launch titles started to hit. David Wu's *Full Auto* hit the stores in February. It sold well, but received mixed reviews. Some gamers appreciated the cool physics, but others thought the game play was repetitive. Mahdi Ashktorab, the 18-year-old student who scored an Xbox 360 at Zero Hour, said he was ecstatic with *Elder Scrolls IV: Oblivion*, which received a 95-percent ranking on Gamerankings.com. *The New York Times* wrote about the game on the cover of its *Arts* section. UbiSoft shipped *Tom Clancy's Ghost Recon 3: Advanced Warfighter* and Electronic Arts shipped

Burnout Revenge.

"With an improving supply, a significant boost in titles, and no PlayStation 3 in sight, I think spring will be really strong for the Xbox 360," said Larson.

Microsoft was now pumping out the consoles. It would probably hit the 4.5 million to 5.5 million units by June 30. That meant it might be able to sell 10 million consoles before Sony sold its first million at the end of the year. That would be a good start, but nothing more. The winner of this console war will likely sell more than 100 million units. That puts the 10 million initial units into perspective.

Moreover, thanks to the chip strategy, Microsoft would probably be able to knock its price for the premium console from $400 to $300 by the fall of 2006. At that time, Sony might be selling its console for anywhere from $400 to $600. Even at those prices, Sony might suffer some big losses on every box. The positions from the previous generation would indeed be switched if that came to pass.

Robbie Bach's plan to launch in 2005 started looking brilliant, accidentally. Microsoft would have a year to consolidate its position. Larry Probst, CEO of Electronic Arts, said that Microsoft got more of EA's development dollars – an equal amount for the first six months of the launch versus the PS3 – because it went a year earlier. If both systems launched in the same season, EA would have devoted more dollars to the PS3.

"They probably got more bandwidth out of us than if they came out at the same time as Sony," said Larry Probst.

But the more Microsoft stumbled with supply after the launch, the more publishers were motivated to move titles to the PlayStation 3. The same thing had happened with the launch of the PlayStation 2 in 2000. Publishers suddenly found it wise to diversify their line-up across a number of titles. If the publishers shifted the weight of the development resources to the PS3 now, Microsoft would feel the pain in a few years.

The wild card in the picture remained Nintendo. It was enjoying huge success with the DS handheld, which was getting a revision in the spring. But Satoru Iwata had gambled big time on the Revolution console. The machine didn't have performance that was faster than Microsoft's or Sony's, and it would display games only in analog, not high-definition digital TV. If gamers were disappointed with the graphics on the Xbox 360, what would they think of the Revolution's graphics? Probst at EA said that he didn't think Nintendo cared about market share. Consequently, EA would devote most of its development dollars to games for the PS3 and the Xbox 360.

Iwata's bet was on innovation. The Revolution's controller, which resembled a TV remote control, had been designed to appeal to non-gamers. Nintendo would have innovative games that exploited an innovative new controller on an inexpensive box. The machine would likely cost around $200 and the games around $40. Nintendo would not only hang on to the kids market with such a console, it might even win over the non-gamers. That was Iwata's grand plan.

Yet for Microsoft, the path to victory wasn't clear. Almost everybody in the industry believed that Bach and company made a huge mistake by failing to postpone the Japanese launch. They launched without their marquee games. Big titles were in the works, but the failure to sell out the paltry amount of units in Japan damaged the brand immensely. If the Japanese saw the Xbox 360 as pathetic now, they would never see it as cool. As long as Sony owned the market in Japan, Microsoft would likely never win a commanding market share in the entire market. And if it was second to Sony, then the business model wouldn't look as good. Sony's advantages in first-party manpower, brand image, and developer loyalty would eventually win out. In April, Microsoft announced more Japanese games for the console, but it was digging itself out of a huge hole.

Sony and Nintendo would continue to clean up and expand the market in the handheld space. Microsoft would likely enter the market with its own handheld, in order to peck away at its rivals' strongholds. But would gamers really buy yet another handheld when all of their friends had the other handhelds?

To really win the console war, Microsoft has to come up with better games, one observer said. At least there were good titles in the works. Larson said that by the end of March, about 51 Xbox 360 and Xbox Live Arcade titles had debuted. Another 82 were scheduled to appear throughout the rest of the year. The most-awaited titles were Epic's *Gears of War, Tom Clancy's Splinter Cell Double Agent*, and *Resident Evil 5*.

The consensus was that Microsoft had a short window of time to come up with the right games. As Sony announces its first-generation PS3 titles, Microsoft can launch its second-generation games. By the time Sony launches the PS3, Rare's *Viva Piñata* would also launch. Titles such as BioWare's *Mass Effect*, Silicon Knight's *Too Human*, Real-Time World's *Crackdown* and a sequel to *Forza Motorsport* were expected to arrive in time for the holidays. Will *Gears of War* compare favorably to Hideo Kojima's next epic on the PlayStation 3, *Metal Gear Solid 4*? Cliff Blezinski at Epic Games is flattered by that idea. And somewhere down the line, as long as Bungie stays Bungie, will come *Halo 3*.

Microsoft can't afford *Halo 3* to be the last bullet in its gun on content. Nintendo and Sony have full clips. Microsoft also can't afford to anger Bungie and squander its most important franchise.

"The gap will be a lot narrower this time," said Alex St. John, CEO of Wild Tangent and the co-creator of DirectX, the technology that led Microsoft to the games business. "It is incredible what they did the last round. They beat Nintendo, the grandfather of gaming. That's a miraculous achievement. For them to be in first place, Sony has to royally screw up."

CHAPTER FIFTY-THREE

THE FUTURE OF GAMES

Predicting the future direction of video games is not an easy task. The industry publishes thousands of games a year, each one of them taking games in a different direction, each one appealing to a different consumer. It's not even easy to get to a definition of games, which span the gamut from simple toys to complex simulations. Is it correct to say that Jordan Weisman's marketing campaigns, such as ilovebees.com, are really games?

"Games are like oxygen," Weisman says. "They are part of every activity, from reading to toys to TV to any kind of experience. That's exciting. There is a much broader platform that people can play on than just the consoles."

That is a hopeful view. There are plenty of rants about what is going wrong with games. Many veterans have become tired of seeing more of the same. Violence is still too easy to lean on as a crutch. Chris Morris, a games columnist at CNN.com, wanted to see the industry break out of its never-ending cycle of repetition, with new World War II games, *Lord of the Rings* clones, or graphically improved versions of the same old franchises. He didn't care if the consoles became the centerpiece of home entertainment. He wanted better games.

Ed Fries tried to steer Microsoft toward making games into a new art form on a brand new platform that was made for the artists. He didn't get a chance to finish that project. But when he spoke at Gamestock in 2001, he posed the eloquent questions that linger in the mind of every game creator. Who would make the Shakespearean art that would enable games to take their rightful place as the greatest form of entertainment? In the case of Fries' own career, art collided with business. Business reality won. Fries left the company and enjoyed trips around the world with his family. He dropped out of the crusade to make important games, conquer the other forms of entertainment, and win the race against Sony and Nintendo.

To the crusaders who remain, the job won't be done until games, like an ever-growing blob, flow into every nook and cranny of popular culture. Five years ago, as he was pitching the original Xbox, Seamus Blackley said that the job of taking over mass culture wasn't done until the *New York Times* ran video game reviews in its *Arts* section. Now, thanks to writers such as Seth Schiesel, the newspaper regularly runs game stories in that section alongside movie, theater, dance, and other kinds of art reviews. Blackley is now an agent at Creative Artists Agency, which packaged Peter Jackson with the *Halo* movie. He still thinks games haven't fulfilled their potential. He still wants to see the industry fulfill its promise of delivering games that can make someone cry, the same way that the finest of motion pictures can.

Life after Zero Hour?

The industry has arrived in many ways, but it has not conquered everything. Many homes still don't own a game console, but gaming is spreading to handhelds, cell phones, laptops, set-top boxes and toys. "The Sims" and "Pokemon" are in a race to be the first game franchise to sell a billion games. Nintendo and Sony measure their collective game sales in the billions of units now. Is it really so ridiculous, then, for J Allard to claim that video games will reach a billion gamers?

It is hard to believe that the games industry can grow that large in the new generation. Even if it misses that pie-in-the-sky target, the future looks bright for the Xbox 360. Doug Lowenstein, president of the Entertainment Software Association and the chief lobbyist (optimist) for the industry, believes that the progress of the games industry is inexorable. It may suffer tough times during a console transition, but at the end of every cycle, there are more people playing. As the Pong generation gets older, the non-gamers are dying off. By 2010, there

will be an estimated 75 million people in the U.S. under the age of 30. These children of the Baby Boomers will more than likely be able to understand the language of gaming.

"If you get caught up in year-to-year changes, you lose sight of where the industry is going," he said. "People become uncertain during transitions. Then, a year or two later, the growth is back at 15 percent or 20 percent a year."

The graphics of games will just keep getting better and better. Will *Gears of War* or *Killzone 2* unleash the next wave of the mass market? They will be new points on the line that stretches from Pong to the ultimate point on the horizon in terms of their ability to render completely realistic games. A good way to stir up gamers in an online forum is to take a side on whether Sony or Microsoft will deliver the first truly movie-like game. How much more movie-like will video games look on the new consoles? Where will they be in ten or twenty years? If you put 9 gigabytes of data on a DVD for an Xbox 360, or 50 gigabytes of data on a PlayStation 3's Blu-ray disk, what will you get?

Kaz Hirai, president of Sony's U.S. game division, says, "We can deliver the cutting edge. Take Gran Turismo 4. It's pretty realistic. What's missing? When the cars whiz by, there is no dirt. You can create some extra ambience, a shaft of light. Those small things. In terms of game play, you can interact with characters by looking at their facial expressions. If they are twitching and blushing, the character might be lying to you. The little things will add up to a real-life experience."

Dirt is a good place to begin thinking about this. Rendering dirt isn't an easy thing to do, given all its visual subtlety. At the 2006 Consumer Electronics Show, Sony showed demos of an off-road racing game, *Motor Storm*, for the PlayStation 3. In the trailer for the game, the dirt was flying everywhere and thick clouds of dust affected the game play by obscuring the vision of the racers who were behind the leaders. But in an actual demo of the game shown at the Game Developers Conference, observers said the dirt didn't look nearly as real. It looked like brown smoke.

David Kirk, chief scientist at Nvidia and a leading thinker on the PlayStation 3, said that the flaws in the current consoles were simply proof that the graphics chip makers had a long way to go before they ever ran out of steam. He said it would be years before graphic artists could perfect imitations of simple things such as dirt.

"There's an infinite opportunity in graphics," he said. "There's some much to do even with offline rendering in film. We can't make a picture of a person that can fool someone on the street. That's great. It gives you opportunity. These are not the last consoles that we're making."

When people try to take gaming forward into the future, they usually move a couple of steps up, one step back. Peter Molyneux, the head of Lionhead Studios in Guilford, England, has been making games for decades, and most of them, from *Black and White* to *Fable*, have sold over a million units. But sitting in the atrium of Electronic Arts' huge game studio in Redwood City, Calif., he felt small and confessed to being worried. The place, he said, looked a whole lot like a movie studio, a city unto itself.

"Game development is becoming impossibly hard," he said, with his heavy British accent. "It's getting so much harder. It's a deep act of true courage to undertake a game. Especially one that is a Triple A in its ambitions. Everything we do has to have absolute quality. Now we're thinking about next-generation games. It's about the emotion we want to give the game player and it's so much like the movies. We're giving players more and more. The next-generation is impossible. The prototypes we are doing of the human face are frightening, modeling pores on the human face and asking if it looks like it does in the movies. Does it talk like the movies? That is the price. Everything is about quality. Even with great tools, it's going to take a lot longer. I'd love to do the Star Trek Holodeck where virtual and real are indistinguishable."

After he said this, Molyneux had to scale back his own plans. His games for the fall of 2005 didn't sell as well as expected, so he had to lay off one of his three game teams at Lionhead. Then he sold his company to Microsoft in April, 2005.

Jed Lengyel was a graphics researcher who worked at Microsoft from 1995 to 2002. His fascination with graphics and photorealism led him to craft new techniques for using 3-D graphics to make things look more realistic. He shifted from research to the Xbox Advanced Technology Group to put some ideas into action, creating code that could realistically render hair, fur, and grass in Xbox video games. The code he generated appeared in games such as *Outlaw Golf* and *NFL Fever*. In those games, the grass looked as good in close-up examination as it did from far away. Lengyel's contribution to realism was just one more step in the decades-long quest to render realistic graphics. Though he left the Xbox team's Advanced Technology Group before work on the Xbox 360 got going, he unplugged from the empire and raised his daughters on a small island near Victoria, Canada. But he still dreams big dreams about games.

Lengyel recalled a famous prediction made by Pixar co-founder Alvy Ray Smith. Smith predicted that "reality begins at 80 million polygons per frame." That is, it would take that many tiny triangles in an image to fully duplicate in 3-D animation the details present in a single snapshot of reality. With his friends at LucasFilm, Smith made the calculation by taking a picture of an object, focusing in on one of the dots within it, then elbowing it up to see just how many polygons were needed to create that single dot. Then he multiplied it across the expanse of a screen. So it was a reasonable stab at how far graphics had to go. Since a second of TV has as much as 30 frames of animation, the number of polygons that a graphics engine had to generate in one second was 2.4 billion. For 60 frames a second, the speed at which the fastest games move, the number becomes 4.8 billion polygons a second.

By one measure, the Xbox 360 can render a little more than a tenth of that now, or 500 million polygons a second. That may seem like it's a long way to go, but it's really only one console generation away before we can truly appreciate digital entertainment that can fool the eye for the longest period of time, says Lengyel.

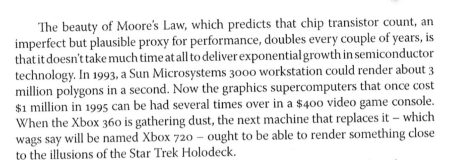

The beauty of Moore's Law, which predicts that chip transistor count, an imperfect but plausible proxy for performance, doubles every couple of years, is that it doesn't take much time at all to deliver exponential growth in semiconductor technology. In 1993, a Sun Microsystems 3000 workstation could render about 3 million polygons in a second. Now the graphics supercomputers that once cost $1 million in 1995 can be had several times over in a $400 video game console. When the Xbox 360 is gathering dust, the next machine that replaces it – which wags say will be named Xbox 720 – ought to be able to render something close to the illusions of the Star Trek Holodeck.

But the "uncanny valley" always gets in the way. Japanese robot designer Masahiro Mori raised this issue in 1970. He saw that the closer an artificial creation comes to duplicating reality, the more disturbing the emotional reaction to it. Lengyel thought of that when he saw the animated film *The Polar Express*. The characters played by Tom Hanks looked close to the real thing, but not quite. By the same token, the closer the Xbox 360 games got to the real thing, the more the flaws stood out. From 10 feet away, no one would guess that Greg Thomas' *NBA 2K6* game was an animated basket ball game. Bill Gates himself said that, "You can't tell the difference between that and a real basketball game on TV."

But to Lengyel's more discerning eye, the question was, how long could you continue to fool someone? The carefully crafted cloth uniforms swayed with the player's movements and the sweat on the players dripped progressively as they got deeper into the game and got more and more tired. But still, somehow their movements were off. The players might move too quickly or their movements might seem wooden, the results of imperfect motion capture. The players might seem real for a second. But would the illusion hold up for a minute?

Human beings are one of the hardest things to recreate. That's why John Carmack, the pioneering graphics wizard at id Software, always chose to animate demons and aliens rather than humans, since no real world comparison would expose the animation as a weak substitute. Lengyel said that the visual quality would improve as animators simulated not only the skeletons and muscles of a person, but the movement of their skin and facial expressions as well. Games also had a long way to go, in terms of reproducing the kind of huge armies that moved like individual soldiers in movies such as *The Lord of the Rings: The Return of the King*. Each soldier in the big battle scenes was programmed to behave in a random way, while in games such as Microsoft's *Kameo: The Elements of Power*, all the trolls in The Badlands seemed to move in the same way. Illusions were so much easier to pull off in movies because they could be rendered offline, whereas game graphics tend to be rendered in real-time, redrawn at 60 frames a second.

In one sense, the screens themselves are the limitations. Simply adding backlights in the form of white light-emitting diodes to flat-panel TVs could improve things by allowing for much higher contrasts between bright and shadowed parts of the screen. These improvements in TVs could make possible scenery that looked a lot more like what the eye would see when someone carried a torch into a dark tunnel, says Kaz Hashimoto, a game technology wizard.

Jim Kajiya, another Microsoft graphics researcher, thought that holographic animations were the best way to present animated illusions, as in the Star Trek Holodeck. But Lengyel thought that much more could be done with screens that had stereoscopic displays. Such screens could render a slightly different image depending on the viewing angle. Imagine that screen replacing the windshield of a car. When the driver looked at the screen, they would see controls needed to navigate the car, as well as the road in front of them. When the passenger looked at the screen, because they had a different viewing angle, they might see a completely different set of controls or, perhaps, a movie. If you took that example to the extreme, you could build a display that supported a thousand different viewing angles, creating the illusion that you were looking through a window. If something is off the screen on one side, shift your position and you'd be able to peer over to get a better look, just as you would if you were looking through a window.

"That would make it much more immersive," Lengyel said. "It would look more like a window into the world."

Indeed, the screen would be less of a barrier than a looking glass through which you could almost move. Such screens would be an enormous consumer of graphics power. It would take Smith's 80 million polygons per frame, multiplied 60 times, and multiplied a thousand fold or more to accommodate the number of viewing angles. The kind of computing power needed to render such images is far beyond what today's consoles could muster.

This is clearly where Sony and Microsoft are heading. Ken Kutaragi saw entertainment and computer colliding on a much higher level. He predicted, in a speech in early 2006, that the same Cell microprocessors inside the PlayStation 3 would one day power supercomputers running the stock market. The result of such powerful supercomputers would be real-time entertainment computing. It was pure brute force, a vision of what you could do with infinite computing power.

There are other ways to improve the illusions. Robert Garriott, president of NCSoft's North American subsidiary, liked the idea of "online invisibility." To Robert and his brother Richard, that meant that as you interacted with the characters in a game, you wouldn't know or care if it was a real person playing the character or an automated computer opponent. A great example of this is Blizzard's *World of Warcraft*, which by the spring of 2006 had snared more than 6 million people, each paying monthly subscription fees to join a fantasy role-playing world.

To others, the graphics vector didn't represent the true path for games. These folks think that the game industry has to vector in on more creativity in games. Will Wright, the creator of *The Sims* and *Sim City*, felt that there were diminishing returns for all of the investment in better graphics. He was working on *Spore*, a PC game that allowed a player to grow from a single-celled animal to a civilization that can take over the galaxy.

"It feels like a solved problem to me," he said. "Now that all games look

beautiful, we should go outside the box. Look at *Katamari Damacy* with its crappy graphics."

"The larger battle is how we make gamers out of non-gamers," he said. "We shouldn't go overboard on the hardcore gamers at the expense of the wider market that has more potential. We are painting ourselves into a corner by appealing to existing gamers. I want to design games my grandmother would play. We should do expressive, open-ended games, social games. I think what Nintendo is doing with innovative software and the controller is a noble attempt. I wish I saw more game companies fighting this battle."

He said his games have always been open ended, where gamers could lend their own creativity to the play. It is in games that people can explore what they only imagined with other kinds of storytelling. It is when gamers get to participate in the story that they truly become creators in their own right.

"The gamer's mindset – the fact that they are learning in a totally new way – means they're treating the world as a place for creation, not consumption. That is the true impact video games will have on our culture." [1]

Wright himself rarely misses with his games, and his latest creations bust open the walls of established genres and they extend a point on the line that leads not to just better graphics, but to better creativity. It is a path that is different from the one that Sony and Microsoft are marching down, and it is closer to the path Nintendo is pursuing.

"If you look at any creative work, like Lewis Carroll, they weren't just kid's books. They appealed to a wide audience. That is what made them enduring. Casting the widest possible net across age and gender. We have such established genres. If someone pitches a game, it's a first-person shooter or real-time strategy. The very first decision you make in choosing a genre feels like you have already resigned."

Games will also advance through input devices that go beyond controllers and keyboards. These could be as simple as the sword-like, remote-like controller for the upcoming Nintendo Revolution to the perfect lip-synching that was researched as "video rewrite" at Paul Allen's now-defunct Interval Research think tank in Silicon Valley. With video rewrite, you could literally put words into the mouth of John F. Kennedy that he never actually said. Smell and sounds could also be brought into the mix to improve the immersiveness of the graphics. Sony's EyeToy researcher Richard Marks contemplates new cameras that can capture many more gestures than the crude imaging system for the EyeToy games on the PlayStation 2. That could free people to really act out the fighting moves that their characters were performing in games.

For every graphics enthusiast, others are nostalgic about the old cartoon style games of the past. Nolan Bushnell, the father of video games and founder of Atari, said in a speech in 2005, "Where is the game play? I'd hate to be the marketing department saying my photorealism is better than your photorealism. Do we really want photorealism? It diminishes the potential for product differentiation. And it will increase the software costs. The blood and gore games will lose their 'cartoon defense.' If you think we've got political problems now, you'll see additional problems with photorealism. At Atari, we had a rule against violence against human beings. It wasn't moralistic. We felt it was good business to stay away from controversy."

Nintendo's Revolution will be the answer for those who think like Bushnell. Better yet, Bushnell thought that women and other non-gamers would enjoy restaurants where they could play casual games on touch screens. He called his chain the "Media Bistro."

Bushnell's chain of restaurants will be targeted at women aged 21 to 45. Bushnell figures if he can get women to come out and play video games again, the men will follow. The first 300-seat restaurant will have tables where couples can sit with two-sided touch screens. While expensive, the touch-screens are a non-intimidating user interface. Bushnell made it clear that the video game industry took wrong turns in the 80s and 90s when it focused on violent, complicated, photorealistic games. It pretty much lost women. But Bushnell thinks that casual games will lure them back.

Among the games he described was a wine-tasting game played on the touch screens. A couple can order a mystery wine and taste it. They can then vote on the characteristics of the wine and talk about their answers. Bushnell said, "The game would be submerged to the conversation." In the wine game, the couple would first see how others in the restaurant voted, then see how wine critics voted, and finally see the name and age of the wine.

How many restaurants would he open? A billion of them, he said. In that respect, the old huckster really did share a common link with J Allard. To look at the dreams of Nolan Bushnell and J Allard is to embrace the totality of games, from beginning to the end, from the light to the heavy, from Pong to the Xbox 360, from the totally creative game that comes out of the imagination, to the totally realistic one that duplicates life. It is to see the simple beginning of games and to foresee their endless march forward.

1.   Dream Machines," by Will Wright, *Wired* magazine, April, 2006.

EPILOGUE

"I haven't been disappointed," said Richard Ouellette, a 40-year-old graduate student in history in Sonoma, California "The 360 and its games look great, the wireless controller feels light and nimble, the machine is powerful. The price is right. I think Microsoft did a terrific job."

Ouellette tossed out his DVD player and was intrigued at the thought of watching DVDs with his friend in Philadelphia and talking about the movie over Xbox Live. He figured out that he could burn CDs, load them onto the 360, and listen to them on surround-sound speakers without turning on the TV.

"My wife remains uninterested in playing video games, but at least the 360 is no longer relegated to the frost of the garage," Ouellette said.

He wasn't happy with the backward compatibility on *Half-Life 2* and *Halo 2*. Glitches in those games were so annoying that he resorted to playing them on the original Xbox instead.

Ouellette had a lot of people to thank for his Xbox 360. If it weren't for Robbie Bach, he wouldn't have bought it in 2005, and if it weren't for Microsoft hardware chief Todd Holmdahl and Flextronics manufacturing executive Jim McKusker, the 360 would never have made it out of China. Ouellette can thank Nick Baker and Jeff Andrews for the machine's power. For the ability to enjoy other entertainment, he can thank people such as Jeff Henshaw, David Reid, and Joe Belfiore. His wife's tolerance of the machine's presence in the house? Well, he can thank her kind nature and the forethought of Jonathan Hayes, Don Coyner, Brett Lovelady, and the folks at Astro Studios and Hers Experimental Design Laboratory. The fact that he can play old games on the new console at all – that is the doing of Drew Solomon and his ninjas. For the fact that it exists at all, he can thank J Allard and hundreds of others on the team. For the games, he can thank Microsoft and its third party publishers.

Perhaps the Xbox 360 will be eclipsed by the PlayStation 3, which

can display games at a higher high-definition resolution than the Xbox 360 can. Or it will be eaten by its own young as Microsoft launches its third console a few short years from now. But the people who created it have made their mark. They are mostly anonymous, but they know that they helped make games move along the road to becoming a "visible, external amplification of the human imagination." [1] Fans are busy enjoying the console in their living rooms. Allard captured the sentiment correctly when he said, "It's not a perfect product, but it's a magical one."

Will the Xbox 360 reach a billion gamers?

In hindsight, it's plausible to conclude that Robbie Bach made the right decision when he decided for the "early rush" strategy that came from *Age of Empires*. But the launch was only a "90-percent success," much like in World War II, when the British airborne went "A Bridge Too Far" in Operation Market-Garden and lost a whole division in Arnhem. The worldwide launch created a frenzy of demand – in just about every place except Japan – and Microsoft lost a lot of goodwill when it failed to execute.

"Why stick with the mistake?" said Hal Halpin, then-president of the Interactive Entertainment Merchants Association, referring to the decision to proceed with the launch in Japan. "I would say it caused a severe strain for retailers."

Halpin thought that Microsoft should be mindful to avoid becoming as arrogant as those that it railed against. That is something that came back to haunt Microsoft, even as it triumphed in personal computer software. Microsoft has succeeded in the past not just with technology, but by exploiting the perceived arrogance of its rivals. As they grow more confident with their decisions, the Xbox team at Microsoft ought to remember that lesson. Only by Sony's own blunder was disaster averted. Now the false hope of delivering a knock-out blow in the first round will have to be replaced by the determination to go 15 rounds with Sony and Nintendo. Microsoft has a golden opportunity with this second chance. It can't afford to waste it. In the long run, Sony has accurately stated that going first has never mattered. At some point in the next few years, Blu-ray may become an asset, not an albatross. And Sony will have a chance to take the high ground back if it has the right technology and the right games.

Many people thought Bach and Peter Moore made a colossal mistake when they decided to launch on schedule in Japan. Bach and Moore have said that they didn't want anyone to feel like a second-class citizen. But was it worse to disappoint consumers in every region? Gamers in the U.S. and Europe loved the Western video games among the launch titles. They were willing to sample the titles even without the blockbuster *Halo* franchise. They took to titles such as "*Call of Duty 2*." But in Japan, Microsoft had no cachet. World War II titles had no appeal there. The absence of *Dead or Alive 4* and *Ninety Nine Nights* meant there was no reason to buy the console. No one was ready to buy the consoles on faith. Now that the Xbox 360 brand has been damaged, labeled by some as "uncool", it will be doubly hard to recover. Could this have been prevented? Numerous parties pleaded with Microsoft to step on the brakes because they saw a train wreck coming. The Japanese game developers that Microsoft tried so hard to recruit may abandon the console once they finish their early games. To recover, Microsoft has to acquire some games headed for other platforms, or make a major acquisition in Japan. It is a measure of desperation.

Without Japan, Microsoft can't rule the world. It can still rush to exploit territories such as Korea and China, but it needs the massively multiplayer online games to achieve long-term growth in those markets. Most observers, including Electronic Arts CEO Larry Probst, think that Microsoft will gain market share. But they doubt Microsoft will beat out Sony for worldwide market share in this generation, especially with the Japan situation. To make the battle more competitive, Microsoft has to follow through on its plans for a handheld. The market is shifting toward handhelds, and Microsoft can't leave those areas for the others to exploit. And if it comes out with a good handheld, it might just stall some of the Apple iPod's growth.

While Bach and Steve Ballmer had the right idea about making money, the rush to make the bottom line profitable was also a poor decision. Microsoft had $34 billion in cash in the spring of 2006. It needed that money to fight a lot of battles. But without committing more cash to the console fight, Microsoft faces certain defeat. Pricing the Xbox 360 and its games at a discount to the PS3 and its games will be a necessity. And adding more soldiers, in this case game developers, will only improve Microsoft's odds. If it is going to invest in hardware, it has to make investments in software.

But the company should not give up. It has come a long way. Microsoft has scratched the surface of new business models with its Xbox Live Arcade, Xbox Live Marketplace, downloadable trailers, episodic content, spectator events, and alternative entertainment via a broadband connection. That is where it has a chance to be the market leader. In the future, there are so many more options available to Microsoft. It can look toward the results of the Halo movie and decide whether it should buy a movie studio to match Sony's own entertainment arsenal, observes Doug Lowenstein.

"They've certainly got the capital to do it," he muses. "Then games and films will become fused together, with audiences overlapping, the talent and the properties migrating back and forth." Or maybe Microsoft will push into handhelds or cell phone games. There are so many worlds to conquer before anyone can declare the game over.

Sony will have a tough time establishing itself this time, particularly as its early games go up against the more mature second-generation Microsoft titles. Nintendo will have a hard time breaking loose from kids, unless its mandate for innovation truly pays off. The Revolution doesn't have the kind of brute force developer support that the other consoles have, but it will succeed if Nintendo finds a way to combine innovation with its library of franchises. In 2007, the gloves will be off. All of the companies will have full production capacity to make as many machines as consumers demand. It may well be the third generation before Microsoft can bring its full might to bear on its competitors, much as it was with Windows 3.1. Now is not the time to let up on the accelerator. It's time to double down again. No one can win a war purely by making fewer blunders than the enemy.

But Microsoft and the games industry are caught in a much deeper problem. Its solution is more elusive. One of the original Xbox thinkers went to a store in November. He looked at the Xbox 360 kiosk, where a couple of gamers were playing "*Call of Duty 2*." Then he looked at the PlayStation 2, where dozens of onlookers were watching two people play "Guitar Hero." That scene captured the essence of what Microsoft failed to achieve with its launch.

This problem of creativity bubbled to the surface in that meeting in 2003, when Ed Fries met with the committee of executives to decide when *Halo* 2 would ship. Fries had argued for giving the game more time. To let the artists finish their art. To build the kind of game that gamers wanted to play. When the committee voted to solve the problem by forcing the talent to ship an unfinished game, all to meet the needs of the platform, no one was happy. Not Fries, not

Bungie, Not Robbie Bach. The committee made the wrong decision. It changed its mind and eventually made the right call. But it was too late to prevent Ed Fries from leaving the company, as well as a number of Bungie employees. Art had clashed with business. The budget and the strategy weren't in alignment with the tactical situation on the ground. At times, the two sides were as far apart as the generals running the Vietnam War and the soldiers fighting it. If it is to win the console war, Microsoft will have to enable Bungie to finish *Halo 3* on time, on budget, and to the satisfaction of the artists and the business executives alike. Microsoft will have to bring its left brain together with its right brain. It has to make the line toward graphics realism and the line toward creativity intersect. If it can make that happen, then *Halo 3* will be a great game. And more great games will follow. That's the only way to win.

1. "Dream Machines," by Will Wright, *Wired* magazine, April, 2006.

DEAN TAKAHASHI

Dean Takahashi has been a business journalist for 17 years, having written for the *Wall Street Journal, Red Herring Magazine,* the *Los Angeles Times, Orange County Register,* and *Dallas Times Herald,* and has appeared on CNN and CNBC. As a die-hard gamer and author of the book *Opening the Xbox: Inside Microsoft's Plan to Unleash an Entertainment Revolution,* Dean is currently a technology and gaming writer for the *San Jose Mercury News.*

For the latest breaking news on the Xbox 360 and the world of video games, check out the "Dean & Nooch on Gaming" blog at:

http://blogs.mercurynews.com/aei/gaming/

PHOTO CREDITS

P. 3 – Courtesy of Microsoft
P. 13 – Courtesy of Microsoft
P. 20 – Courtesy of Microsoft
P. 25 – Courtesy of Microsoft
P. 29 – Courtesy of Dean Takahashi
P. 41 – Courtesy of Microsoft
P. 42 – Courtesy of Microsoft
P. 49 – Courtesy of Microsoft
P. 71 – Courtesy of Microsoft
P. 88, L – Courtesy of Electronic Arts
P. 88, R – Courtesy of Cam Ferroni
P. 93 – Courtesy of Dean Takahashi
P. 97 – Courtesy of Microsoft
P. 117 – Courtesy of Microsoft
P. 118 – Courtesy of Microsoft
P. 137 – Courtesy of Dean Takahashi
P. 168 – Courtesy of Cliff Blezinski
P. 177 – Courtesy of Microsoft
P. 181 – Courtesy of Dean Takahashi
P. 183 – Courtesy of Microsoft
P. 193 – Courtesy of Microsoft
P. 207 – Courtesy of Microsoft
P. 213 – Courtesy of Microsoft
P. 217 – Courtesy of Dean Takahashi
P. 223 – Courtesy of Dean Takahashi
P. 233 – Courtesy of Microsoft
P. 235 – Courtesy of Microsoft
P. 242 – Courtesy of Microsoft
P. 244 – Courtesy of Microsoft

P. 245 – Courtesy of Microsoft
P. 246 – Courtesy of Microsoft
P. 247 – Courtesy of Microsoft
P. 254 – Courtesy of Electronic Arts
P. 257 – Courtesy of Activision
P. 258 – Courtesy of Sega
P. 272 – Courtesy of 42 Entertainment
P. 291 – Courtesy of Microsoft
P. 294 – Courtesy of Microsoft
P. 301 – Courtesy of Microsoft
P. 302 – Courtesy of Microsoft
P. 306 – Courtesy of Microsoft
P. 308 – Courtesy of Dean Takahashi
P. 311 – Courtesy of Microsoft
P. 331 – Courtesy of Microsoft
P. 332 – Courtesy of Microsoft
P. 335 – Courtesy of Microsoft
P. 351 – Courtesy of Dean Takahashi
P. 352 – Courtesy of Dean Takahashi
P. 353 – Courtesy of Dean Takahashi
P. 354 – Courtesy of Microsoft
P. 356 – Courtesy of Dean Takahashi
P. 357 – Courtesy of Dean Takahashi
P. 358 – Courtesy of Dean Takahashi
P. 360 – Courtesy of Microsoft
P. 361 – Courtesy of Microsoft
P. 369 – Courtesy of Electronic Arts
P. 378 – Courtesy of Microsoft
P. 386 – Courtesy of Microsoft

INDEX

Printed in the United States
58396LVS00019B/134

9 780977 784219